THE ARDEN SHAKESPEARE

GENERAL EDITORS: HAROLD F. BROOKS
HAROLD JENKINS AND BRIAN MORRIS

PERICLES

Being

The true History of the Play of *Pericles*, as it was
lately presented by the worthy and an-
cient Poet *John Gower*.

John   *Gower.*

At London.
Printed by T.P. *for* Nat:Butter
1608.

From the title-page of Wilkins'
The Painfull Aduentures of Pericles Prince of Tyre

THE ARDEN EDITION OF THE
WORKS OF WILLIAM SHAKESPEARE

PERICLES

Edited by
F. D. HOENIGER

METHUEN

LONDON and NEW YORK

The general editors of the Arden Shakespeare have been
W. J. Craig (1899–1906), R. H. Case (1909–1944)
and Una Ellis-Fermor (1946–1958)

Present general editors: Harold F. Brooks, Harold Jenkins
and Brian Morris

F. D. Hoeniger's edition of *Pericles* first published in 1963 by
Methuen & Co. Ltd
11 New Fetter Lane, London EC4P 4EE
Reprinted 1966

First published as a University Paperback 1969
Reprinted 1977 and 1979

Published in the USA by Methuen & Co.
in association with Methuen, Inc.
733 Third Avenue, New York, NY 10017

Editorial matter © 1963 Methuen & Co. Ltd

ISBN (hardbound) 0 416 47570 1
ISBN (paperback) 0 416 27850 7

Printed and bound in Great Britain by
Richard Clay (The Chaucer Press), Ltd
Bungay, Suffolk

CONTENTS

PREFACE

No ONE would include *Pericles* among Shakespeare's masterpieces. But after long neglect, it seems recently to have come into its own again, as one would gather from several dramatic productions, at Stratford, at Birmingham, at the Old Vic, and by lesser-known companies in England as well as abroad, and from the critical essays about the play which have appeared in literary journals. To explain this growing interest in *Pericles* in terms of our age's predilection for old and neglected works, many of which should have been left buried in the dust of antiquity, would hardly be just. Rather, our generation has been peculiarly attracted to Shakespeare's romances or last plays, more especially to their vision of suffering and rebirth. To us, the last plays are more than old wives' tales with which Shakespeare tried to cheer his old age.[1] Among these plays, *Pericles* is the first and least, but looks forward to no lesser achievements than *The Winter's Tale* and *The Tempest*. To all those who are drawn to Shakespeare's romances, it should have a special interest, for in *Pericles* one might expect to find the hints of what Shakespeare was to say and accomplish consummately later. Here we might perhaps see Shakespeare's imagination groping, reaching out for the vision to which he gave masterly form in *The Winter's Tale* and *The Tempest*. Though *Pericles* can reward the student in its own right, it is suggested, then, that it be read with the greater plays that were to follow it in mind.

There is, however, much in *Pericles* that is far from happy or clear. In trying to appreciate its form or meaning, one is sadly hampered by what is, to all appearances, a most uneven and puzzling text. Before discussing the literary aspects of the play, it seems therefore desirable not merely to consider such factual matters as its sources, date of composition, and the circumstances surrounding its first publication, but also to deal fairly thoroughly with the more controversial problems of the nature and reliability of the text, and of the possibility of mixed authorship. Unfortunately, these problems are extremely complex, to some extent inter-

1. See G. L. Strachey, 'Shakespeare's Final Period', *Books and Characters*, 1922, 51–69.

involved, and, external evidence being almost completely wanting, scholars have not reached agreement on them. One cannot discuss them adequately without being technical and rather lengthy. Moreover, in the interest of clarity, it has sometimes seemed wise not to deal consecutively with issues that are closely interrelated. The student will therefore, I trust, not mind the occasional resort to cross-reference through the footnotes, which will help him to judge the force as well as implications of the argument. This section of the introduction is obviously designed more for the advanced student than the general reader. Once these controversial and technical issues have been dealt with, we can turn with some confidence as well as relief to the more literary aspects of *Pericles*, and try to assess its dramatic structure and purpose in the context of Elizabethan drama and more especially in that of Shakespeare's work as a whole.

ACKNOWLEDGEMENTS

IT WAS Professor Una Ellis-Fermor, the former General Editor, who asked me to prepare this edition of *Pericles*. She was the supervisor of my London doctoral thesis, a chapter of which contains in essence the interpretation of the play offered in my Introduction. During the years of my work under her, her personality itself was a stimulus to creative thinking. I dedicate this edition to her memory. Like all other Arden editors of recent years, I owe a deep gratitude to the acute criticism as well as encouragement of the present General Editors, Dr Harold Brooks and Professor Harold Jenkins. The latter has taught me much in style; the former sent me a wealth of suggestions for the Commentary and parts of the Introduction. Both have saved me from errors. Mr Ernest Schanzer scrutinized the Commentary at an early stage and suggested several welcome changes and additions. Mr J. C. Maxwell, with thoughtful kindness, let me see his New Cambridge edition of *Pericles* in page-proof, and since then has shared with me his new discoveries. I have enjoyed the community of Arden editors, many of whom have helped me in minor ways. The same is true of several other scholars whose contributions are acknowledged in the notes. I am also indebted to K. Deighton for some of his acute notes in the original Arden edition. Dr James McManaway encouraged me all along, and gave me the opportunity of testing my ideas on the play's authorship through the *Shakespeare Quarterly*. Some of these pages are reprinted, with adjustments, in Appendix B.

Part of the work towards this edition was done in the British Museum during 1956–7, when I was holder of a fellowship of the Humanities Research Council of Canada; part of it at the Folger Library, which granted me a fellowship during the summer of 1959. To both my gratitude. Throughout, I have benefited from the encouragement of my colleagues at the University of Toronto, especially from that of my principal and former teacher, Northrop Frye.

F. D. H.

Toronto, June 1961

For the first reprint of this edition, a number of corrections have been made and a few extra notes added at the end. I am happy to acknowledge further help from Prof. J. C. Maxwell and Dr Ernest Schanzer. Prof. John P. Cutts drew my attention to a gross mis-quotation in the important note to v. i. 237 which has now been corrected.

F. D. H.

Toronto, March 1966

ABBREVIATIONS

The abbreviated titles of Shakespeare's works are those of C. T. Onions, *A Shakespeare Glossary*, p. x; line numbers and texts of passages cited or quoted as in *Complete Works*, ed. P. Alexander (London, 1951), unless otherwise indicated. Editions of Shakespeare and *Pericles* from Rowe to the present day are referred to by the name of their editors, with the exceptions of the Cambridge (1863) and Globe (1864) editions by W. G. Clark and W. A. Wright (Camb. and Globe respectively) and the edition of *Pericles* in *The Yale Shakespeare* (Yale) by A. R. Bellinger (1925). The customary abbreviations are used for periodicals.

Abbott	E. A. Abbott, *A Shakespearian Grammar* (3rd edn), 1870.
Arcadia	Sir Philip Sidney, *Arcadia*, as reprinted by A. Feuillerat, 1922.
Beaumont and Fletcher	A. R. Waller (ed.), *The Works of Beaumont and Fletcher*, 1910.
C.A.	John Gower, *Confessio Amantis*, Book VIII, as in G. Macaulay (ed.), *The Works of John Gower*, Vol. III, 1901.
Cowl	R. P. Cowl, *The Authorship of Pericles*, n.d.
D.	K. Deighton (ed.), *Pericles* (old Arden edn), 1907.
Day	A. H. Bullen (ed.), *The Works of John Day*, 1881 (unless original quarto editions are cited).
Dekker	F. Bowers (ed.), *The Dramatic Works of John Dekker*, 1953–61.
E.S.	Ernest Schanzer, privately.
Edwards	Philip Edwards, 'An Approach to the Problem of *Pericles*', *Shakespeare Survey 5*, 1952, pp. 25–49.
Franz	W. Franz, *Shakespeare Grammatik* (3rd edn), 1924.
Green, *Emblem Writers*	H. Green, *Shakespeare and the Emblem Writers*, 1870.
Halliwell-Phillips, Scrapbook	A Scrapbook on *Pericles*, containing unpublished notes, now at the Shakespeare Birthplace, Stratford-upon-Avon.
H. F. B.	Harold Brooks, General Editor.
Hastings	W. Hastings, 'Shakespere's Part in *Pericles*', *Sh. Assoc. Bul.* XIV, No. 2 (1939), pp. 67–85.
Hazlitt's Dodsley	W. C. Hazlitt, *A Select Collection of Old English Plays*, 1874.
Jonson	C. H. Herford, Percy Simpson, and Evelyn Simpson (edd.), *Ben Jonson*, 1925–52.
Kökeritz	H. Kökeritz, *Shakespeare's Pronunciation*, 1953.
loc.	locale, location.

M.E.	Middle English.
M.S.R.	Malone Society Reprint.
Mason	J. M. Mason, *Comments on the Last Edition of Shakespeare's Plays*, 1785 and (enlarged) 1807.
Maxwell	J. C. Maxwell (ed.), *Pericles*, New Cambridge Shakespeare, 1956.
Middleton	A. H. Bullen (ed.), *The Works of Thomas Middleton*, 1885.
n.	note in Commentary.
N.C.S.	New Cambridge Shakespeare.
Nashe, *Works*	R. B. McKerrow and F. P. Wilson (edd.), *The Works of Thomas Nashe*, 1958.
O.E.	Old English (Anglo-Saxon).
O.E.D.	*The Oxford English Dictionary*, 1884–1928.
On.	C. T. Onions, *A Shakespeare Glossary* (2nd edn), 1949.
P.A.	George Wilkins, *The Painfull Aduentures of Pericles, Prince of Tyre*, 1608, ed. K. Muir, 1953.
pple	participle.
Round	P. Z. Round (ed.), *Pericles*, The Henry Irving Shakespeare, VIII, 1890.
S.D.	Stage-direction.
S.H.	Speech-heading.
Sisson	C. Sisson, *New Readings in Shakespeare*, 1955, II, pp. 286–300.
Theobald MS	Unpublished marginalia by L. Theobald, in copies of Q4 (at present at the Folger Library, Washington), and Q6 (at present in the Library of the University of Pennsylvania, Philadelphia).
Tilley	M. P. Tilley, *A Dictionary of the Proverbs in England*, 1950.
Twine	L. Twine, *The Patterne of Painefull Aduentures*, n.d. (1594?), reprinted in J. P. Collier, *Shakespeare's Library* (2nd edn), 1875, vol. IV.
S. Walker	Sidney Walker, *A Critical Examination of Shakespeare's Text*, 1860.
J. D. Wilson	Notes quoted in J. C. Maxwell's ed. of *Pericles*.

INTRODUCTION

I. SOURCES

1. Sources of the Fable and Analogues

The ultimate source of *Pericles* is the romance of Apollonius of Tyre, one of the best-known stories of the Middle Ages and the Renaissance. Of about a hundred mediaeval Latin manuscript versions of the romance, the earliest is of the ninth century, but allusions to the tale have been found in works dating several hundred years earlier, and one may reasonably assume that the original was a Hellenistic novel somewhat like those by Xenophon, Heliodorus, and Achilles Tatius.

The early popularity of the romance is further indicated by a number of adaptations and translations, including one in Anglo-Saxon and one in Middle English.[1] Godfrey de Viterbo used the story in his *Pantheon* (ca. 1186). In the fourteenth century it became, notwithstanding its great length, part of the famous collection of the *Gesta Romanorum*. John Gower, the English poet, retold it in his *Confessio Amantis*. Even Chaucer's reprobation in the Introduction to *The Man of Law's Tale*,

> But certeynly no word ne wryteth he
>
> .   .   .   .   .   .
>
> of Tyro Apollonius,
> How that the cursed king Antiochus
> Birafte his doghter of hir maydenhede,
> That is so horrible a tale for to rede,
> Whan he hir threw up-on the pavement,[2]

seems not to have lessened its fame. Such stories, the Man of Law remarks, are 'unkinde abhominaciouns', a judgment apparently shared less by Shakespeare than by some of his later readers.

1. An eleventh-century MS in the library of Corpus Christi College, Cambridge, ed. by Zupitza, *Archiv. f. d. Stud. der n. Sprachen u. Lit.*, 1896, vol. 97, pp. 17–34; and a fragment of a M.E. poem in MS, printed by Halliwell in *A new boke about Shakespeare and Stratford-upon-Avon*, 1850. More recently, both works have been edited by J. Raith in *Die alt- und mittelenglischen Apollonius-Bruchstücke*, Munich, 1956.

2. Ll. 77–85.

Throughout the Renaissance, the story's appeal remained as great as ever, as new adaptations in many languages, in prose, verse, and drama, and the scholarly edition of the early romance, *Historia Apollonii regis Tyrii*, by Velserius testify.[1] We today, like Ben Jonson, may regard it as a 'mouldy tale', but in some parts of the world the story of Apollonius of Tyre is still passed on from mouth to mouth.[2] For a treatment of its fascinating history, and of the many shapes this romance has taken, the student is directed to three studies: A. H. Smyth's *Shakespeare's Pericles and Apollonius of Tyre* (Philadelphia, 1898), S. Singer's *Apollonius von Tyrus* (Halle, 1895), and E. Klebs' *Die Erzählung von Apollonius aus Tyrus* (Berlin, 1899).[3]

My discussion must necessarily confine itself to a few versions which have some bearing on our play. It has recently been argued that *Pericles* was based on an earlier, lost play. But about such a source we can at best theorize.[4] The two main recognized sources of *Pericles* are John Gower's tale in Book 8 of *Confessio Amantis* and Lawrence Twine's *The Patterne of Painefull Aduentures*, a translation from a French version which in turn had been a translation of the 153rd story of the *Gesta Romanorum*. Gower's and Twine's are the only versions whose use by the dramatist of *Pericles* can be demonstrated with certainty. Of the two, Gower's exercised by far the greater influence. Written late in the fourteenth century, it was printed twice in the sixteenth, in 1532 and 1554.[5] It was the *Con-*

1. M. Welser, *Narratio Eorum Quae Contigerunt Apollonio Tyrio*, 1595.

2. See R. M. Dawkins, 'Modern Greek Oral Versions of Apollonius of Tyre', *MLR*, xxxvii, No. 2 (1942), 172 ff.

3. Klebs' is the best and Smyth's the least reliable of these studies. None of them should be trusted for their account of the immediate sources of *Pericles*, but the German books at least are otherwise trustworthy.

4. See the discussion on the 'Ur-Pericles', pp. xlvii–xlix below.

5. The text Shakespeare knew was probably that of the 1554 edn, printed by Berthelette. Berthelette's dedication bears quoting: '. . . And who so euer in redynge of this warke, doth consider it well, shall fynde, that it is plentifully stuffed and fournished with manifolde eloquent reasons, sharpe and quicke argumentes, and examples of great auctoritee, perswadynge vnto vertue. . . There is to my dome no man, but that he maie by readinge of this warke get right great knowlage, as well for the understandynge of many and diuers auctours, whose reasons, sayenges, and histories are translated in to this warke, as for the pleintie of englishe wordes and vulgars, beside the furtherance of the life to vertue. Whiche olde englishe wordes and vulgars no wise man, because of their anti-quitee will throwe aside. For the writers of later daies, the which began to loth and hate these olde vulgars, whan they them selfe wolde write in our english tonge, were constreigned to bringe in, in their writynges, newe termes (as some call them) which thei borowed out of latine, frenche, and other langages, which caused that they that vnderstode not those langages, from whens these new vulgars are fette, coude not perceiue their writynges. And though our most alowed olde autors did otherwhile use to borowe of other langages, either because

fessio Amantis, of course, which suggested to the playwright—we will call him Shakespeare for simplicity's sake—the Chorus Gower, whose spirit returns for two hours to present this dramatization of an ancient story. A fairly large number of passages in the play can be shown to have been paraphrased from Gower, especially the Riddle in I. i, Pericles' letter at III. ii. 70–7, the first half of Marina's epitaph in IV. iv, and some of the choruses, especially III. Ch.,[1] but only in a few instances does the play follow Gower's wording closely.[2] Most of the place-names and certain of the characters' names were probably suggested by Gower; for instance Cerimon, Helicanus, Dionyza, Lychorida, Thaisa (Thaise is the daughter in Gower), and Philoten. The main outline of the plot is like Gower's, and about half of the scenes follow the order of events in Gower's narrative. Yet there are a few notable exceptions. Gower has nothing to correspond to I. ii; in his story, Helicanus is introduced much later, and then only briefly. He has no tournament scene, which appears in no version of the tale before *Pericles*. Gower has only one fisherman, and thus little to anticipate the colourful dialogue at the beginning of II. i of *Pericles*. Nothing in Gower hints at the argument between Dionyza and Cleon set forth in IV. iii. In fact, the whole of Act IV appears in Gower in a much shorter form: in the brothel scenes he has no female Bawd, only a pandar and servant, and Athenagoras (who corresponds to Lysimachus) never enters the brothel but meets Marina only on the day of Neptune's festival. Generally speaking, therefore, it is some of the most striking episodes in the play that are least anticipated in Gower—the comedy of the fishermen and of the scenes in the brothel; and the same holds true for the passages of highest poetic merit, notably in III. i, IV. i, and V. i. On the other hand, the play cuts to a minimum the story of Antiochus' incest before the Prince of Tyre's arrival.[3] Moreover, what in Gower and other versions is a fairly long episode —the hero as Thaisa's music-master—is only alluded to in the play. (The episode at the beginning of II. v of the play is prepared far

---

of their metre, or elles for lacke of a feete englishe worde, yet that ought not to be a presidente to vs, to heape them in, where as nedeth not, and where as we haue all redie wordes approued and receiued, of the same effecte and strength. The which if any man wante, let hym resorte to this worthy olde writer *Iohn Gower*, that shal as a lanterne giue him lighte to write cunningly, and to garnishe his sentences in our vulgare tonge...'

1. See also Commentary for I. Ch. 39–40, I. ib. 156, II. Ch. 14, II. iii. 109–10, II. v. 16–17, III. iii. 27–9, IV. vi. 181, etc.

2. See Commentary for II. Ch. 31, III. ii. 107, IV. iv. 34–43, IV. vi. 193, V. Ch. 14, V. i. 84.

3. Some people regret that the episode was not cut altogether—witness Nugent Monck's production at Stratford in 1947, which began at I. iv.

better in Gower than in *Pericles*—unless a mute episode between
scenes iv and v, of Pericles playing a musical instrument, was omitted in the printed text.) Lastly, the play's moral epilogue, however
much it may recall Gower's manner, has little in common with
Gower's ending. It was Gower's ostensible, if not real, purpose to

> liere
> What is to love in good manere,
> And what to love in other wise:
> The mede arist of the servise;
> Fortune, thogh sche be noght stable,
> Yit at som time is favorable
> To hem that ben of love trewe.

Lust, according to Gower, meets with its due punishment, while
the true lover, though he may have to endure suffering galore,
eventually reaches happiness. However one interprets *Pericles*, that
is not its meaning.

Twine's novel was probably printed at least three times between
1576 and 1607,[1] but it is not possible to say which edition the
dramatist used.[2] Twine's influence was considerable only upon
three scenes in the fourth act, iv. i, iv. iii (especially), and iv. vi.
The passages in his novel corresponding to these scenes will be
found in Appendix A. The reader will notice that in Twine, unlike Gower, Athanagoras (= Lysimachus) does visit the brothel,
though there he is Marina's first visitor, and though Twine's story
has nothing corresponding to large parts of iv. vi (namely lines
1–94, 117–40, and 147–79). Elsewhere in the play the wording
only seldom echoes that of Twine.[3] Thus the play's debt to Twine
was small—infinitely smaller than that of Wilkins who, in his
novel, *The Painfull Aduentures of Pericles, Prince of Tyre*, took over
about one-third of his predecessor's text *verbatim*.

This treatment of the play's two main sources has revealed two
noteworthy facts: first, the playwright of *Pericles* followed, on the
whole, the outlines of his story—a very undramatic story at that!—
more closely than was Shakespeare's usual custom in romantic
comedy or tragi-comedy; but secondly, the best passages and episodes in the play, both in prose and in verse, are largely of the

1. It was entered in the Stationers' Register in 1576, but no copy bearing
that date survives; an undated edition was published about 1594; it was reprinted in 1607, and then ascribed to Thomas Twyne, the author's brother.

2. The edition of 1607 may have been the immediate cause for the play, or the
play may have been the immediate cause for it. As Twine's novel is an indirect
translation of the story in the *Gesta Romanorum*, some passages in the play that
appear to be derived from Twine may in fact come from a different source.

3. It does so at i. Ch. 18, i. iii. 27–8, v. i. 71–5, and v. iii. 8 and 75.

dramatist's creation. Shakespeare's Marina, above all, is given a far more prominent role in the play that the corresponding Thaise or Tharsia in the sources. When considering the play's purpose and meaning, it will be well to keep some of these changes in mind.

A few other versions of the story, some of which may have been known either to Shakespeare or to members of his audience, deserve brief mention here. (i) Robert Copland's *King Appolyn of Tyre*, a translation from French prose, printed in 1510, which left no trace on *Pericles*. (ii) F. de Belleforest's retelling of the story in French from a manuscript of the *Gesta Romanorum* in 1595.[1] Again, no trace of influence can be found. (iii) The version in the Latin *Gesta Romanorum* itself, which work, judging from contemporary references, enjoyed a new vogue of interest about 1600. It was perhaps because of the story's length that R. Robinson did not include it in his translation of parts of the *Gesta*,[2] but the Latin is simple and would have presented the pupil of Stratford Grammar School with no difficulty. Two slight pieces of evidence indicate that this version was perhaps known to the dramatist. The heading of the story in the *Gesta, De tribulacione temporali, que in gaudium sempiternum postremo commutabitur*, suggests more closely the treatment of the story in *Pericles* than does either Gower or Twine. In neither Gower nor Twine is there any attempt to find meaning in human suffering. What matters to Gower is that the good fare well in the end and the wicked are punished. Twine's sole concern is with the revelation of the arbitrary ups and downs of Fortune. Secondly, the word *bitumed* at III. i. 71 and III. ii. 57 seems to have been derived from a Latin source, for it occurs neither in Twine nor in Gower.[3] (iv) Another Latin version of some interest is J. Falckenburgk (Germanus), *Britannia, Sive de Apollonice Humilitatis, Virtutis et Honoris Porta . . .*, London, 1578. Dedicated to Leicester and Lord Burghley, this book contains many laudatory verses to Elizabeth, and on the title-page quotes *Psalm* 33: *Multae sunt tribulationes iustorum, sed ex omnibus his liberat eos Dominus*.

That a major lost source is at least a possibility was argued by

1. *Le Septiesme Tome des Histoires Tragiques*, 1595, Histoire Troisiesme, pp. 59–111v.

2. R. Robinson's translation of part of the *Gesta* appeared in 1595, 1610, 1620, and later edd. It contains a version of the bond-story used in *Mer. V*. See Intro. to Arden edn of *Mer. V*.

3. Pointed out by Malone; Twine uses 'seare'. In the *Gesta Romanorum* and *Pericles*, the inscription in Thaisa's coffin is reported in the context of III. ii only; in Gower in that of III. i; in Twine twice, in those of both III. i and III. ii. But this is weak evidence.

S. Singer,[1] who noticed two strange 'coincidences' of names in *Pericles* and distant analogues: the hero in a French manuscript version (MS 3428, Wiener Hof bibliothek) for two years calls himself 'Perillie', while in Gower and all other versions, his name throughout is Apollonius; and Cerimon's assistant Philemon (not in Gower, 'Machaon' in Twine) has a counterpart named Filominus in a fourteenth-century German poem by H. von Neustadt, and one named Silemon in Slavic folktales.[2] To this one might add that a Greek rimada, printed in 1534 and 1603, introduces, like *Pericles* but unlike its acknowledged sources, a tournament in the Western style of chivalry at Pentapolis.[3] Not too much should be made of these distant parallels, but they may suggest that Shakespeare knew some folklore version of the tale unknown to us.

Lastly, it should be of some interest that soon after Shakespeare's play two dramatized versions of the same story appeared on the continent: in Holland, Pieter Bor's *Twee Tragi-commedien in prosa, d'Eene van Appolonius, Prince van Tyro, Ende d'ander van denselven onde van Tharsia syn Dochter*, 1617 and 1634; in France, J. Bernier de la Brousse, *Les Heureuses Infortunes*, 1617.[4] These analogues provide some idea of how much a play on the story of Apollonius of Tyre must have been 'in the air' when *Pericles* was first staged. It also had its own imitators: the play gave rise to Wilkins' novel, *The Painfull Aduentures of Pericles, Prince of Tyre*.[5] The tournament scene, at least, made sufficient impression on one other, though minor and anonymous, English dramatist for him to imitate it closely in *The Impartiall Law*[6]; and there are numerous minor adaptations from *Pericles* in the *Valiant Scot*, 1637.[7]

It hardly needs saying that many other works exercised some minor influence on certain of the play's episodes. Such works hardly deserve to be called 'sources', and I shall mention only a few of the more obvious. The most noteworthy biblical echoes are of *2 Maccabees*, ix, where the fate of Antiochus IV is described in terms resembling those of II. iv, and of the Book of *Jonah*, where some of

1. 'Appolonius of Tyrus' in *Aufsätze und Vorträge*, 1912, pp. 79–103.

2. Klebs (*op. cit.*, p. 382) comments: 'eine rein zufällige Übereinstimmung' —a purely accidental likeness. See below, Commentary to *Dramatis Personae*, under *PERICLES* and *PHILEMON*.

3. Dawkins, *ibid.*, p. 172. See also Commentary, introductory n. to II. ii.

4. The suggestion that Gil Vicente's *Comedia de Rubena*, ca. 1521, is a close analogue to *Pericles* rests on no foundation.

5. See Section II. 6 below.

6. First printed by B. Dobell in 1908. The MS of about 1615–30 is in the Folger Library, Washington.

7. By the mysterious J.W.

the dialogue of the fishermen in II. i is anticipated, though this
scene is even more specifically indebted to John Day's *Law Tricks*.[1]
Other biblical echoes are listed in the commentary. The description of the famine at Tharsus owes something, either directly or
indirectly, to the account of the famine of Jerusalem in Josephus or
Nashe. Elizabethan prose-romances, especially Sidney's *Arcadia*,
exercised considerable influence on the play's language. And for
his treatment of Marina in her predicament at Mytilene, the playwright may have been slightly indebted to an account of a similar
triumph of chastity in Seneca the Elder's *Controversia*, I. 2, or in L.
Piot's translation of van der Busche's *Orator* (1596, Declamation
53). This list is of course nowhere nearly complete, but it does give
some idea of the large variety of reading which may have influenced
the poet while at work.[2]

2. *The Choric Convention*

So much for the sources and analogues of the story or plot of
Pericles. I shall now turn from the influence of story-material to
that of dramatic convention; more specifically, to the origins of the
peculiar device in *Pericles* of reincarnating the mediaeval poet
Gower. Gower is employed in a manner quite unlike that of the
chorus of Greek or Senecan tragedy. The ultimate origins of this
device are rather to be looked for in mediaeval religious drama.
But leaving this matter for later,[3] let us focus our attention at present on some more immediate prototypes.

Our first glance will naturally be at Shakespeare's own work,
and more particularly at the only other play in which he makes
more than occasional use of a chorus: *Henry V*. Certain similarities
in treatment will at once be apparent. Like Gower, the Chorus of
Henry V acts both as prologue and epilogue and appears on the
stage before each act. He is both presenter and, to some degree,
interpreter. Like Gower, he narrates essential parts of an action
which contains 'the accomplishment of many years' and 'much
jumping o'er times', and which involves much movement from
place to place. In his epilogue, he briefly summarizes the remainder
of Henry V's reign and reminds the audience that England was to

---

1. See App. B, pp. 172–3.

2. Minor sources are discussed in the following articles: W. Elton, '*Pericles*:
A new Source or Analogue', *JEGP*, XLVIII (1949), 138–9; E. M. Waith, '*Pericles*
and Seneca the Elder', *MLN*, L (1951), 180–2; R. J. Kane, 'A Passage in *Pericles*',
MLN, LXVIII (Nov. 1953), 483–4; N. Nathan, ' "Pericles" and "Jonah" ',
N&Q, n.s. III, No. 1 (vol. 200), (1956), 10–11. See also M.A. thesis by V. S.
Prooth in the University library, Leeds.

3. See below, section VI, pp. lxxxviii ff.

be less happy under Henry VI—again much like Gower's epilogue, if one allows for the very different types of plot.

Since the Chorus of *Henry V* introduces a play utterly unlike *Pericles*, we are not surprised to find some differences in handling. For instance, the Chorus of *Henry V* does not present any dumb-shows; they would have been unsuitable in a realistic historical drama. But the main difference is the lack of individuality of the Chorus in *Henry V*. He does not, like Gower, speak for the author, but represents his company of actors who, aware of the limitations of their stage and the impossibility of presenting the events in life-like grandeur, use him as their spokesman to ensure the imaginative appeal of their acting. An interplay between the action and his personality is not even faintly suggested.[1]

Yet the appeal by the Chorus of *Henry V* to the audience to assist the actors with their imagination is not unparalleled in *Pericles*. It is, to be sure, both stronger and more successful in *Henry V*, where the events presented concern the audience intimately, unlike those of *Pericles*. But in *Pericles*, too, Gower several times suggests that the audience's sympathetic and imaginative co-operation is essential to the spectacle's success:

> Be attent,
> And time that is so briefly spent
> With your fine fancies quaintly eche   (III. Ch.)

> Which never could I so convey,
> Unless your thoughts went on my way   (IV. Ch.)

> In your supposing once more put your sight;
> Of heavy Pericles, think this his bark ...   (V. Ch.)

> ... think his pilot thought;
> So with his steerage shall your thoughts grow on ...,
>   (IV. iv)

for which last passage, compare:

> Follow, follow!
> Grapple your minds to sternage of this navy.
>   (*H5*, III. Ch. 17–18)

Several minor echoes, listed in the Commentary, confirm the impression that the Chorus of *Henry V* was in the mind of the writer who composed the choruses of *Pericles*.

However, what has just been said about Gower's attitude towards the audience applies in *Pericles* only from Act III on. The first two choruses resemble those of *Henry V* much less. They contain no

---

1. For Gower in *Pericles*, see below, pp. lxxvi–lxxvii.

reference to the audience's imagination nor any exhortation to them, but rather suggest that the spectacle will be worth watching whatever the limitations of the verse:

> ... What shall be next,
> Pardon old Gower,—this 'longs the text.
>
> (II. Ch. 39–40)

Such an attitude is not anticipated in *Henry V*.

There are, however, even more immediate prototypes for the device of Gower in two plays which must have been produced very shortly before *Pericles*: Barnabe Barnes's *The Divil's Charter* (performed early in 1607 and printed later that year), and *The Travailes of the Three English Brothers*, of the same date, by John Day, William Rowley, and George Wilkins. The choruses of these two plays resemble the chorus of Gower more closely than any others in contemporary drama, except for the chorus of Homer in three plays by Heywood, *The Golden Age*, *The Silver Age*, and *The Brazen Age*. These we may ignore, since it is highly probable that they were not acted before late in 1609. They exercised no influence on *Pericles* but, on the contrary, may have been influenced by it.

Barnes's source for *The Divil's Charter* was Guicciardini's *Historie of Italie* in Fenton's translation. He took from it not merely the main incidents for his 'Life and Death of Pope Alexander the Sixth', the subject of his play, but also recreated its original author as chorus, just as the writer of *Pericles* was to do with Gower. Commanded by the muse to present his tragedy on earth, Guicciardine is

> Sent from the Christall Palace of true *Fame*,
> And Bright Starre-Chamber of eternall soules,
> Seuerd from Angels fellowship awhile,
> To dwell with mortall bodies here on earth.   (sig. A2)

So in *Pericles*, 'From ashes ancient Gower is come, / Assuming man's infirmities'. Like Gower, Guicciardine acts as prologue, narrates intervening action, points to spectacular incidents, comments on the poetic justice of the course of events, indicates frequent shifts in time and place, occasionally employs a dumbshow to abbreviate the action, and in the epilogue provides a general moralistic comment on the events, as well as narrating further action. Except for the fact that he is less romantic, since he speaks in the idiom of the Renaissance, Guicciardine is Gower's exact, even if rather pale, prototype. The likelihood that Shakespeare or his collaborator was influenced in his delineation of Gower by Barnes's Guicciardine is strengthened by some detailed resemblances in the attitudes and

wording of the two choruses. For instance, they introduce their
dumbshows with similar words:

> And first by what ungodly means and art
> He did attain the triple diadem,
> This vision offered to your eyes declares.   (sig. A2)

and: But tidings to the contrary
> Are brought your eyes.   (II. Ch. 15–16)

They announce the continuation of the dramatic action in a
similar manner:

> The life of action shall explain the rest   (sig. A2v)

and: I nill relate, action may
> Conveniently the rest convey.   (III. Ch. 55–6)

Both plead with the audience to attend to their stories patiently:

> What follows, view with gentle patience   (F4v)

and: Patience, then,
> And think you now are all in Mytilen.
> (IV. iv. 50–1)[1]

Both picture forth the rewards of evil actions:

> Unnatural murthers, cursed poisonings,
> Horrible exorcism and invocation
> In them examine the reward [of sin.]   (F4v)

and: In Antiochus and his daughter you have heard
> Of monstrous lust the due and just reward.
> (Epil. 1–2)

Even more frequently than in *The Divil's Charter*, Gower is anticipated in both attitude and wording by the chorus of *The Travailes of the Three English Brothers*. Setting forth an extremely rambling narrative of small dramatic but great spectacular potentiality,
this chorus exercises the same basic functions as those of *The
Divil's Charter* and of *Pericles*. The only important difference is the
less personal contribution of the chorus of *Travailes* in assuming the
shape of the allegorical figure of Fame.[2] Among the many detailed
resemblances I shall only mention some which are not also shared
by the Chorus of *Henry V*. (i) In both *Pericles* and *Travailes*, the
chorus presents the action to the 'judging eyes' of the audience.
Compare

1. But see end of the first chorus in *H5*.
2. Guicciardine in Barnes's play descends from 'the Christall Palace of true
Fame'.

> What now ensues, to the judgment of your eye
> I give my cause, who best can justify   (I. Ch. 41–2)

with: to your just censures then,
> We offer up their travels and our pen   (A2v)

and with 'in your judging eyes' (2nd chorus, C4v). (ii) The words 'please your eyes' (*Per.*, I. Ch. 4) repeat those of the third chorus in *Travailes* (sig. Dv). (iii) Both choruses refer to the actors as 'shadows', and to the swiftness of 'thought' with which actors are transported from one country to another.[1] (iv) Like Gower in *Pericles*, Fame in *Travailes* several times contrasts dumbness with speech:

> What's dumb in show I'll plain with speech   (III. Ch. 14)
> Our scene lies speechless, active but yet dumb   (A2).

(v) Both refer to 'winged time' repeatedly, and at least once to the 'shortening' of time and space:

> Thus time we waste, and long leagues make short   (IV. iv. 1)
> Time now makes short their way   (Dv).

Enough has been said to indicate beyond doubt that the choruses of *Pericles* were strongly influenced not merely by *Henry V* but also by *The Divil's Charter* and by *Travailes*.[2] It seems probable that the dramatic convention of the loose travelogue or romance narrated by a choric figure was begun by Barnes and so successfully developed in *Pericles* one or two years later that Heywood was persuaded to apply the same technique in his plays on the *Ages*.

2. THE TEXT

1. The Publication of the Substantive Quarto

The first reference to the printing of a text of *Pericles* is an entry in the Stationers' Register for 1608:

> 20 Maij. Edward Blount. Entred for his copie vnder thandes of Sir George Buck knight and Master Warden Seton A booke called. *The booke of PERICLES prynce of Tyre.* vj^d.[3]

From the expression 'A booke called The booke . . .' it can be inferred with reasonable certainty that the copy was the play's

---

1. See *Pericles*, IV. iv. 18–22, *H5*, III. Ch. 1–3, and the opening chorus in *Travailes*, 'on the full sailes of thought'.
2. See further discussion of this play in App. B.
3. Ed. Arber, III. 167v.

prompt-book.[1] Blount, a reputable printer, likewise entered *Antony and Cleopatra* on the same day. But he seems never to have printed either play. There appeared instead in 1608 a novel by one George Wilkins, a minor dramatist and hackwriter of the time, entitled *The Painfull Aduentures of Pericles Prince of Tyre*, which claimed on the title-page to be 'The true History of the Play of *Pericles*, as it was lately presented by the worthy and ancient Poet *Iohn Gower*'. And in the following year was published, without any indication of an authorized transfer of the printing rights, what is nowadays referred to as the first Quarto of *Pericles* (here designated Q), with the following title-page:

> THE LATE, and much admired Play, Called Pericles, Prince of Tyre. With the true Relation of the whole Historie, aduentures, and fortunes of the said Prince: As also, The no lesse strange, and worthy accidents, in the Birth and Life, of his Daughter *MARIANA*, As it hath been diuers and sundry times acted by his Maiesties Seruants, at the Globe on the Banck-side. By William Shakespeare.
>
> Imprinted at London for *Henry Gosson*, and are to be sold at the signe of the Sunne in Pater-noster row, &c. 1609.

Henry Gosson was a minor publisher who mainly dealt in ballads and pamphlets and who had apparently not ventured into the publication of plays before. *Pericles* evidently proved attractive to him because of its success on the stage during the preceding year, and because Shakespeare's name was attached to it. Gosson's quarto indeed sold so well that he reprinted it during the same year. Before *Pericles*, only two Shakespearean plays had been printed twice during the same year—*Richard II* and *1 Henry IV*, both in 1598.

The facts surrounding the first publication of *Pericles* will make us suspicious from the outset about the trustworthiness of the text. First of all, it seems strange that Edward Blount, who registered the play's prompt-book for his copy, did not proceed with the printing. It has been suggested that we are here confronted with a blocking entry, in other words with an attempt on the part of Shakespeare's company 'to protect themselves against an anticipated piracy by employing a friendly publisher . . . to register his copyright in the plays "under the hands of" His Majesty's Censor of Plays and the Warden of the Stationers'[2]—a precaution which proved inadequate for *Pericles*. This may well have been the case. But the possibility also suggests itself that Blount's was a regular entry; that he intended to print both *Pericles* and *Antony and Cleopatra* but was

---

1. See W. Greg, *Editorial Problems in Shakespeare*, p. 106.
2. J. D. Wilson, ed. *Antony and Cleopatra*, N.C.S., p. vii.

prevented, perhaps because soon after the registration he had to move his shop.[1] At any rate, no text of *Pericles* was ever to be printed from the prompt-book or a transcript of it. Was it lost soon after Blount's entry? We do not know.

Another factor which may have influenced the first publication of *Pericles* was the plague, which was bad enough in London during 1608–9 for the theatres to be closed for more than a year.[2] At such a time, one would expect to find not merely a large number of plays rushed to the printers by needy playwrights, but also much irregular printing, for the temptation of piracy must have been especially great for the unemployed minor dramatist, actor, or bookkeeper of theatrical companies. Moreover the plague must have affected the printing trade too. Again, we must rest content with observations, without arriving at specific conclusions.

One point, however, can be made with reasonable conviction. It would seem highly improbable that either Shakespeare or his company first encouraged Blount to register for a copy of *Pericles*, and then in the following year, and without official transfer of licence, asked a minor publisher—described by Greg as 'a purveyor chiefly of the more ephemeral types of popular literature'— to print an authoritative text. This consideration makes me from the outset sceptical of the view that the copy for Q was 'Shakespeare's foul papers'.[3] This could only have occurred if Shakespeare was singularly negligent about what happened to his rough drafts. Rather, it would seem probable that Gosson's copy, or at least a large part of it, was surreptitiously obtained. If this reasoning is sound it will in turn permit one at least a guess why the play was not included by Heming and Condell in the First Folio of 1623. They were evidently unable to procure more satisfactory copy than Gosson's printed text, which they held to be unreliable. By 1619 three more quartos of *Pericles* (Qq 2–4) had appeared, but all these are derived directly or indirectly from Q without recourse to any manuscript copy. This might have been sufficient reason for the exclusion of *Pericles*, though other factors may have had a decisive influence upon their judgment.[4]

---

1. Blount moved in 1608 from 'over against' the Great North Door of St Paul's to the Black Bear, St Paul's Churchyard (McKerrow, *Dict. of Printers and Booksellers 1557–1640*, 1910).

2. From 28 July 1608 to Dec. 1609. See J. T. Murray, *English Dramatic Companies*, 1910, and F. P. Wilson, *The Plague in Shakespeare's London*, 1927.

3. See below, p. xxxix.

4. For instance, doubts about Shakespeare's authorship of large parts of the play; or possibly Ben Jonson's objection.

2. *The Printing of Q*

Since all later quartos and other texts of *Pericles* can be shown to be derived from Q, Q represents the only substantive text of our play. Students of the play will therefore wish to know everything that can be discovered about the condition of this text, about how it was printed, and what kind of copy was used.

For the printing Gosson hired William White, whose ornaments appear on the title-page and on A2. Judging from his position as master warden of the Stationers' Company for several years, White enjoyed a reputation in his profession. In the previous year he had seen Q4 of *Richard II* through the press, and in the following year, 1610, he was to print one of the later quartos of Kyd's *Spanish Tragedy*. We cannot be certain, however, that White supervised the printing of the entire play, for there is strong evidence to show that the printing was divided between two shops. On sheets A and C–E, the running title corresponds to the head-title: 'The Play of / Pericles Prince of Tyre', while the pages of the remaining sheets are simply headed 'Pericles Prince of Tyre'. The pages in sheets A and C–E contain 37 lines, those of the remaining sheets 35. Moreover the fount of type in these two groups of sheets is different.[1] These variations suggest that the play was set up by compositors of different training, who were working in different shops.

As has recently been demonstrated,[2] at least three compositors shared in the printing of Q. Sheets A and C–E were composed by one compositor, from now on to be called *x*, while the remaining sheets were shared by two compositors, *y* and *z*. We have already seen that the work of *x* is distinguished by its peculiar running titles and the setting up of 37 lines per page. His spelling differs from that of the other compositors, and he observed the peculiar habit of adding a dot after his signatures.[3] What is more significant, he set up the text as verse almost all the way, and most of the time correctly, though with two significant exceptions: not realizing at once the change over from verse to prose in the fishermen scene, II. i, he turned most of the prose into verse; and he evidently became greatly perplexed in Act III (most of which appears on sheet E), for while he persists in printing verse, it becomes

---

1. This is best revealed by a study of the italics. Swash capital letters abound in sheets A and C–E but, with the exception of *M* and *G*, are absent in the other sheets. The same applies to italic digraph *es* and to a peculiar small italic *w*, in which two of the slanting strokes are extended upwards.

2. By P. Edwards, 'An Approach to the Problem of Pericles', *Shakespeare Survey 5*, 1952, pp. 25–49. Much of what follows is indebted to his article.

3. This custom may have been a peculiarity of White's shop rather than of compositor *x* only.

impossibly irregular from the middle of E3 (roughly III. ii. 14) on.

Compositor z, on the other hand, printed all the verse, both in Act I and Acts IV–V, as prose, and compositor y did the same three-quarters of the time. The main reason for this was probably that they failed to recognize the verse in their copy, though they may also have been influenced by the fact that they had to fit into only 35 lines per page the quantity of text which compositor x spread over 37 lines. y and z can be differentiated from each other by their preferential abbreviations in speech-headings and certain spellings. But the most obvious difference between the two is z's unusual habit of indenting speech-headings very deeply.[1]

Surprisingly enough, though y and z collaborated on each of sheets B and F–I and roughly did equal amounts of work, they did not divide their work by outer and inner formes, as was normal in Elizabethan printing of quartos.[2] Rather, each printed four, and sometimes more, consecutive pages. Edwards lists their shares as follows:

y: B–B2v, F–F2v, G–G2v, H3–I2
z: B3–B4v, F3–F4v, G3–H2v, I2v–I3v.[3]

Such a procedure meant that the two compositors collaborated on every outer and inner forme, an awkward method. One may further infer that their copy had not been cast off page by page, but only very roughly, by half-sheets, if that. Whether y and z worked simultaneously or alternately I have not been able to decide on the basis of a comparison of the type used. The former seems more probable.

Two problems still remain to be answered: why was the printing of the play shared by two shops, and why was sheet B printed in the second shop and not, as one would expect, by compositor x in White's own establishment? The probable answer to the second question is that sheet B was first printed in White's shop and then for some reason cancelled and reprinted in the other shop by

1. Pointed out to me by Mr Richard Hosley.

2. Compositor x proceeded in the normal manner. For instance, he printed the outer forme of D before the inner forme, where initial capital italic K is replaced by lower-case k.

3. Edwards' account of the play's compositors on which the foregoing description has been largely based is accurate but for two pages, signatures F3 and F4v. Not having heavily indented speech-headings, these pages were probably not set up by z, as Edwards claimed, but either by y or by some fourth compositor, who helped out in these two pages alone. A reason for doubting that F4v was set up by y is the spelling of the speech-headings for the Bawd with a w. On the signature immediately following, y spells this word six times with a u, in spite of the fact that the catchword on F4v reads *Bawd*.

compositors y and z. An analysis of the running titles reveals that sheet B in its final form was printed last, after the incomplete sheet I.[1] Furthermore, the type of paper used for all sheets is the same. What probably happened, therefore, is that White was commissioned by Gosson to print *Pericles*, and that he in turn arranged with some other printer for the printing of roughly the play's second half, namely sheets F–I, and later, after the decision to cancel sheet B, also for the reprinting of that part. The identity of this other printer I have not been able to establish.

3. The Condition of the Text

The knowledge that Q was set up by three compositors of different habits can be useful to the play's modern editor only if one can reach a fair state of certainty as to the nature of the copy from which they printed. As has been indicated, the play's irregular publication makes it exceedingly doubtful that the copy was in any way authorized, and thus 'good'. For further knowledge, we depend primarily on clues afforded by a thorough examination of the Q text itself, and to a lesser degree on the different ways in which the compositors reacted to apparent difficulties in their copy.

To begin, then, with a description of the more obvious characteristics of the text. At once its most pronounced and bewildering feature is the extreme unevenness in the literary quality of its language. For stiffness and triteness of verse most of the scenes of Acts I and II, and some in the later acts, afford no equal elsewhere in Shakespeare. On the other hand, some parts in Acts III and V are of the highest order. They more than reward the student who has patiently plodded through the mediocrity of the early acts. What bewilders the reader of *Pericles* is the mixture of long passages one would not consider worthy of Shakespeare the apprentice, not to mention the mature dramatist, with scenes like V. i, which in its undeniable poetic power recalls nothing so much as Shakespeare's last plays, *The Winter's Tale* and *The Tempest*. From almost any page in the first two acts instances of trite verse such as these could be cited:

> Antioch, farewell! for wisdom sees, those men
> Blush not in actions blacker than the night,
> Will shew no course to keep them from the light.
>
> (I. i. 135–7)
>
> The which when any shall not gratify,
> Or pay you with unthankfulness in thought,

1. Mr John Crow drew my attention to this point and other details in this section.

> Be it our wives, our children, or ourselves,
> The curse of heaven and men succeed their evils!
> Till when,—the which I hope shall ne'er be seen—
> Your grace is welcome to our town and us.   (I. iv. 101–6)

Typical of Acts I and II is also the jog-trot rhythm of such lines as:

>   but thou know'st this:
> 'Tis time to fear when tyrants seem to kiss.
> Which fear so grew in me, I hither fled,
> Under the covering of a careful night,
> Who seem'd my good protector; and, being here,
> Bethought me what was past, what might succeed.
> I knew him tyrannous; and tyrants' fears
> Decrease not, but grow faster than the years.
>   (I. ii. 78–85)[1]

A few verse-lines rise above the general low level of the first two acts, notably the image,

>   The blind mole casts
> Copp'd hills towards heaven, to tell the earth is throng'd
> By man's oppression; and the poor worm doth die for't.
>   (I. i. 101–3)

But the only pleasant interlude in the mediocre verse-drama of the play's first half is the dialogue of the fishermen in II. i. Its racy prose could have been written by any of a dozen writers of the period, but is nevertheless far superior to most of the surrounding verse.

The average literary standard of the play's second half, Acts III–v, is much higher. The opening speech of III. i marks a dramatic and welcome change from the earlier humdrum verse:

> The god of this great vast, rebuke these surges,
> Which wash both heaven and hell; and thou that hast
> Upon the winds command, bind them in brass,
> Having call'd them from the deep! O, still
> Thy deaf'ning, dreadful thunders; gently quench
> Thy nimble sulphurous flashes! . . .
> .   .   .   .
>   The seaman's whistle
> Is as a whisper in the ears of death,
> Unheard;   (III. i. 1–10)

and it is not least the beauty and evocative power of the verse that make the scene of Marina's recognition by her father a deeply

---

1. Similarly, see I. iii. 31–9.

moving experience, comparable in tenderness of feeling with that
of Lear's reunion with Cordelia. Yet the writing of the later acts
continues to be markedly uneven. Some scenes, especially III. iv,
seem flat and undistinguished. There are still many botched-up
lines, and some passages are quite as bad as the worst of Acts I and
II, notably the last lines of the epitaph, devised by Dionyza for
Marina, which Gower recites in IV. iv. This striking unevenness of
the play's literary quality calls for an explanation. First, however,
let us note certain other peculiarities of the Q text.

Almost as bewildering as the text's uneven literary quality is the
highly irregular manner in which it is set up. Entire scenes are
printed in prose which were manifestly intended as verse, such as
IV. i, v. iii, and most of v. i. Many other passages are set up in highly
irregular verse, some of which no modern editor has succeeded in
turning into convincing blank verse (which no doubt was originally
intended):

> I hold it euer Vertue and Cunning,
> Were endowments greater, then Noblenesse & Riches;
> Carelesse Heyres, may the two latter darken and expend;
> But Immortalitie attendes the former,
> Making a man a god:
> T' is knowne, I euer haue studied Physicke:
> Through which secret Art, by turning ore Authorities,
> I haue togeather with my practize, made famyliar,
> To me . . .   (III. ii. 26–35)

The chaotic setting up of the end of IV. iii,

> Yere like one that supersticiously,
> Doe sweare too'th Gods, that Winter kills
> The Fliies, but yet I know, youle
> doe as I aduise,

is typical of much of the play, though in this case the rhyme points
to the correct lineation. On the other hand, several passages intended as prose, such as part of the dialogue of the fishermen (II. i.
16–47), are set up as verse. Badly arranged verse, verse set up as
prose, or prose set up as verse, are not uncommon features in the
dramatic texts of Shakespeare's age. But few of them parallel the
extent of misarrangement in Q of *Pericles*.

As for stage-directions, they are notable for their frequent omission. Some of the entries are bare to the point of vagueness, e.g.
Enter Bawdes 3 at the beginning of IV. ii (i.e. Pandar, Bawd, and
Boult) and *Enter two Sailors* at v. i, without indication whether they
belong to Pericles' ship or are from Mytilene. Particularly ambigu-

ous are the stage-directions for the opening dialogue of III. ii at Cerimon's house, which have hitherto been wrongly interpreted.[1] This lack of precision affects some of the speech-headings as well. The speeches of the fishermen, and of the sailors in both III. i and v. i, are indicated merely by numerals, and in the latter case at least the modern editor will have to decide upon the precise identity of the speakers. There are also several instances of omitted speech-headings (e.g. I. i. 57 and I. iii. 30) and the misattribution of speeches (see v. iii. 50, collation). At some places the dialogue has become utterly confused by the misplacement of phrases. In III. i, where Pericles says to the 1st Sailor

> As you thinke meet; for she must ouer board straight:
> Most wretched Queen,

the words 'for she must ouer board straight' ought evidently to have been printed at the end of the Sailor's previous speech. Worse still is the confusion at v. i. 32–4, where Helicanus answers Lysimachus' request to be allowed to see Pericles,

> You may, but bootlesse. Is your sight, hee will not speake to any,
> yet let me obtaine my wish.

Again, however, editors have solved the problem easily.

A last characteristic of the Q text to be mentioned in this preliminary survey is the very considerable number of gross errors, some of which have remained unsolved cruces. Often the text of Q makes sheer nonsense, as in 'The which the Gods protect thee, Fame may defend thee:' (II. i. 128), or

> . . . thinke this Pilat thought
> So with his sterage, shall your thoughts grone
> To fetch his daughter home, who first is gone
> Like moats and shadowes, see them
> Moue a while . . .   (IV. iv. 18–21)

Punctuation, likewise, is frequently chaotic. Often the compositors seem to have been so much at a loss that they simply resorted to punctuating the end of each line, whether the sense required it or not. As in the above quotation after 'gone', full-stops or semi-colons are sometimes lacking, while at other places words which belong together are severed by a heavy punctuation mark.

4. The Causes of Corruption

Enough has been said to show that Q is a highly imperfect text. As early as 1780, Malone commented:

1. See Commentary, III. ii, opening n.

... the earliest printed copy appears in so imperfect a form, that there is scarcely a single page of it undisfigured by the grossest corruptions. As many words have been inserted, inconsistent not only with the author's meaning, but with any meaning whatsoever, as many verses appear to have been transposed, and some passages are appropriated to some characters to whom manifestly they do not belong, so there is great reason to believe that many words or even lines were omitted at the press; and it is highly probable that the printer is answerable for more of these ellipses than the poet. The same observation may be extended to the metre, which might have been originally sufficiently smooth and harmonious, though now, notwithstanding the editor's best care, it is feared it will be found in many places rugged and defective.[1]

Steevens thought similarly of the text, but attributed its many gross mistakes to the 'faithful copies of frequent early transcriptions in the playhouses'.[2]

Later scholars have not quarrelled with their description of the text, though their explanations, which are mere guesses, have proved inadequate, and Steevens' theory is untenable in the light of present-day knowledge of Elizabethan dramatic manuscripts. Malone's view, as will be shown, is too simple but should not be neglected.

A more thorough examination of the problem of the text was made by some nineteenth-century scholars, but it did not provide a solution. On the basis of a comparison between the play and Wilkins' novel, which is a contemporary report of it, both Collier and Mommsen arrived at the view that parts of the play, notably the scene of Lysimachus' visit to the brothel, have reached us in a cut and otherwise mangled form. It will be best to discuss this theory, which still has some followers, in a later section dealing with Wilkins' novel, and only remark here that the length of the printed text of *Pericles* does not differ appreciably from the average for early seventeenth-century plays, which makes it unlikely that cutting, if any was made, was extensive. The other main development was the attempt to explain the play's great unevenness of style in terms of mixed authorship. This opens up an entirely new problem, which will also be deferred till a later section.

The peculiar contribution of twentieth-century criticism to the problem of the text has been to seek an explanation mainly in terms of printer's copy. Modern bibliographical scholarship has

1. Supplement to edn of Shakespeare's plays by Steevens of 1778, 1780, II, p. 183.
2. *Ibid.*, p. 179.

made us aware of the different kinds of manuscript copy from which plays in Shakespeare's age were printed; and though scholars do not as yet see eye to eye as to the copy in the case of *Pericles*, they are agreed that the main cause of the high incidence of textual corruption must be sought in it. It is not the printer who is to be held mainly responsible, as Malone had supposed, but his copy.

Such an approach to the play, however, is fraught with difficulties. The ideal material for the study of printer's copy, an extant manuscript designed for such a purpose, does not exist for any of Shakespeare's plays, and the unsatisfactory Quarto of *Pericles* was not replaced by a better text, as happened within a few years in the case of such bad quartos as Q1 of *Hamlet* and Q1 of *Romeo and Juliet*. The test of comparison with a superior text is therefore not available and the only procedure left is to analyse the printed text, and *indirectly*, by comparing its characteristics with those of other corrupt dramatic texts where analysis is easier, to reach some hypothesis about its underlying copy. In such a study, moreover, the possibility of mixed authorship presents a further complicating factor.

It is then no wonder that some of the most learned modern scholars of Elizabethan dramatic texts have shrunk from a detailed analysis of *Pericles*, and have confined themselves to brief and extremely cautious comments. To Pollard and Chambers the large amount of verse that is either mislineated or printed as heavily punctuated prose 'suggests a report, possibly with the aid of shorthand', and Chambers adds: 'There may have been some omissions'.[1] In his introduction to a modern facsimile of Q, Greg expresses himself even more cautiously: 'it seems possible that the text is a reported one, though it cannot be said to manifest the same state of disintegration as the recognized "Bad Quartos".'[2] Such a view is of course reconcilable with the data of the play's irregular printing. That we can now be much less vague about the copy and some aspects of the printing is mainly owing to Philip Edwards, who recently published the only thorough examination of the text on bibliographical grounds.[3] Edwards found sufficient marks of inaccurate reporting to make it highly probable that the text was 'assembled without reference to an authorized manuscript'.[4] Foremost among these is the manifest confusion, at a number of points in the play, of the action within a scene, of which the first

1. A. W. Pollard, *Shakespeare's Folios and Quartos*, 1909, p. 62. E. K. Chambers, *William Shakespeare*, 1930, I, p. 521.

2. *Pericles 1609*, Shakespeare's Quartos in Collotype Facsimile No. 5, 1940.

3. See *op. cit.* on p. xxvi above.   4. *Ibid.*, p. 26.

sixty lines of I. ii furnish the clearest example. Edwards not merely demonstrates convincingly how this confusion has come about, but gives an outline of the probable order of events and speeches in the original. An attempt at reconstruction, along similar lines, will be found in Appendix C, where this matter is discussed at some length. A second token of corruption, he notes, is the frequent repetition of phrases, a feature commonly found in texts that are regarded as memorial reconstructions. For instance the opening of one of Pericles' most moving speeches, 'I am great with woe / And shall deliver weeping' (v. i. 105), is echoed fifty lines later by Marina: '. . . as my good nurse Lychorida hath oft Deliver'd weeping'. Similarly, the resemblance of v. i. 12–13 and v. iii. 59–61 is close enough to make one suspicious.[1] One should of course be wary of attributing every repetition in wording to the reporter. Such repetitions may be due to hasty writing,[2] may be deliberate—as they are throughout the F text of *Antony and Cleopatra*, and occasionally in our text (Q) of *Pericles*[3]—or may be blamed on the sleepy compositor. But the evidence Edwards has marshalled leaves us in no doubt that Q was set up from corrupt reported copy.

Edwards then examined the many instances in Q of misaligned verse. He was struck by the fact that such inaccuracy occurs more frequently in the later acts. In the first two acts, only about 10 per cent of the verse appears to be misaligned, while in Acts III–V the faulty proportion is no less than 70 per cent. More precisely, he marks the turning point half way through sig. E3, that is to say, soon after the opening of III. ii. This fact, together with the rather greater incidence of misplacements and of gross textual errors, suggested to him that the play's compositors found much more trouble in setting up the last three acts than in the first two; and, as the change can be traced in the work of all three compositors who had a share in the play's printing, he made the further inference that 'the latter half of the manuscript was prepared by a different hand from that responsible for the first half.'[4] From this he in turn deduced that the two parts of the play were assembled by two reporters, who differed greatly in capacity and in the legibility of their handwriting. For convenience' sake in this summary, let me call them A and B. Reporter A, who was responsible for Acts I and II, Edwards argues, remembered his scenes so badly that he was

---

1. Other examples are 'rough' (III. ii. 81), repeated at III. ii. 90; 'That the gods Would set me free from this unhallow'd place' (IV. vi. 98–9), closely paraphrased at IV. vi. 178–9; and IV. vi. 125–7, repeated substantially at IV. vi. 152–4.

2. See Commentary, I. iv. 17.

3. E.g. 'prosperous' at v. i. 72 and 79 (by Shakespeare), and 'countless', I. i. 32 and 74 (not by the reporter, though not by Shakespeare either).

4. Edwards, p. 34.

often driven to glue fragments of the original into verse of his own making. Only the prose of the fishermen in ii. i did he recall with fair accuracy. His reconstructed scenes are thus comparable to the worst in the first Quarto of *Romeo and Juliet*. However, he had at least the virtues of presenting fairly legible copy, and of setting out his verse as verse. B, in charge of Acts iii–v, was a much better reporter, which may largely account for the better average aesthetic quality of many of the later scenes:

> He knows the text better than his predecessor, and he sets about his work in a style that, had it been maintained beyond the first ninety lines, would have given us very little indeed to grumble at. But his eagerness to get all right flags, and he writes down what he recalls partly in verse, partly in prose, and so we lose sight, presumably for ever, of the genuine version of the last three acts, from the opening of iii. ii.[1]

The copy he produced was much more crowded than A's, and his handwriting worse, thus causing the compositors to make more mistakes of their own. Lastly, Edwards suggests that 'the different aptitudes of the two reporters [may be] the *sole* cause of the difference in literary value between the two halves of the play'.[2]

The evidence Edwards has marshalled for the view that Q is a report presenting the original in mangled form is considerable and much of it convincing. But when he implies that Q is as bad a text as Q1 of *Romeo and Juliet* or worse, and that reporting is a sufficient explanation for the play's worst scenes, his conclusions should not go unchallenged. The second of these deductions may surely be rejected outright; for that two entire acts of a Shakespearean drama should be reduced by a reporter to what Acts i and ii of *Pericles* are, with hardly anything reminding one of Shakespeare's gifts of language, not to mention other attributes, is simply incredible. No parallel can be found for it even in the worst of Shakespeare's quartos. His conclusion that Q is an extremely bad text is likewise debatable. If by any chance the original of the first two acts was not composed by Shakespeare but in the main by one of his minor fellow-dramatists, we should not be surprised to find the verse set up more regularly by the reporter, for anyone could have set it up more easily than Shakespeare's much freer and more complex lines. Hence Edwards' pivotal point, that not one but two reporters compiled the manuscript, is shaky.[3] If it is true, as Edwards contends, that the condition of the play's text should be kept in mind in any investigation of its authorship, the reverse is

1. *Ibid.*, p. 38.   2. p. 45.

3. Nothing in the spelling of Q suggests that its copy was in two different hands. But such negative evidence carries little weight.

equally true. The problem of authorship cannot be settled by a purely bibliographical approach. Conclusions about multiple or single reporting in a play must remain suspect as long as there seem good reasons for possible mixed authorship.

A last point in this thesis that seems doubtful is the contention that for the first two acts the copy must have been much cleaner and the handwriting more legible than for the last three. For, like the rest of the text, Acts I and II contain a large number of errors which seem to have arisen from the compositors' misreading of copy or from haste or negligence on their part. As this fact has been underplayed, a list of some of the more striking errors of this kind in the first two acts may be of interest: 'the stint' for *th'ostent* (I. ii. 26), 'once' for either *care* or *am* (I. ii. 31), 'doo't' for *doubt it* (I. ii. 86), 'too sauers' for *two summers* (I. iv. 39), 'thee' for *thou* (I. iv. 58), 'That' for *Hath* (I. iv. 67), 'hymnes' for *him's* (I. iv. 74), 'sau'd one' for *sends word* (II. Ch. 22), 'What, to pelch' for *What, ho, Pilch!* (II. i. 12), 'more:or' for *moreo'er* (II. i. 83), 'Pompey' for *pompae* (II. ii. 30), 'I' for *To* (II. iii. 3). Numerous smaller errors resulting from misreading could be added to these examples, and there are also several major errors in punctuation; for example at I. i. 155–6, I. iv. 5, 65, and 105, II. Ch. 32, and II. iv. 22. These errors are distributed over the sheets set up by the different compositors and can therefore not be blamed on the exceptional ineptitude of any one of them. From a comparison with the not much larger number of similar errors in Acts III–V, one can only conclude that the handwriting of the copy for the two first acts was quite as bad as that for the last three.

While, with the notable exception of II. v, graphic errors are numerous throughout the text, auditory errors are remarkable for their scarcity, if not absence. Nothing comparable can be found to such errors as 'in sight' for *incite*, or 'do so bade in office' for *dog's obeyed in office* in Q1 of *Lear*, a text which resembles that of our play in the high degree of misarranged verse and prose. The only possible instances of errors resulting from mishearing which I have been able to find in *Pericles* are: 'All day' for *holidays* (II. i. 81), 'kee' for *che* (II. ii. 27), 'ayre' for *e'er* (III. i. 62), 'art' for *heart* (IV. Ch. 10), 'bed' for *bird* (IV. Ch. 26), and 'Verollus' for *Verolles* (IV. ii. 104); and some of these instances could be explained in other ways. At any rate, a few apparent sound-confusions in a text do not establish a likelihood of an oral stage in its transmission; as is now recognized, among the substitutions that can be made by a copyist working from MS or print are substitutions of syllables associated by sound with those he ought to have set. If the report was made with the help of notes during a theatrical performance, as Pollard and others have suggested, no direct evidence can be found. One can only guess, in general terms, in what manner and by what kind of person the report was made. All that can be stated safely is that this report often represents the original inaccurately, and that it was written down in a confused and badly legible manner so that the copy used in the printing shops must have looked somewhat like bad 'foul papers'.

It would, however, be quite wrong for this reason to blame textual corruption of Q almost entirely on the reporter and his unsatisfactory copy. There is good reason to believe that Q's compositors did not take enough trouble in deciphering their copy sensibly, and that they were otherwise careless.[1] For instance, they several times provided question-marks after phrases beginning with *who* or *what*, even if these obviously introduce a subordinate clause, not a question. They often omitted words (e.g. at i. i. 8 and 128, i. ii. 45, 83, and 121, ii. i. 157, ii. iv. 56). Several times speech-headings were omitted at the beginning of a page because they failed to supply correct catchwords (e.g. i. i. 57, i. iii. 30, v. i. 180).[2] An entire line is missing at i. ii. 122 and, though less certainly, at several other places. For many other errors it is impossible to decide definitely whether compositor or reporter should be held responsible. The point I wish to make is that it has been customary to blame the reporter too freely for the corruptions in the text: the compositors contributed a good share, and not only because of their difficult copy.

A further indication of hasty and careless work in the two printing shops is the very casual proof-reading of the text. In the nine copies of Q that have come to my attention, only the following variants can be found:[3]

1. Q2, which was also printed by W. White (at least in part), but of course from copy that provided no difficulty in legibility, can be fruitfully studied for this purpose. There, in Marina's epitaph (iv. iv. 39), *Thetis* becomes 'That is', and twice, for a reason hard to fathom, the word 'daily' slips into the text.

2. The inadequate catchwords were provided by compositors *x*, *z*, and *y*, in that order. Another speech-heading is missing at i. i. 170. Two other catchwords are erroneous; those on E4v (iii. iii. 32, '*Cler.* 1') and on G3 (iv. v. 1, '*Gower*', an obvious error which was caught by the press-corrector), but both are followed by the correct speech-headings. R. A. Foakes comments that the large number of these errors may be indicative of a rather unusual MS copy in which speech-headings were placed far over in the margin.

3. The nine copies included in this survey are in the following libraries: British Museum (B.M.), Bodleian (Bod), Public Library, Boston, Mass. (Bos), Capell Collection, Trinity College, Cambridge (C), Folger Library, Washington (F), Huntington Library, California (H), private library of John Murray, the publisher, Albemarle Street, London W.1 (M), Stratford Birthplace (Flower copy) (S), and Elizabethan Club, Yale, New Haven, Conn. (Y). M was purchased by Mr Allerton C. Hickmott of West Hartford, Conn., in 1964.

Signature (Q) and Line Reference	1st State Copies	2nd State Copies	3rd State Copies
Title Page	diuers aad sundry F only	diuers and sundry all except F	—
C1v (II. Ch. 24)	hid in Tent to murdred Bod, S	had intent to murder B.M., C, F, H, M, Y, Bos	—
C3v (II. i. 119, 120, 145, 150)	pary ... yeat ... di'e ... youle Bod only	pray ... yeat ... di'e ... you'le F, H, S	pray ... yet ... do'e ... you'le B.M., Bos, C, M, Y
E2 (III. i. 43)	Slake Bod only	Slacke all except Bod	—
F2 (IV. i. 12)	resolu'de Y only	resolude all except Y	—
G3, Catchword	*Gower* B.M., Bod, Bos	2. *Gent.* C, F, H, M, S, Y	—
H2v (v. Ch. 20 and v. i. 11)	former ... *Hell.* B.M., C	former ... *1. Say.* Bod, Y	feruor ... *1. Say.* Bos., F, H, M, S
H3 (v. i. 33)	sight see, will B.M., C, Y	sight, hee will Bod, Bos, F, H, M, S	—

Of the nine copies of Q I have consulted, only Murray's has all the variant formes in the corrected state. The Huntington copy has all except for C3v, which is in its second state. No copy known consists only of uncorrected sheets. None of the corrections made is such as to provide clear evidence that the press-corrector consulted the original manuscript copy. From these corrections one can infer that the proof-reading was fairly intelligent but entirely inadequate. How a contemporary could go about correcting an obviously imperfectly printed text is demonstrated by Q4, where hundreds of passages are changed, quite a number convincingly. In the known copies of Q of *Lear*, which was also printed badly, no fewer than 150 variants have been found. Everything, then, points in the case of *Pericles* to hasty and careless printing, a fact to which, it will be remembered, Malone already gave emphasis, but which modern scholars, preoccupied with the reporter, have tended to minimize.

These observations may do something to moderate one's view of the 'badness' of the copy. Corrupt it certainly was, but whether as corrupt as Edwards' thesis would imply, at least for part of it, is doubtful. Yet it is one thing to question the degree of badness of the report and quite a different thing to postulate a different kind of copy, as both Craig and Sisson have recently done. Independently, they have expressed the belief that the copy for Q was, at least in part, Shakespeare's 'foul papers' or rough draft.[1] The theory that Shakespeare revised *Pericles* from an older play, on which Craig's new theory of the copy partly depends, deserves separate treatment.[2] But it can be said categorically here that no theory of 'foul papers' applied to *Pericles* can claim conviction unless it counters adequately the considerable evidence Edwards and others have found for reported copy. In a note,[3] Sisson remarks that many of the errors evidently arose from the compositors' misinterpretation of the handwriting, and that certain confusions in the printed text can be explained in terms of author's corrections *currente calamo* in the copy. But as has been shown, neither of these two features is necessarily alien to the copy of a report. And, one may observe, most texts believed to have been printed from foul papers are far superior to Q of *Pericles*.

5. Early Reprints

Gosson's experiment with Q was evidently successful, for he published a second Quarto (Q2) during the same year. Q2 was evidently printed from a copy of Q, for title-page and head-title are identical and, though the entire type was set up anew, the text reproduces that of Q page by page and line by line, with only minor alterations. Of the substantial variant readings, some are simple corrections, others new errors. The retention of a number of obvious gross errors of the earlier edition makes it probable that the compositors of Q2 did not reconsult the original MS copy. If they did, they must have used it for occasional checking only. The regularization of the running-title to 'The Play of Pericles Prince of Tyre' is one of the few marks which enable one to decide the priority of Q over Q2. But the standard manner of distinguishing between the two editions is by referring to the first entry in the play, 'Enter Gower', which was carelessly rendered as 'Eneer Gower' in Q2.

All later editions in the seventeenth century are directly or indirectly derived from Q2. Four more quarto editions appeared, in

1. See H. Craig, '*Pericles* and *The Painfull Aduentures*', *SP*, xlv (1949), 100–5; and his 'Review of Shakespearean Scholarship in 1952', *Sh.Q.*, iv, No. 2 (1953), 122, where he rejects Edwards' thesis 'as an error in the major proposition'; also G. E. Seiler, 'Shakespeare's Part in Pericles', Abstract of Ph.D. Thesis, Missouri, 1951, in *Dissertation Abstracts*, vol. xii, pp. 309–10. This thesis was written under Craig's supervision.

2. See pp. xlvii–xlix below.

3. Note to iv. i. 4–7 in *New Readings in Shakespeare*, 1955, ii, p. 296. For details see Commentary.

1611, 1619, 1630, and 1635 (Qq 3–6). Each reprints the edition immediately preceding it, except for Q6, which made some use of Q4. Apart from Q4, they introduced only a few minor changes in the text. Q4, printed by William Jaggard for Thomas Pavier in 1619, was designed to form part of Pavier's collection of Shakespearean and pseudo-Shakespearean plays, as evidenced by its signatures, which continue those of the 1619 quarto of the Second and Third parts of *Henry VI*. The compositor of Q4 made numerous small changes in the text, quite a number of which have been accepted by modern editors as convincing corrections, though there are also a few which make obvious nonsense. But even the best of the changes are purely the result of guesswork, and editors need to be especially wary of them, for the workman responsible was the same as the notorious compositor B of the First Folio. The fact that at two or three places Q4 continues manifest misprints introduced into the text by Q2 or Q3 suggests that Jaggard's compositor consulted neither Q nor any manuscript source more closely related to the original.

The play's absence from the First Folio is notable. It was added in the second impression of the third folio (F3), together with a number of plays spuriously associated with Shakespeare. F3 depended on Q6 for its text, and in 1685 F4 reprinted again, this time from F3. Both folios introduced a few changes into the text, mainly in the interest of grammar and more regular metre. In the eighteenth century, Rowe accepted the play into his three editions of 1709 and 1714, but then it was omitted by Pope, Theobald, Warburton, Dr Johnson, Capell, and others, though Sewell printed it in Pope's second edition of 1728, and two unimportant texts appeared in duodecimo in 1734, printed by Tonson and Walker. Only towards the end of the eighteenth century was the play admitted again into the regular canon of Shakespeare, when Malone took Farmer's advice and printed it in the supplement to Steevens's edition of 1778–80. Since then it has been allowed a place in most editions of Shakespeare's complete works.

6. *Wilkins' 'Painfull Aduentures'*

For the sake of clarity, my treatment of the text has so far left out of consideration a work which is closely related to it, and which for several reasons should be of great interest to students of *Pericles*: George Wilkins' contemporary novel, *The Painfull Aduentures of Pericles Prince of Tyre*, which appeared in 1608, one year before Q of *Pericles*.

Unfortunately, the precise relation between novel and play is not easily analysed and, in spite of a number of learned studies, scholars have not reached agreement.[1] A few matters, however, are clear. The novel is obviously not a source of *Pericles*, either direct or indirect, as was assumed by Dugdale Sykes.[2] For not only does the novel's title-page announce 'The true History of the Play of *Pericles* as it was lately presented by the worthy and ancient Poet *John Gower*'—a statement which one might argue was added fraudulently by the printer, after the play itself had been staged, to help the book's sales—but at several points the novel's phrasing leaves no doubt that it was in fact a report of a play. An instance occurs in the following passage, corresponding to IV. vi: 'he [the Pandar] told them, that the Lorde *Lysimachus* was come, and as if the word Come had beene his kew, he entred the Chamber with the master bawde, . . .' (87. 19–22). Moreover, the novel's narrative includes episodes of a kind one would hardly expect in a work composed independently of a play, pieces of dialogue which are proper within the artistic conventions of drama but alien to the novel form. Such an episode is Cleon's description of the famine at Tharsus to his wife Dionyza, hardly the person to stand in need of such information.[3]

The novel, then, is based on a play for certain. Whether that play was *Pericles*, however, or some earlier dramatization of the story before it reached the hands of Shakespeare, an 'Ur-Pericles' as Muir has called it, is a matter less easy to decide.

The degree of correspondence between Wilkins' novel and the play as we know it is considerable. The names of all the characters are identical, a likeness which, among all versions of the story, only Wilkins' novel shares with the play. The list of 'the Names of the Personages in this Historie' at the beginning of the novel might just as well have formed the *Dramatis Personae* of *Pericles* itself. It includes Pericles, called Apollonius or by some similar name in all previous versions, Thaisa, Marina, John Gower the presenter, Cleon, Dionyza, Simonides, Lysimachus, etc. The only difference is that Boult is referred to simply as 'a leno' in Wilkins' list. The novel, furthermore, echoes the play's language frequently, though close verbal parallels are fewer than one would expect if it were unquestionably based directly on *Pericles*. What is no less relevant, how-

---

1. Wilkins' novel has recently appeared in a convenient reprint by K. Muir, *Liverpool Reprints*, No. 8, 1953. Page and line references are to this text. It is both reliable (except for minor mistakes in spelling) and inexpensive.

2. In *Sidelights to Shakespeare*, 1919, pp. 143–203.

3. See S. Spiker, 'George Wilkins and the Authorship of *Pericles*', *SP*, xxx (1933), 560, one of the best treatments of the subject; and K. Muir, ed. *P.A.*, pp. iv–v.

ever, is that these parallels are spread over the whole work, echoing
not merely those scenes whose authorship has been widely questioned but also passages indubitably by Shakespeare. Among lines
of the play's first two acts echoed in Wilkins are: I. Ch. 30, 'custome
of sinne made it accompted no sinne' (*P.A.*, 13. 18); I. iv. 45-7,
'heere standes one weeping, and there lies another dying, so sharpe
are hungers teeth' (*P.A.*, 25. 9-11); and II. iii. 81-5, which Wilkins
follows more closely than any other passage of similar length in the
play: '*Pericles* . . . thus returneth what hee is, that hee was a Gentleman of *Tyre*, his name Pericles, his education beene in Artes and
Armes, who looking for aduentures in the world, was by the rough
and vnconstant Seas, most vnfortunately bereft both of shippes and
men, and after shipwrecke, throwen vpon that shoare' (*P.A.*, 40.
1-9). Echoes of passages that have always been regarded as Shakespeare's include: 'Poore inch of Nature (quoth he) thou arte as
rudely welcome to the worlde, as euer Princesse Babe was, and hast
as chiding a natiuitie, as fire, ayre, earth, and water can affoord
thee' (59. 4-7; cf. *Per.*, III. i. 30-4)[1]; 'I haue bin tossed from wrong
to iniurie' (105. 22-3, in the middle of a passage taken from Twine;
cf. *Per.*, v. I. 130); and 'he [Pericles] . . . thanketh *Lysimachus* that
so fortunately had brought her to begette life in the father who
begot her' (106. 26-107. 1; cf. *Per.*, v. i. 195). Other parallels will
be found listed in the commentary. The identical names of the
characters in *Pericles* and the novel and the echoes in the novel of
passages which are manifestly Shakespeare's are not merely further reasons for rejecting the theory that the novel was the play's
main source, but also would seem to provide good grounds for believing that Wilkins based his novel on the play as we know it and
not on some earlier dramatic version.

But this is by no means the whole story concerning Wilkins. At a
number of points his novel is quite different from the play. There
would be no problem if this were merely owing to the difference in
form, or to Wilkins allowing a free rein to his own powers of invention by elaborating a few of the episodes as they appealed to him.[2]
But it is mainly due to his liberal use of a second source, Twine's
earlier novel on the same subject. Rather than 'the true History of
the Play of Pericles', Wilkins' novel is a hybrid creation, the pro-
duct of heterogeneous cross-breeding. It was Twine's novel which

---

1. For the words, 'Poor inch of nature', see n. to III. i. 34 in the text.

2. Examples are Wilkins' account of the banquet at Simonides' court, where
Pericles is presented with a steed and spur (though it may be argued that this
incident belonged to the original play, and fitted in after II. iii. 91); and of the
recognition in v. i. In Wilkins, Marina, unabashed by Pericles' morose and
aggressive bearing, proceeds 'with morall precepts to reproue him' (*P.A.*, p. 104).

suggested to Wilkins his title, *The Painfull Aduentures*, which gave
him the idea of dividing his work into chapters, each headed by a
brief summary, and which supplied a convenient narrative for
certain incidents which are only briefly alluded to by Gower, the
play's chorus. For these episodes Wilkins did not hesitate to copy
entire paragraphs from Twine almost word for word.[1] Muir provides a sound summary of those passages where Wilkins' dependence on Twine is most in evidence:

> He relies most obviously on the earlier novel in the opening
> chapter, describing events before the beginning of the play; in
> the description of the statue, barely mentioned in the play; in the
> description of the wedding, not dramatized; in Lychorida's rela-
> tion of Marina's parentage, omitted in the play; in Marina's
> song and in her conversation with her father; and in the final
> chapter, describing events after the end of the play.[2]

His conclusion, however, that 'Wilkins obviously followed the play
when he could, only falling back on the novel when the play was
deficient', does not quite meet the case. The distribution of verbal
echoes of Twine over all but a few pages of *The Painfull Aduentures*—
the only longer section free from such echoes spreads from about
the middle of Chapter IV to the end of Chapter V, a passage corresponding roughly to half of Act II in the play—would rather indicate that Wilkins consulted a copy of Twine almost constantly
while at work on his own version. His dependence on Twine was
indeed greater than his reliance on the play itself. And this makes
one wonder whether there was perhaps no other way for Wilkins;
whether his memory of the play was so faulty that he needed Twine
to be able to write his novel at all.[3]

The fact that a number of episodes in the play's action are treated
in Wilkins' novel in a manifestly inferior manner strengthens this
suspicion. In his account of I. iii, the episode of Thaliard's arrival
at Tyre after Pericles' departure, Wilkins differs strikingly from the

1. For evidence that Wilkins also knew Gower, see Commentary, III. ii. 92n.

2. Muir, *op. cit.*, p. v.

3. It is perhaps of some interest that *The Painfull Aduentures* is not Wilkins' only
work where he shows such excessive dependence, without acknowledgement, on
another author. His translation of the *Historie of Iustine*, 1606, but for slight
changes and some small elaborations, merely reprints Golding's earlier translation of the same work.

Another matter is the use Wilkins' printer, Thomas Purfoot, made of Twine,
to which E. A. J. Honigmann drew attention in a review of Muir's edn of *P.A.*—
see *Sh.Q.*, VI, No. 1 (Winter 1955), 98–100. It may be significant that the
original printing of Wilkins' novel contains two ornamental borders identical
with those of Twine's novel, as printed by Valentine Simmes. But the known
facts are insufficient to warrant any far-reaching conclusions.

play. In the novel, Thaliard never reveals himself to Helicanus, as he does in the play, but discovers Pericles' departure by witnessing the lamentations of the people of Tyre. His report of the scene does not contain a single echo of *Pericles* but, significantly enough, is strongly indebted to Twine. Even if he depended on a version of the play earlier than that known to us, one would be driven to conclude that his memory of this small scene was weak. At II. iv. 45 in the play Helicanus pleads with the Lords of Tyre, who are impatient for a new ruler, to wait 'A twelvemonth longer', while in Wilkins he asks for three months' forbearance (*P.A.*, 43. 24). The ensuing action, as treated in both versions, makes 'three months' appear much less probable than 'twelve'. In the rendering of the incidents of III. ii, leading up to Thaisa's awakening by Cerimon, the novel is strikingly inferior to the play. In *The Painfull Aduentures*, it is Cerimon himself who, while walking on the beach, discovers Thaisa's chest. Then follows a tasteless description, taken largely from Twine, of how Cerimon discovered some remaining life in her (*P.A.*, p. 64) and how he himself carried Thaisa to his chamber. Similar instances of notably inferior treatment, accompanied by considerable reliance on Twine, are Wilkins' versions of the incidents which form III. iii, IV. i, and IV. iii in the play. Enough has been said to show that, whether the play Wilkins depended on was *Pericles* or an earlier version of it, his report is a patched up and highly inaccurate affair.

Nevertheless, it is with good reason that Collier and many scholars since have urged students of *Pericles* to give close study to Wilkins' novel. For if the novel is only a very inferior and thus undependable report of the play, so is, as has been shown in the previous section, the play's first quarto, its only substantive text. It need not surprise us, therefore, that notwithstanding the line of argument of the previous paragraphs, Wilkins' version can at a few points be shown to be superior to that of the play. It has long been recognized, for instance, that the text of the novel can be useful to an editor for restoring readings that are corrupt in the play. Here are some examples: 'two summers' (I. iv. 39), 'uncomely' (I. i. 129), 'bitumed' (III. ii. 57), 'unscissor'd . . . hair' (III. iii. 29). Furthermore, it can be relied upon for supplementing Q's all too bare stage-directions at many points.

Though, for reasons now obvious, extreme caution is needed, one should show an open mind even to the possibility that in one or two instances Wilkins' account of entire episodes may be more accurate than that of Q. A fairly clear example is provided by the play's second scene, Pericles' conference with Helicanus and his preparations for the flight from Tyre. As I noted earlier,[1] something must have gone wrong in the transmission of this scene, especially the opening sixty lines. Wilkins' report confirms this impression. It leaves unmentioned the Lords whose speeches provide such a puzzle of inconsistencies in the play, so that Pericles lets only Helicanus into the secret of his impending departure—which, in view of the later development of the action, is more probable than the play's version. Wilkins' report also omits any mention of Pericles' anger towards Helicanus at his boldly critical intervention. On the other hand, it includes what may be a lost line of the original: 'Absence abates that edge that presence whets'. Such stock phrases are typical of the early parts of the play. In Appendix C, an attempt has been made to reconstruct the scene with the help of Wilkins.

The case of II. ii, the scene in which the six knights present their shields to Thaisa and the King before the triumph, is rather different; but here again, Wilkins' account seems in some respects better than that of the play. Q's stage-directions for this scene are quite inadequate. It is from Wilkins that we learn that 'the King himselfe, with the Princesse his daughter, haue placed themselues in a Gallery, to beholde the triumphes' (36. 19–21),[2] that '5. seuerall princes (their horses richly caparasoned, but themselues more richly armed, their Pages before them bearing their Deuices on their shields) entred then the Tilting place' (36. 28–37. 2), that upon the knights passing by with their squires, the shields were 'by the knights Page deliuered to the Lady, and from her presented to the King her father' (37. 6–7). Though here as elsewhere Wilkins may have added his own embellishments, his description is confirmed by II. ii. 40 in the play, and the great detail of his ensuing account of the six knights and their shields increases one's confidence that he is reporting the stage spectacle with at least a fair degree of accuracy. In Q, the episode proper opens with the King's question to Thaisa concerning the first knight, who is passing in front of them with his squire. Thaisa answers, 'A knight of Sparta', describes the device on his shield, and reads the Latin motto. The King in turn translates the motto, similarly asks Thaisa about the second knight, who by then is approaching, and so the episode continues until all the knights have passed. But there seem to be some omissions. Not all the foreign mottoes are translated by the King,

---

1. pp. xxxiii–xxxiv.
2. The gallery on the Elizabethan stage was probably too high for this episode, and Wilkins may be referring to a pavilion placed on the stage. In Q the King and Thaisa 'withdraw' to the 'gallery' at the end of II. ii. But the whole matter is controversial. See Commentary, II. ii loc. and 57–8.

only those of the first and fourth knights and of Pericles; and Thaisa does not introduce the place of origin of the fourth and fifth. The former omission may be deliberate, to shorten what is an undramatic episode; the latter looks unintentional.

In Wilkins, on the other hand, all the knights are presented in the same manner. We are told the identity of each one, and not only is the device on every shield described, but the King 'made playne to her the meaning of each imprese' (37. 8–9)—that is, he translates the mottoes. Might one then make use of Wilkins to fill out what look like unintentional omissions in Q's report? The answer, unfortunately, is not a simple 'yes', for though the devices and mottoes in Wilkins and in Q are the same, their order is not, and it is hardly possible to decide which of the versions is in this respect the more accurate.[1]

An episode where Wilkins' novel departs even more strikingly from the play has been reserved for the end of this discussion, since it has played a large rôle in rival theories both about the source of the novel and about the nature of the play's text. As Collier and Mommsen long ago pointed out, the treatment of the brothel scenes, and especially of Marina's encounter with Lysimachus, is quite different in Wilkins and in the play, and the difference in this case cannot be explained in terms of Wilkins' reliance on Twine, for echoes of Twine in the relevant pages are relatively few. The whole passage in Wilkins—Chapter x of his novel—merits close reading, but a summary will indicate the main issue sufficiently. Unlike his counterpart in the play, Lysimachus sees Marina first when she is displayed by her keepers in the market place. Surprised by her beauty, he first pities her and ruminates with himself that 'she was rather a deseruing bed-fellow for a Prince, then a play-fellow for so rascally an assembly'. However, 'being inflamed with a little sinnefull concupiscence' and realizing that she is anyhow destined to fall, he sends word to the bawd to keep Marina from the multitude, and to reserve her for him until he can come to the brothel disguised under cover of darkness. The bawd is of course most pleased and proceeds to give Marina instructions (in a passage which has several verbal echoes of the play), until Lysimachus arrives, disguised as in the play. He 'distributed golde among them, and then roundly demaunded for that same peece of stuffe'. Being left alone with Marina, he asks for 'the performaunce of that for which he came', whereupon Marina throws herself at his feet and, pleading for pity, narrates all her misadventures, except for the death of her parents and the story of her own birth. He, however,

1. For Wilkins' version of II. ii, see App. C.

thinks this is all mere artfulness and begins 'to be more rough with her'. Marina responds by reminding him of his high honourable station, and with the kind of melodramatic morality of which Wilkins is fond, she urges him not to stain his good name by impoverishing hers. Lysimachus is still not content, but a second moral speech from Marina, almost a page in length, succeeds in converting him. He lifts up Marina 'saying aside: Now surely this is Virtues image . . .' He then urges upon her to be steadfast and of good courage, gives her gold, and speaks to her the words, 'I hither came with thoughtes intemperate, foule and deformed, the which your paines so well haue laued, that they are now white' (*P.A.*, 91. 12–15), words whose tenor is strikingly different from those in the play ('Had I brought hither a corrupted mind, Thy speech had alter'd it', IV. vi. 103–4). Thereupon Lysimachus pretends to leave the brothel, but proceeds to eavesdrop upon Marina from an adjacent chamber to see whether her morality withstands the importunities of other suitors equally well. Later, he leaves the brothel, after having expressed his displeasure to the bawd in terms similar to those in the play. The remainder of Wilkins' chapter follows the events in the play fairly closely.

It will be clear from this summary that Wilkins presents Lysimachus as a cruder and more obviously sensual man than he is in the play. Strange as it may seem, it is Wilkins who keeps what may be regarded as the episode's main purpose, the demonstration of the power of Marina's virtue, more constantly in mind. In the play, the reasons for Lysimachus' visit to the brothel are left somewhat ambiguous; at any rate, his sensual motives are treated more delicately. This difference in the presentation of a fairly important character is one reason why some scholars, including Hardin Craig and Kenneth Muir, believe that Wilkins' report is at least partly based on an earlier play, which Shakespeare later refashioned into the *Pericles* we know. 'The reviser,' Craig states, 'intended to make him (i.e. Lysimachus) an acceptable lover for the chaste Marina'.[1] Lysimachus is transformed into a figure more 'like the Duke in *Measure for Measure*'. He is turned into a 'gentleman'.[2] Though rather overstating the case, this contention deserves some scrutiny, if only because an independent study of the play's text will lead one to suspect that in IV. vi a number of lines have dropped out and that others are misplaced.

That the different treatment of the episode in the brothel sug-

1. H. Craig, '*Pericles* and *The Painfull Aduentures*', *SP*, XLV (1949), 100–5. He also sees signs of revision elsewhere in the play which cannot be discussed here for lack of space.
2. H. Craig, privately.

gests an earlier play or 'Ur-Pericles' as Wilkins' source has been
argued independently by Muir.[1] The main further support he
found for such a hypothesis is a number of passages in Wilkins'
novel, especially in the part corresponding to IV. vi, which allow
themselves easily to be turned into blank verse.[2] Though they are
not found in *Pericles*, Muir contends that these lines must have been
copied or adapted from some play. One relevant passage occurs in
Marina's lecture to Lysimachus: 'If as you say (my Lorde) you are
the Gouernour, let not your authoritie, which should teach you to
rule others, be the meanes to make you mis-gouerne your selfe: If
the eminence of your place came vnto you by discent, and the
royalty of your blood, let not your life prooue your birth a bastard'
(*P.A.*, 89. 10–16).[3] Muir furthermore noted a piece of dialogue in
this same episode where 'Lysimachus drops suddenly from indirect
to direct speech, because Wilkins carelessly neglected to alter his
pronouns',[4] namely: 'or *his* displeasure punish at *his* own pleasure,
which displeasure of *mine*, *thy* beauty shall not priuiledge *thee*
from . . .'.[5] Muir also suggests that in two instances words seem to
be repeated for no apparent reason except to complete a blank
verse line.[6] And he links these items of evidence to the general
observation on the scene: 'The dialogue of the play is jerky, a
mingling of prose and verse with many short and irregular lines; it
reads as though it had been condensed. On the other hand, the
dialogue of the novel runs smoothly and naturally'.[7]

The evidence Muir has assembled is fairly considerable, yet his
thesis should, I think, be rejected. The passages of 'blank verse
fossils' he lists[8] do not resemble any of the verse in the play's first
two acts, which, if there were an 'Ur-Pericles', one would have good
reason to believe were taken over almost unchanged into the play
we know (though one must of course allow for the reporter's
mangling of the text and for possible multiple authorship of the
'Ur-Pericles'). Moreover, one is able to judge fairly safely, from a
comparison between these two acts and Wilkins' report of them,
to what extent he tended to quote the play's verse literally. The
longest passage of literal correspondence which this part of the
novel reveals extends over barely five lines, those reporting II. v.

1. K. Muir, 'The Problem of Pericles', *English Studies* (Amsterdam), xxx
(1949), 65–83, and Intro. to his edn of *P.A.* Muir does not accept Craig's
unorthodox views on the nature of Q's copy. He restates his views in *Shakespeare as
Collaborator*, 1960.

2. I am less convinced than Muir about this. For instance, the passage cited
three lines below strikes me as typical early seventeenth-century prose.

3. Other such blank verse 'fossils' are 51. 9–12 and 90. 16–26.

4. Muir, *English Studies*, p. 71.   5. Italics mine.   6. Muir, p. 71.

7. *Ibid.*, p. 76.   8. See collation and notes in his edn of *P.A.*

81–5. This makes it rather hard to believe that he quoted much longer passages almost word for word from the hypothetical older version in Act IV. We have noted, moreover, that on several occasions in his novel Wilkins gave rein to his own fancy, and there seems no special reason why he should not have done so in his account of Lysimachus' conference with Marina. He liked dramatizing and moralizing, and this passage would have suited him well! Lastly, one may question on general grounds whether in a euphuistic novel like Wilkins', much can be made of passages whose rhythm is closely akin to that of blank verse.

To account for the identical names of Wilkins' characters and those of *Pericles*, including such evidently Shakespearean names as Marina, Muir was driven to postulate that upon finishing his novel, Wilkins made some adjustments, bringing it a little closer in line with Shakespeare's revised play, which by then had been staged. Such a theory might be plausible if only applied to the characters' names, but it seems an unsatisfactory explanation for those passages in Wilkins' novel which are unquestionably Shakespearean. All points considered, therefore, it appears more probable that Wilkins based his report, however imperfectly, directly on the play as we know it. There may well have been an earlier play which Shakespeare refashioned,[1] but in that case no reliable evidence can be found in Wilkins which would permit one to reconstruct any of its scenes and thus to estimate the kind of changes which Shakespeare made.

7. *This Edition*

The text of this edition is based on that of Q, the play's only substantive text. But, for more than one reason, fairly considerable changes have been made. In line with the other Arden editions, modernization in spelling and regularization of punctuation according to current practice have been introduced, and such changes have been listed in the collation only in those instances where the interpretation seemed in any way open to question, or where a peculiarity of Q might be of special interest.

In the majority of scenes, the spelling has been modernized completely.[2] Certain scenes, however, it seemed advisable to treat differently. As will be discussed more fully in the interpretative part of this introduction, *Pericles* is endowed with an archaic atmosphere. One of the main devices for creating this mood is the introduction, especially in the speeches of Gower the chorus, of older

1. Such an 'Ur-Pericles' was already postulated by Collier, W. C. Hazlitt, and later by Brandes. See also pp. liii and lxiii below.

2. Old forms, such as *spake*, *ere*, and *wrack'd*, have been retained.

forms of expression which must have struck Shakespeare's own audience as archaic. Not to retain these would have meant obscuring some of the play's very intention and character. Secondly, a few words forming part of the racy dialogues of some of the play's low characters, such as the fishermen and the keepers of the brothel, have been reproduced in their unusual and obsolete spelling, if there was reason to believe that the spelling was employed for the sake of colour or forcefulness of expression; *di'e* for 'do ye' (II. i. 145) and *a conscience* for 'on my conscience' (IV. ii. 19–20) are examples. Elsewhere in the play, modernization has been carried out consistently.

A much more difficult problem for the modern editor is the fact that the play's only substantive text, Q, is grossly corrupt. As has been shown, it is a report representing the original in a mangled form, and it was moreover printed very badly, which resulted in much further deterioration of the text. Editors of no other Shakespearean play have to depend mainly on such an unreliable text, and they have therefore better hope of giving an authoritative version of the play fairly completely. On this account, the principles of emendation one should follow in editing *Pericles* must be rather different from those usually adopted. The proper answer to the question, 'What kind of changes is an editor justified in introducing into his text?' is, one would think, not the same for *Pericles* as for any other of Shakespeare's plays.

Fortunately, other scholars have in recent years given some thought to the peculiar problem of editing such plays as *Pericles*. Textually, *Pericles* is unique in Shakespearean drama, but the rest of Elizabethan drama affords several similar cases. In his introduction to one of them, Dekker's *Sir Thomas Wyatt*, Fredson Bowers has set forth his views on editorial procedure. A scholarly edition of a play that exists only in what bibliographers call a 'bad' text, he argues, must necessarily be more conservative than that of a good one. The editor should not 'attempt emendation when, on the evidence, there is little chance of lighting on the authentic reading of the lost autograph'.[1] But he may try to emend errors 'which there is some reason to assign to the compositor', even though such changes may merely result in restoring 'the equal impurity of the underlying printer's copy',[2] for thereby he will remove at least one stage of corruption. In lineation, he should follow the substantive text conservatively.

This procedure is theoretically sound, and may be desirable in practice for editions in original spelling which aim at a purely

1. *Dramatic Works of Thomas Dekker*, 1953, I, p. 413.   2. *Ibid.*, p. 402.

scholarly audience. But too rigorous an adherence to it would often result in unintelligibility. It is the duty of an Arden editor, whenever possible, and of course with a minimum of textual changes, to make sense of the text, and therefore to draw cautiously but liberally on the large body of interpretation and conjectural emendation by earlier editors. A balance between these two principles has therefore been struck. In the majority of cases where the Q text seemed doubtful and yet permitted some kind of reasonable paraphrase, it has been retained, sometimes contrary to the practice of other modern editors. On the other hand, the emendations incorporated into the text are fairly numerous.

More specifically, emendations were adopted whenever a reading in Q could be attributed convincingly to error on the part of the compositor; that is to say, where it could be presumed to have arisen either from misreading of MS copy or from demonstrable carelessness. In passages manifestly corrupted by the reporter, emendations were only introduced if they could be supported with some good evidence, such as a close parallel from Wilkins' novel (which, as has been shown, is also a report of the play, though one still further removed from the original) or, in a few instances, especially in the more Shakespearean scenes, a parallel in some other Shakespearean play. But for the vast majority of lines that can be attributed to the reporter, there is no alternative to conservative reprinting. In some other instances again, where a corruption seemed to be confined to a brief phrase or one line, the best-seeming correction yet suggested has been adopted, even if no precise explanation of the nature of the error offered itself and even if some doubts remained in my mind as to whether the original was restored correctly—doubts which will be found expressed in the commentary. In these cases it seemed preferable to print some sense rather than to reprint manifest nonsense, though, of course, such procedure was applied cautiously and sparingly. Examples are III. iii. 5–7 and IV. i. 4–6. A few similar passages, on the other hand, have been retained in their original though unintelligible form, because the great doubtfulness of any emendation yet suggested put the scales in favour of Bowers' principle of a conservative text; because, that is, the adoption of an emended reading would have been particularly open to the criticism of misleading future readers who might, for all we know, find more light than either previous editors or myself. In these cases possible solutions will be found discussed in the Commentary. Some highly debatable readings have been marked with an obelisk.

One further matter deserves perhaps special emphasis. From F3 on, and particularly during the eighteenth century, editors were especially fond of making small changes in the text for the sake only of regularizing the metre. Unless such changes could be justified on other grounds, they have not been accepted into this edition, for they are almost always mere guesses, and we know now that Shakespeare's verse was often much freer than his earlier editors supposed.

The principle of a conservative text has not been applied to lineation. Modern editors are agreed that the arrangement of verse and prose in over half of Q is chaotic, and also that, though the original lineation seems often irrecoverable, much of the text can be arranged into reasonably convincing dramatic verse. It would seem therefore pedantic to reject the great pioneering work in this field by earlier editors, especially Malone. No doubt, their work of arrangement can, here and there, be questioned and possibly improved, but much of it is sound. Some bolder reconstructions of passages, chiefly by Harold Brooks, where omissions or transpositions by the reporter seem to have thrown the verse out completely, are provided in Appendix D.

In the stage-directions I have not departed from Q unless there seemed to be good cause, but as Q is very bare, many additions, most of them from Malone, have been introduced in square brackets. The only major change is made at the beginning of III. ii. In act and scene headings, which were first introduced in the Third Folio, this edition follows Malone, except for the division of an extra scene, Act I, Scene 1b, the reasons for which are given in the commentary.[1]

The collation lists all substantive changes made from Q. Of variants in other texts, only a critical selection is presented: mainly a number of readings which, in my opinion, have some just claim to be considered as alternatives to the text adopted.

3. AUTHORSHIP

1. Reasons for assuming Mixed Authorship

In his prologue to *Marina* (1738), an adaptation of the last two acts of *Pericles*, George Lillo announced:

> We dare not charge the whole unequal play
> Of Pericles on him; yet let us say,
> As gold though mix'd with baser matter shines,

1. It is highly doubtful whether *Pericles* was planned by its authors as a five-act drama. Rather, it seems to have been intended either as a play in two parts (as in the production at court in 1619—see p. lxvi below), or in seven tableaux or acts, each separated by a chorus.

So do his bright inimitable lines
Throughout those rude wild scenes distinguish'd stand,
And shew he touch'd them with no sparing hand.

This judgment was adopted by Dr Farmer in 1766, who in turn persuaded Malone to include *Pericles* for this reason in his Supplement to Steevens' edition of Shakespeare. It was shared likewise by Coleridge. *Pericles* illustrates, he said,

> the way in which Shakespeare handled a piece he had to refit for presentation. At first he proceeded with indifference, now and then only troubling himself to put in a thought or an image, but as he advanced he interested himself in his employment, and the last two acts are almost altogether by him.[1]

The majority of present-day scholars still hold to a similar view. They believe that Shakespeare had little or nothing to do with Acts I and II, but that he wrote either completely or in large part Acts III–V. Two possible alternatives suggest themselves: either *Pericles* was a new play, which for some reason Shakespeare decided to write only in part, assigning the first two acts to other, and certainly minor, dramatists; or the play reached Shakespeare in a complete or nearly complete state, and he decided to rewrite only the second part; perhaps because his imagination was only aroused then, perhaps because the thing had to be done in a hurry—one can only speculate. The latter possibility seems more attractive, for it is hard to conceive that the mature Shakespeare would assign the important first two acts of a new play to minor collaborators. Yet if an earlier play existed, all we can safely say is that Shakespeare transformed its verse into dramatic poetry of sometimes the highest order. About any other changes, nothing can be inferred.[2]

The whole matter is incapable of being finally decided for the simple reason that external evidence is wholly wanting. We do not know what justification Henry Gosson had for assigning the play to Shakespeare alone in the quarto, nor do we know why Heming and Condell excluded it from the Folio. The view of mixed authorship must needs rely primarily on the general impression of the play's uneven style, part of which looks as if it could have been written only by Shakespeare, and part of which seems like the work of a third-rate writer. I have already discussed at length the reasons for believing that the enormous differences in the average quality

1. Henry Crabb Robinson's Diary, commenting on Coleridge's Lectures, as cited in T. M. Raysor, *Coleridge's Shakespearean Criticism*, II 209.

2. See pp. xlvii–xlix above for the rejection of the view that Wilkins' description of Lysimachus' visit to the brothel is based on a pre-Shakespearean version of that episode, in an 'Ur-Pericles'.

of the verse in the play's two parts cannot be accounted for in terms of corruptions of a play entirely by Shakespeare.[1] The style of whole scenes in the first two acts shows a considerable degree of consistency (noticeable even in this corrupt text), which strongly suggests a different author. Even if, as we shall find, it is very hard to identify this author (or these authors), the assumption that there was such a man remains reasonable.

2. Shakespeare's Part in 'Pericles'

About one matter there can at any rate be no doubt: Shakespeare wrote most or all of Acts III–V. His hand is most obvious in III. i, the scene of the storm and the casting overboard of Thaisa's body, and in V. i, the first recognition scene. The two brothel scenes are also clearly by him, even if the Victorians disliked them. Their prose and their humour are Shakespearean. They resemble parts of *Measure for Measure* and *All's Well* much more than any scene with similar low characters elsewhere in Jacobean drama.[2] Leaving the Gower choruses aside for the moment, Shakespeare' late style is likewise evident in most other scenes of Acts III–V though much of it has been obscured by the reporter's inadequate transmission. These observations will be shared by every sensitive reader. They require no defence.

On the other hand, it is very doubtful whether Shakespeare contributed anything to Acts I and II. Here judgments differ. Categorically, it can only be stated that passages which reflect Shakespearean style are very few. The longest piece of good writing in Acts I–II is the Fishermen's comic dialogue in II. i. In quality this is not unworthy of Shakespeare, perhaps, but in this case, as will be shown,[3] strong evidence pointing to other authorship is available. Of the rest, the following lines have often been attributed to Shakespeare:

> The blind mole casts
> Copp'd hills towards heaven, to tell the earth is throng'd
> By man's oppression, and the poor worm doth die for't.

They may indeed have been Shakespeare's; yet we must not blind ourselves to the fact that a dozen dramatists of Shakespeare's day were capable of occasional flights of poetry equal to them. In view of the possibility that Shakespeare may have added occasional touches to the first two acts, no treatment is necessary here of the few other lines of real merit.

The Gower choruses represent a special case. In view of their

1. See above, pp. xxxv–xxxvi.   2. See also below, pp. lxx–lxxi.
3. See App. B.

sometimes close, sometimes less close imitation of Gower's own style, and of their uniqueness of manner in Shakespearean drama, can one decide with any degree of assurance that Shakespeare did or did not write any of them? It is perhaps of some relevance that certain changes in the manner of the choruses are observable from Act III on. The style of the first two choruses is stiffer, more regular, than that of the later acts, with the notable exception of the chorus between the two recognition scenes (V. ii), which seems to revert largely to the earlier manner. The predominantly end-stopped tetrameter lines of the first two choruses yield to a freer handling of the verse, with more pentameter lines and lines of nine or eleven syllables, and with significantly more syncopation and variation in the use of the caesura.[1] Contrast with any passage in the opening choruses:

> This maid
> Hight Philoten; and it is said
> For certain in our story, she
> Would ever with Marina be:
> Be't when she weav'd the sleided silk
> With fingers long, small, white as milk;
> Or when she would with sharp neele wound
> The cambric, which she made more sound
> By hurting it; or when to th' lute
> She sung, and made the night-bird mute
> That still records with moan; (IV. Ch. 17–27)

The change in style is accompanied by a difference in attitude towards the audience. The later choruses, especially that of IV. iv, remind us much more of the Chorus in *Henry V*. Gower no longer merely presents the scenes to our eyes and judgment: he asks us to co-operate imaginatively with the actors.[2] All this is not enough to make it certain that Shakespeare contributed to the later choruses, or even that he had nothing to do with the earlier ones. Other playwrights in their choruses echoed *Henry V*.[3] And there may have been a simpler reason for adjusting and 'freeing' Gower's style, once the character of the chorus had been adequately created in the opening acts. After Act III there was less need for such a chorus to continue perfectly in his stiff, archaic idiom and verse. Yet it seems very possible that Shakespeare wrote some of the later choruses.

This feeling is strengthened by the realization that the play's

1. The significance of some of these changes was first pointed out to me by Mr Henry F. Wolff.
2. See also above, pp. xx–xxi, and Commentary for IV. iv.
3. E.g. Wilkins, Day, and Rowley in *The Travailes of the Three English Brothers*.

third chorus echoes closely Puck's speech near the end of *A Midsummer Night's Dream*. The two passages have in common a complex cluster of images, a feature which in recent years has come to be thought of as one of the most reliable literary criteria for authorship.[1]

As for specific textual parallels between Shakespeare's other plays and *Pericles*, the evidence corroborates one's impression that Shakespeare had little to do with Acts I and II, and much with Acts III–V. Rare in Acts I–II, such parallels are frequent later. Of twenty-three anticipations of the phrasing of *Cymbeline*, *The Winter's Tale*, and *The Tempest*, some of them very remarkable, only three occur in Acts I and II.[2] While hardly any passages in the first two acts of *Pericles* can be said to echo *Macbeth*, a play written shortly before *Pericles*, many can be found in the later acts, especially in Act IV. The same general pattern applies to echoes of Shakespeare's other works. Such an observation is significant, even if in a reported text one has reason for regarding textual echoes with special caution. And it will take on extra significance, if it can be shown that the works of some other contemporary dramatist are frequently echoed in Acts I–II of *Pericles*, but seldom or not at all in the remainder of the play. In that case we should surely have further reason for believing in divided authorship.

3. Shakespeare's Collaborators : Basic Difficulties

To say that mixed authorship in *Pericles* is probable is one thing; to discover the identity of Shakespeare's collaborator or collaborators is another. In the complete absence of external evidence bearing on this problem, we depend solely on such internal matters as the stylistic characteristics of the opening two acts, the dramatic techniques evident in them, and most of all, perhaps, detailed literary echoes in the work of some other dramatist, if such can be found. Our belief that the printer's copy was a surreptitious reported text, full of corruptions, will make us aware of yet another obstacle in this quest. Certain stylistic peculiarities may be the reporter's rather than the author's; even unquestionable textual echoes may be due to the reporter alone, for such men were notoriously liable to eke out their faltering memories with passages from other plays. Moreover, spellings in such a text can tell one nothing about authorship. One may apply spelling tests as a guide to authorship in *Henry VIII* or the Fletcher–Massinger plays,

1. See Commentary for III. Ch. 1, and for the general theory, E. A. Armstrong, *Shakespeare's Imagination*, 1946.

2. Namely at I. iv .24 (to *Tp.*), II. i. 20–1 (*Wint.* and *Tp.*), and II. iii. 17 (*Wint.*); see Commentary for these and later parallels.

all printed from good texts: here such a procedure would be useless.

Critical confidence has been further discouraged because cases have been argued, sometimes at length, for at least three possible collaborators, Heywood, Wilkins, and William Rowley, and these tend to undermine each other, at least in part. We are now more aware than some earlier scholars that these three dramatists, like many of their contemporaries, depended on a large common stock both of technique and idiom, and showed no reluctance to imitate each other. Yet I feel that we should not merely, as some have done, postulate some 'unknown' collaborator. As long as we remain on our guard, and examine each piece of internal evidence by careful criteria of quality and quantity, we may hope to make some progress towards a solution. And in my view, at least, a few fairly confident conclusions about Shakespeare's collaborators can be reached.

4. Exeunt Rowley and Heywood

The case for Rowley has been by far the vaguest,[1] and it can be dismissed at once. I suppose Rowley's name has been brought up by two or three critics merely because of a general impression that in its rough humour the melodramatic situation of Marina's defence of her chastity in a brothel would have greatly appealed to Rowley. My own examination of Rowley's plays (including those in which he collaborated) has revealed no evidence whatsoever which would justify the linking of his name with *Pericles*.

Much more has been made of Thomas Heywood,[2] and some scholars persist in seeing Heywood's hand, even if vaguely, in *Pericles*. But the attribution, it must be categorically stated, rests on a very feeble basis. The most elaborate and influential article advocating Heywood's collaboration[3] may impress readers unacquainted with much of Heywood's work but is a glaring example of the critical tendency to squeeze all the juice out of the lemons of evidence without first ascertaining that the lemons are good. It is argued that the ten plays of Heywood nearest in time to *Pericles* are all similar dramatized narratives, full of episodic, romantic adventures. Yet on examination, we discover that most of them are uncertain in date, were probably staged after *Pericles*, and certainly

---

1. E.g. by S. Lee, *A Life of William Shakespeare*, 1904, p. 252.
2. See D. L. Thomas, 'On the Play of Pericles', *Englische Studien*, xxxix, 210–39; and H. D. Gray, 'Heywood's Pericles', *PMLA*, xl (1925), 507–29. Thomas's views were rejected by J. Q. Adams in *MP*, xvi (1918), 273–4 and by A. M. Clark in *Thomas Heywood*, p. 331.
3. Gray, *ibid.*

after other plays of similar kind and structure (or rather, absence of structure). Next, it is contended that *The Golden Age*, *The Silver Age*, and *The Brazen Age* make use of choruses and dumbshows similar to those in *Pericles*. But so does Barnes' *The Divil's Charter*,[1] which was almost certainly produced before *Pericles*, while all the evidence points to Heywood's plays on the Ages as not having been staged before late in 1609.[2] Gray makes much of the many storms and banquets in Heywood's plays, as if such incidents were rare in Shakespeare. He spends considerable space on listing parallel incidents in *Pericles* and in Heywood's plays, most of which are mere stock situations of romance, as common in Sidney's *Arcadia* as in *Pericles*. Still feebler is the argument that Edward IV's association with a character of low station, Hobs, in Heywood's play is significantly paralleled by Pericles' attitude in the fishermen scene; we need only recall Prince Hal. Most of the 'parallel passages' listed by critics fail to convince.

It is however quite true that Heywood's later play, *The Captives*, reminds us at several points of *Pericles*. Heywood's play includes a storm, a fisherman who catches valuable belongings in his net, and a daughter who for much of the play is separated from her parents and who has to defend her chastity against the owner of a brothel (though the latter incident takes place off stage). It includes a passage, by Palaestra,

> Alas I never yet wrong'd man or child
> Woman or babe . . . ,

which seems to be a real echo of Marina's words in *Pericles*, IV. i. 74ff.[3] Yet the inference from this resemblance that Heywood collaborated in *Pericles* is likewise mistaken. The relevant incidents are all taken over directly from Heywood's source, Plautus' *Rudens*. And even if *Pericles* influenced Heywood in his composition of *The Captives* fifteen or more years later, why should it not? Throughout his life, Heywood was an imitator of his betters. As early as 1594, he closely imitated *Venus and Adonis* in his own *Oenone and Paris*. The

1. *The Divil's Charter* was produced before royalty on 2 Feb. 1607, and perhaps earlier on the public stage.

2. See Clark, *op. cit.*, 64–5, and A. Harbage, *Annals*, entries under 1610–12. The contention by some critics that Heywood's two plays on *The Iron Age* were written much earlier rests on very slim evidence. E. Schanzer, 'Heywood's Ages and Shakespeare', *RES*, n.s. XI, No. 41 (Feb. 1960), 18–28, argues strongly for 1611 as the date of Heywood's three first *Ages*.

3. Palaestra's complaint against fortune in Heywood's play, however, is otherwise quite unlike anything Marina says. It is both wordy and conventionally Christian in its sentiments.

two parts of *The Iron Age* frequently echo *Troilus and Cressida*.[1] *Pericles* had been a success: that would be enough to spur Heywood to imitate it. On the other hand, we have not the slightest bit of evidence that Heywood was associated with Shakespeare's company during the years surrounding the first staging of *Pericles*. And if he had collaborated in *Pericles*, one would have expected him to protest at the omission of his name in the first three quartos, judging from the annoyance he expressed with Jaggard in the *Apology for Actors* for misattributing two of his poems to Shakespeare.[2] To summarize: the positive evidence for Heywood carries little weight, and other factors make his participation in *Pericles* improbable. Scholars in future should be safe in excluding Heywood from consideration.

5. George Wilkins: pro and contra

The case for Wilkins' collaboration in *Pericles* is stronger but also much more complex. First examined by Delius in 1868,[3] it is still a matter of controversy.[4] Not a few scholars have rejected Wilkins primarily because the very idea that Shakespeare should have collaborated with such a minor dramatist near the end of his career was repugnant to them—if there must be a collaborator, then Heywood. On the other hand, Wilkins' dates fit the issue better than Heywood's. All his extant works are dated between 1606 and 1608. More important, his name is closely linked to the play by his novel, *The Painfull Aduentures of Pericles Prince of Tyre*, which, as we have shown, is partly based on the play itself. And thirdly, a certain George Wilkins, who may well have been the dramatist, is mentioned, along with Shakespeare, in the Belott–Mountjoy suit of 1612. He is there described as 'of the parishe of S^ct Sepulchers London victuler of the Age of thirtye Syxe yeres or th^r aboutes', and as one who had known the plaintiff and defendant for seven years—Shakespeare had for ten.[5]

1. See Schanzer's article cited on the previous page.

2. This point is made by J. G. McManaway in his review of Maxwell's edition of *Pericles* (N.C.S.) in *MLR*, LII (1957), No. 4, 583–4.

3. In *Shakespeare Jahrbuch*, III (1868), 175–204.

4. Some of the major contributions to this controversy are: R. Boyle, in *Transactions of the New Sh. Soc.*, 1880–5, Pt II, 323–40; P. Z. Round, Intro. to Praetorius Facsimile of Q2 of *Pericles*, 1886; H. Dugdale Sykes, *Sidelights on Shakespeare*, 1919, pp. 143–204; Sina Spiker, in *SP*, XXX (1933), 551–70; W. T. Hastings, in *Sh. Assoc. Bul.*, XI, No. 2 (1936), 67–83, and XIV, No. 2 (1939), 67–85; K. Muir, in *English Studies* (Amsterdam), XXX (1949), 65–83.

5. See C. W. Wallace, 'Shakespeare and his London Associates as Revealed in Recently discovered Documents', *The Univ. Studies of the U. of Nebraska*, X (1910), No. 4, 261–360, especially 288–9. It is quite possible that George Wilkins was the

Most of the evidence marshalled for Wilkins' collaboration consists of textual parallels between the first part of *Pericles* and Wilkins' works. Of these, apart from *The Painfull Aduentures*, the only ones extant are two plays, *The Miseries of Inforst Marriage*, 1607 (by Wilkins alone), and *The Travailes of the Three English Brothers*, 1607 (by Day, Wilkins, and Rowley)[1]; a pamphlet entitled *Three Miseries of Barbary*, n.d. (1606?); a translation, *The Historie of Iustine*, 1606[2]; and parts of *Jests to Make you Merry*, 1607 (with Dekker). Critics have ransacked these works for possible textual parallels to *Pericles* and have listed a large number, many of which on closer examination reveal themselves as insignificant, because either they are not close or they consist of stock or proverbial phrases, common in other works of the time. Yet a few are striking and must be attributed to something else than coincidence:

(i) *Three Miseries of Barbary*, sig. D2, includes an account of the effects of famine in part closely resembling that of the famine at Tharsus in *Pericles*, I. iv. Common to both are 'mouths', 'are now ready', and the reference to cannibalism. Also striking is the similarity of 'they could scarce stand on their legs' to I. iv. 49. On C3v, Wilkins says it is impossible 'to afford them burial'.[3]

(ii) The following passage in *The Miseries of Inforst Marriage*[4] closely resembles *Pericles*, II. v. 87–92:

> *Scarborough.*   And are all pleas'd?
> *All.*   We are.
> *Scarborough.*   Then if all these be so,
> I am new wed, so ends old marriage woe;
> And in your eyes so lovingly being wed,
> We hope your hands will bring us to our bed.

(iii) Similarly, compare the following lines from *Miseries*[5] with *Pericles*, I. Ch. 29–30:

'Poet' who lived in St Giles, Cripplegate, in 1605. See Mary R. McManaway, 'Poets in the Parish of St. Giles, Cripplegate', *Sh.Q.*, IX, No. 4 (1958), 561–2.

1. It has also been argued, on tenuous evidence, that Wilkins wrote *A Yorkshire Tragedy* and collaborated with Day in *Law Tricks*, *Humour out of Breath*, etc.

2. By G.W. That this G.W. was probably Wilkins was pointed out to me by E. A. J. Honigmann. The translation purports to be from the Latin but is an even more blatant example of plagiarism than *The Painfull Aduentures*, for in most parts it adopts closely the wording from Arthur Golding's *Abridgement* of 1564 (reprinted in 1570 and 1578). G.W. adds, however, 'An Epitomy of the Emperors Liues'. Certain phrases and images in the original sections of the work parallel Wilkins' other works closely. The *Short-Title Catalogue* lists the work under 'Trogus Pompeius'.

3. See, however, Commentary to I. iv. 42–4.

4. Hazlitt's *Dodsley*, IX. 576; the last lines of the play.

5. *Ibid.*, 512; sig. D4v in Q 1607.

Who once doth cherish sinne, begets his shame,
　　For vice being fosterd once, coins Impudence,
Which makes men count sinne, Custom, not offence.

(iv) The lines almost immediately following in *Pericles*,

To seek her as a bed-fellow,
In marriage-pleasures play-fellow,　　(i. Ch. 33–4)

are echoed in *The Painfull Aduentures* in a very different context,
namely when Lysimachus is speaking of Marina in Chapter x,
p. 85:

She was rather a deseruing bed-fellow for a Prince, than a play-
fellow for so rascally an assembly.

(v) A less impressive parallel, to *Pericles*, i. i. 74, is afforded by
these lines in *Travailes*:

The silver moon and those her countless eyes
That like so many servants wait on her.[1]

But while the scene in *Travailes* is usually ascribed to Wilkins, the
lines cannot safely be attributed to him.

Dugdale Sykes, who includes these five in a much longer list of
parallels, provides also a pertinent comparison of the style of Acts
i–ii of *Pericles* and that of Wilkins' acknowledged works, listing the
following similarities. (i) There is frequent ellipsis of the relative
pronoun in the nominative case. There are fourteen instances in
Acts i–ii alone of *Pericles*, far more than in any entire play by Shakespeare, and *Miseries* has twenty instances. (ii) The tendency for
verbal antitheses to run riot is equally marked in *Pericles* i–ii,
Miseries, and those scenes of *Travailes* which are probably by
Wilkins. Further, many of these antitheses (soul . . . body, heart
. . . eye, eyes . . . hands, live . . . die, life . . . death) tend to recur in
the three works. (iii) Many of the favourite rhymes of *Miseries* and
Travailes appear also in the opening two acts of *Pericles*: e.g. 'will-
ill' (five times in *Miseries*, twice in *Travailes*, three times in *Pericles*),
and such less common rhymes as 'dead–buried', 'consist–resist',
'him–sin'. Of these three observations, the first seems truly significant. Much less weight is to be attached to the two others, for
verbal antitheses were extremely popular at this time, and most of
the rhymes listed by Sykes are also found elsewhere in Shakespeare,
not to mention other plays. Yet Sykes gives a much longer list of
rhymes than has been provided here, and it is surely a matter of
some significance that Wilkins' two plays should have so many
rhymes in common with the two short first acts of *Pericles*.

1. Act ii; p. 23 in Bullen's edn of Day; sig. B4v in Q 1607.

The reader should note that the evidence advanced by many scholars for the collaboration of Wilkins has been represented here in greatly abbreviated form. Cumulatively, this evidence is just about as considerable as any internal evidence can be. It would seem an incredible coincidence if all these similarities in style and close textual echoes between *Pericles* and Wilkins' work should have arisen accidentally. Rather, they strongly incline one to the belief that Wilkins did have a share in *Pericles*.

And yet there are two considerations which make it difficult to suppose that Wilkins wrote the whole of the first two acts. The first rests on a comparison between these first two acts and the corresponding chapters in *The Painfull Aduentures*. For as we have seen, Wilkins in his novel quotes only brief passages from the play, the longest one in the first two acts being five lines, namely II. iii. 81–5, while on the other hand he follows Twine's earlier novel word for word in about a third of his book. It would be odd if a habitual plagiarist were to follow his own composition so very much less than someone else's![1] On the other hand, if he remembered another author's play only in scraps, he would naturally eke out his narrative with long bits from an earlier prose version of the same tale. A second fact militating against Wilkins is the discovery that some scenes and phrases in *Pericles* are even more closely paralleled in the work of John Day, a dramatist who has until recently not been linked with the problem of its authorship.

6. A New Case for John Day

As this hypothesis[2] is my own and is too recent to have run the test of critical scrutiny by other scholars, it seems proper merely to summarize it here, and to present the detailed evidence in an Appendix (= B). The case there presented shares with similar arguments for the collaboration of other dramatists the weakness that it depends purely on such internal evidence as textual parallels or echoes, similarities in syntax and in idiom, and plays on words. Yet this claim should, I believe, be more persuasive than any other made hitherto for a collaborator in *Pericles*, because of the quality and quantity of the evidence presented, and because it is confined to the few scenes where the similarities are impressive. It suggests that Day is the author of II. i, II. iii, and possibly of I. ii, the available evidence not warranting a judgment on the remaining scenes of the first two acts. But the reader must judge for himself.

1. Other critics have overlooked this obvious point.
2. F. D. Hoeniger, 'How Significant are Textual Parallels? A New Author for *Pericles*?', *Sh.Q.*, XI, No. 1 (1960), 27–37.

7. Conclusion

We have insufficient evidence to warrant a final solution to the problem of authorship. But the evidence set forth above and in Appendix B suggests to me the following hypothesis. Some time during 1607, soon after their collaboration in *The Travailes*, Day and Wilkins (with perhaps yet a third dramatist) decided to put Gower's narrative of Apollonius of Tyre into loose dramatic form, with the help of a chorus similar to that used in *The Travailes*.[1] Whether they completed their draft or not, Shakespeare soon became sufficiently interested in their venture to assume responsibility for the last three acts of *Pericles*, giving them the shape in which, the reporter's corruptions apart, they have come down to us. If such a view is incapable of proof, it seems at least more sensible, in the light of all the data we have examined, than any other that might suggest itself.

4. DATE

For a long time the belief persisted that *Pericles* was one of Shakespeare's earliest works. The main source for this opinion was undoubtedly Dryden's statement,

> Shakespear's own Muse her *Pericles* first bore,
> The Prince of *Tyre* was elder than the *Moore*:
> 'Tis miracle to see a first good Play
> All Hawthorns do not bloom on *Christmas-day*,[2]

to which eighteenth-century scholars attached more authority than was probably warranted. Dryden, it was argued, must have known, for he was a friend of Davenant, who had met the dramatist. But it is usually thought today that Dryden merely depended on his judgment of the play's verse and characterization. For some time, scholars believed they had found further support for an early date in the anonymous *Pimlyco or Runne Red-Cap*, a contemporary pamphlet which contains one of the earliest references to *Pericles*.[3] Warton in his *History of English Poetry* had dated this pamphlet 1596.[4] But, as Malone pointed out in 1821, the only known copies

---

1. See above, pp. xxii–xxiii. If this hypothesis is right, Wilkins seems to have left his mark most clearly in I. iv, II. ii, and II. v, judging from style, textual parallels, and a comparison with *The Painfull Adventures*.

2. Prologue to Davenant's *Circe*, 1677.

3. See below, Stage History, p. lxvi.

4. The same error is found in Malone's edn of *Pericles* in the Supplement (1780) to Steevens' edn of 1778, and in Lowndes, *Bibliographers' Manual*.

bear the date of 1609, and it was only then licensed for printing.[1]
It is of course possible that an earlier Shakespearean version of our
play existed in the 1590's. But evidence for such a view is very slight.
Considering the play's obvious popularity from 1608 on, we might
have expected, in that case, some allusion to it at an earlier date.
There is none we know of. As for parallels in the language and
plot of *Pericles* to other plays of Shakespeare's, they are mainly to
Macbeth and the last plays, rather than to the early comedies.
There is, however, one significant exception. As noted long ago,
the frame-story of *The Comedy of Errors* is in some ways remarkably
like the story of *Pericles*. Egeon, in the earlier play, has also lost his
wife and children for many years; and his wife has become an
abbess at no other place than Ephesus. This resemblance, it must
be admitted, makes it likely that when at work on *The Comedy
of Errors* Shakespeare was already acquainted with the tale of
Apollonius of Tyre.

Whether *Pericles* existed in an earlier form or not is, as has been
shown, a matter of pure speculation. What can be stated with some
conviction is that *Pericles*, as we know it, was written and staged
some time between 1606 and 1608. This is now the general view of
scholars, who place it at the beginning of the Romances or 'Last
Plays', after *Macbeth* and *Antony and Cleopatra*, and before *Cymbeline*
and *The Winter's Tale*.[2] The later limit of 1608 is decided by three
factors: the play's entry in the Stationers' Register on 20 May
1608; the appearance in that year of Wilkins' novel, which claims
to be a report of the play, and uses Shakespeare's names for the
characters; and a contemporary reference to a performance by
Giustinian, who was Venetian ambassador to England from
5 January 1606 to 23 November 1608.[3] Besides the printing of the
play, we might note that there are two further contemporary allusions to *Pericles* in 1609–10.[4] On the other hand, we know of no
earlier reference than in 1608. These facts point to a date late in
1607 or early in 1608, before the closing of the theatres by royal

1. The Stationers' Register, 15 April 1609, ed. Arber, III. 406; quoted by
E. K. Chambers, *William Shakespeare*, 1930, II, p. 217.

2. It cannot be ascertained whether *Pericles* was written before or after *Timon*
and *Coriolanus*, which are usually dated about 1607–8. There is no reason why
Shakespeare should not have begun experimenting with a romance while still at
work on his later tragedies.

3. See *Venetian State Papers*, x. 310 and xi. 195; referred to in Chambers *op. cit.*,
I, p. 522 and II, p. 335. Giustinian saw the play in the company of de la Boderie,
French ambassador from May 1606 on, and of his wife, of whose presence in
England nothing is known before April 1607.

4. See below, p. lxvi.

decree in March 1608 or at any rate their re-closing on account of
the worsening of the plague on 28 July 1608.[1]

A case has, however, been argued for late in 1606, by T. S.
Graves.[2] Upon examining the activities of Giustinian, who saw the
play during his residence in England, Graves noted that late in
1606 this Venetian ambassador tried hard to get permission for a
ship of corn to be sent from England to Venice and Tuscany in
order to relieve a famine there. He further noted that the episode
of the relief of the famine at Tharsus has much more made of it in
the play than in the sources. From this, he deduced that the play's
scene has bearing on the contemporary situation, that in fact the
playwright through it tried to help stir up popular support for
Giustinian's mission. About another historical allusion, Graves is
less certain, but he believes that II. ii, the tournament scene, is a
veiled compliment to King James, who in a tournament given in
honour of King Christian IV in July 1606 had showed poorly.
Graves concludes that *Pericles* was first performed about December
1606. His argument leaves me unconvinced.[3] If *Pericles* was meant
to help Giustinian's cause, it seems odd that in his otherwise
thorough report of his activities Giustinian made no reference to
this fact. And the parallel to James's tournament is not at all close.
The facts we do know, and the close link between *Pericles* and the
last plays, make a date late in 1607 or early in 1608 more probable.

5. STAGE HISTORY[4]

Pericles was evidently popular in its day. According to the title-page
of Q, it was 'diuers and sundry times acted by his Maiesties Seruants, at the Globe on the Banck-side'. If this reference is to be
trusted—and I do not see why not, even in a bad quarto—it must
refer to the months immediately before the closing of the theatres

1. The king closed the theatres in March on account of two plays, including
Chapman's *Biron*, which had given offence. In July theatres were closed, this
time for over a year, when the weekly death-rate from the plague rose above
forty.

2. In 'On the Date and Significance of *Pericles*', *MP*, XIII, No. 9 (Jan. 1916),
177–88.

3. James was not exactly popular in 1606. And courtly tournaments were frequent; e.g. the one in 1607 during which Carr, the later favourite, broke his leg.
Yet Graves presents his case cautiously.

4. See the excellent treatment of this subject by C. B. Young in J. C. Maxwell's
edn of *Pericles* (C.U.P.), to which these pages are much indebted. Young
describes in greater detail several productions which are only briefly referred to
here.

owing to the plague on 28 July 1608. The very facts that the play was printed twice during 1609, and that Wilkins produced his prose rendering of *Pericles* in 1608, are testimony to its early stage success. In *Pimlyco or Runne Red-cap*, 1609, an anonymous pamphlet largely in Skeltonics, we read:

> Amazde I stood, to see a Crowd
> of *Ciuill Throats* stretched out so lowd; ...
> So that I truly thought all These
> Came to see *Shore* or *Pericles*.

Moreover we know that the Venetian and French ambassadors to England saw a performance of *Pericles* probably in 1607 or early in 1608,[1] and that it was produced again by the Cholmeley players, a respectable company of travelling actors, at Gowthwaite Hall, Nidderdale, Yorks., on Candlemas (i.e. 2 February) 1610.[2] We possess records of two further performances before the closing of the theatres in 1641, of which the first has some special interest. According to a letter by Sir Gerald Herbert to Sir Dudley Carleton at The Hague on 24 May 1619, a visiting French ambassador and his retinue were entertained at Whitehall on 20 May with various shows and banquets, including a two-part performance of *Pericles*:

> In the Kinges greate chamber they went to see the play of Pirracles, Prince of Tyre, which lasted till two a clocke. After two actes, the players ceased till the French all refreshed them with Sweetmeates brought on chynay voiders, and wyne and ale in bottelles. After, the players begann anewe.[3]

As sumptuous spectacle, the play must have competed on this occasion with the rest of the entertainment, at a time when the court was used to expensive masques and other 'shows'. The arrangement of an interval after Act II was perhaps unique to the occasion yet is highly interesting considering that the play naturally falls into two parts. We know further that *Pericles* was played at the Globe at least once between 1625 and 10 June 1631.[4] In the *Ode to Himselfe*, printed in the same year, Ben Jonson complains that people were flocking to 'some mouldy tale, Like *Pericles*', while neglecting his own more serious work. No wonder that by that time the quarto had been four times reprinted. There are few plays by Shakespeare for which as much evidence is available to testify to

1. See E. K. Chambers, *William Shakespeare*, II 335, and note 3 on p. lxiv above.
2. See C. J. Sisson, 'Shakespeare's Quartos as Prompt-copies', *RES*, XVIII (April 1942), 129–43.
3. Cited in J. O. Halliwell's edn of *A Copy of a Letter of News* ..., 1865, p. 11.
4. Chambers, *op. cit.*, II. 348, and see Young, p. xxxii.

their popularity on the stage during the early decades of the seventeenth century.

This popularity, however, hardly lasted beyond the Restoration. It is true that *Pericles* was probably Shakespeare's first play to be staged after the Restoration, Betterton, then a young actor of about twenty-five, being 'highly applauded in the title-rôle'. And he staged it again with the Duke's company at Salisbury Court Theatre in early 1661.[1] But after this, the play is not heard of for nearly eighty years, and then in a completely refurbished version by Lillo, the author of *George Barnwell*. Believing only the play's second half to be by Shakespeare, and in line with the prevailing eighteenth-century attitude that one could do greater justice to Shakespeare by rewriting him than by fidelity to his text, he wrote a three-act play based mainly on Acts IV and V of *Pericles*. He omitted Cleon and Cerimon, added several episodes, and melodramatized the rôle of Lysimachus. The whole was reduced 'to a single tale'; 'Charming Marina's wrongs [began] the scene'; and the two recognition scenes in *Pericles* were telescoped into one. In other words, Lillo's *Marina* was a typical eighteenth-century refurbishing of Shakespeare. It was produced at Covent Garden on August 1, 4, and 8, 1738.[2]

The only nineteenth-century production of importance was the bold revival by Samuel Phelps at Sadler's Wells on 14 October 1854. The play had a run of several weeks. Like most of Phelps' productions, *Pericles* was staged as an elaborate spectacle, and successfully so, judging from the reviews. Unfortunately, Gower was omitted, the brothel scenes were compressed into one and heavily expurgated to suit Victorian taste, and other scenes were strung together. Douglas Jerrold's comment on the brothel scenes deserves quotation:

> The fourth act, so dangerous to represent, has been disinfected of its impurities in a manner that would win the praise of the most fastidious member of the most moral Board of Health that ever held its sittings within the camphored precincts of Exeter Hall. The greatest theatrical purist need not be afraid to visit that foul room at Mitylene, since it has been whitewashed and purified by the pen of Mr. Phelps.[3]

Yet one gathers from the extant prompt-book and various con-

---

1. See John Downes, *Roscius Anglicanus* (1708), Montague Summers's edn, pp. 17–18, and A. Nicoll, *A History of English Drama, 1660–1900*, I, pp. 352–3. More details are provided by Young.

2. For further detail, see Young.

3. In *Lloyd's Weekly London News*, reprinted in W. M. Phelps and J. Forbes-Robertson, *Life of Samuel Phelps*, 1886, p. 143.

temporary reviews that the production was impressive in many ways. Henry Morley, for instance, comments on how the scene-painter and machinist constantly reinforced the impression of *Pericles* as a sea-play, by reproducing the rolling of the billows, the whistling of the wind, and the tossing of the ship. The many glittering dances, banquets, and trains of courtiers created the atmosphere of an Eastern story. Such effects do justice to the play, as I and others interpret it today, even if the means can be less elaborate. There seem only to have been three other productions of *Pericles* before World War I: two of them in Germany, at Munich in 1882 and 1904,[1] and a quite unsuccessful one by Benson at Stratford in 1900, with John Coleman in the title-rôle.[2]

The number of revivals since 1920 testify to the play's growing popularity in our century. Perhaps the first unexpurgated production was the excellent one by Robert Atkins at the Old Vic in May 1921. It was followed by presentations at the New Scala in 1926; at the Maddermarket Theatre, Norwich, on an Elizabethan type of stage in 1929; at the Festival Theatre, Cambridge, in February 1933; and at Regent's Park in an open-air production during the summer of 1939. Between the two wars, *Pericles* was also produced several times in Germany,[3] and at least twice in the United States: a shortened adaptation by amateurs at Smith College in April 1920, and a more professional production at the Pasadena Playhouse from 29 June to 4 July 1936.

This growing interest in *Pericles* in the theatre has continued to our own day. Nugent Monck produced it successfully at Stratford in 1947, omitting Act I wholly but little else. Paul Scofield and Daphne Slater as the principals received high praise. They acted again in a moving production by the Under Thirty Group in the Rudolph Steiner Hall, London, on 2 July 1950. Meanwhile, the play had been done at least once by an amateur student group in Sydney, Australia, in 1948. During the summer of 1954, the Birmingham Repertory Theatre staged the whole play impressively, with a few additions from Wilkins' novel. For many who saw it, both the scholarly and the unscholarly in the audience, this production was a profound experience.[4] The sea seemed to provide a unity to the play, linking the first part to the second. The chorus Gower delivered his lines slowly in sing-song fashion, without lute

1. These productions were liberally prepared by E. von Possart, and were reviewed in *Shakespeare Jahrbuch*, XVIII. 209, and XLI. 308.

2. See Young.

3. E.g. at Kiel and Mannheim in 1924; see *Shakespeare Jahrbuch* for 1925.

4. Not having seen the production, I made a point of speaking to several people of both kinds who did.

accompaniment. The brothel scenes were oriental. Lysimachus'
conversion by Marina was fully serious and moving. The climax in
the recognition scene moved many to tears. The whole effect was
fairytale-like, to which the colour of the costumes and the lights
contributed skilfully.

Other recent productions can only be listed briefly: by Arthur
Lithgow at Antioch, Ohio, in 1954; at Ashland, Oregon, in 1957;
by René Dupuy at the Ambigu in Paris in 1957; and an impressive
one at Stratford in 1958 with Richard Johnson as Pericles and
Geraldine McEwan as Marina, who 'made the recognition as
poignantly beautiful as the Lear–Cordelia scene'. The audience
was continually reminded of the sea theme, which 'anchors the
rambling yarn to an atmosphere.'[1] It appears that never since
Shakespeare's own generation has *Pericles* met with so much
acclaim on the stage as it does today.[2]

6. LITERARY INTERPRETATION

1. Past and Present Attitudes to 'Pericles'

The history of critical reaction to *Pericles* parallels its stage-
history. Jonson's bitter comment, 'a mouldy play', merely betrays
the enthusiastic reception *Pericles* received on the Jacobean and
early Caroline public stage. But during the ensuing centuries,
criticism with few exceptions was either negative or confined itself
to the non-aesthetic problems of the play. And just as recent
decades have witnessed a remarkable revival of interest in the play
on the stage, so literary critics have suddenly begun to proclaim its
artistic power. I shall follow the trend in this introduction, though
perhaps the play's neglect by so many previous generations should
put us on our guard, lest it be only the preoccupations and tastes
peculiar to our own time, and not any broader, more objective
literary judgment, that attract us to *Pericles*.

In the eighteenth and nineteenth centuries stage-producers and
literary critics alike regarded it as a poor play, unworthy of comparison with almost any other of Shakespeare's work. It was
generally held to be lacking in original or lively characterization
and to contain little thought; the action was thought to be too
sprawling and too improbable for it to achieve a unified and powerful dramatic effect. Such charges have persisted to our own time

1. Both quotations are from M. St Clare-Byrne's review in 'The Shakespeare
Season at the Old Vic, 1957–58 and Stratford-upon-Avon, 1958', *Sh.Q.*, IX, No. 4
(Autumn 1958), 520–3.
2. Since this was written, two further productions have come to my notice: at
Barnard College, New York, in April 1960, and at Gniezno, Poland, in May 1960.

and must not be ignored, even if we can afford to smile at the extremity of Steevens' judgment, addressed in a letter to his fellow-editor Malone:

> . . . the valuable parts of *Pericles* are more distinguished by their poetic turn, than by variety of character, or command over the passions. Partial graces are indeed almost the only improvements that the mender of a play already written can easily introduce; for an error in the first concoction can be redeemed by no future process of chemistry. A few flowery lines may here and there be strewn on the surface of a dramatick piece; but these have little power to impregnate its general mass. Character, on the contrary, must be designed at the author's outset. . . . In genuine Shakespeare, it insinuates itself everywhere. . . . But the drama before us contains . . . very few traces of original thought. . . . *Pericles*, in short, is little more than a string of adventures so numerous, so inartificially crouded together, and so far removed from probability, that, in my private judgment, I must acquit even the irregular and lawless Shakespeare of having constructed the fabrick of the drama, though he has certainly bestowed some decoration on its parts.[1]

This comment indicates why most eighteenth-century editors' including Pope, Dr Johnson, and Capell, excluded the play from Shakespeare's canon. While nineteenth-century editors followed Malone in grudgingly allowing it a place in their texts, Victorian taste was, if anything, even more hostile to *Pericles*; for the brothel scenes outraged the moral sense. Such an attitude must have discouraged people's appreciation even of Marina. It took a while for the sanity of Sir Walter Raleigh's defence of these scenes early in our own century to spread:

> *Measure for Measure* and the fourth act of *Pericles* (which no pen but his could have written), prove Shakespeare's acquaintance with the darker side of life of the town, as it might be seen in Pickt-hatch or the Bankside. He does not fear to expose the purest of his heroines to the breath of this infection; their virtue is not ignorance; 'It is in grain: 'twill endure wind and weather'. In nothing is he more himself than in the little care he takes to provide shelter for the most delicate characters of English fiction.[2]

To this one might add that the comic power of these scenes is Shakespearean:

---

1. *The Plays and Poems of Shakespeare*, edited by Boswell and Malone, 1821, vol. XXI, pp. 227–8.

2. *Shakespeare* (English Men of Letters), Macmillan & Co. Ltd, 1928 (first published 1907), p. 53. Even Dowden found those scenes 'offensive to our taste'.

Bawd. How now, what's the matter?
Boult. Worse and worse, mistress; she has here spoken holy
      words to Lord Lysimachus.
Bawd. O abominable!   (IV. vi. 131–4)

In the last forty years several critics and poets have given testimony to the play's moving power. T. S. Eliot's poem *Marina* was suggested by the treatment of recognition between father and daughter in Act v of *Pericles*. This theme of recognition, so prominent in *Lear* and all Shakespeare's Romances, has been a major theme in Eliot's work. More recently, a critic has referred to

> the remarkable manner in which this tale of long ago and the far
> away induces in the reader or spectator a semi-hypnotic state in
> which everything is experienced as in a dream. This quality,
> which is shared by *The Tempest*, invests the narrative and dra-
> matis personae with significances far in excess of the surface
> values of the lines.[1]

Still others have claimed for the play a unity of structural design[2] and a profound underlying theme.[3] This rise of the play in recent critical estimation has been accompanied by a growing confidence that Shakespeare took a large share in it, that he did much more than what Steevens had contemptuously called 'decoration'. Students have sensed Shakespeare's hand in the play not merely in the more moving passages of dramatic poetry in III. i and v. i, but in the very design and underlying thought of the whole.

2. Its Kinship with the Last Plays

A further justification for a serious approach to *Pericles* is its close kinship to Shakespeare's other 'Romances'. It seems that already when at work on *Pericles*, Shakespeare's mind was occupied with certain areas of experience which were to be crucial to his final plays. *Pericles* anticipates *Cymbeline*, *The Winter's Tale*, and also, though less obviously, *The Tempest* in a number of characteristics which justify one in speaking of these plays as a group different from the earlier comedies, tragedies, and histories. Superficially, the Romances may look like a return on Shakespeare's part to his former mode of romantic comedy after the 'dark' tragedies. But structurally and otherwise, they are quite unlike the romantic

1. J. G. McManaway, review of N.C.S. edn of *Pericles*, *MLR*, LII, No. 4 (Oct. 1957), 583.
2. J. Arthos, '*Pericles, Prince of Tyre*: A Study in the Dramatic Use of Romantic Narrative', *Sh.Q.*, IV (Summer 1953), 257–70.
3. Especially J. M. S. Tompkins, 'Why Pericles?', *RES*, n.s. III, 12 (Oct. 1952), 315–24 and M. D. H. Parker, in *The Slave of Life*, 1955.

comedies. They share with them romantic plots with happy endings and certain similar conventions, but there the likeness ends.

What sets the last plays apart from Shakespeare's romantic comedies is primarily their kind of action, or rather actions. *Pericles*, *Cymbeline*, and *The Winter's Tale* are characterized by a peculiar kind of double plot which is found nowhere else in Shakespeare, and hardly anywhere else in Elizabethan drama. Two actions are intertwined, the protagonists of which are a king or duke and his daughter or, as in *Cymbeline*, his several children and son-in-law. While the relative weight given to these two actions and to the dangers, struggles, and misfortunes sustained by their protagonists differs appreciably among the three plays, in each the fortunes of a king take a sudden happy turn near the end, as a result of some act of the children which brings about, though without their foreknowledge, their recognition and restoration to their father. In none of these plays, therefore, does a love-action, as so often in Shakespeare's earlier comedies, constitute the main issue. They do not so much present the fortunes of individuals, even if these are momentarily stressed in the course of the play, as those of a family of parents *and* children, husband *and* wife. References to family affection are accordingly frequent. Each play tells the story of a family whose various members are for many years scattered, in the end to be miraculously reunited. The central figure is usually a king or prince—least clearly so in *Cymbeline*—who, at any rate by the end of the action, is well on in middle age, and who becomes the joyful witness of his daughter's marriage. In romantic comedy on the other hand, the chief protagonists are almost invariably attractive and marriageable young men and women. Older people are either in the background, or represent the chief antagonists, like Shylock in *The Merchant of Venice* and Duke Frederick in *As You Like It*.[1]

The peculiar nature of the action and choice of protagonists in *Pericles* and the other Romances explains the markedly different handling of time in them. While the unity of time is not observed in Shakespeare's earlier comedies, the action is spread at most over a few months, enough time for the young lovers to disentangle themselves from their predicaments or outwit their antagonists. At the end, the protagonists are not much older, though perhaps a little wiser, than they were at the beginning. In *Pericles*, by contrast, the action takes about sixteen years, enough time for *Pericles* to woo and marry Thaisa, and for their child Marina to be born and grow up to marriageable age. A similar lapse of time occurs in the middle

1. This distinction applies least to *All's Well*.

of *The Winter's Tale*, to allow the baby Perdita to grow up into a shepherdess wooed by Florizel. Though the technique of construction is different, the stories of *Cymbeline* and *The Tempest* likewise involve many years, sufficient for the two royal princes and for Miranda to grow up. Long passages of recollected antecedent action in these plays correspond to the opening acts of *Pericles* and *The Winter's Tale*. The injustice righted by Prospero in the classically-constructed *Tempest* occurred some twelve years earlier.

The romantic comedies and the last plays are also different in mood, but this is much less easily defined, because of the great individuality and variety of the plays themselves. The romantic comedies are far from being always gay—we need only think of the trial scene in *The Merchant* or the wedding scene in *Much Ado*. Nevertheless they contain nothing to correspond in seriousness or sinister suggestion to the opening scene of *Pericles* or the treatment of Leontes' jealousy in *The Winter's Tale*. In all the last plays we are made aware of the frightening shape and power of evil to an extent alien to the very spirit of the romantic comedies. In the comedies our response to evil is always mitigated, either by giving the evil little emphasis, or by endowing evil characters with 'humorous' traits that make them appear as at least partly comic. The aim of romantic comedy was to delight, and Shakespeare never forgot this even in the most serious scenes.

Linked with this stronger impression of evil in the last plays is the sense, conveyed especially in *Pericles*, *Cymbeline*, and *The Winter's Tale*, of man as the plaything of Fortune or of the gods. Pericles is not in control of his fortunes: he endures them. Similarly, Leontes' destructive jealousy is such as to render all human forces of sanity and good will helpless. It is a mental fever. Only time and 'recognition' can bring Hermione and Perdita back to Leontes, after Apollo's anger has been allayed. Many, though not all, of Pericles' sufferings are directly caused by angry Neptune, and Marina is likewise helpless against the strokes of fate, however strongly she withstands human attempts to undermine her purity. The action of all the last plays is overshadowed by supernatural forces, who seem to be willing to grant to the protagonists enduring happiness only after years of suffering. Supernatural forces, on the other hand, have no share in Shakespeare's earlier comedies, except for *A Midsummer Night's Dream*, where they take a different shape and act upon human beings in a manner peculiar to that play.

This emphasis on man's subservience to supernatural forces is one of the reasons why the world of the last plays seems very remote from that of everyday existence. By its very nature, of course, romance places us in fanciful surroundings, in Illyrias or Bohemias with a sea-coast. Yet this sense of remoteness is much more marked in the last plays than in the earlier romantic comedies. Though Viola's adventures are pure make-believe, we soon encounter in the world of *Twelfth Night* much that is familiar. The play is infused with a realistic spirit which, while most clearly apparent in the scenes of the subplot (Olivia's household is recognizably English), affects the atmosphere of the whole. The very individuality of Viola makes her a half-realistic character. And sometimes in *Twelfth Night*, as even more obviously in *As You Like It*, the realistic spirit turns critical, questioning some of the very assumptions of romantic attitudes.

Of such a spirit there is little in the last plays and least of all in *Pericles*. Only in the dialogue of the fishermen in II. i and in the brothel scenes are we brought back to a world of familiar reality. In *The Winter's Tale* and *The Tempest*, the realistic element is somewhat stronger, but in them also we are only for brief moments allowed to forget the essential strangeness of their world, a world more like that of our dreams than that of normal outward experience. We are no longer in surroundings where healthy wit and sanity can get us very far. The characters of the last plays seem so much more to depend on the good will of the gods—or, in *The Tempest*, of Prospero, whose magic is sanctioned by Providence and who takes over many of the functions of the supernatural characters in the other Romances—and this good will becomes clear to them only in the final act, after much suffering.

While the spirit of gaiety is not excluded from their world, it is of necessity less prominent than in the romantic comedies. A Rosalind cannot be imagined in the last plays: she manages her own fate with too much wit and common sense. Instead, a more lyrical heroine enters. *Pericles* can hardly have been intended by its creator to delight audience or reader in the sense the comedies do. Rather its appeal is to our sense of wonder, a wonder which reaches its high point in the scenes of recognition.

3. *The Basic Problem of Construction: Spectacle vs. Drama*

To become fully appreciative of the task Shakespeare faced in the Romances, one must be aware of their uniqueness in the drama of their time. As tragi-comedies, they stand by themselves. None of Beaumont and Fletcher's plays, for instance—to mention merely the pair of dramatists who are sometimes said to have exercised an influence on Shakespeare during his 'last phase'—contains the most characteristic structural element of the Romances: the double plot involving parents and children. As the first of Shakespeare's Romances, then, *Pericles* represents a completely new experiment in drama on the Elizabethan stage.

It must have been an experiment fraught with unusual difficulties, as we shall realize if we reflect on the plot in the play's primary source, Gower's *Confessio Amantis*, Book 8. The long time-span of the action, the multiplicity of its incidents and their loose organization, the many ups and downs in the fortunes of the protagonists—all of these must have seemed to Shakespeare, as they seem to us, unusual obstacles to effective dramatization. As Ker has said, Romance by 'itself is a kind of literature that does not allow the full exercise of dramatic imagination'.[1]

This basic obstacle was not overcome by Shakespeare, it seems, in *Pericles*. In dramatic power it is inferior to most of Shakespeare's plays. In the tragedies and comedies, the action is usually organized around some central and highly concentrated conflict. The norm of structure in such plays, followed in most though not in all instances, is to prepare for the main issue in the opening act, then to involve the leading characters in increasing complications up to the climax, which usually occurs shortly after the middle, and finally to carry the action through to its catastrophe or resolution, with often a second climax near the end. A structure of this kind is designed largely with a view to creating dramatic suspense and sustaining it over most of the play. The action usually moves from one group of characters to another, from protagonist to antagonist, from intriguers to those intrigued against, thereby widening more and more the possibilities for irony, by which dramatic suspense is often enhanced. But in *Pericles*, dramatic irony is used sparingly and, what is even more peculiar, there is no central conflict. If it is a unified play in any sense, it is so not by virtue of a single action but because almost all the incidents directly affect the well-being of Pericles and Marina.

Yet *Pericles* cannot simply be dismissed by saying that Shakespeare and his collaborators chose a wrong type of plot for drama. There was evidently something about the tale of Apollonius of Tyre that fascinated Shakespeare sufficiently to hazard writing a new kind of play. Working to a plot so very unlike those he had employed in either comedy or tragedy before, with few opportunities for dramatic complication or suspense, he seems to have decided to attempt something quite different. How can one otherwise explain the (for Shakespeare) unusual loyalty to the plot of his source, and the employment of such an obviously undramatic

1. W. P. Ker, *Epic and Romance*, p. 33, cited by Arthos, p. 264.

makeshift as the chorus of Gower? If *Pericles* could not hold its audience by suspense, perhaps it could appeal to it by other devices.

One of these devices is the evocation of John Gower, the author of the main source, as chorus of the play. As has already been stressed,[1] Shakespearean drama offers no precedent for such a device, for in the only other play that employs a chorus more than once or twice, *Henry V*, the chorus is the impersonal spokesman for the company of actors in an epic drama of dimensions too vast for complete or realistic presentation on the stage. Gower, on the other hand, reincarnates the original mediaeval poet. On first reflection he may seem to us a mere makeshift device, and very undramatic at that, for holding the play's sprawling action together. But his entry must have had a striking effect on the Jacobean audience. Presumably he wore a garb somewhat like that pictured on the woodcut of Gower in Wilkins' prose version of the play, *The Painfull Adventures* (reproduced in the frontispiece to this edition). This woodcut may well have been based on an original which was familiar to Elizabethans, for the portrait accords in some detail with 'The Description of Iohn Gower' in Robert Greene's *Vision*:[2]

> Large he was, his height was long;
> Broad of brest, his lims were strong;
> But couller pale, and wan his looke,—
> Such haue they that plyen their book:
> His head was gray and quaintly shorne,
> Neately was his beard worne.
> His visage graue, sterne, and grim,—
> Cato was most like to him.
> His Bonnet was a Hat of blew,
> His sleeues straight, of that same hew;
> A surcoate of a tawnie die,
> Hung in pleights ouer his thigh:
> A breech close vnto his dock,
> Handsomd with a long stock;
> Pricked before were his shoone,
> He wore such as others doone;
> A bag of red by his side,
> And by that his napkin tide.
> Thus *John Gower* did appeare,
> Quaint attired, as you heere.

Here was the author of the play's story himself, revived from ashes, presenting it anew to an audience two hundred years after his

1. See pp. xix–xxi.

2. Grosart's edn of Greene (Huth Library), XII. 210. I do not think that this description was based on Gower's monument at St Saviour's, Southwark.

death. Any estimate of the play's total impact will have to allow for the vivid incarnation of its presenter, who steps out of an archaic world, quaint yet with its own kind of wisdom.

An audience might indeed wonder to what extent the play is Shakespeare's and to what extent Gower's—Shakespeare seems to be merely endowing Gower's episodes with an idiom fitting for the new age. This is obviously not the complete truth, yet the impression is strongly produced at the beginning, and if we forget it in the course of some scenes, Gower returns with some moralizing comment in the mediaeval (or pseudo-mediaeval) vein. The play is Gower's narrative in visual form, and Gower asks us, his audience, to judge it kindly. The dominant technique of *Pericles* is therefore indirect and narrative from the outset, and only episodically, as in the brothel scenes, is the play allowed to become truly dramatic.

Many of the play's episodes affect us as 'pictures more than drama'.[1] The play opens spectacularly with the scene of the riddle at Antioch against the background of the 'grim looks' of the former suitors. The famine at Tharsus in the fourth scene is conveyed descriptively rather than dramatically, through the dialogue of Cleon and Dionyza. Scenes of hunger are presented to our visual imagination, the only touch of drama being provided by Pericles' unexpected arrival with ships bearing food. Pericles' first shipwreck again is described, not enacted: contrast the opening scene of *The Tempest*. The scene of the lists, where the various knights through their squires present their shields with devices and mottos to Thaisa and Simonides, is purely spectacular—a more undramatic episode is hard to imagine. In some of the later and Shakespearean scenes, the dramatic element is stronger, but the dominant narrative and pictorial method persists. We are the witnesses of such varied spectacles as the dumbshow of Pericles' return to Tharsus (where he learns of Marina's death), the vision of Diana, and the ceremonial final scene culminating in Pericles' reunion with Thaisa. Moreover, the fact that as early as III. ii we learn of Thaisa's revival by Cerimon (another romantically spectacular episode), deprives the final scene of the dramatic tension it might otherwise have had. If the scene moves us at all, it is for other reasons.

Truly dramatic scenes, then, are few in the play: the storm at the opening of Act III, Marina's encounter with Lysimachus in the brothel, the extended and deeply moving scene of Pericles' gradual recognition of his daughter. But of the rest it seems hardly just to say, negatively, that spectacle compensates for the paucity of dramatic situation. Rather, the dramatist is deliberately aiming at

1. Arthos, *op. cit.*, p. 265.

an effect that is something else than dramatic. It is more like that of *The Magic Flute* than that of *Macbeth* or *As You Like It*. Such a comparison is appropriate in view of the large rôle of music in *Pericles*. In addition to the visual effects, sound effects contribute a great deal. One of the play's first incidents is the entry of Antiochus' daughter to music. Later, Cerimon calls for music, when he tries to revive Thaisa:

> The still and woeful music that we have,
> Cause it to sound, beseech you.
> The viol once more; how thou stirr'st, thou block!
> The music there! (III. ii. 90–3)

If the song Marina was intended to sing when she is brought by Lysimachus before the speechless Pericles had not been lost, we can be sure the play would be enriched. And near the end of the same scene, Diana's vision is anticipated, for fifteen lines before her appearance, by 'most heavenly music'. I should think that we in the audience are meant to hear it, even if Pericles' companions do not. Furthermore, in trying to reconstruct as well as possible the play's performance in Shakespeare's own time, we should surely attend to the emphasis laid on the musical accomplishments of both Pericles and Marina. Simonides praises Pericles as 'music's master':

> I am beholding to you
> For your sweet music this last night. I do
> Protest my ears were never better fed
> With such delightful pleasing harmony.
>
> (II. v. 25–8 and 30)

In the play as we have it, we are merely told this. But does it not seem probable that the original presented Pericles at least once with a musical instrument in his hand, playing an Elizabethan air? The sources, which make much of Pericles as Thaisa's music-teacher, might easily have suggested such an episode to the playwright. As for Marina, the audience perhaps had to wait until the recognition scene, its appetite whetted by Gower's description in the fourth chorus:

> or when to th' lute
> She sung, and made the night-bird mute
> That still records with moan. (IV. Ch. 25–7)

There are other scenes, including the last, where some use of music would seem fitting. But whether these speculations prove acceptable or not, the important contribution of music to the play's total effect is not in question. Though Shakespeare was fond of music, nowhere else did he use it as often and as widely except in the great play which *Pericles* so clearly anticipates, *The Tempest*. In both we are presented with music and with storms. When the storms subside, music takes over.

4. Characterization; The Pattern of Pericles' Adventures

The dominantly narrative and spectacular technique of *Pericles* partly dictates and is partly conditioned by the manner of presentation of its most important characters. The play is unified by its central figure, Pericles, rather than by its plot. It is a romantic biography. It presents us with Pericles' adventures over a period of many years, and to a lesser degree with those of Marina (Thaisa's are barely sketched). All other characters are strictly subordinate and most of them in fact episodic, drifting into Pericles' life on only one or two decisive occasions. There is therefore no room for the development of the minor characters. They are mere type-figures, though the realistically portrayed fishermen and brothel-keepers become obviously more alive than the more romantic figures, of whom only Cerimon has any individuality. They are presented not so much for themselves as for their impact on Pericles and Marina. If the play is informed by any deeper significance, it must then be sought in the 'pattern'—to employ Twine's and Wilkins' term—of Pericles' experiences, and the way in which they affect him.

The basic rhythm of Pericles' adventures may be described as one of love, loss, and restoration. We first see him as a young prince in quest of love who makes the ghastly discovery that the fairness of the lady he woos is a cover for tyrannous and incestuous lust. Recoiling from the shock, Pericles plunges into profound melancholy, which however does not blind him to the necessity of flight. Next we encounter him in his generous act of relieving the famine at Tharsus. His trail of suffering, however, has only begun. In a shipwreck, he loses his companions and all his possessions, except for his armour. Yet this shipwreck turns out to be a blessing in disguise, for soon after his rescue he encounters true love in Thaisa, whom he marries at the end of Act II.

Everything seems set for his happy return to his native land, when a severe storm at sea deprives him of his wife in the very act of childbirth. All he has left to cheer him is the new-born Marina, whom he entrusts to Cleon and Dionyza for her upbringing. What happens during the ensuing fifteen or sixteen years we are not told, and it is thus of no interest. When after this interval Pericles returns to Tharsus, he is persuaded by the monument and by Cleon and Dionyza's simulated sorrow that his daughter, too, has died. Departing in utter grief, and withdrawing from all society into his cabin, he this time 'rides out' a storm at sea, and as a result of a series of rapid and fortunate events discovers that his daughter and his wife are both alive and is reunited to them. They all live happily to old age, we feel sure.

Even this sketchy summary will indicate how many of Pericles' changes in fortune are caused by supernatural intervention. Some are caused by human agents: Pericles flees from Antiochus' wrath after unmasking his guilty secret; his success at Simonides' court is the direct outcome of his accomplishments and character; later, he is taken in by Dionyza's story of Marina's death; and it is Marina who rescues him from utter despair. Yet these events seem no more significant than the storms and shipwrecks caused by Fortune or angry Neptune and the vision of Diana which leads Pericles back to Thaisa. Clearly the course of Pericles' life is shaped mainly by Providence and only secondarily by his human contacts and his own actions. There is moreover ample justification for regarding certain human characters in the play, notably Cerimon, as tools of the divine purpose. Some significance may also be attached to the fact that Pericles' reunion with Marina occurs on the day of Neptune's festival, even if it is not possible to define this significance more precisely than to point out that there is one day in the year when Neptune's anger is allayed.

In accord with this evidence of the gods, or Providence, controlling the main changes in his fortune is the generally passive portrayal of the hero. While the leading characters of Shakespeare's comedies and tragedies are drawn as preponderantly active figures, as men and women who make decisions or show fateful indecision, thus contributing to a chain of events which eventually leads to their happiness or ruin, in *Pericles* the events usually happen to the protagonists. One can infer from Pericles' talents and activities that he is a man of unusual gifts, a skilful soldier as well as a great musician, a man of great authority among his subjects, and of generous dealing. But he is revealed mainly as the plaything of Fortune and the gods. He does not create his fortune in any important sense: he endures Fortune's blows and accepts her gifts. Such a manner of characterization is only partly explained by his indirect presentation through Gower. It is inherent in the nature of the play's action, and thus indicative of the view of life which informs it.

Besides being presented mainly passively, Pericles is drawn as an impeccably good man, a man without defect, which constitutes another essential difference from the characterization of Shakespeare's tragic heroes, and foreshadows the idealized figures of Imogen and Hermione. Pericles cannot be said in any sense to deserve misfortune or suffering, let alone the immensity of loss that lies in store for him. He is drawn without moral weakness—at any rate up to Act IV—and without even any ambivalent passion; that is partly why he does not strike us as especially interesting. Nor is his daughter Marina in any sense responsible for her misfortunes, though her eloquent chastity safeguards her from worse. Both Pericles and Marina undergo intense suffering, though both are wholly good.

My reason for emphasizing this point is that some contemporary scholars have been unwilling to face its implications, but instead have tried, in one way or another, to discover a trace of guilt in Pericles, Thaisa, or Marina. These critics see Pericles following the course of guilt, chastisement, atonement, and restoration, like Leontes in *The Winter's Tale*. G. Wilson Knight, for instance, in an otherwise illuminating essay on *Pericles*,[1] argues that Pericles is somehow infected by the evil of Antiochus' daughter whom he tried to woo, and therefore has to undergo purification through suffering. But when was a character ever conceived as worthy of the gods' chastisement whose only wrong had been to discover another's evil and who recoiled from it at once? Pericles is truly a man 'on whom perfections wait' (I. i. 80). Kenneth Muir's imaginative suggestion that in the original uncorrupted text it was clearly indicated that Thaisa upon suddenly marrying Pericles broke a vow to Diana[2] is equally misleading. That Pericles and his family should be chastised by the gods on account of some broken vow or because they have come into contact with evil men—such an interpretation is irreconcilable with any known form of the story and, it seems to me, with the whole spirit of the play. Pericles suffers as a good man and for reasons beyond human comprehension. He is more like Job or like Tobit in the Apocrypha than like Leontes.[3] As Gower puts it simply, Pericles' sufferings serve to show how 'those in troubles reign, Losing a mite, a mountain gain' (II. Ch. 7–8). To seek for a moral cause of Pericles' troubles is to assume the rôle of Job's comforters.

When we first encounter Pericles, he is a young prince of already exceptional insight. He solves Antiochus' riddle, which had

1. In *The Crown of Life*, 1947, pp. 32–75.
2. In *Shakespeare as Collaborator*, 1960, pp. 80–1.
3. See also below, pp. lxxxix–xci.

baffled a hundred suitors,[1] and conveys his solution to Antiochus diplomatically so as to gain time to flee from his murderous wrath. By the end of the play, he has undergone all the practical education a philosopher-king might desire. That aspect of Pericles' career, however, receives only secondary emphasis. It is indicated rather than impressed upon the spectator's mind. What matters is the pattern of sudden changes in Pericles' fortune, his severe losses, the sufferings which ensue, and his restoration to joy. Twine had portrayed the pattern of these basic experiences merely for the sake of illustrating the whimsical and melodramatic power of the goddess Fortune. But the playwright used the same material for a deeper purpose, as we shall see.

As is to be expected, the blows Pericles undergoes increase in severity and in their crushing effect upon his happiness. In his first shipwreck he loses his companions and most of his goods, and is reduced to nakedness, begging for help among fishermen. But his armour is soon cast up again by the sea, though heavily rusted, and before long he has not merely achieved victory at the tournament organized by the local king but also gained the affection of his daughter. Pericles' response to the first storm is utterly unlike Lear's. Lear challenges the storm heroically. First he actually encourages it:

> Blow, winds, and crack your cheeks! rage! blow!
>
> .   .   .   .
>
> Strike flat the thick rotundity o' th' world.
> Crack Nature's moulds . . .   (*Lear*, III. ii. 1–8)

Then, after his dramatic exclamation of his own helplessness in the face of the elements—'Here I stand your slave. A poor, infirm, weak, and despis'd old man'—he proceeds to denounce them for collaborating with the forces of ingratitude:

> But yet I call you servile ministers,
> That will with two pernicious daughters join
> Your high-engender'd battles 'gainst a head
> So old and white as this!   (III. ii. 21–4)

This, by contrast, is how Pericles addresses the gods of thunder:

> Yet cease your ire, you angry stars of heaven!
> Wind, rain, and thunder, remember, earthly man
> Is but a substance that must yield to you;

---

1. There is no implication that the former suitors were all fools. We must accept the convention that the riddle was difficult, even if its verses seem translucent to us.

And I, as fits my nature, do obey you.

.   .   .   .

Let it suffice the greatness of your powers
To have bereft a prince of all his fortunes;
And having thrown him from your wat'ry grave,
Here to have death in peace is all he'll crave. (II. i. 1–11)

Lear never expresses obedience or submission to the angry elements. If in his play one looks for a parallel to 'death in peace is all
he'll crave', one must turn to Kent's words near the end. Soon,
however, Pericles' fortunes take a turn for the better again, and he
has reason to thank the gods for having sent him to Pentapolis.

His address to the second storm, before he learns the bitter news
of Thaisa's death, is more urgent, though again quite unlike that of
Lear:

The god of this great vast, rebuke these surges,
Which wash both heaven and hell; and thou that hast
Upon the winds command, bind them in brass,
Having call'd them from the deep! O, still
Thy deaf'ning, dreadful thunders; gently quench
Thy nimble, sulphurous flashes!   (III. i. 1–6)

Pericles is now concerned more about the safety of his wife than
about his own well-being. When Lychorida informs him that the
queen has died, she implores him: 'Patience, good sir; do not assist
the storm'. And after his brief outburst,

O you gods!
Why do you make us love your goodly gifts,
And snatch them straight away? We here below
Recall not what we give, and therein may
Use honour with you,   (III. i. 22–6)

she again urges him, this time successfully: 'Patience, good sir,
Even for this charge'. Awareness of new responsibilities towards his
daughter quickly calms any rebellious mood to which his mind
might have been prone. He even yields without long debate to the
sailors' request that his queen be at once buried at sea. But his
wholehearted submission to inevitable fate finds its clearest expression in the following scene at Tharsus, where, upon recalling the
death of Thaisa, he says to Cleon and Dionyza:

We cannot but obey
The powers above us. Could I rage and roar
As doth the sea she lies in, yet the end
Must be as 'tis.   (III. iii. 9–12)

His words of stoic resignation recall Edgar's in *King Lear*:

> Men must endure
> Their going hence, even as their coming hither:
> Ripeness is all.

So far Pericles has borne his misfortunes steadfastly. Yet one more tragedy is to overtake him, for on returning to Tharsus he is led by the tomb erected in her memory to believe that his daughter Marina is dead. Now his patience has reached an end, at least for a while. The occasion is presented in dumbshow only, but the stage-direction clearly conveys the violence of Pericles' grief: '. . . whereat Pericles makes lamentation, puts on sackcloth, and in a mighty passion departs'. After this event he no longer washes his face, and, as we learn at the beginning of the fifth act, he refuses food. He withdraws from human society altogether, not speaking a word to anyone. Yet he does no violence to himself, and as if Fortune had by now done her worst, he survives the next tempest without physical harm; Gower relates that

> He bears
> A tempest, which his mortal vessel tears,
> And yet he rides it out.   (iv. iv. 29–31)

In the scene of the reunion with Marina, the note of endurance is struck clearly again at a vital moment. After Marina's first words Pericles pushes her firmly away—how firmly appears from her lines,

> I said, my lord, if you did know my parentage,
> You would not do me violence.   (v. i. 99–100)

Pericles evidently has not yet mastered his grief so far as to bear it with restraint. Yet though he will not let himself believe, at first, that her story could 'prove the thousandth part Of my endurance' (v. i. 135–6), something in her face and general bearing, which reminds him of Thaisa, persuades him to listen to her. As she speaks on and he contemplates her face, his doubts dissolve, and he expresses his emotion in an image at once beautiful and deeply meaningful:

> yet thou dost look
> Like Patience gazing on kings' graves, and smiling
> Extremity out of act.   (v. i. 137–9)

Wilson Knight's comment on this passage will bear quoting in full:

> We remember Viola's 'Patience on a monument smiling at grief' (*Twelfth Night*, ii. iv. 116); but these lines hold a deeper penetration. The whole world of great tragedy ('kings' graves') is subdued to an over-watching figure, like Cordelia's love by the

bedside of Lear's sleep. 'Extremity', that is disaster in all its finality (with perhaps a further suggestion of endless time) is therefore negated, put out of action, by a serene assurance corresponding to St. Paul's certainty in 'O death, where is thy sting?' Patience is here an all-enduring calm seeing *through* tragedy to the end; smiling through endless death to ever-living eternity.[1]

The idea of 'Patience . . . smiling Extremity out of act' is indeed one that carries us beyond the world of Shakespeare's tragedies.[2] One would search in vain for it among Beaumont and Fletcher's tragi-comedies, which differ from Shakespeare's romances not only in structure, as has been pointed out, but, more fundamentally, in the vision of life they contain. When Wilson Knight relates Pericles' words to those of St Paul, he points, I believe, to a very real analogy For while the series of Pericles' adventures is not to be regarded as a deliberate allegory of the life of the good Christian, as traditionally conceived, it can hardly help reminding us of it. Pericles and Spenser's Red Cross Knight have different personalities and different duties.[3] But both are subjected to a series of tribulations, for a time alternating with brief episodes of good fortune, progress, or comfort. In the lives of both, tribulation reaches an extreme, before they are freed from it by outside help and are prepared for a joy which outbalances any hardship, tragic loss, and loneliness they had to endure. Often in religious literature, the Christian protagonist is presented more passively than Spenser's Knight of St George; for instance St John of the Cross relates[4] that the believer must pass through the ordeal of extreme negation, or utter darkness, before he can receive the light of redemption. Like so many mediaeval Christian saints and figures in the Old Testament, Pericles is fitted with the quality of passive endurance. His indirect presentation, however undramatic, appears therefore singularly appropriate.

But Marina, aided by the grace of Diana, the play's presiding goddess, becomes the main instrument in the freeing of Pericles, her father, from his condition of inward darkness after extreme tribulation. She enables him to see beyond tragedy. The extent of her sufferings bears comparison with his, and her expression, like

1. *Op. cit.*, p. 65.

2. It is however anticipated, as J. M. S. Tompkins (*op. cit.*) noticed, in *Cor.*, IV. i. 7–9.

3. Unlike Pericles, the Red Cross Knight is undertaking a pilgrimage and has to be cured of sin.

4. In *Obras Espirituales*, first published in 1618. As is well known, T. S. Eliot drew heavily on this work for his *Ash Wednesday*, which contains a similar passive treatment of the process of purgation in the soul.

'Patience . . . smiling Extremity out of act', is the living image of
her powers of calm endurance, and more, of her capacity to tran-
scend tragic experience. But as his daughter, Marina is part of
Pericles' own personality, a symbol of the fruition of his marriage
with Thaisa. She clearly represents—though this is probably only
part of her function in the play—that hope man can find in the
younger generation, more especially in his children, of renewal,
which reconciles him to life even after he has undergone severe
disillusionment. Some creative power at work in this world can
take him beyond tragedy to reaffirmation and joy. But the tragic
experience brings with it humility, sympathy, and wisdom,
all of which qualities are in the course of the play stressed in
both Pericles and Marina. As to Marina, let Pericles' own words
speak:

> Falseness cannot come from thee, for thou look'st
> Modest as Justice, and thou seem'st a palace
> For the crown'd Truth to dwell in.   (v. i. 120–22)

To give an expression of this creative, renewing principle closely
related to ordinary human experience is the function of the double
plot in *Pericles*.

5. Shakespeare's Emphasis on the Theme of Patience and Redemption

The contention that the theme of patience is important to the
understanding of the play's informing idea or vision receives support from a comparison of *Pericles* with its sources; for in neither
Gower nor Twine, nor in any other possible source, is the idea of
enduring suffering with patience emphasized. On the contrary, in
all these versions Pericles' prototype, Apollonius, bursts out in a
frantic display of grief on the occasion of his wife's death. In
Gower, Apollonius' reaction is the opposite, as nearly as it can be
conceived in the context of the story, to that of Pericles quoted
earlier:

> Ha, thou Fortune, I the defie,
> Now hast thou do to me thy worst.
> Ha, herte, why ne wolt thou berst.
> That forth with her I mighte passe?
> My paines were well the lasse.
> In such weping and suche crie
> His dede wife which lay him by
> A thousand sithes he her kiste.
>
> .   .   .   .   o
>
> He fell swounende as he that thought
> His owne deth, which he besought

> Unto the goddes all above
> With many a piteous word of love.[1]

The brief episode of Lychorida's entreating Pericles to have patience for the sake of his child has no parallel in Gower. In the *Gesta Romanorum*, on which Twine based his version, Apollonius, when beholding the corpse of his wife, 'tore his garments from his breast and cast himself with tears and groans upon her inanimate body'.[2]

These quotations should suffice to convince anyone that the conception of the character of Pericles in Shakespeare's play, at any rate from the beginning of Act III on, differs considerably from that in his sources. To clinch the argument, in Gower, Twine, and Wilkins, immediately before the recognition the hero gives a more violent expression to his anger at his daughter's persistence. He does not merely push her off: he smites her with his hand. In Twine's and Wilkins' novels, she falls on the floor and wounds her cheek. Such a melodramatic display might have pleased Beaumont and Fletcher; not Shakespeare. Lastly, we note that the passage, 'Patience . . . smiling Extremity out of act', is not anticipated by any similar description in Shakespeare's sources. Its underlying idea, as well as the beauty of its expression, are Shakespeare's alone.

The changes Shakespeare made in the plot of Apollonius of Tyre seem, at first sight, so small as to have only limited importance. But, as has been shown, some of these changes alter the basic conception of the hero's character and project into the play a new theme which appears strongly enough to affect the response of the sensitive reader to the play as a whole. In Shakespeare's *Pericles*, though not so clearly as in some of his plays, the story or plot is mainly a means to an end. The story of *Pericles* is very much like the story of Apollonius of Tyre: the purpose to which it is put is different. The view of life *Pericles* contains is new, and of Shakespeare's making.

That view of life is not unlike the traditional Christian view of the sufferings man must undergo before he can penetrate to a full vision of God's goodness and purpose for him. The story of Apollonius of Tyre, like that of the *Odyssey*, which, I believe, strongly influenced its original version, presents a pattern of the course of human life partly analogous to the biblical one. If Shakespeare's play, with its emphasis on the place of patience and creative

---

1. *Confessio Amantis*, VIII. 1066–80.

2. So in Swan's modernized English version. Twine describes this incident as follows: '. . . like a madman distracted he tare his cloths, and rent his haire' (sig. E3v in undated (1594?) edn).

redemption in human life, suggests a still closer analogy to the Christian or biblical view, it is not because he wanted his play to be more Christian—that would be a preposterous deduction. But as he conceived the significance of the tragi-comic pattern of the story of Apollonius of Tyre more deeply than did Gower or Twine or Wilkins or even the author of the *Gesta Romanorum*, he was led to a view of the place of suffering in a great man's life more like that of another profound view, the Christian one. His play remained secular in content and intention.

6. Pericles and the Miracle Play

So far, I have stressed the uniqueness of *Pericles*, both in relation to Shakespeare's earlier work and to the play's sources. The interpretation I have offered receives some oblique support from a direction where scholars have so far refused to look. The play is curiously, and I think significantly, like the vernacular religious drama in its later, more developed, and less rigid forms, especially the Saint's play. One could argue that from plays of this kind, with which Shakespeare was surely acquainted, most of the broad structural features of *Pericles* are derived. They are at any rate paralleled; among them the device of the choric presenter in the person of a poet,[1] the building up of the action out of a large number of loosely related episodes, the treatment of the play as a 'pageant' rather than a work of highly concentrated action around a central conflict, the tragi-comic development of the action, the large part taken in it by supernatural powers, and the construction of the whole so as to serve an explicit didactic end.

If this observation is sound, it has far-reaching implications for our understanding of *Pericles*. It would mean that not only its story-material and its presenting chorus are mediaeval, but also its essential dramatic form. And if this is the case, can it perhaps be said to echo the spirit of the bygone age in its underlying thought or purpose also? Earlier, the play's effect was tentatively described as one of wonder at the mysteries and miracles of existence. A look at the play's opening chorus reveals its basic intentions: 'The purchase is to make men glorious'. It seems no accident that this line also describes adequately the basic aim of the Legends of the Saints and of the miracle plays derived from them.

An introduction like this is not the place for presenting in great detail all the evidence for the assertion that the structure of *Pericles* closely parallels that of certain miracle or saint's plays.[2]

---

1. See also pp. xix ff. above.
2. See my unpublished London doctoral dissertation.

Here, a few general observations must suffice. English saints' plays have been somewhat ignored because only very few have survived. But it is known that many were performed all over England from about 1100 to 1580, and such a long tradition can hardly have failed to make an impact on the professional writers for the Elizabethan stage. Moreover, much can be inferred about the general nature of many of the lost plays by examining analogous continental plays, such as those in the *Miracles de Notre Dame*. I believe it was J. M. Manly who first recognized the full importance of these miracle plays for our understanding of Elizabethan drama. Miracle plays, as he defines the term, deal with subjects drawn from the legends of saints and martyrs, and thus can be sharply differentiated from the cyclic plays of Chester, York, and elsewhere, which deal with subjects drawn from Scripture. He claimed that 'these miracle plays . . . were more important for the development of the drama in England than the great Scripture cycles'.[1]

A qualification applies to those plays based on the Apocrypha, notably the Book of Tobit, which resemble saints' plays rather than cycle plays. But whether drawing for its material on the *Legenda Aurea* or the Apocrypha, 'the most important fact concerning the miracle play is that its material was essentially romantic'. Their stories were thus essentially like that of *Pericles*. The shift from a religious to a more broadly secular emphasis came easily in the Renaissance.

That Elizabethan secular romantic drama was in large part inspired by continental precedents, especially in Italy, is not in question. Yet one must recognize that this influence had been prepared for natively by the established tradition of the miracle play. All that was needed in *Pericles* was to carry one step further the process of secularization, already much in evidence in some of the later miracle plays: to replace God or Christ by Diana or Neptune, and the Christian saint or apocryphal character by a prince or princess; for there is no greater difference between the saints' legends and the romance of Apollonius of Tyre. They are both biographical romances. The fate of Pericles, like that of St Andrew or Mary Magdalene or Tobit, is governed by Providence. Like them, he undergoes manifold adventures, which bring upon him great suffering. Like them, he is lifted out of despair by a miraculous-seeming intervention of a god—a Christ or a Diana.

Of the few surviving English miracle plays, the one which reminds one most closely of *Pericles* is the Digby play of *Mary Mag-*

---

1. 'The Miracle Play in Mediaeval England', *Essays by Divers Hands*, n.s. VII (1927), 133-53.

dalene. Roughly equal to *Pericles* in length, it divides, like *Pericles*, sharply into two parts, though this is probably pure coincidence. The first part is in twenty scenes. The opening five set forth the tyrannous pride and covetousness of Emperor Tiberius, lord of this world. Under him Satan flourishes. Satan's forces beset the Castle of Maudlyn, and Lechery succeeds in tempting Mary Magdalene, one of its inmates and owners. The later scenes present her redemption and the revival of her brother Lazarus, both by Jesus. Margaret, Martha, and Lazarus return to their castle. The second part is devoted mainly to the rôle played by Mary Magdalene in the conversion of the king of Marcyll (Marseilles). The final six scenes carry her life to its conclusion, showing how she was sustained in the desert by food from heaven and ending in the burial of her body and the ascension of her soul. But it is the section dealing with Marcyll's conversion that has greatest interest for us. In a vision, Magdalene is commanded by Christ to go by ship to Marcyll in order to convert the Mohammedan king. There she persuades the King and the Queen to cast off their allegiance to the heathen gods. As a consequence, the Queen's desire to be with child is miraculously fulfilled. They prepare for a voyage to the Holy Land, but on the way a violent storm overtakes them, and the Queen dies even while giving birth to her child. Similarly as in III. i of *Pericles*, the ship's crew demand that both Queen and child be set on a rock. The King himself safely reaches the Holy Land, where he is baptized by Peter. On his return voyage he discovers his babe unharmed on the rock, and his wife suddenly returns to life as if awaking from a trance. They return joyfully, and bless Mary Magdalene, who exhorts them to lead a steadfast Christian life.

It will be seen that in both *Mary Magdalene* and *Pericles* the action is biographical. In both, the protagonist is involved in a series of extraordinary adventures and turns of fortune. Both have a happy ending, largely effected by supernatural intervention. The episodes in both are loosely co-ordinated, and sometimes of a highly spectacular nature. And there are some remarkable correspondences in the detailed incidents.[1] Yet apart from the Christian emphasis of the Digby play, there is of course one further significant difference. The double plot of two generations is not found in the

1. As D. A. Stauffer makes clear in the opening chapter of *English Biography before 1700*, 1930, early biography was almost exclusively that of saints or of royal persons, and hagiography exercised a strong influence on the biographies of kings. It is not surprising, then, that a narrative and biographical drama like *Pericles* should partake of the saint's 'life' and be in the tradition of the Saint's play. Pericles, like the converted Marcyll in *Mary Magdalene*, is something of the royal saint, uniting the royal 'life' with the hagiographical 'life' (from H. F. B.).

earlier play. Nor is it part of any other miracle play, with the exception of certain plays based on the apocryphal story of Tobit.[1] We know that the authors of *Pericles* took it over from the narrative source.

And so this discussion has come full circle. However much the structure of *Pericles* may owe to the mediaeval tradition of miracle plays, the basic feature of its double plot of two generations can safely be said to be peculiar to it and the other Romances of Shakespeare's last period, and with this plot the theme of loss and restoration. This theme was to be treated by Shakespeare both more clearly and with greater dramatic effectiveness in the plays after *Pericles*, which are of Shakespeare's sole authorship. In them Shakespeare's final vision becomes clearer. And as it becomes clearer, it becomes also something different, as we should expect from Shakespeare, who never simply repeated himself. For instance, there is hardly a hint in *Pericles* of the consciousness of guilt and contrition that haunts certain characters in *Cymbeline* and in *The Winter's Tale*. Yet this does not lessen the extreme interest *Pericles* must have for students of *The Winter's Tale* and *The Tempest*. For in the earlier play Shakespeare can be seen groping for much that was to be given consummate expression in his final work.

---

1. No early English play on this story is extant but we know of one having been performed at Lincoln (E. K. Chambers, *The Mediaeval Stage*, II. 131), and of another referred to in Henslowe's Diary in May and June 1602 (ed. Greg, I. 166–8). A full-length sixteenth-century French play on the story is Mlle de Roches, *Acte de la Tragi-comedie*. Like Pericles, it has a double plot of two generations, with loss and restoration.

PERICLES

DRAMATIS PERSONÆ

ANTIOCHUS, *King of Antioch.*
PERICLES, *Prince of Tyre.*
HELICANUS, ⎱ *two lords of Tyre.*
ESCANES, ⎰
SIMONIDES, *King of Pentapolis.*
CLEON, *Governor of Tharsus.*
LYSIMACHUS, *Governor of Mytilene.*
CERIMON, *a lord of Ephesus.*
THALIARD, *a lord of Antioch.*
PHILEMON, *a servant to Cerimon.*
LEONINE, *a servant to Dionyza.*
Marshal.
A Pandar.
BOULT, *his servant.*

The Daughter of Antiochus.
DIONYZA, *wife to Cleon.*
THAISA, *daughter to Simonides.*
MARINA, *daughter to Pericles and Thaisa.*
LYCHORIDA, *nurse to Marina.*
A Bawd.

Lords, Ladies, Knights, Gentlemen, Sailors, Pirates,
Fishermen, and Messengers.
DIANA.
GOWER, *as Chorus.*

SCENE : *dispersedly in various Countries.*

DRAMATIS PERSONAE] first
listed in F3, as 'The Actors names'.
Antiochus is there described as 'a
Tyrant of Greece'. Then follows
'Hesperides, *Daughter* to Antiochus'.
Dionyza is called 'Dionysia', and
Mytilene 'Metaline'. Another char-
acter is included, *viz.* 'Philoten,
Daughter to Cleon'. The errors and
omissions were corrected partly by
Rowe and partly by Malone, who also
added 'SCENE . . . *Countries*'. Unless
specially noted below, the names of the
characters resemble closely those in

Gower's version of Appolinus of Tyre
in *C.A.*, the play's main source.

Antioch] now Antakieh, in the pro-
vince of Aleppo, Syria. Founded
about 300 B.C. by Seleucus. Antiochus
the Great (223–187 B.C.) enlarged it,
as did also his son Antiochus Epiphanes. One of the largest cities of the
Middle East between 200 B.C. and
A.D. 300; then overshadowed only by
Rome and Alexandria (from Round).

PERICLES] in the sources called
Appolinus (Gower) and Apollonius
(Twine, *His. Apolloni regis Tyri*). Until

fairly recently, the theory was widely held that the name was suggested by Sidney's Pyrocles, one of the heroes of the *Arcadia* (Steevens and Malone; the latter cites an epigram by R. Flecknoe in 1670 'on the Play of the Life of *Pyrocles*'). Recently, it has been convincingly argued that the name was rather derived from Plutarch's life of the Athenian statesman, who is drawn as a model of patience (J. M. S. Tompkins, in *RES*, n.s. III (1952), 322–4). It is probably sheer coincidence that in a French analogue of the story, *Du noble roy apolonie* (= MS 3428, Wiener Hofbibliothek), Apollonius, when asked for his name by the princess at Pentapolis (= Thaisa in the play), calls himself *Perillie*: 'il luy dist ... que il auoit este perillie sur mer. Et il auoit nom perillie Et ainsi fut nomme le perillie par lespace de deux ans' (cited by S. Singer, *Aufsätze und Vorträge*, Tübingen, 1912, p. 91). But it may well be that the association of the hero's name with 'peril' or Latin 'periculum' was in Shakespeare's mind.

SIMONIDES] called Artestrates in Gower, and Altistrates in Twine. Simonides of Ceos was an influential poet in fifth-century (B.C.) Greece, only fragments of whose works are extant, but who is referred to in Plutarch and many other classical authors.

Pentapolis] = Cyrenaica. Round remarks that in the Latin *Historia Apolloni*, the place is called 'Pentapolitanae Cyrenaeorum terrae'. Cyrene, the first of the five towns from which this district took its name, was the chief Hellenic colony in Africa. But in this play, it is taken to be a city in Greece (see II. i. 64—so Round).

CLEON] called Stranguilio in Gower and Twine; Cleon is a common name in Greek drama.

Tharsus] a wealthy city in the fertile plain of Cilicia, now part of Turkey; lay on both sides of the river Cydnus; of semitic origin but Hellenized later. Cleopatra first met Mark Antony at Tharsus. The inhabitants had the reputation of being vain, effeminate, and luxurious—see I. iv. St Paul came from Tharsus.

LYSIMACHUS ... Mytilene] This name occurs neither in Gower nor in Twine. It was probably suggested by a passage in Barnabe Riche's *Souldiers Wishe*, 1604. The relevant quotation is given in a n. to I. iii. 3–6. But the name of this powerful king occurs often in North's Plutarch (especially in the 'Life of Demetrius') and in other authors of classical histories. For some time, a Lysimachus was actually ruler of Mytilene on the island of Lesbos, which is now part of Turkey. For the spelling of *Mytilene*, see IV. ii. 3n.

Ephesus] site of a famous shrine to Diana in classical times.

CERIMON] so in Gower and the other sources. The name seems appropriate, suggesting as it does ceremony. Both III. ii and v. iii, where Cerimon officiates, are ceremonious scenes. Shakespeare's interest in ceremony is also reflected in Prospero's emphasis on holy 'ceremony', when addressing Ferdinand, *Tp.*, IV. i. 14–19. Ceremonious scenes occur in all of the last plays, and especially in *The Two Noble Kinsmen* (see G. W. Knight, *The Sovereign Flower*, p. 196).

PHILEMON] not in Gower. In Twine, Cerimon's 'pupil' is called Machaon, but Dionyza's daughter bears the name of Philomacia. Oddly enough, in a very distant analogue of *Pericles*, Cerimon's servant bears the name of Filominus, and in another that of Silemon. But similar names were common in romance literature. See Intro., p. xviii, and Pudmenzky, *Shakespeares Pericles und der Apollonius des Heinrich von Neustadt*, 1884.

LEONINE] The name of the owner of the brothel at Mytilene in Gower.

BOULT] not in the sources; perhaps invented by the dramatist.

THAISA] In Gower, Pericles' wife is not given a name, but the daughter (= Marina in the play) is called Thaise.

MARINA] not in Gower or Twine, where she is called Thaise and Tharsia respectively. The name, both appropriate and beautiful, was probably chosen by Shakespeare. But it is common in eastern and southern Europe. Considering the character of Shakespeare's heroine, it seems worth mentioning that there were lives or legends of more than one saint called Marina. One was a virgin martyr at Antioch, also called St Pelagia, St Margaret, and 'Pearl of the sea' (see M. E. C. Walcott, *Westminster Memorials*, 1849, pp. 113–16). But it seems improbable that Shakespeare had heard of her.

On the title-page, Qq1–3 printed the name as 'Mariana'; perhaps because this is a common name in Elizabethan plays; e.g. *Meas.*, *All's W.*, *Fair Em.*, etc. See also IV. iii. 33. It seems relevant, however, that in *Meas.* Mariana's brother Frederick 'was wreck'd at sea' (III. i. 212), thus contributing to her misfortunes.

DIANA] The goddess is referred to only twice in Gower and in Twine, but about a dozen times in the play, which may be significant.

GOWER] a resurrection of the fourteenth-century poet. See the discussion of the Chorus in Intro., pp. xix–xxiii and lxxvi–lxxvii.

PERICLES, PRINCE OF TYRE

[ACT I]

Enter GOWER

[Before the Palace of Antioch, with heads displayed above the entrance.]

To sing a song that old was sung,
From ashes ancient Gower is come,
Assuming man's infirmities,
To glad your ear, and please your eyes.
It hath been sung at festivals,   5
On ember-eves and holy-ales;

ACT I

ACT I] *Malone; not in* Q *; Actus Primus Scena Prima F3.*   Location] *Malone subst.;
not in* Q.   6. holy-ales] *Theobald MS, Malone, conj. Farmer;* Holydayes Q.

ACT I] Q indicates no act or scene
divisions, except for a horizontal line
across the page at the end of what are
now Acts I and II. Act divisions were
first introduced in F3, scene divisions
by Malone. Modern edd. have uniformly accepted Malone's divisions,
which, but for a minor change in Act I,
this ed. also follows. It is, however,
doubtful whether the play was originally intended to have a five-act structure—see Intro., p. lii, n. 1.

S.D. Location] With a few exceptions, this ed. follows the S.D.s des-
criptive of locale introduced by
Malone. The reader should however
be aware that the notion of a well-
defined locale was foreign to the Elizabethan stage, and that therefore descriptions of setting are not found in the
early printed texts of *Pericles*. They

were introduced only after the bare
and flexible stage of Shakespeare's
theatre had given way to the more
elaborate proscenium theatre.

1. *old*] of old; used adverbially, perhaps for archaic effect.

3. *Assuming man's infirmities*] putting
on again the frail body of mortality
(D.). For this temporary 'restoration' of Gower in the flesh, as the play's
presenter, see Intro., pp. lxxvi–lxxvii.

6. *ember-eves*] the evenings before
ember-days, the four three-day periods
of fasting in the Church calendar.

holy-ales] 'ales' were rural festivals—
cf. Jonson, *A Tale of a Tub*, Prologue,
l. 9. Though restoring the rhyme, the
emendation of Q 'Holydayes' to *holy-
ales* is questionable, for while there
are many references to 'church-ales',
'Whitsun-ales',   'Midsummer-ales',

5

And lords and ladies in their lives
Have read it for restoratives:
The purchase is to make men glorious,
Et bonum quo antiquius eo melius.   10
If you, born in these latter times,
When wit's more ripe, accept my rimes,
And that to hear an old man sing
May to your wishes pleasure bring,
I life would wish, and that I might   15
Waste it for you like taper-light.
This Antioch, then, Antiochus the Great
Built up, this city, for his chiefest seat,
The fairest in all Syria—
I tell you what mine authors say.   20
This king unto him took a peer,

---

11. these] *Q2;* those *Q.*   17. then,] *Q2;* then *Q;* then; *Round.*   21. peer] *Q;*
pheere *Theobald MS, Malone;* fere *Dyce.*

---

etc., no other instance of 'holy-ales'
has been found. Yet most edd. have
adopted this reading which Theobald
and Dr Farmer arrived at independently.

9. *purchase*] gain, profit.

glorious] If this word is to be understood literally, the play opens with an
immense promise to the audience or
reader. See Intro., p. lxxxviii.

10. *Et . . . melius*] And the older a
good thing is, the better it is. A common saying, usually with 'communius'
for 'antiquius'. Maxwell refers to T.
Lodge, *Wits Miserie,* 1596, p. 11,
where it is quoted as an 'axiome of
ARISTOTLE'. It also occurs in Marston,
The Dutch Courtezan (1605), I. i.

11-13. *If you . . . that*] *that* is the
equivalent of a second *if.*

11. *these*] The emended reading
seems preferable, but Q 'those' is
possible.

12. *wit*] intelligence, knowledge.

16. *like taper-light*] like a candle
which consumes itself while offering
light freely. A common saying (Tilley
C 39), used at least twice by Shakespeare:

The lamp that burns by night

Dries up his oil to lend the world
    his light.   (*Ven.,* 755-6)
and
Heaven doth with us as we with
    torches do,
Not light them for themselves;
              (*Meas.,* I. i. 33-4)
For similar passages in *The Travels of
Three English Brothers,* see App. B.

17. *then,*] so Q subst. and most edd.,
but a semi-colon would make 'the sentence much more direct' (Round).

18. *chiefest seat*] This phrase occurs
in Twine but not in Gower, whom
the authors otherwise followed more
closely in the opening acts. Note however G.W.'s (Wilkins'?) *The Historie of
Iustine,* 1606, p. 34, 'the chief seate of
his kingdome', translating the Latin
'regni sedem statuit'.

20. *I . . . say*] a clear imitation of
Gower; cf. *C.A.,* 274-6 (Yale). The
phrase 'as my Aucthor saies' occurs in
Nashe, *Choise of Valentines,* l. 46,
Works, III, p. 405 (Maxwell, pri-
vately).

21. *peer*] companion, mate. See
*O.E.D.*3, where several examples are
cited. Edd. have emended the term
unnecessarily, referring to *Tit.,* IV. i.

Who died and left a female heir,
So buxom, blithe and full of face
As heaven had lent her all his grace;
With whom the father liking took,   25
And her to incest did provoke.
Bad child, worse father, to entice his own
To evil should be done by none.
But custom what they did begin
Was with long use account'd no sin.   30
The beauty of this sinful dame
Made many princes thither frame,
To seek her as a bed-fellow,
In marriage-pleasures play-fellow;
Which to prevent he made a law,   35
To keep her still, and men in awe;

29. But] *Q; By Malone.*   30. Was] *Q; Made Maxwell.*   account'd] *Q;* counted *F3;* account *Malone.*

89, 'wofull feere' (both Q 1594 and F).

23. *buxom*] cheerful, brisk.

full of face] *O.E.D.*3 defines 'beautiful', with a query, and alternatively 'full-faced, florid'. Perhaps 'with a healthily round face'.

29. *custom*] i.e. by custom.

29–30. *custom . . . sin*] a paraphrase of Gower, *C.A.*, 345-6, 'And such delit he tok thereinne, / Him thoghte that it was no Sinne'. A common saying; cf. Tilley C 934, who quotes Greene, *Disputation between a He and She Conny Catcher*, ed. A. Grosart, x, p. 270, 'Custome of sin, tooke away the feeling of the sin'. See also *Cæs.*, III. i. 270 (Maxwell). Wilkins' version of the line is 'The custome of sinne made it accompted no sinne' (*P.A.*, 13. 17–18), which Maxwell may be right in regarding as evidence that the line in *Per.* was corrupted by the reporter. Yet *was* seems natural enough in its context, and one has to be cautious in drawing such deductions from Wilkins who paraphrased quite as often as he quoted literally.

account'd] reckoned; Q's spelling, which is a compromise between the more common trisyllable 'accounted' or 'accompted' and the occasional shortened pple form 'account', has been retained. Most modern edd. read 'account', to indicate the bisyllabic pronunciation.

32. *frame*] direct their course, betake themselves (*O.E.D.*7d); seldom so used, but see Spenser, *Faerie Queene*, III. i. 20, 'A stately castle . . . / To which her steps directly she did frame'.

33–4. *bed-fellow . . . play-fellow*] Cf. *P.A.*, 85. 10–11, 'that she was rather a deseruing bed-fellow for a Prince, then a playfellow for so rascally an assembly'. The echo in what is a completely different context in Wilkins' novel (i.e. that of IV. vi) is indicative of Wilkins' fondness for this pair of terms. Whether it is also to be regarded as evidence that Wilkins had a part in I. Ch. of the play is debatable.

36. *To . . . awe*] To keep her always to himself and to deter others (Malone subst.). It is probably mere coincidence that the phrase *To keep her still* is anticipated in a reference to a similarly incestuous relation, that of Herod to his brother's wife, in Lydgate's *Story of Thebes*, Pt I :

That whoso ask'd her for his wife,
His riddle told not, lost his life.
So for her many a wight did die,
As yon grim looks do testify.   [*Pointing to the heads*.]   40
What now ensues, to the judgement of your eye
I give my cause, who best can justify.   *Exit*.

[SCENE I.—*Antioch*.]

Enter ANTIOCHUS, *Prince* PERICLES, *and Attendants*.

Ant. Young prince of Tyre, you have at large receiv'd
      The danger of the task you undertake.
Per. I have, Antiochus, and, with a soul
      Embolden'd with the glory of her praise,

38. told not, lost] *Q2;* tould, not lost *Q*.   39. a] *F3;* of *Q*.   40. S.D.] *Round subst.; not in Q*.   42. give my cause, who] *Q; give, my cause who Malone*.

Scene I

SCENE I] *Malone; not in Q*.   Location] *not in Q; Antioch. A room in the palace | Malone*.   Entry. *Attendants*] *Malone; followers | Q*.   3–5. I . . . enterprise] *As Malone;* emboldned / hazard, / enterprise *Q*.

And holy writte, recordeth in
  sentence
How Herode falsly, in his life
By violence tooke, his brothers
  wife
For she was faire and pleasant to
  his sight
And kept her still, by force
  through his might
Although to her, title had he
  non.
        (Chaucer's *Works*, ed. 1561,
        fol. 360 a.1)
38. *told not*] 'not having been ex-pounded' (Round).
39–40. *So . . . testify*] closely para-phrased from Gower, *C.A.*, 368–9.
39. *a*] Q 'of', which may be a pseudo-archaism; cf. II. Ch. 35 (Maxwell). The opposite, *a* for 'of', is often found in Elizabethan texts.
41–2. *What . . . justify*] Malone changed the meaning by moving the comma, so that *justify* governs *cause*.

But Q makes sense with the original punctuation. E.S. sends a pertinent note: 'Commentators have overlooked the series of legal metaphors in these lines. They are set off by *testify* in l. 40 (and possibly *a law* in l. 35), which then suggested *judgment, cause* and *justify*; *O.E.D.* defines *cause* (2. 7) as "the case of one party in a suit", and *justify* (4) as "to absolve, acquit, excul-pate". The meaning of the lines is therefore: "In what ensues, I submit my case to the judgment of your eye, as you are in the best position to acquit me" (of the charge of having told an incredible tale)'. A second meaning of the passage may be: 'I present my theme to the judgment of your eyes, you who are best able to confirm its truth (for seeing is believing)' (Max-well subst.).

Scene I

1. *at large receiv'd*] learned fully.

Think death no hazard in this enterprise.   5
Ant. Music!   [*Music.*]
Bring in our daughter, clothed like a bride,
For the embracements even of Jove himself;
At whose conception, till Lucina reign'd,
Nature this dowry gave: to glad her presence,   10
The senate-house of planets all did sit
To knit in her their best perfections.

Enter Antiochus' Daughter.

Per. See, where she comes apparell'd like the spring,
Graces her subjects, and her thoughts the king
Of every virtue gives renown to men!   15
Her face the book of praises, where is read
Nothing but curious pleasures, as from thence

6–7. Music! / Bring] *this ed.;* Musicke bring *Q;* Bring *Malone.*   6. S.D. *Music*]
Malone; not in Q.   8. For the] *Malone;* For *Q;* Fit for *conj. anon. apud Camb.*
10. this] *Q;* rich *conj.* D.

---

8. *For the*] not a certain emendation, but the compositor probably omitted *the.*

9. *At . . . reign'd*] that is, during her mother's pregnancy, between her conception and her birth. *Lucina* is the goddess of childbirth.

10–12. *Nature . . . gave: to . . . perfections*] a construction characteristic of Day. Her *dowry* is that she was conceived and born at the astrologically most propitious time, and would thus all her life remain under the beneficial influences of the planets; *to glad her presence* probably means either: 'to make her stay in this world a happy one', or 'to make her presence delightful (to those about her)' (Maxwell subst.). But it is possible that *her presence* refers to *Nature* whose very bounty is demonstrated and 'gladdened' by the perfect woman she and her agents (the *planets*) have created; cf. opening lines of Surrey's sonnet, 'The golden gift' (No. 8 in Padelford's edn). Steevens noted the parallel in *Arcadia,* II. 6 (p. 189): 'The senate house of the planets was at no time to ["so" in

modern edd.] set, for the decreeing of perfection in man'. Not quite so close in wording, but remarkable because applied to a similar context, are the following lines from the third stanza of *A Woman's Birth* (*Roxburgh Ballads,* I, p. 466):

The privy Counsell of the heavens
    and Planets
Whose Counsell governes all
    affaires on earth
They held a consultation in their
    Senats, . . .

The double parallel suggests that this elaborately conceived image was a common conceit of the time.

15. *gives*] which gives. Ellipsis of the relative in the nominative case occurs frequently in the first two acts of this play, and has been described as a characteristic of Wilkins' style—see Intro., p. lxi.

16. *the book of praises*] a common metaphor for a beautiful woman's face in Elizabethan literature.

17. *curious*] exquisite.
as] as if.

Sorrow were ever raz'd, and testy wrath
Could never be her mild companion.
You gods, that made me man, and sway in love,   20
That have inflam'd desire in my breast
To taste the fruit of yon celestial tree
Or die in the adventure, be my helps,
As I am son and servant to your will,
To compass such a boundless happiness!   25
Ant. Prince Pericles—
Per. That would be son to great Antiochus.
Ant. Before thee stands this fair Hesperides,
With golden fruit, but dangerous to be touch'd;
For death-like dragons here affright thee hard.   30
Her face, like heaven, enticeth thee to view
Her countless glory, which desert must gain;

---

18. raz'd] *Dyce;* racte *Q1-2;* racket *Q3;* rackt *Q4-6;* ras'd *Malone.*   23. the]
Q3; th' *Q.*   25. boundless] *Rowe;* bondlesse *Q.*   26. Pericles—] *Malone;*
Pericles. Q.   30. death-like] *Theobald MS, Malone;* Death like *Q.*

17–18. *as . . . raz'd*] Contrast the
accounts of Marina in v. i. 129 and ff.,
and see n. to v. i. 195. Not only are the
relations between fathers and daughters at the beginning and near the end
of the play dramatically opposed, but
some of Pericles' words to Antiochus'
daughter would never have been
addressed by him to Thaisa or
Marina.

18. *raz'd*] erased; cf. *Mac.*, v. iii. 42,
'Raze out the written troubles of the
brain' (Malone). *raze* was often spelt
'race' in the seventeenth century, and
thus the past pple *racte*. Cf. *O.E.D.*
race v. 3.3 and *raze* 3. The mistake
made by Qq 3–6 and Ff 3–4 indicates,
however, that Q's spelling was open to
misinterpretation.

19. *mild companion*] the companion of
her mildness (Mason); that is 'of her
who is mild'.

20. *, and . . . love*] Considering Q's
comma before *and*, this phrase may
mean 'and who sway in love', though
most edd. by dropping the comma
seem to interpret, and perhaps rightly:
'and who made me sway in love'.

22–30. *To taste . . . hard*] Cf. *All's W.*,
II. i. 162–3 and *LLL.*, IV. iii. 341n. in
Arden edn (David): 'The final labour
Hercules was called upon to perform
was to enter the garden of Hesperus,
overcome a guardian dragon, and
pick the apples from the tree.' None
of the play's sources anticipates this
passage. See the account of Hercules' last labour in Diodorus Siculus
(Loeb edn), iv. 26–7. Also cf. Dekker, *Old Fortunatus*, I. iii. 92. 'And taste
the fruit of this alluring tree', and
Ovid, *Metamorphoses*, IX. 190 and
XI. 114.

24. *As*] As surely as.

28. *Hesperides*] See 22–30n. above.
The daughters of Hesperus are here
identified (or confused with) the
garden, as frequently in Elizabethan
literature.

32. *countless glory*] the stars. Edwards
(p. 28) believes this to be a reporter's
anticipation of l. 74. But the authors of
Acts I and II were excessively fond of
this or similar phrases and the metaphor of which they form part. Cf. also
II. iii. 39 and see App. B.

And which, without desert because thine eye
Presumes to reach, all the whole heap must die.
Yon sometimes famous princes, like thyself,   35
Drawn by report, advent'rous by desire,
Tell thee, with speechless tongues and semblance pale,
That without covering save yon field of stars,
Here they stand martyrs slain in Cupid's wars;
And with dead cheeks advise thee to desist   40
For going on death's net, whom none resist.

Per. Antiochus, I thank thee, who hath taught
My frail mortality to know itself,
And by those fearful objects to prepare
This body, like to them, to what I must;   45
For death remember'd should be like a mirror,
Who tells us life's but breath, to trust it error.
I'll make my will then; and, as sick men do,
Who know the world, see heaven, but feeling woe
Gripe not at earthly joys as erst they did: 50
So I bequeath a happy peace to you
And all good men, as every prince should do;
My riches to the earth from whence they came;
[*To the Princess.*] But my unspotted fire of love to you.
Thus ready for the way of life or death,   55

---

34. all the] *Q;* all thy *Malone.*   35. sometimes] *Q;* sometime *Malone.*
54. S.D.] *Malone subst.; not in Q.*

34. *all the whole heap must die*]
Malone's emendation, 'thy' for *the*,
does not improve the passage. Sisson's
paraphrase and comment on ll. 33–4
are sound: 'Because your eye (a part of
you) presumes without desert to look
upon her face, the whole of you must
die for the fault of the part. This use of
heap, meaning "the whole mass", is
perhaps more unfamiliar to modern
readers than to Shakespeare who was
nearer to the wider uses of the word in
mediaeval English or in Anglo-Saxon'
(*New Readings*, II, p. 287).

35. *sometimes*] once, formerly.
'Shakespeare has both "sometimes"
and "sometime" in this sense' (D.).

41. *For*] for fear of; (or simply) from;
cf. *O.E.D. For* (prep.) 23c, d.

going on] Clarke's interpretation,
'driving headlong on', though too
emphatic, accounts for the somewhat
unusual *on*.

42. *thee, who hath*] for third person
verb with second person antecedent,
see Abbott §247.

43. *My . . . know itself*] Cf. *Tp.*, v. i.
212–13.

45. *must*] sc. face, encounter; i.e.
inevitable death.

47. *Who*] i.e. death who.

49–50. *Who . . . did*] The expression
is compact and the syntax obscure, but
the meaning is evidently: who, though
they felt very much at home in the
world, now that they are in pain and
have a glimpse of heaven, grasp no
longer at earthly pleasures.

I wait the sharpest blow, Antiochus.

Ant. Scorning advice, read the conclusion then:

> [*Angrily throws down the Riddle.*]

Which read and not expounded, 'tis decreed,
As these before thee thou thyself shalt bleed.

Daugh. Of all, 'say'd yet, may'st thou prove prosperous!   60
Of all, 'say'd yet, I wish thee happiness.

Per. Like a bold champion I assume the lists,
Nor ask advice of any other thought
But faithfulness and courage.

[*He reads*] *the Riddle.*

I am no viper, yet I feed   65
On mother's flesh which did me breed.

56–7. blow, Antiochus. | *Ant.* Scorning] *Alexander;* blow (*Antiochus*) | Scorning
Q; blow. | *Ant.* Scorning *Malone.*   57. S.D.] *this ed.; not in Q.*   60, 61. 'say'd]
Collier (i), *conj. Percy;* sayd *Q;* said *Q4.*   64. S.D. *He . . . Riddle*] *Steevens; The
Riddle* | *Q.*   66. which] *Q;* that *Maxwell.*

56–7. *blow, Antiochus.* Ant....] Alexander's emendation, adopted by both
Sisson and Maxwell, seems slightly
preferable to Malone's, for it is more
probable that the compositor in Q
simply omitted the speech-heading
than that he misinterpreted his copy
so badly as to move it into the text of
the previous line. The brackets in Q,
however, may betray his bewilderment.

57. *conclusion*] riddle.

S.D. Angrily . . . Riddle] Cf. *P.A.*,
16. 20–3: 'which the tyrant receiuing
with an angry brow, threw downe the
Riddle, bidding him, since perswasions could not alter him, to reade and
die . . .'

60, 61. '*say'd*] who have yet assayed.
For the omission of the relative, see
15n. above. The initial syllable of
verbs opening in a vowel was often
elided by Elizabethan dramatists. Cf.
The Puritan (1607), sig. D3, 'to say on a
new Doublet'.

63–4. *Nor . . . courage*] Cf. *Arcadia*,
III. 8 (p. 391), 'asking no advice of
no thought, but of faithfulness and
courage' (Steevens).

65–72. *I . . . you*] Wilkins reports
this riddle in full in *P.A.* The three
substantial variants are listed in the
collation above. For a discussion of the
riddle's sources, see P. Goolden, 'Antiochus's Riddle in Gower and Shakespeare', *RES*, n.s. VI (1955), 245–51.

65–6. *viper . . . breed*] one of the many
references in Elizabethan literature to
the belief, ultimately derived from
Herodotus and other classical sources,
that vipers at birth eat their way out of
the mother's body. It is also alluded to
in Wilkins' *Miseries of Inforst Marriage*
and frequently in the works of Day,
who (mistakenly?) refers to it as
'Aesop's fable'. Cf. I. i. 131–4. Also see
v. i. 195n.

66–8. *which . . . in*] Maxwell's emendations are derived from *P.A.* As one
cannot be sure about Wilkins' authorship of the riddle, the Q text, which
makes sufficient sense, has been retained. E.S. comments that *kindness*
may have the double meaning
of 'affection' and 'close kinship'
(*O.E.D.*1), in which case *in* would certainly be preferable to 'from'. See also
the following n.

I sought a husband, in which labour
I found that kindness in a father.
He's father, son, and husband mild;
I mother, wife, and yet his child: 70
How they may be, and yet in two,
As you will live, resolve it you.

[*Aside.*] Sharp physic is the last: but, O you powers
That gives heaven countless eyes to view men's acts:
Why cloud they not their sights perpetually,   75
If this be true, which makes me pale to read it?
Fair glass of light, I lov'd you, and could still,
Were not this glorious casket stor'd with ill.
But I must tell you, now my thoughts revolt;
For he's no man on whom perfections wait   80
That, knowing sin within, will touch the gate.

---

68. in] *Q*; from *Maxwell.*   71. they] *Q*; this *Maxwell, conj. Mommsen.*   73.
S.D.] *Camb.*; *not in Q.*   powers] *Camb.*; powers! *Q.*   74. gives] *Q*; give
Malone.   81. touch] *Q*; ope *conj. J. D. Wilson.*

71. *How they . . . in two*] These words
can only mean: 'How they can represent so many different people, and yet
be only two persons.' If one follows
Wilkins and adopts 'this' for *they*, as
Mommsen and Maxwell suggest, the
meaning of *in two* needs to be explained.

73. *the last*] i.e. the last condition of
the riddle.

74. *gives*] For third person plural in
-*s*, see Franz §155 and Abbott §333.
This grammatical form is common in
the First Folio, e.g. *Ham.*, III. ii. 199,
'his favourites flies'; it also occurs frequently in the works of King James,
e.g. 'they that reades' and 'they who
ignorantly proues' (*Daemonologie*, ed.
G. B. Harrison, 1924, p. 15) but there
it presumably descends from the old
Northern plural in -*s*.

heaven . . . eyes] For the image of the
stars as heaven's eyes, see also *Wint.*,
II. i. 132, *R3*, II. i. 82 and *MND.*, III. ii.
188. The ultimate source is probably
biblical. M. Abend ('Some Biblical
Influences on Shakespeare's Plays',

N&Q, 195 (1950), 554–8) cites *Eccl.*,
xxiii. 19, 'the eyes of the Lord are ten
thousand times brighter thē the Sunne,
beholding all the waies of mē'
(*Geneva Bible*, 1560).

75. *Why . . . sights*] Cf. *Mac.*, I. iv.
50, 'Stars, hide your fires!' (Steevens).

77. *glass of light*] Schmidt's 'image of
light' does not wholly explain the
metaphor. *Glass* points forward to
glorious casket. Both are images of the
daughter's outward beauty, which
stands in such sharp contrast with her
inward evil.

78. *glorious . . . ill*] See previous n.
Cf. the references to Portia's golden
casket in *Mer. V.*, especially II. vii. 65–9
and III. ii. 73–7; but the passage may
only be a memory of Pandora's box, of
which the phrase would be a precise
description (H.F.B.).

81. *touch*] J. D. Wilson proposes
'ope', because of the anticipation of
touch in l. 88. But though sometimes
due to piratic reporting, such repetitions are common among minor Eliza-

You are a fair viol, and your sense the strings,
Who, finger'd to make man his lawful music,
Would draw heaven down and all the gods to hearken;
But being play'd upon before your time,   85
Hell only danceth at so harsh a chime.

> [*Turning towards the princess.*]

Good sooth, I care not for you.

Ant. Prince Pericles, touch not, upon thy life,
For that's an article within our law
As dangerous as the rest. Your time's expir'd: 90
Either expound now or receive your sentence.

Per. Great king,
Few love to hear the sins they love to act;
'Twould braid yourself too near for me to tell it.
Who has a book of all that monarchs do,   95
He's more secure to keep it shut than shown;
For vice repeated is like the wand'ring wind,
Blows dust in others' eyes, to spread itself;
And yet the end of all is bought thus dear,
The breath is gone, and the sore eyes see clear   100

---

86. S.D.] *this ed.; not in Q.*   100–1. clear ... them.] *Steevens, conj. Mason;* cleare: ... them, *Q.*

bethan dramatists, including both Wilkins and Day. E.S. suggests that the image behind *touch the gate* 'is that of the wise traveller who refuses to enter a town, knowing it to be stricken by the pestilence'.

82. *viol*] a six-stringed instrument, the Renaissance counterpart to the modern violin.

sense] collective singular, as in *Meas.*, II. ii. 169 and *Oth.*, IV. iii. 92.

86. S.D.] Pericles' movement or gesture accounts for Antiochus' anxious answer.

87. *Good sooth*] in truth.

90. *dangerous*] rigorous, severe (*O.E.D.*1a).

94. *braid*] upbraid; the aphetic form of the obsolete 'abraid'. Cf. Hutton, *Discovery of a London Monster* (1600), sig. B3v: 'And then he gan with basest terms to braide' (Halliwell-Phillips, Scrapbook.)

97–101. *For vice ... them*] *repeated* = talked about; *Blows* = which blows; *to spread* = in spreading. The *eyes* in ll. 98, 100 are those of the sinners. The remainder of the image is clear but infelicitous. Mason paraphrases ll. 100 f., 'The breath is gone, and the eyes, tho' sore, see clear enough to stop for the future the air that would annoy them'. This is sound enough, but it will be readily seen that the image does not fulfil its intended purpose well, which is to show the danger, not merely the uselessness, of revealing the king's crime. The image, however, occurs elsewhere in Shakespeare: *Lr.*, IV. ii. 30–1, 'You are not worth the dust which the rude wind / Blows in your face', and *All's W.*, v. iii. 53–5: 'That she whom all men prais'd ... / ... was in mine eye / The dust that did offend it' (C. Spurgeon, unpublished notes).

To stop the air would hurt them. The blind mole casts
Copp'd hills towards heaven, to tell the earth is throng'd
By man's oppression; and the poor worm doth die for't.
Kings are earth's gods; in vice their law's their will;
And if Jove stray, who dares say Jove doth ill?   105
It is enough you know; and it is fit,
What being more known grows worse, to smother it.
All love the womb that their first being bred,
Then give my tongue like leave to love my head.
Ant. [*Aside.*] Heaven, that I had thy head! he has found
        the meaning;   110
But I will gloze with him. [*Aloud.*] Young prince of
        Tyre,

110. S.D.] *Steevens; not in Q.*   111. S.D.] *Steevens; not in Q.*

101–3. *The blind . . . for't*] Many edd.
regard this passage as Shakespeare's,
even if they find no sign of the master's
hand elsewhere in this scene. The
musical appeal of the image, and its
note of mixed indignation and compassion, recall to one such passages as
'And the poor beetle, that we tread
upon / In corporal sufferance finds a
pang as great / As when a giant dies'
(*Meas.*, III. i. 80–2), and the reference
to the deer in *AYL.*, II. i. 22, as 'poor
dappled fools', who also suffer injustice like that suffered in the human
commonwealth. Yet Day at his best
would have been quite capable of
these lines. And though very evocative,
the image seems not altogether happy
in its context. Maxwell privately
points out the following parallel from
Middleton, *A Game of Chesse* (1624), IV.
iv. 95 ff. (ed. Bald):

> As the blinde Mole, the properst
>   Son of earth
> Who in the casting his Ambitious
>   hills up
> Is often taken, and destroide ith
>   midst
> Of his aduanced worke, twere well
>   wth thee
> If like that verminous Labourer,
>   wch thou Imitatst
> In hills of pride and malice . . .

Another passage that comes to mind is
Marlowe, *Tamburlaine*, II. vi. 1–4:

> What means this devilish shepherd,
>   to aspire
> With such a giantly presumption,
> To cast up hills against the face of
>   heaven,
> And dare the force of angry
>   Jupiter?   (Hastings, p. 83)

But these parallels seem closer to the
image in *Pericles* than they reveal themselves to be on more precise analysis.
In Middleton, the mole's activity is an
image of ambitious 'pride and malice'.
In *Pericles* the mole is a victim, a 'poor
worm'. As the context of the image
makes clear, the mole represents not
Antiochus with his ambitious pride,
but Pericles, who has good reason *to tell
the earth is throng'd*, to warn others of
oppressors, but realizes that all he
would thereby accomplish is his own
death at the hands of the tyrant.
copp'd = peaked (as frequently in
Elizabethan drama); *throng'd* = tyran-
nized, oppressed (cf. II. i. 73; a favourite word of Day's); *worm* = creature,
an expression of pity as in *Tp.*, III. i. 31,
'Poor worm, thou art infected'
(Steevens).
    111. *gloze*] use specious language;
cf. *LLL.*, IV. iii. 366.

Though by the tenour of our strict edict,
Your exposition misinterpreting,
We might proceed to cancel of your days,
Yet hope, succeeding from so fair a tree   115
As your fair self, doth tune us otherwise:
Forty days longer we do respite you;
If by which time our secret be undone,
This mercy shows we'll joy in such a son;
And until then your entertain shall be   120
As doth befit our honour and your worth.

Exeunt all but Pericles.

Per. How courtesy would seem to cover sin,
When what is done is like an hypocrite,
The which is good in nothing but in sight!
If it be true that I interpret false,   125
Then were it certain you were not so bad
As with foul incest to abuse your soul;
Where now you're both a father and a son,
By your uncomely claspings with your child,—

112. our] *F3;* your *Q.*   114. cancel of] *Malone;* counsell of *Q;* cancell off *F3.*
121. S.D.] *Malone subst.; Manet Pericles solus | Q.*   128. you're] *F3 subst.;* you
Q.   129. uncomely] *Maxwell, conj. Delius;* untimely *Q.*

112. *our*] Q 'your' can hardly be right. The compositor perhaps anticipated 'your' in the next line.

114. *cancel of*] the cancelling of. The emendation is defensible on graphic grounds, and demanded by the context.

115. *hope*] i.e. the hope that Pericles will interpret the riddle correctly and thus become Antiochus' heir—a gross lie, of course.

succeeding] proceeding, naturally issuing. See *O.E.D. Succeed* 5b.

117. *Forty*] 'Thirty' in Gower and Twine, but *P.A.,* 18. 20 confirms Q.

118. *secret be undone*] riddle be solved.

119. *joy*] rejoice.

120. *entertain*] entertainment. This shortened form of the noun occurs nowhere in Shakespeare, but is not uncommon in the plays of other Elizabethan dramatists, including Day, Heywood, and Porter.

122. *would seem*] would speciously endeavour (D.); cf. i. ii. 78.

124. *The which*] The relative was commonly so used; see Abbott §270.

sight] outward appearance.

128. *Where*] whereas.

129. *uncomely*] Q 'untimely' must be corrupt. It would make sense, if it were applied specifically to the daughter's loss of chastity, as in l. 85, *play'd upon before your time*; but here it refers to the father's actions. The error may be due to memorial corruption or to the compositor's misreading of 'ti' for *co*, a not uncommon mistake in Elizabethan printing. Or it may have arisen from the author's inadvertence. The emendation *uncomely* sounds rather feeble, but at least makes good sense and finds some support in *P.A.,* 19. 6–8, 'Hee was become both father, sonne, and husband by his vncomely and abhorred actions with his owne child'.

Which pleasures fits a husband, not a father;   130
And she an eater of her mother's flesh,
By the defiling of her parent's bed;
And both like serpents are, who though they feed
On sweetest flowers, yet they poison breed.
Antioch, farewell! for wisdom sees, those men   135
Blush not in actions blacker than the night,
Will shew no course to keep them from the light.
One sin, I know, another doth provoke;
Murder's as near to lust as flame to smoke.
Poison and treason are the hands of sin,   140
Ay, and the targets, to put off the shame:
Then, lest my life be cropp'd to keep you clear,
By flight I'll shun the danger which I fear.   *Exit.*

130. pleasures] *Q; pleasure Rowe* (iii).   135. sees, . . . men] *F3;* sees . . . men, *Q.*
137. shew] *Q;* 'schew *Theobald MS, conj. Malone;* shun *Malone.*

130. *pleasures fits*] Most edd. read 'pleasure fits', which is more appealing to the ear. Yet for the grammar, cf. I. i. 74n.

131–4. *And she . . . breed*] See I. i. 65–6n. For the image of the serpent, no doubt a commonplace at the time, cf. Greene's *Vision*, 1592, sig. B2v, 'the serpent . . . for that he sucketh poyson from that Odorifferous flower, from whence the painefull Bee gathers her sweete Honnie'.

135–7. *those . . . light*] Cf. *Mac.*, I. iv. 51, 'Let not light see my black and deep desires'. Both passages echo the Gospel of St John, iii. 20, 'For euerie man that evil doeth, hateth the light' (*Geneva Bible*, 1560, cited by M. Abend, 'Some Biblical Influences in Shakespeare's Plays', *N&Q*, 195 (1950), 554–8).

136. *Blush*] who blush; see l. 15n. above.

137. *shew*] so Q. Most edd. either follow Malone's emendation 'shun', or less often, like Theobald, interpret 'eschew', of which *shew* might be the aphetic form (see *O.E.D.*). But the word may well be an old form of 'shy',

derived from A.S. 'sheoh' (cf. Dutch 'shuw'), a plausible assumption considering the fact that 'shy' as a verb came into English only in the 18th century (*O.E.D.* lists no earlier examples). My interpretation finds further support in two other passages in Elizabethan literature, where modern edd. have likewise tended to emend *shew* to 'shun': Dekker, *Patient Grissil* (1604), I. i. 44–5, 'So fares it with coy dames, who great with scorne / Shew the carepined hearts, that sue to them' (*Works*, I, p. 214); and Dekker and Wilkins, *Jests to Make You Merry* (1607, Grosart edn, II, p. 333), '. . . when presently he [a pickpocket] will perceiue himselfe to be smoked . . . and so shew from you'. Though in an Elizabethan hand, 'shun' might be misread as *shew*, it seems therefore more likely that one meaning of *shew* in Shakespeare's day was 'shy' in the sense of 'shun' than that the error was made so often. If this argument is rejected, 'schew' is the more plausible alternative.

141. *targets*] light shields.
put off] avert.

[SCENE Ib—*The same.*]

Enter ANTIOCHUS.

Ant. He hath found the meaning,
　　　For which we mean to have his head. He must　　145
　　　Not live to trumpet forth my infamy,
　　　Nor tell the world Antiochus doth sin
　　　In such a loathed manner;
　　　And therefore instantly this prince must die;
　　　For by his fall my honour must keep high.　　150
　　　Who attends us there?

Enter THALIARD.

Thal.　　　　　　　　　Doth your highness call?
Ant. Thaliard,
　　　You are of our chamber, Thaliard, and our mind
　　　　partakes

Scene ib

SCENE Ib . . . *same*] *this ed.; not in Q.*　　145–6. For . . . infamy] *arranged this ed.;*
head: / infamie *Q.*　　152–6. Thaliard . . . gold] *As Collier;* Chamber, *Thaliard,* /
actions, / faythfulnes, / *Thaliard:* / Gold *Q.*　　153. Thaliard] *Q; not in Q4.*

SCENE Ib] Malone included this
scene in Sc. 1, and all edd. have done
so since. But when, after 1. i. 143,
Pericles leaves, the stage is empty.
Wilkins' report indicates likewise that
Antiochus' entry should mark the beginning of a new scene: 'he [Pericles]
resolued himselfe with all expedition
. . . to flie backe to *Tyre*, which he
effecting, and *Antiochus* being now
priuate in his lodging, and ruminating
with himselfe, that *Pericles* had found
out . . .' (*P.A.*, 19. 16–21). The new
scene has been called *SCENE Ib*, and
not Scene 2, so as not to make reference to concordances and to other
editions difficult.

144–8. *He . . . manner*] irregular verse,
which may well be the reporter's.
Apart from placing *He must* at the end
of l. 145, no convincing rearrangement seems possible.

151. *Who . . . there?*] 'A frequent
idiom in calling for a servant; cf.

2H4, I. i. 1' (Maxwell).

152–9. *Thaliard . . . done*] Though set
up as verse in Q, this speech was perhaps intended as prose, in accordance with ll. 163–8. Compositor *x*, who
set up these lines (but not ll. 163–8),
more than once betrays an inclination
to set up what was prose in his copy as
verse, as manifestly in the dialogue of
the fishermen in II. i. Yet in this instance one cannot be certain, and Q's
verse, except for some needed relineation, has therefore been followed.

152–3. *Thaliard . . . Thaliard*] Many
edd. have followed Q4 in eliminating
this repetition, yet cf. *John*, III. iii. 19
(Maxwell). Proper names are sometimes extra-metrical.

153. *of our chamber*] our chamber-
lain; directly paraphrased from
Gower, *C.A.*, 504: 'which was his prive
consailer'; cf. *Mac.*, II. iii. 99 (D.).

partakes] imparts. Cf. *Wint.*, v. iii.
132 (D.).

Her private actions to your secrecy;
And for your faithfulness we will advance you.   155
Thaliard, behold here's poison, and here's gold;
We hate the prince of Tyre, and thou must kill him:
It fits thee not to ask the reason why:
Because we bid it. Say, is it done?
Thal. My lord, 'tis done.
Ant.   Enough.   160

Enter a Messenger.

Let your breath cool yourself, telling your haste.
Mess. My lord, prince Pericles is fled.   [*Exit.*]
Ant. As thou wilt live, fly after; and like an arrow shot
from a well-experienc'd archer hits the mark his eye
doth level at, so thou never return unless thou say   165
"Prince Pericles is dead".
Thal. My lord, if I can get him within my pistol's
length, I'll make him sure enough: so, farewell to
your highness.
Ant. Thaliard, adieu!   [*Exit Thaliard.*]
Till Pericles be dead   170
My heart can lend no succour to my head.   [*Exit.*]

155–6. you. Thaliard,] *Malone;* you, *Thaliard*: Q.   158–9. why: / Because]
F3; why? / Because *Q;* why, / Because *Malone.*   160. *Ant.* Enough. S.D.]
Dyce; S.D. *Anti.* Enough. Q.   162. S.D.] *Malone; not in* Q.   163–9.] *As Q;
verse, Malone and Dyce.*   163. like] *Q;* as *F3.*   170. *Ant.*] *Q4; not in* Q.   S.D.]
Rowe; not in Q.   171. S.D.] *Q2; not in* Q.

156. *poison . . . gold*] paraphrased
from Gower, *C.A.*, 506–7, 'The king a
strong puison him dihte / Withinne a
buiste and gold therto'.

160–1. *Enough . . . haste*] Dyce's rearrangement of the S.D. is surely
right. L. 161 probably means: 'Tell
me the reason for your haste, and that
will calm your panting'.

165. *level*] aim.

167. *pistol*] an anachronism of a

kind common in Elizabethan drama.

168. *length*] range.

170. Ant.] The omission of the
speech heading in Q is due to the careless compositor. In Q, Antiochus'
speech marks a sudden change-over
from prose to rhymed verse.

171. *My heart . . . head*] freely paraphrased: 'I shall have no calm of
mind'.

[SCENE II.—*Tyre*.]

Enter Pericles with his Lords.

Per. Let none disturb us. [*The Lords withdraw*.]
Why should this change of thoughts,
The sad companion, dull-ey'd melancholy,
Be my so us'd a guest, as not an hour
In the day's glorious walk or peaceful night, 5
The tomb where grief should sleep, can breed me quiet?
Here pleasures court mine eyes, and mine eyes shun
them,
And danger, which I fear'd, is at Antioch,

Scene II

Scenr ii] *Malone; not in Q.* Tyre] *not in Q; Tyre. A room in the palace | Malone.*
Entry] *Q; Enter Pericles, Helicanus, with other Lords | F3; Enter Pericles | Camb.*
1. S.D.] *Alexander subst. (Exeunt Lords), this ed.; not in Q; To those without | Dyce;*
Aside | Yale. 1–2. Let...thoughts] *As Q4; one line Q.* 2. change] *Q (chāge);*
charge *Steevens.* 4. Be my] *Dyce;* By me *Q.*

Entry and 1 S.D.] so Q. But the
entry is hard to reconcile with the S.D.
at l. 34, a matter which worried the
printer of Q4 sufficiently for him to
omit the later S.D. completely. This
problem constitutes only the first of
many in this badly corrupted scene.
For instance, the Lords in Q are stated
to enter twice and, what is still more
bewildering, they appear to know of
Pericles' impending departure before
the Prince himself has reached a decision (see ll. 36–7). Drastic changes in
the order of the text and the S.D.s
would be necessary to clarify these and
other passages—see Intro., pp. xxxiii-
xxxiv. Such a reorganization has been
attempted in App. C, but in the text
itself Q has been followed conservatively.

Should the Entry and opening S.D.s
be correct in the text as it stands, the
Entry can be interpreted in two ways:
either the Lords enter only for a
moment, leaving again after l. 1 or
withdrawing to some distant part of
the stage, later to re-enter or move up
when Pericles has ended his mono-
logue; from the dramatic point of view

this would be clumsy indeed! Or it is to
be understood as a mass-entry, that is
to say, a listing at the beginning of the
scene of all the characters participat-
ing in it, even though some of them
enter only part way through; at which
point, a second entry is marked. (For a
discussion of 'mass-entry', see W.
Greg, *The Shakespeare First Folio*, 1955,
p. 241, and cf. the S.D.s in *LLL.*, ii. i
and, as they refer to Helena, in Q of
MND., i. i.) Of these two interpretations, the first is more plausible, as a
mass-entry is difficult to account for in
a reported text. The S.D. at the end of
l. 1 is in accord with the first interpretation.

2–3. *Why . . . companion*] Cf. *Mac.*,
iii. ii. 9–10, 'Of sorriest fancies your
companions making, Using those
thoughts, . . .' (Hastings). *Change of
thoughts*: i.e. from his usually serene
frame of mind (D.). Cf. 'Though we
laugh and live at ease / Change of
thoughts assayleth' in *A Friend's
Advice*, Pt 2 (*Roxburgh Ballads*, i, p. 117)
which supports the text.

4. *Be my*] Q's 'By me' can be attributed to the compositor.

Whose arm seems far too short to hit me here;
Yet neither pleasure's art can joy my spirits,　　　　10
Nor yet the other's distance comfort me.
Then it is thus: the passions of the mind,
That have their first conception by mis-dread,
Have after-nourishment and life by care;
And what was first but fear what might be done,　　　15
Grows elder now and cares it be not done.
And so with me: the great Antiochus,
'Gainst whom I am too little to contend,
Since he's so great can make his will his act,
Will think me speaking, though I swear to silence;　　20
Nor boots it me to say I honour him,
If he suspect I may dishonour him;
And what may make him blush in being known,
He'll stop the course by which it might be known.
With hostile forces he'll o'erspread the land,　　　25
And with th'ostent of war will look so huge,
Amazement shall drive courage from the state,
Our men be vanquish'd ere they do resist,
And subjects punish'd that ne'er thought offence:
Which care of them, not pity of myself,—　　　　30
Who am no more but as the tops of trees

12. the passions] *Q*; that passions *Q2*.　　　14. after-nourishment] *hyphened Tonosn 1734; unhyphened Q*.　　17. me: the] *Q4* (me; the)*; me the Q*.　　21. honour him] *Rowe*; honour *Q*.　　26. th'ostent] *Malone, conj. Tyrwhitt; the stint Q*.　　31. am] *Malone; conj. Farmer; once Q; care Sisson*.

9. *arm . . . short*] Cf. Tilley K 87, 'Kings have long arms', and *R2*, IV. i. 11–13, 'I heard you say, "Is not my arm of length, / That reacheth from the restful English Court / As far as Calais, to mine uncle's head?"'. The ultimate source of the saying is probably Ovid, *Heroides*, XVII. 166, 'An nescis longas regibus esse manus?', quoted in Edwards, *Damon and Pithias*, 1571, l. 432.

16. *cares*] takes anxious care that; with a word-play on *care* in l. 14; the conjunction is omitted.

19. *can*] that he can; see n. above.

21. *boots it me*] does it help me; is it of any avail to me.

honour him] *him*, supplied by Rowe, provides the rhyme and completes the line metrically.

23–4. *And what . . . known*] The first phrase stands in a genitive relation to the second; *blush in being known* = blush if it were known.

26. *th'ostent*] a certain emendation. Q's compositor misread his MS copy.

27. *Amazement*] terror; *O.E.D.*3 cites Spenser, *Faerie Queene*, I. ix. 24, 'adding new / Fear to his first amazement'.

31–2. *Who . . . them*] The image was a commonplace; cf. *3H6*, v. ii. 11–15.

31. *am*] Q 'once' makes nonsense;

Which fence the roots they grow by and defend them—
Makes both my body pine and soul to languish,
And punish that before that he would punish.

Enter [HELICANUS *and*] *all the Lords to Pericles.*

1. Lord. Joy and all comfort in your sacred breast!   35
2. Lord. And keep your mind, till you return to us,
    Peaceful and comfortable!
Hel. Peace, peace, and give experience tongue.
    They do abuse the king that flatter him,
    For flattery is the bellows blows up sin;   40
    The thing the which is flatter'd but a spark,
    To which that blast gives heat and stronger glowing;
    Whereas reproof, obedient and in order,
    Fits kings, as they are men, for they may err.
    When Signior Sooth here does proclaim a peace,   45

---

34. S.D.] *Dyce; Enter all the Lords to Pericles* | *Q ; not in Q4.*   42–3. To . . . order]
As Q4; stronger | order *Q.*   42. blast] *Collier, conj. Mason;* sparke *Q;* breath
Malone; spur *Sisson.*   45. a peace] *Malone;* peace *Q.*

of many suggested emendations,
Farmer's *am,* adopted by most modern
edd., seems best, though Sisson's *care*
is attractive—for see ll. 14–16 and
30.

   32. *fence*] protect.

   34. *And punish . . . punish*] 'and
afflict myself by fearful anticipation'
(D.).

   34. S.D. Enter . . . Pericles] See
opening note to this scene.

   35–51. 1. Lord . . . *us*] See the rearrangement of this section in App. C.
Helicanus' speech seems quite un-
called for after the Lords have expressed their wishes. Wishes, however
much they may be merely for for-
mality's sake, are not flattery; and
considering l. 106, it is astonishing
that the Lords should know of
Pericles' impending journey. See also
Edwards, pp. 26–7.

   39. *abuse*] disgrace.

   42–3. *To . . . order*] Q's incorrect
lineation is evidently due to the com-

positor, who, finding insufficient room
in his stick for *glowing,* placed the
word at the opening of the following
line.

   42. *blast*] Q 'sparke' makes no sense,
and was obviously 'recollected' from
the preceding line. The mistake may
have been the reporter's—for such
recollections are a recognized feature
of reported texts—or the compositor's. Mason's conj. *blast,* accepted by
Collier and most edd., fits the metaphor well.

   43. *obedient . . . order*] i.e. 'when
accompanied with reverence and
decorum' (D.).

   44. *as . . . err*] Cf. Tilley E 179, who
cites Jonson, *Every Man Out,* II. ii. 17,
'Humanum est errare'.

   45. *Signior Sooth*] Sir Appeasement,
Sir Flattery. Cf. *R2,* III. iii. 136, 'words
of sooth'. The *-th* is voiced as in 'sooth-
ing'. Also cf. 'Sir Smile' in *Wint.,* I. ii.
196 (Malone).

   a peace] Malone's addition of *a* seems

He flatters you, makes war upon your life.
Prince, pardon me, or strike me, if you please;
I cannot be much lower than my knees.   [*He kneels.*]
Per. All leave us else; but let your cares o'erlook
What shipping and what lading's in our haven,   50
And then return to us.   [*Exeunt Lords.*]
                                  Helicanus,
Thou hast mov'd us; what seest thou in our looks?
Hel. An angry brow, dread lord.
Per. If there be such a dart in princes' frowns,
How durst thy tongue move anger to our face?   55
Hel. How dares the plants look up to heaven, from whence
They have their nourishment?
Per.   Thou know'st I have power
To take thy life from thee.
Hel.   I have ground the axe myself;
Do but you strike the blow.
Per.   Rise, prithee, rise;
Sit down; thou art no flatterer;   60
I thank thee for't; and heaven forbid

---

48. S.D.] *Collier ii; not in* Q; *Kneeling (at l. 58) Malone.*   50. lading's] *Rowe;*
ladings Q.   51. S.D.] *Malone; not in* Q.   56. dares the plants] Q; dares the
planets Q2; dare the plants *Steevens and Malone.*   56–8. How . . . thee]
As Malone; heauen, / nourishment? / thee Q.   59. but you] Q; you but
Q4.   59–60. Rise . . . flatterer] *As Steevens; one line* Q.   61. heaven] Q2;
heaue Q.

---

convincing, for not only does it make
the expression more natural, but it also
improves the scansion; yet the more
emphatic *peace* (without *a*) is just
possible.

48. S.D. He kneels] The propriety of
this S.D. is clearly indicated by its context. Helicanus remains kneeling until
l. 59 (E.S.). Most edd. follow Malone
in providing the direction only at
l. 58.

49. *All . . . else*] everybody else.

50. *lading's*] cargo is. It is, however,
just possible that the term is to be
interpreted as a simple plural,
the omitted 'are' being understood.

56–60. *How . . . flatterer*] The linea-

tion of most modern edd., originally
proposed by Malone, has been followed for lack of a more satisfactory
solution.

56. *dares*] for inflections in *-s* preceded by a plural subject, see Abbott
§335.

59. Per. *Rise . . .*] Wilkins describes
this incident as follows: 'When
Pericles no longer suffring such
honored aged knees to stoope to his
youth, lifting him vp, desired of him,
that his counsell now would teach
him . . .' (*P.A.*, 22. 14–18). If Wilkins'
report is to be trusted at this point, it
suggests a stage-direction: 'Lifting
him up'.

That kings should let their ears hear their faults hid!
Fit counsellor and servant for a prince,
Who by thy wisdom makes a prince thy servant,
What would'st thou have me do?

Hel.   To bear with patience
Such griefs as you do lay upon yourself.   66

Per. Thou speak'st like a physician, Helicanus,
That ministers a potion unto me
That thou wouldst tremble to receive thyself.
Attend me then: I went to Antioch,   70
Whereas thou know'st, against the face of death
I sought the purchase of a glorious beauty,
From whence an issue I might propagate,
Are arms to princes and bring joys to subjects.
Her face was to mine eye beyond all wonder;   75
The rest, hark in thine ear, as black as incest;
Which by my knowledge found, the sinful father

---

64. makes] *Q;* mak'st *Malone.*   65–6. To . . . yourself] *As Knight; prose Q.*
66. you] *Steevens;* you yourself *Q.*   71. Whereas] *Q;* Where as *Q2;* Where, as
Theobald MS, Malone 1790, conj. Mason.

62. *let . . . hid*] i.e. allow themselves
to listen to flatteries which cover up
their faults.

64. *makes*] Many edd. adopt
Malone's emendation 'mak'st', which
fits *would'st* in l. 65. But the syncopated
form of the second person sing. present
is found elsewhere in Shakespeare,
though, as Franz §152 emphasizes, it
occurs commonly only when either
following 'thou' or when preceding a
word which opens with a consonant.
At least one instance, however, in F
provides strong support for *makes*:
'thou do'st stone my heart, / And
makes me call . . .' (*Oth.,* v. ii. 66–7).

66. *you*] Steevens' emendation has
been adopted, as in the New Cambridge edn, for it improves the line in
every respect. If this is sound, the
compositor of Q anticipated *yourself* at
the end of the line.

70. *Attend*] listen to.

71. *Whereas*] where (as fairly frequently in Elizabethan literature);

cf. I. iv. 70. In support of Mason's
interpretation 'where, as', it might be
said that already Q2 prints two words,
'where as', and that the sense becomes,
to us at any rate, more pregnant. Yet
the parallel provides strong support
for Q, and Q2's objection to it must be
rejected as a narrow interpretation.

73–4. *an issue . . . Are*] issue, as still in
modern English, can be understood as
a plural. The relative is omitted before
Are. Because of the harshness of the
expression, S. Walker postulated the
omission of an entire line, which he
phrased: 'Worthy to heir my throne;
for kingly boys'. Yet though such
omissions have probably occurred at
more than one place in this corrupt
scene (see l. 122n. below), Walker's
clever line must be relegated to the
realm of pure speculation. For all we
know, l. 74 may be wholly out of place
in the text.

74. *arms*] i.e. 'additional strength to'
(Mason).

Seem'd not to strike, but smooth; but thou know'st this:
'Tis time to fear when tyrants seem to kiss.
Which fear so grew in me, I hither fled,　　　　　　　80
Under the covering of a careful night,
Who seem'd my good protector; and, being here,
Bethought me what was past, what might succeed.
I knew him tyrannous; and tyrants' fears
Decrease not, but grow faster than the years.　　　　　85
And should he doubt, as no doubt he doth,
That I should open to the list'ning air
How many worthy princes' bloods were shed,
To keep his bed of blackness unlaid ope,
To lop that doubt he'll fill his land with arms,　　　　90
And make pretence of wrong that I have done him;
When all, for mine if I may call offence,
Must feel war's blow, who spares not innocence:

79. seem] *Q2;* seemes *Q.*　　83. Bethought me] *Rowe;* Bethought *Q.*　　84. fears]
F4; feare *Q.*　　86. doubt, as] *Malone;* doo't, as *Q;* thinke, as *Q4;* doubt it, as
Steevens; doubt, as 'tis *Maxwell;* doubt, as doubt *conj. H.F.B.*　　92. call] *Q;*
call't *Malone.*　　93. spares] *Q;* feares *Q2.*

78. *Seem'd*] pretended.

79. *seem*] Maxwell defends Q
'seemes' on similar grounds to 'gives'
at I. i. 74. But though instances of
singular inflections governed by plural
nouns are especially frequent in this
play, a corruption by either reporter or
compositor appears likely to me for
reasons of euphony.

81. *careful*] protecting; with possibly
an additional suggestion of 'full of
care'.

83. *Bethought me*] It appears probable that Q's compositor omitted *me*,
which has been restored by Rowe. It
not merely improves the metre
but also makes the expression more
natural.

86. *doubt, as*] suspect, as. Q 'doo't,
as' is a common graphic error, though
it puzzled Pavier, the printer of Q4,
sufficiently for him to substitute
'think'. The emendation is justified by
lop that doubt in l. 90. Steevens' 'doubt
it, as' and Maxwell's 'doubt, as 'tis'
aim primarily at regularizing the

metre, and are to be distrusted (see
Intro., p. lii). The following suggestion by H.F.B. is more plausible: that
the line in the true text read, 'And
should he doubt, as doubt no doubt he
doth'. This is good metre, and the
rhetoric is typically Elizabethan. If
H.F.B. is right, the error can be
explained in terms of haplography.
Cf. *LLL.*, I. i. 77, 'Light seeking light
doth light of light beguile', where 'of
light' is omitted in F2.

89. *unlaid ope*] undisclosed.

92. *for . . . offence*] for my offence, if I
may call it that. Malone's 'call't' for
call is tempting.

93. *who*] which.

spares] Q2's 'feares' provides a good
example of how a compositor could
mangle the text on his own. Apparently 'feares' arose from association with
'feel' in the same line and 'fears' in
l. 84. Such an association was further
encouraged by the resemblance in
Elizabethan script between initial long
s and *f*.

Which love to all, of which thyself art one,
Who now reprov'dst me for't,—

Hel.   Alas, sir!   95

Per. Drew sleep out of mine eyes, blood from my cheeks,
Musings into my mind, with thousand doubts
How I might stop this tempest ere it came;
And finding little comfort to relieve them,
I thought it princely charity to grieve them.   100

Hel. Well, my lord, since you have given me leave to speak,
Freely will I speak. Antiochus you fear,
And justly too, I think, you fear the tyrant,
Who either by public war or private treason
Will take away your life.   105
Therefore, my lord, go travel for a while,
Till that his rage and anger be forgot,
Or till the Destinies do cut his thread of life.
Your rule direct to any; if to me,
Day serves not light more faithful than I'll be.   110

Per. I do not doubt thy faith;
But should he wrong my liberties in my absence?

Hel. We'll mingle our bloods together in the earth,
From whence we had our being and our birth.

Per. Tyre, I now look from thee then, and to Tharsus   115
Intend my travel, where I'll hear from thee,

---

95. reprov'dst] *Q ;* reprovest *Malone.*   for't,—] *Malone ;* fort. *Q.*   100. grieve
them] *Q5 ;* griue for them *Q.*   105–10. Will . . . be] *As Rowe ; prose Q.*

---

95. *now reprov'dst*] just now has re-
proved. *Now* is similarly used in *John*,
II. i. 502 (Maxwell). But Malone's
'reprovest', which sounds pleasant to
the ear, is defensible, as in Elizabethan
handwriting *e* can easily be misread
for *d*.

96. *Drew . . . cheeks*] It was believed
that sighs and tears did actually
impoverish the heart (and thus *cheeks*)
of blood; cf. *3H6*, IV. iv. 21 and *Wint.*,
v. ii. 97. For similar passages in Day,
see App. B.

99–100. *relieve them . . . them*] For the
rhyme, cf. *Err.*, II. i. 38–9, 'grieve
thee / relieve me', and Jonson, *Sejanus*,

III. iii. 37–8, 'sway him / obey him'.

100. *grieve them*] If Q5's emendation
is correct, Pericles may well mean that
he is 'grieving' his subjects so as to save
them the greater distress of an invasion
by Antiochus (Maxwell subst.; see
*O.E.D.*5). But edd. usually interpret
grieve = grieve for, giving the word an
unusual sense, though with some support from *O.E.D.*8b. In that case, it
would seem wiser to retain Q's awkward 'griue for them'.

109. *direct*] assign.

112. *liberties*] royal rights, preroga-
tives (Schmidt).

116. *Intend*] direct.

And by whose letters I'll dispose myself.
The care I had and have of subjects' good
On thee I lay, whose wisdom's strength can bear it.
I'll take thy word for faith, not ask thine oath;   120
Who shuns not to break one will crack both.
But in our orbs we'll live so round and safe,
That time of both this truth shall ne'er convince,
Thou show'dst a subject's shine, I a true prince'.   *Exeunt.*

[SCENE III.—*Tyre.*]

Enter THALIARD *alone.*

Thal. So this is Tyre, and this the court. Here must I kill
King Pericles; and if I do it not, I am sure to be
hang'd at home: 'tis dangerous. Well, I perceive he

121. will crack] *Q;* will sure crack *F3;* will crack them *Maxwell.*   122. we'll]
Malone; will *Q;* we *Q2.*   124. subject's] *Malone;* subjects *Q;* subject *conj.*
Mason.   prince'] *Maxwell;* Prince *Q.*   124. S.D.] *Rowe; Exit | Q.*

Scene III

SCENE III] *Malone; not in Q.*   Location] *not in Q; Tyre. An antechamber in the*
palace. Malone.   Entry. *alone*] *Q (solus).*

121. *will crack both*] Since F3, most
edd. have assumed that a word is
missing. Two possible restorations are
indicated in the collation, but as they
are pure guesswork, Q's text has been
left standing.

122. *But . . . safe*] Malone's supposi-
tion that a line before this, rhyming
with *safe*, has been lost, is convincing.
'will' may therefore be sound, but
Malone's emendation *we'll* has been
adopted as a necessary stop-gap.
round and safe echoes Horace, *Satires*,
II. 7. 86, 'totus, teres atque rotundus'
(Theobald MS and Steevens).

orbs] spheres of action; a metaphor
from the Ptolemaic cosmology still
current in Shakespeare's time. The
heavenly spheres were believed to
move concentrically—thus *round.* Cf.
v. i. 228n.

123. *of . . . convince*] 'shall never con-

fute this truth regarding both of us'
(E.S.). *Convince* is here used in the
original sense of 'overcome', from
Latin *convincere.*

124. *subject's . . . shine . . . prince'*]
shine = shining example, as in *Tim.*,
III. v. 101 (D.). Mason's interpretation
of this word as a verb necessitating the
dropping of the final *s* in *subject's* is less
convincing. In support for *prince'*,
Maxwell cites the genitive 'prince' at
II. Ch. 21.

Scene III

3–6. *I . . . secrets*] Cf. I. i. 95–6. As
Steevens noted, the source is probably
Barnabe Riche, *Souldiers Wishe to*
Britons Welfare, 1604, p. 27 (= sig.
E2): 'I will therefore commende the
Poet *Philippides*, who being demaund-
ed by King *Lisimachus*, what fauour
hee might doe vnto him for that he

was a wise fellow and had good discretion that, being bid to ask what he would of the king, desir'd he   5
might know none of his secrets: now do I see he had
some reason for't; for if a king bid a man be a villain,
he's bound by the indenture of his oath to be one.
Husht! here comes the lords of Tyre.

Enter HELICANUS, ESCANES, *with other Lords.*

Hel. You shall not need, my fellow peers of Tyre,   10
  Further to question of your king's departure.
  His seal'd commission, left in trust with me,
  Doth speak sufficiently he's gone to travel.
Thal. [*Aside.*] How? the king gone?
Hel. If further yet you will be satisfied   15
  Why, as it were unlicens'd of your loves,
  He would depart, I'll give some light unto you.
  Being at Antioch—
Thal. [*Aside.*]   What from Antioch?
Hel. Royal Antiochus, on what cause I know not,
  Took some displeasure at him; at least he judg'd so;   20

9. Husht] *Q; ; Hush Malone.*   comes] *Q; ;* come *F4.*   10–24. You ... death]
As Rowe; prose Q.   11. to question of] *Maxwell; ;* to question mee of *Q; ;* to question *Steevens.*   14. S.D.] *Malone; ;* not in *Q.*   17. depart,] *Malone; ;* depart? *Q.*
you.] *Rowe; ;* you, *Q; ;* you; *Q4.*   18. Antioch—] *Rowe; ;* Antioch. *Q.*   S.D.]
Malone; ; not in *Q.*

loued him, made this answere to the
King, that your Maiestie would neuer
impart vnto me any of your secrets'.
As Maxwell pertinently comments,
this passage is preceded by several
pages of dialogue on the subject of
flattery which, though commonplace
and without any clear echo, may have
influenced I. ii.

The story is also related several
times by Plutarch, notably in his *Life
of Demetrius*, ch. xii, p. 252 (Nonesuch
edn, 1930), where Lysimachus says:
'What wilt thou have me give thee of
my things, Philippides?', who answers:
'even what it shall please thee, O King,
so it be none of thy secrets'. Antioche,
Antiochus, Tyr, Tarsus, Miletum
are all mentioned in this life.

See also *Dramatis Personae*, n. on
Lysimachus.

8. *indenture*] a contract between servant and master; cf. IV. vi. 175 and
Ham., v. i. 105.

9. *Husht!*] so *Shr.*, I. i. 68; still used
in some dialects.

comes] third person plural in -*s*, as
frequently in this play. It is significant
that the grammatical correction was
not made before F4.

11. *to question of*] to call in question
(not: to ask for information). Maxwell's simplification of the Q text
seems preferable to Steevens' and scans
well enough, but possibly the word *to*
should also be omitted. (See p. 188.)

16. *unlicens'd ... loves*] without your
loving assent.

And doubting lest he had err'd or sinn'd,
To show his sorrow he'd correct himself;
So puts himself unto the shipman's toil,
With whom each minute threatens life or death.

Thal. [*Aside.*] Well, I perceive I shall not be hang'd now,   25
although I would.
But since he's gone, the king's ears it must please,
He 'scap'd the land, to perish at the seas.
I'll present myself. [*Aloud.*] Peace to the lords of Tyre!

Hel. Lord Thaliard from Antiochus is welcome.   30

Thal. From him I come
With message unto princely Pericles;
But since my landing I have understood
Your lord has betook himself to unknown travels,
My message must return from whence it came.   35

Hel. We have no reason to desire it,

---

21. lest he] *Q;* lest that he *Steevens;* that hee *Q4.*   24. or death] *Q;* with death
conj. *Daniel.*   25. S.D.] *Malone; not in Q.*   27–9. But . . . Tyre] *As Malone;
prose Q.*   27. king's ears it] *Dyce;* Kings seas *Q;* king it sure *Steevens.*   28. seas.]
Steevens, conj. Percy; Sea. *Q.*   30. *Hel.*] *Q4; not in Q.*   31–9. From . . . Tyre]
As Rowe; prose Q.   34. betook] *Q2;* betake *Q.*   35. My] *Q4;* now *Q.*

21. *doubting*] fearing; possibly trisyllabic.
lest] Steevens' 'lest that' can be justified on metrical grounds only. In as
irregular a play as *Pericles*, it is best not
to tamper with metre.
25–6. *I . . . would*] Thaliard surely
means that considering Pericles' probable death at sea, Antiochus will be
satisfied, and it will thus be safe for him
to return. But not all edd. have read
the passage this way.
27–8. *king's ears . . . seas*] Sisson
retains Q, interpreting 'King's seas
. . . please' as an ethical dative, and its
meaning, if I understand him rightly,
as 'it must be the pleasure of the king's
seas'; i.e. Pericles will be at their
mercy. But the seas on which Pericles
travels are not owned by Antiochus.
The text has been plausibly restored
by Dyce. The source for this passage is
Twine, not Gower.
30. S.H. *Hel.*] The omission in Q
occurs at the top of sig. B3v, and is

anticipated by the incomplete catchword ('Lord') on B3. Again, it is the
compositor who is guilty.
31–9.] Rowe's lineation has been
followed in this as in all modern edd. Q
prints prose. That the final two lines
were intended as verse is certain because of the rhyme, but the same is
not necessarily true of the remainder,
which can be set up as tolerably regular verse—and as exceedingly stodgy
verse at that—only with the help of the
short l, 31. Something may have been
omitted by the reporter; yet a sudden
change over from prose to two final
rhyming lines is not rare in Elizabethan drama.
34. *betook*] The early correction has
been adopted, for it suggests that at
least one person in the printing
shop must have been puzzled. Yet Q
'betake' may be right, for see Abbott
§343–4 and cf. *H8,* II. iv. 152–3, 'have
. . . spake'.
36–8. *desire . . . desire*] awkward repe-

Commended to our master, not to us;
Yet ere you shall depart, this we desire,
As friends to Antioch, we may feast in Tyre.   [*Exeunt.*]

[SCENE IV.—*Tharsus.*]

Enter CLEON *the Governor of Tharsus, with his wife* [DIONYZA]
and Attendants.

Cle. My Dionyza, shall we rest us here,
　　And by relating tales of others' griefs,
　　See if 'twill teach us to forget our own?
Dio. That were to blow at fire in hope to quench it;
　　For who digs hills because they do aspire　　　　　5
　　Throws down one mountain to cast up a higher.
　　O my distressed lord, even such our griefs are;
　　Here they are but felt, and seen with mischief's eyes,
　　But like to groves, being topp'd, they higher rise.

---

39. S.D.] *Q2; Exit | Q.*

Scene IV

SCENE IV] *Malone; not in* Q.　　Location] *Malone; not in* Q *; Tharsus. A Room in the Governor's House. Steevens.*　　Entry. *Dionyza and Attendants] Steevens; and others | Q.*
5. aspire] *Camb.; aspire?* Q *; aspire,* Q4.

tition which smacks of the reporter.
　37. *Commended*] it being commended (D.).

Scene IV

Location] Almost all edd. since Steevens have placed this scene in Cleon's house. But the text does not specify locale, as indeed was unnecessary for such a scene on the bare Elizabethan stage. In Wilkins, moreover, Pericles encounters Cleon 'in the market place' (*P.A.*, 26. 21–2), though his version does not indicate whether Cleon went there on purpose to receive him (Round subst.).

　Entry] This may be a mass-entry, in which case *and Attendants* (Q and most edd.) should be omitted.
　4. *blow . . . it*] proverbial; see Tilley F 251, 'Do not blow the fire thou wouldst quench' and cf. *Cor.*, III. i. 197,

'This is the way to kindle, not to quench'.
　5. *who digs hills*] he who endeavours to lessen by digging (D.).
　5–6. *aspire . . . higher*] *aspire* = rise high (*O.E.D.*5). For the rather unusual rhyme, cf. Dekker, *The Whore of Babylon*, 1607, sig. G3v, '. . . conspire | The higher villaines climbe, they fall the higher'. The parallel in J.W.'s *The Valiant Scot*, 1637, sig. C4, 'For as a ball's thrown down to raise it higher | So death's rebound shall make my soule aspire', is noteworthy considering the detailed echoing in that play of *Per.*, II. i—see Intro., p. xviii.
　8. *mischief's eyes*] misfortune's eyes; i.e. the griefs are seen 'merely as they are' (D.); see following n.
　9. *But . . . rise*] *topp'd* = lopped, the top cut off for pruning (*O.E.D.*1). The

Cle. O Dionyza,   10
    Who wanteth food, and will not say he wants it,
    Or can conceal his hunger till he famish?
    Our tongues and sorrows to sound deep?
   †Our woes into the air, our eyes to weep,
    Till lungs fetch breath that may proclaim them louder?
    That, if heaven slumber while their creatures want,   16
    They may awake their helps to comfort them.

13. sorrows] *Q;* sorrows cease not *conj. Schanzer.*   13–14. to . . . to] *Q;* doe . . . to
Q2; too . . . do *Malone 1780.*   14. weep,] *Q3;* weepe. *Q.*   15–17. Till . . .
them] *As Collier;* proclaime / while / awake / them *Q.*   15. lungs] *Steevens;*
tongues *Q.*   louder?] *this ed.;* louder, *Q.*   17. helps] *Malone;* helpers *Q.*

comparison suggests that any attempt to forget the griefs (ll. 2–3) by relating those of others would only result in aggravating them.

13–16. *Our . . . That*] a passage that has been interpreted and emended in several ways. It seems memorially corrupt. *To sound* = to proclaim (*O.E.D.* 10). The following lines from a contemporary ballad show that at any rate one should not read 'do' for *to* in either l. 13 or 14:

   Which makes our woes still to
      abound
     trickling with salt teares in my
       sight,
   To heare his name in our eares *to*
     sound.

(from 'A Lamentable new Ballad upon the Earle of Essex Death', stanza 6, in *The Shirburn Ballads,* 1907, No. LXXIX; italics are mine; *To heare* = on hearing).

If Q is retained, except for changes in punctuation, and Steevens' *lungs* for 'tongues' in l. 15 (which the compositor seems to have repeated from l. 13), and if the passage is interpreted as depending on *conceal* in l. 12, an at least possible meaning can be extracted: '(Who . . . or conceal) our lamentations from ringing out loudly, our sufferings from filling the air, (and) our eyes from weeping, until the time when our lungs are able to gather enough breath to proclaim them louder, so that . . .' (Sisson subst.,

but he unconvincingly retains Q 'tongues').

I have emended thus conservatively, considering the 'badness' of the play's text. But the involved syntax of such a reading makes it appear very doubtful. E.S. suggests the interesting solution that two words have dropped out in l. 13, which in the original read: 'Our tongues and sorrows *cease not* to sound deep'. To emend accordingly would both restore the metre and leave the remaining passage clear. Yet I find it hard to believe that *sorrows* was intended as the subject of *woes*. More probably, as H.F.B. suggests, *sorrows* is the reporter's intrusion in a passage whose original sense was: 'therefore let our tongues now sound deep our woes . . . , our eyes weep, until . . .' The true text is irrecoverable.

16. *if heaven slumber*] For heaven with plural verb, cf. *Mac.,* II. i. 4–5, 'There's husbandry in heaven; / Their candles are all out' (D.).

17. *helps*] Malone's emendation has been adopted, but Q 'helpers' is possibly correct considering *appearer,* an even more unusual noun, at v. iii. 18. Yet 'helpers' would make bad metre. H.F.B. suggests that Q's mistake may have arisen from the compositor's expansion of a non-existent contraction. The repetition of *help* in ll. 19 and 31 looks suspicious, yet in both lines the word seems to come naturally and the

I'll then discourse our woes, felt several years,
And wanting breath to speak help me with tears.
Dio. I'll do my best, sir.   20
Cle. This Tharsus, o'er which I have the government,
A city on whom plenty held full hand,
For riches strew'd herself even in her streets;
Whose towers bore heads so high they kiss'd the clouds,
And strangers ne'er beheld but wond'red at;   25
Whose men and dames so jetted and adorn'd,
Like one another's glass to trim them by—
Their tables were stor'd full to glad the sight,
And not so much to feed on as delight:
All poverty was scorn'd, and pride so great,   30
The name of help grew odious to repeat.
Dio. O, 'tis too true.
Cle. But see what heaven can do by this our change:

---

18. our] *Q; of conj. Staunton.*   22–3. hand, . . . streets;] *Malone;* hand: . . .
streetes, *Q.*   23. her] *Q; the Q3.*   27. by—] *Q2* (by:)*; by, Q.*   33. do . . .
change:] *Q subst.;* do! . . . change, *Malone.*

---

metre is regular. The repetition, therefore, may reflect hurried writing on the
part of the scene's second-rate author,
rather than contamination by the reporter. See Intro., p. xxxiv.

19. *help me*] probably short for: do
you help me; not: 'help myself'. See
l. 17n. above.

21. *This Tharsus*] probably: This is
Tharsus (H.F.B.); otherwise the sentence begun by these words is not
completed. 'This is' was often pronounced as one syllable in Chaucer's
time, and may have been similarly
slurred still in Shakespeare's day. At
any rate, the abbreviation was still
common; cf. *Lr.,* IV. vi. 184, 'This a
good block'. H.F.B. further comments
that 'This is Tharsus' is also a pointed
announcement to the audience who
have not yet heard what place this
dignitary is magistrate of.

22. *on*] over.

23. *riches*] singular and feminine,
derived from French 'richesse'; cf.
Oth., II. i. 83 and *Sonnet* 87. 6, 'And for

that riches where is my deserving?'
(Malone).

her] Q3's 'the' improves the line,
but one suspects that the reporter is
not to be blamed for every weakness
in the verse of this inferior scene.

24. *kiss'd the clouds*] echoes *Troil.,* IV.
v. 220–1, 'Yond towers, whose wanton
tops do buss the clouds, / Must kiss
their own feet' (Malone); also cf. *Tp.,*
IV. i. 152, 'cloud-capp'd towers'. But
the source of the image is surely the
Tower of Babylon.

25. *ne'er . . . at*] Cf. *1H4,* III. ii. 57,
'Ne'er seen but wond'red at' (Cowl).

26. *jetted*] strutted; a common
Elizabethan term.

27. *glass . . . by*] mirror to dress in
front of (because each could see his
image in another similarly dressed).

31. *repeat*] mention.

33. *see . . . change*] As the meaning is
clear, Malone's changes in punctuation are not necessary: 'Note the
power of the gods by this example of
our change'.

These mouths, who but of late earth, sea and air,
Were all too little to content and please,   35
Although they gave their creatures in abundance,
As houses are defil'd for want of use,
They are now starv'd for want of exercise;
Those palates who, not yet two summers younger,
Must have inventions to delight the taste,   40
Would now be glad of bread, and beg for it;
Those mothers who, to nuzzle up their babes
Thought nought too curious, are ready now
To eat those little darlings whom they lov'd.
So sharp are hunger's teeth, that man and wife   45
Draw lots who first shall die to lengthen life.
Here stands a lord, and there a lady weeping;
Here many sink, yet those which see them fall
Have scarce strength left to give them burial.
Is not this true?   50
Dio. Our cheeks and hollow eyes do witness it.
Cle. O, let those cities that of plenty's cup
And her prosperities so largely taste,
With their superfluous riots, hear these tears!
The misery of Tharsus may be theirs.   55

---

34. These] *Q;* Those *Dyce.*   36. they] *Q2;* thy *Q.*   39. two summers]
Theobald MS, Steevens, conj. Mason; too sauers *Q.*   42. nuzzle] *Q* (nouzell);
nousle *Steevens.*

34. *These*] Many edd. have adopted Dyce's 'Those', emended by analogy with ll. 39 and 42; but Elizabethan English could change in this
way.

39. *not yet two summers younger*] 'When
they were' is understood. Theobald's
MS emendation, arrived at independently by Mason, is confirmed by
Wilkins' 'not two summers younger'
(*P.A.,* 24. 9–10). The error arose from
misreading of longhand copy.

40. *inventions*] ingenious novelties.

42–4. *Those mothers . . . lov'd*] This
gruesome detail may have been suggested by a contemporary account of
the famine of Jerusalem in the time
of Vespasian, the desolation of which

was epitomized by Miriam's eating of
her own son, which 'was neuer till this
ever heard from *Adam*'. See for instance Nashe, *Christs Tears over Jerusalem,* 1593, pp. 31v–36v (*Works,* ii,
pp. 69–71).

42. *nuzzle up*] bring up (*O.E.D.* v.2.
3), as in 'Whom . . . He nousled up in
life and manners wilde' (Spenser,
Faerie Queene, i. vi 23.8). Most edd.
have wrongly followed Steevens in
interpreting Q 'nouzell' as a corruption of 'nurstle' (nurse).

43. *curious*] exquisite.

46. *to lengthen*] i.e. the other's.

54. *superfluous*] See *O.E.D.*1 and 2.

riots] 'wanton, loose, or wasteful
living' (*O.E.D.*2), indulgence.

Enter a Lord.

Lord. Where's the lord governor?
Cle. Here.
  Speak out thy sorrows which thou bring'st in haste,
  For comfort is too far for us to expect.
Lord. We have descried, upon our neighbouring shore,   60
  A portly sail of ships make hitherward.
Cle. I thought as much.
  One sorrow never comes but brings an heir
  That may succeed as his inheritor;
  And so in ours: some neighbouring nation,   65
  Taking advantage of our misery,
  Hath stuff'd the hollow vessels with their power,
  To beat us down, the which are down already,
  And make a conquest of unhappy men,
  Whereas no glory's got to overcome.   70
Lord. That's the least fear; for, by the semblance
  Of their white flags display'd, they bring us peace,
  And come to us as favourers, not as foes.
Cle. Thou speak'st like him's untutor'd to repeat:
  Who makes the fairest show means most deceit.   75

57–9. Here . . . expect] *As Malone; prose Q.*   58. thou] *Q4; thee Q.*   60–1. We . . . hitherward] *As Q4; prose Q.*   65. ours:] *Rowe;* ours, *Q;* ours; *Q2.* 67. Hath] *Rowe;* That *Q.*   the] *Q;* these *Malone.*   69. men] *Malone;* mee *Q; we conj. Steevens.*   71–3. That's . . . foes] *As Malone; prose Q.*   74. him's] *Malone;* himnes *Q.*

58. *thou*] Q's compositor misread 'thee'.

61. *portly sail*] stately fleet; cf. *Mer. V.*, I. i. 9.

63–4. *One . . . inheritor*] a proverbial phrase. Cf. Erasmus, *Adagia*, 1208E, 'Mala malis eveniunt' (Tilley M 1012) and *Ham.*, IV. v. 75–6, 'When sorrows come, they come not single spies, / But in battalions' (Steevens).

67. *power*] armed forces.

69. *men*] Malone's emendation has been adopted because in the context Cleon speaks of all collectively and it seems improbable that he should refer to himself alone here. Q's error 'mee' is easily explained if we postulate that the MS read 'mē', a common contraction; an example is cited in I. i. 74n. above.

70. *Whereas*] where.

71. *semblance*] a trisyllable, as in *Err.*, v. i. 357.

74. *him's . . . repeat*] *him's* (Malone) seems certain, but corruption may lie deeper. 'You talk like him who has never been taught the lesson' (Round). For *repeat* = recite, like a repeater, see *O.E.D.* 2b. In l. 31 above, the word is used in a more common sense.

75. *Who . . . deceit*] proverbial; cf. Pettie, *A Petite Palace*, 'in fairest speech is falsehood and feigning rifest' (ed. Gollancz, 1908, I. 116, quoted by Tilley, C 732).

But bring they what they will and what they can,
What need we fear?
Our ground's the lowest, and we are half-way here.
Go tell their general we attend him here, to know for
what he comes, and whence he comes, and what he   80
craves.

Lord. I go, my lord.   [*Exit.*]
Cle. Welcome is peace, if he on peace consist;
If wars, we are unable to resist.

Enter [Lord, with] PERICLES *and Attendants.*

Per. Lord governor, for so we hear you are,   85
Let not our ships and number of our men
Be like a beacon fir'd t'amaze your eyes.
We have heard your miseries as far as Tyre,
And seen the desolation of your streets;
Nor come we to add sorrow to your tears,   90
But to relieve them of their heavy load;
And these our ships, you happily may think

---

76. and what they can] *Q; not in Steevens.*   77. fear?] *Q4 subst.;* leaue *Q.*
78. Our] *Q;* the *Q4;* On *Maxwell.*   79–81. Go . . . craves] *As Q;* here, / comes, /
craves *Rowe.*   81. S.D.] *Malone; not in Q.*   84. S.D. Lord . . . and] *this ed.;*
Pericles with / Q.   90. tears] *Q;* hearts *conj. Walker.*

76–81. *But . . . craves*] The text is so
corrupt that the original is probably
irrecoverable. Not only does Q's
'leave' make nonsense, but the extreme wordiness of the passage, 'bring
they what . . . and what . . . What . . .
And we . . . to know for what . . . and
whence . . . and what', suggests serious
deterioration by the reporter. For
this reason, Steevens' omission in
l. 76 of *and what they can,* which would
also restore the metre, is very attractive.

78. *Our ground's . . . there*] Cf. Tilley
G 464, 'He that lies upon the ground
can fall no lower.' One of the closest
parallels Tilley lists is from *2 Fair Maid
of the West,* 'Being on the ground, lower
we cannot fall' (Pearson's ed. of Heywood, p. 388, but wrongly attributed
to Heywood), and note also Heywood,
2 Edward IV, 1600, sig. L6v, 'Lower

then now we are, wee cannot fall'.
Hastings drew attention to the less
marked parallel in *Lr.,* IV. i. 2–6.

79. *attend*] await.

83. *on peace consist*] is disposed for
peace, 'stands on peace. A Latin
sense' (Malone). Cf. *2H4,* IV. i. 187.

84. S.D.] The change made in this
direction is called for by the context,
and in line with Wilkins' report: 'he
[Pericles] demaunded of the fellow
[i.e. the Lord], where the Gouernour
was, and foorthwith to be conducted
to him' (*P.A.,* 26. 19–21).

87. *Be . . . eyes*] Cf. Dekker, *Whore of
Babylon,* 1607, sig. B3, 'Hold Beacons
in their eyes (blazing with fire of a hot-
seeming zeal)'.

amaze] alarm (*O.E.D.*3).

90. *tears*] Walker's 'hearts' would
suit the following line better.

92. *happily*] haply, perhaps.

Are like the Trojan horse was stuff'd within
With bloody veins expecting overthrow,
Are stor'd with corn to make your needy bread,　　　95
And give them life whom hunger starv'd half dead.

All.　The gods of Greece protect you!

                [*Cleon, Dionyza, and Lords of Tharsus kneel.*]

And we'll pray for you.

Per.　　　　　　　　　　Arise, I pray you, rise;
We do not look for reverence, but for love
And harbourage for ourself, our ships and men.　　　100

Cle.　The which when any shall not gratify,
Or pay you with unthankfulness in thought,
Be it our wives, our children, or ourselves,
The curse of heaven and men succeed their evils!
Till when,—the which I hope shall ne'er be seen—　　105
Your grace is welcome to our town and us.

Per.　Which welcome we'll accept; feast here awhile,
Until our stars that frown lend us a smile.　　　　　*Exeunt.*

---

93. was stuff'd] *Q;* war-stuff'd *Steevens.*　　94. veins] *Q;* views *Malone;* banes *Collier;* arms *conj. D.*　　expecting] *Q;* importing *conj. D.*　　97. S.D.] *this ed.; not in Q.*　　98–100. Arise . . . men] *As Rowe; prose Q.*　　105. when,—the] *Malone subst., Camb.;* when the *Q;* when, the *Q2.*　　ne'er] *Rowe;* neare *Q;* nere *Q2.*

93–4. *was stuff'd . . . overthrow*] which was filled with bloody arteries (or entrails; a metaphor for the blood-thirsty Greek warriors) awaiting the moment for the overthrow (i.e. of Troy). The double omission of the relative, a feature very common in the early scenes of this play (see 1. i. 15n.), has confused past editors. It is unnecessary to emend *expecting* to 'importing', as D. does. If my interpretation is correct, *overthrow* is used in an active sense. For *bloody*=bloodthirsty, cf. *2H4*, IV. i. 34, 'led on by bloody youth'.

95. *your needy bread*] i.e. 'bread for your needy subjects' (Percy).

97. S.D.] Cf. Wilkins, *P.A.*, 26. 29–27. 2, 'at which the feeble soules not hauing strength enough to giue a showte for ioy, gazing on him, and heauen, fell on their knees, and wept'.

101. *gratify*] show gratitude for.

102. *in thought*] in so much as thought.

105. *ne'er*] For Q's spelling, cf. III. ii. 6. See Edwards, p. 49, for odd *ea* spellings by compositor *x* (Maxwell).

[ACT II]

Enter GOWER.

Here have you seen a mighty king
His child, I wis, to incest bring;
A better prince and benign lord
That will prove awful both in deed and word.
Be quiet then, as men should be   5
Till he hath pass'd necessity.
I'll show you those in troubles reign,
Losing a mite, a mountain gain.
The good in conversation,
To whom I give my benison,   10
Is still at Tharsus, where each man

ACT II

ACT II] *Malone; not in Q; Actus Secundus / F3.*   4. That will prove] *Q; Prove
Steevens.*   7. troubles reign,] *Q subst.* (raigne;); trouble's reign, *Malone.*
11. Tharsus] *Q4; Tharstill / Q.*

2. *I wis*] derived from O.E. '3ewis' =
certainly, the sense of which has been
partly obscured. Cf. *Shr.*, I. i. 62, 'Iwis
it is not halfway to her heart', and
Mer. V., II. ix. 68.

4. *That will prove*] The omission of
That will would regularize the metre,
but this is not the only five-stress line
in Gower's early choruses; cf. l. 14n.
below.

awful] inspiring awe, commanding
respect.

5–6. *men . . . he*] As in M.E., *men* is
here used as an indefinite pronoun,
like the modern 'one'; thus the singular *he* follows naturally; cf. German
'man', and see Franz §349. (See p. 188.)

6. *pass'd necessity*] gone through
extreme hardship. *Necessity* is frequently used in this sense; see *O.E.D.*
10 and 11.

7–8. *I'll show . . . gain*] The play's
underlying thought and purpose is
hinted at in these two lines, for which
see Intro., p. lxxxi. Malone pertinently
comments: 'I suspect our author had
here in view the title of the chapter in
Gesta Romanorum, in which the story of
Apollonius is told, though I will not
say in what language he read it. It is
this: "De tribulatione temporali quae
in gaudium sempiternum postremo
commutabitur".' One can understand
reign either as a verb, as in this edn, or
as a noun (Malone). (See p. 188.)

9. *conversation*] conduct; used similarly in the Bible, e.g. *Peter*, iii. 1–2.

11. *Tharsus*] It is possible that the
original read 'Tharshish', which Q's
compositor misread as 'Tharstill'.
'Tharshish' was one of the biblical
names for *Tharsus*; cf. 'Tharsis' in l. 25

37

Thinks all is writ he spoken can;
And, to remember what he does,
Build his statue to make him glorious.
But tidings to the contrary   15
Are brought your eyes; what need speak I?

DUMB SHOW

Enter, at one door, PERICLES, *talking with* CLEON; *all the train with*
them. Enter, at another door, a Gentleman, with a letter to PERICLES;
PERICLES *shows the letter to* CLEON; PERICLES *gives the Messenger*
a reward, and knights him. Exit PERICLES *at one door, and* CLEON
at another.

Good Helicane hath stay'd at home,
Not to eat honey like a drone
From others' labours; for he strives

12. spoken] *Q;* speken *Grant White.*   17. Helicane] *Malone;* Helicon / *Q;*
Hellican *Q3.*   hath] *Steevens;* that *Q.*   19. for he strives] *this ed., conj.* H.F.B.;
for though he striue *Q;* though he strive *Hudson;* but doth strive *conj. Maxwell.*

below. A different and plausible
theory is Maxwell's who suggests that
the compositor was influenced by the
preceding *still.*

12. *writ*] Holy writ (Malone), gospel
truth.

spoken can] Literally: has skill to
speak; see Abbott §349, but M.E.
'speken' may well be imperfectly recreated here.

13. *to remember*] in commemoration
of.

14. *Build . . . glorious*] Though decasyllabic, this seems to be a four-stress
line. Gower's verse was strictly octo-
syllabic, but his verse was probably
not so read in Shakespeare's time. For
glorious, cf. I. Ch. 9; for the whole
passage, cf. Gower, *C.A.,* 563–4.

15. *tidings . . . contrary*] The phrase is
odd, but evidently means: news of contrary import (for Pericles, which
makes him leave Tharsus).

17. *hath*] Steevens' emendation,
paralleling that of I. iv. 67, is the only
way of restoring syntax in the sentence,
Good . . . Tyre, but corruption may lie
deeper, for see 19 n.

18–19. *to eat . . . labours*] Cf. II. i. 48–9.
A proverbial image, also echoed in
2H6, IV. i. 109. Its frequent occurrence
in the writings of both Wilkins and
Day is unsuitable evidence for decid-
ing authorship, as the proverb was
exceedingly common.

19. *for . . . strives*] Edd. are agreed
that Q does not make sense. The halting metre of Q's line confirms the
impression that it is corrupt. Emendation is therefore called for, but all previous suggestions are unconvincing:
Hudson's change in the text improves
the metre without clarifying the sense;
Maxwell's conj. involves too great a
change to be editorially acceptable.
But to my mind, H.F.B.'s solution is
convincing. In defence of it, he writes:
'Helicanus acts not like a drone but
like a good bee, which kills drones and
helps to preserve the King (i.e. Queen
bee). My conjecture (i) allows us to
postulate an original reading that
made both sense and metre; (ii) one
that had an irregularity—a not unpre-
cedented irregularity—which would
provoke miscorrection; (iii) and it

To killen bad, keep good alive;   20
And to fulfil his prince' desire,
Sends word of all that haps in Tyre:
How Thaliard came full bent with sin
And hid intent to murder him;

21. prince'] *Malone;* prince *Q;* prince's *Rowe.*   22. Sends word] *Theobald MS,*
Steevens; Sau'd one *Q.*   24. hid intent . . . murder] *Q2–3;* hid in Tent . . .
murdred *Q uncorrected;* had intent . . . murder *Q corrected,* Q4.

suggests a likely process of corruption
resulting in the reading of Q. One
could find other instances in Elizabethan drama of imperfect plural-
singular rhymes. In the process of
transmission, someone thinks the
rhyme should be perfect: *alive*—it
must be "strive". Hence the intrusive
"though", wrecking sense and metre.
Attention to one or two features (here
the postulated imperfect rhyme),
without regard to the context, is one of
the commonest causes of miscorrection. The corrector narrows his field of
vision to the focal irregularity, which
he gets rid of regardless of the effect on
sense and metre.' In support of this
conjectural reading, adopted in the
text, one can further point to the fre-
quency of imperfect rhymes, particularly n–m rhymes, in this play. S.
Walker, I. 143–5, remarks that plural-
singular or similarly imperfect rhymes
occur often in Fulke Greville and in
some sections of Hall's *Satires,* and
sometimes, though seldom, in other
Elizabethan authors. He cites several
passages from Spenser; e.g. *Shepherd's*
Calendar, IV. 5–8, 'yeare / rayne? /
teares / paine', but finds only two
'mitigated' instances (i.e. bisyllabic
rhymes) in Shakespeare: *Gent.,* III. i.
92–3, 'sent her / contents her, and *Lr.,*
III. vi. 112–13, 'defile thee / reconciles
thee' (Q only, not F); yet note *2H4,*
v. iii. 139–40, where 'they' rhymes
with 'days'. See, however, 17 n. above.

22. *Sends word*] The emendation is
confirmed by *P.A.,* 28. 19–21, 'Good
Helycanus . . . let no occasion slip wherein hee might send word to Tharsus'.
Q's error resulted from misreading of
what must have been almost illegible

longhand copy. This error like many
others should put the reader on his
guard not to attribute every corruption in the text to the reporter; see
Intro., p. xxxvi.

23. *bent with*] intent upon (On.).

23–4. *sin . . . him*] Edd. have voiced
the belief that the imperfect rhyme is
used with archaizing intention. This
may be true in other instances in the
play, but probably not here, for cf.
Troil., III. iii. 212–13 'win/him' (Dyce).
Elizabethan drama affords many
other examples of m–n rhymes. Gower's version of the story of Appolinus,
on the other hand, affords none.

24. *hid . . . murder*] so Q2. The reading is debatable, for Q first printed
'hid in Tent . . . murdred' which the
press-corrector changed to 'had intent
. . . murder', a plausible alternative to
Q2. But *hid* seems preferable on both
literary and bibliographical grounds.
If it were necessary to interpret it, as
Sisson does, as a verb in the past tense,
the resulting line would have undue
emphasis. But it can also be taken as a
past pple—'he came with . . . hid
intent'—which improves the verse
(E.S.), and which I take to be the
meaning here. Bibliographically, *hid*
is preferable to 'had', because of the
general tendency in Elizabethan
printing, and probably in the printing
of this text, to do much of the press-
correcting haphazardly, without recourse to the MS copy. As originally
printed, the line made nonsense, but
the corrections *murder* for 'murdred'
and *intent* for 'in Tent' must have suggested themselves immediately. The
press-corrector then took the further
step of replacing *hid* by the more

And that in Tharsus was not best   25
Longer for him to make his rest.
He, doing so, put forth to seas,
Where when men been, there's seldom ease;
For now the wind begins to blow;
Thunder above and deeps below   30
Makes such unquiet that the ship
Should house him safe is wrack'd and split;
And he, good prince, having all lost,
By waves from coast to coast is toss'd.
All perishen of men, of pelf,   35
Ne aught escapend but himself;

---

25. Tharsus] *F3; Tharsis* | *Q*.   31. Makes] *Q; Make Rowe (iii).*   32. safe is]
Camb.; safe; is *Q*.   wrack'd] *Q* (wrackt); wreck'd *Malone*.   36. aught]
Steevens; ought *Q*.   escapend] *Q; escapen Steevens, conj. Percy.*

---

natural-seeming 'had'. Moreover, as Maxwell suggests, 'conceivably *murdred* was a misreading of an archaic *murdren* rather than of the simple *murder*'. The most probable explanation for Q2's text is that the relevant page was printed from an uncorrected sheet of Q, the printer making the two more obvious changes in which Q's press-corrector had anticipated him.

25. *Tharsus*] For the Q reading, see l. 11n.

27. *doing so*] acting accordingly.

27-8. *seas . . . ease*] A similar rhyme, 'please / seas', is used in Day, Wilkins, and Rowley, *The Travels* (1607), sig. D4 (Bullen's Day, p. 44).

28. *been*] are; the Midland form of the plural in early English; see Abbott §332.

31. *Makes*] For the grammar, see I. i. 74n. The line is based on Gower, *C.A.*, 605.

31-2. *ship* | *. . . split*] This false rhyme has no equal even in this play. It may have been introduced for archaic effect.

32. *Should*] For the omitted relative, see I. i. 15n.

wrack'd] Considering the deliberate use of archaism in the Prologue, it has seemed wise not to modernize this

term. Many modern edd. retain 'wrackt' and 'wrack' in *Mac.*, I. iii. 29 and v. v. 51.

35. *perishen*] perish; the Midland form of the third person plural in early English; cf. l. 28n. above.

pelf] possessions.

36. *escapend*] escaping. The form occurs nowhere else in Shakespeare, which is not surprising considering the many archaic expressions in this chorus. It seems here to be present pple, not past pple as numerous edd. have asserted; for in O.E. and often still in M.E., present pples ended in *ende* or *inde*, and the context mingles present and past tenses. Spenser employs 'glitterand' for 'glittering' five times, though always as an adjective rather than participle; e.g. *Shepherd's Calendar*, July, 177, and *Faerie Queene*, I. iv. 16.9. In J.W.'s play, *The Valiant Scot*, 1637, the suffix *-and* appears as the ending of various tense-forms with four instances of present pple (see *Studies in English Drama*, 1st Series, publ. of the Univ. of Pennsylvania, 1917, p. 100).

Yet Percy's emendation 'escapen', interpreting the word as a third person plural similar to *perishen*, may be correct; the matter is further complicated by the fact that past pples ending in

Till fortune, tir'd with doing bad,
Threw him ashore, to give him glad:
And here he comes. What shall be next,
Pardon old Gower,—this 'longs the text.   [*Exit.*]   40

[SCENE I.—*The Sea-side, Pentapolis.*]

Enter PERICLES, *wet.*

Per. Yet cease your ire, you angry stars of heaven!
Wind, rain, and thunder, remember, earthly man
Is but a substance that must yield to you;
And I, as fits my nature, do obey you.
Alas, the seas hath cast me on the rocks,   5
Wash'd me from shore to shore, and left me breath

40. 'longs] *Theobald MS, Singer, conj. Mason and Douce;* long's *Q.*   40. S.D.]
Malone; not in Q.

Scene 1

SCENE I . . . *Pentapolis*] *Malone subst.; not in Q.*   5. seas] *Q* (Seas); sea *Rowe (iii).*
6. me breath] *Malone;* my breath *Q.*

-*en* were common in the North Midland dialect; cf. Spenser, *Shepherd's Calendar,* August, 134: 'To him be the wroughten mazer alone'.

38. *glad*] gladness; another pseudo-archaism (*O.E.D.*).

40. '*longs*] belongs to; see *O.E.D.* 2.2, which cites Day, *Law-Tricks,* sig. H3v, 'vnto what great Prince / Christian or Pagan longs this mansion'.

Scene 1

1–11. *Yet . . . crave*] Gower's story contains no equivalent of this speech. Though the wording is quite different, it was probably suggested by the following passage in Twine (Chapter IV), 'And when he had recouered to land, wearie as he was, he stoode vpon the shoare, and looked vpon the calme sea, saying: O most false and vntrustie sea! I will choose rather to fall into the handes of the most cruell king Antiochus, than venture to returne againe by thee into mine owne Countrey:

thou hast shewed thy spite vpon me, and deuoured my trustie friendes and companions, by meanes whereof I am nowe left alone, and it is the prouidence of almightie God that I haue escaped thy greedie iawes. Where shall I now finde comfort? or who will succour him in a strange place that is not knowen?' Twine's version is in turn an extended paraphrase of that in the *Gesta Romanorum.* But the play departs from these sources in one important point. Pericles does not weigh the perils of the sea by comparing them with the threats of Antiochus. If he did, his later voyage with Thaisa would seem extremely foolhardy. Twine was apparently not troubled by this thought.

5. *seas hath*] For the grammar, see Franz §156. *hath* for 'have' occurs also in *Cor.,* IV. vi. 64 (F text); 'Doth' was used similarly for 'Do'.

6. *me breath*] Q 'my breath' is possible, if *breath* is taken to mean 'life',

Nothing to think on but ensuing death.
Let it suffice the greatness of your powers
To have bereft a prince of all his fortunes;
And having thrown him from your wat'ry grave,   10
Here to have death in peace is all he'll crave.

Enter three Fishermen.

1. Fish. What, ho, Pilch!
2. Fish. Ha, come and bring away the nets!
1. Fish. What, Patch-breech, I say!
3. Fish. What say you, master?   15
1. Fish. Look how thou stirr'st now! come away, or I'll
    fetch'th with a wanion.
3. Fish. Faith, master, I am thinking of the poor men that
    were cast away before us even now.

12. What, ho, Pilch!] *Malone, conj. Tyrwhitt;* What, to pelch? *Q;* What's to,
Pilch? *conj. Trent.*   16–47. Look . . . honey] *As Malone; irregular verse Q.*
17. fetch'th] *Q;* fetch thee *Q4.*

but the correction is plausible and has been generally followed.

9. *fortunes*] perhaps a reporter's paraphrase of 'dowers' (= dowries), rhyming with *powers*.

11. S.D. three] Gower and Twine introduce only one fisherman, and give a very short account of what corresponds to this scene. The playwright probably drew some inspiration from the dialogue of the fishermen in Act II of Plautus' *Rudens* (Yale).

What, ho, Pilch!] a sensible correction of Q's 'What, to pelch?', which is probably a misreading of MS copy. The name *Pilch* jocularly signifies an outer garment, usually made of leather or skin, or 'a coarse shagged piece of rug laid over a saddle for ease of a rider' (Bennett's *Glossary*, MS Lansdowne 1033, quoted by Halliwell-Phillips, Scrapbook). In the *Untrussing of the Humorous Poet* or *Satiro-Mastix* (1602), Dekker pokes fun at Jonson for wearing a pilch: 'Thou hast forgot how thou amblest (in leather pilch) by a play-wagon, and took'st Ieronimoes

part, to get seruice among the Mimickes' (IV. i. 130–2, *Works*, I, p. 351) (D.). See also l. 14n. on a similar name.

13. *bring away*] bring here. Cf. *R2*, II. ii. 107.

14. *Patch-breech*] Cf. l. 12n. and also the remarkable combination of the terms from which the fisherman's names are derived in Nashe, *Lenten Stuffe*, 1599, sig. Ev–E2: 'The poorer sort make it three parts of their sustenance: with it for his dinner, the patchedest *leather-piltche laboratho* may dine like a Spanish duke' (*Works*, III, p. 179).

16. *how thou stirr'st now!*] aren't you moving yet?

come away] 'get a move on'.

fetch'th] fetch thee, as in Q4. The original though unusual spelling has been retained, for contractions are fairly numerous in this play, and fit the colloquial dialogue.

17. *with a wanion*] with a vengeance. For its interesting derivation, consult *O.E.D.*

1. Fish. Alas, pour souls, it griev'd my heart to hear 20
    what pitiful cries they made to us to help them, when,
    well-a-day, we could scarce help ourselves.

3. Fish. Nay, master, said not I as much when I saw the
    porpoise, how he bounc'd and tumbled? they say
    they're half fish, half flesh; a plague on them, they 25
    ne'er come but I look to be wash'd! Master, I marvel
    how the fishes live in the sea.

1. Fish. Why, as men do a-land: the great ones eat up the
    little ones. I can compare our rich misers to nothing
    so fitly as to a whale: a' plays and tumbles, driving 30
    the poor fry before him, and at last devours them all
    at a mouthful. Such whales have I heard on a'th'

24. porpoise] *Q* (Porpas); porpus *Rowe.*   31. devours] *F4;* deuowre *Q.*
32. a'th'] *Q* (a'th); o'the *Dyce.*

20–1. *Alas . . . them*] Cf. *Tp.*, I. ii. 8–9, 'O, the cry did knock Against my very heart! Poor souls, they perish'd' (D.), and *Wint.*, III. iii. 88–9 (Malone).

22. *well-a-day*] ah, woe, alas! 'wayloway' in Gower.

23–4. *when . . . porpoise*] This was commonly regarded as foreboding a storm. Cf. Webster, *Duchess of Malfi,* III. iii. 63–4, 'He lifts up's nose, like a fowle Por-pisse before A storme' (Malone) and *Eastward Ho,* III. iii. 153–5, 'there was a *porepisce* even now seen at London Bridge, which is always a messenger of tempests, he says' (D.).

25. *half fish, half flesh*] Cf. the description of the otter in *1H4,* III. iii. 126–7 (D.).

28–9. *the great . . . ones*] proverbial; see Tilley F 311, and W. Parsons, 'Lest Men, like Fishes . . .', *Traditio,* III (1945), 380–8 (who traces the proverb back to the early Christian fathers), and M. E. Borish, 'John Day's *Law Tricks* and George Wilkins', *Mod. Phil.*, XXXIV (1936–7), 255, n. 34 (who quotes, among others, three passages from mediaeval plays). Whitney's *Choice of Emblems*, the source of some of the mottos in II. ii, contains on p. 52 a picture of dolphins devouring 'the

little fry'.

The closest parallels in Shakespeare are *2H4*, III. ii. 330–1, 'If the young dace be a bait for the old pike', *Lr.*, IV. ii. 49–50, 'Humanity must perforce prey on itself Like monsters of the deep', and *Troil.*, v. v. 22–3, 'they fly or die, like scaled sculls Before the belching whale'. Closer still is *Sir Thomas More*, 'men like ravenous fishes Would feed on one another', which in the MS occurs among the three pages almost certainly in Shakespeare's handwriting (= ll. 86–7 of W. Greg's transcript in *Shakespeare's Hand in the Play of Sir Thomas More*, 1923, pp. 230 ff.). But the immediate source here is probably Day's *Law Tricks*, for which see App. B. A similar passage in Dekker and Middleton, *The Roaring Girl*, 1611, sig. G4 ('all that liue in the world, are but great fish and little fish, and feede vpon one another, some eate vp whole men, a Seriant cares but for the shoulder of a man . . .'), may well be indebted to *Pericles*. See also ll. 39–43 and n. below.

30. *a'*] he.

32–4. *Such . . . all*] See n. to ll. 28–9 above. The immediate source of the passage is probably Day's *Law Tricks*.

land, who never leave gaping till they swallow'd the
whole parish, church, steeple, bells, and all.

Per. [*Aside.*] A pretty moral.   35

3. Fish. But, master, if I had been the sexton, I would
have been that day in the belfry.

2. Fish. Why, man?

3. Fish. Because he should have swallow'd me too; and
when I had been in his belly, I would have kept such   40
a jangling of the bells, that he should never have left
till he cast bells, steeple, church, and parish up
again. But if the good King Simonides were of my
mind—

Per. [*Aside.*] Simonides?   45

3. Fish. We would purge the land of these drones, that
rob the bee of her honey.

Per. [*Aside.*] How from the finny subject of the sea
These fishers tell the infirmities of men;
And from their wat'ry empire recollect   50

---

33. they swallow'd] *Q;* they've swallow'd *Malone;* they ha' swallowed *Maxwell,*
conj. Camb.   35. S.D.] *Dyce; not in Q.*   45. S.D.] *Dyce; not in Q.*   48. finny]
Tonson; fenny *Q.*

Yet the development of the image possibly owes much to the tradition of
Tudor polemic against enclosures, as
expressed in a famous passage in
More's *Utopia,* Book I: 'Your sheep,
that were wont to be so meek and
tame, and so small eaters, now, as I
hear, be become so great devourers,
and so wild, that they eat up and
swallow down the very men themselves. They consume, destroy, and
devour whole fields, houses, and cities
. . . [Nobles, gentlemen, and even
abbots] . . . throw down houses; they
pluck down towns; and leave nothing
standing but only the church, to make
of it a sheephouse' (The *Utopia* of Sir
Thomas More, ed. J. H. Lupton, 1895,
pp. 51–2, spelling modernized).

32. *on a'*] of on.

33. *they swallow'd*] Q's text has been
retained, as all attempts to make the
fishermen speak grammatical English
are to be discouraged.

35. *moral*] story of moral import.
Maxwell suggests that 'the exact repetition at II. ii. 44 savours of the
reporter'.

39–43. *Because . . . cast . . . up again*]
cast . . . up = vomited. This passage,
with the image of a man in the whale's
belly, and the whale throwing up
again what he has swallowed, must
have recalled Jonah to the audience.
Oddly enough, this point seems to have
been overlooked by previous edd., but
see N. Nathan, '*Pericles* and *Jonah*',
N&Q, n.s. III, No. 1 (1956), 10–11.

46–7. *drones . . . honey*] i.e. 'our rich
misers'. See II. Ch. 18–19n.

48. *finny*] The correction is con-
firmed by *P.A.,* 33. 3. Cf. further *The
Puritan,* 1607, sig. D (II. i), 'And the
Seas scalde their finnie labourers'.

subject] subjects, citizens; a collective singular, frequently so used in
Elizabethan drama.

50. *recollect*] gather up, collect.

All that may men approve or men detect!—
Peace be at your labour, honest fishermen.

2. Fish. Honest! good fellow, what's that? If it be a day
fits you, search out of the calendar, and nobody look
after it.　　　　　　　　　　　　　　　　　　　55

Per. May see the sea hath cast upon your coast—

2. Fish. What a drunken knave was the sea to cast thee in
our way!

Per. A man whom both the waters and the wind,
In that vast tennis-court, hath made the ball　　　60
For them to play upon, entreats you pity him;
He asks of you, that never us'd to beg.

53–5. Honest . . . it] *As Malone; verse Q.*　　53. Honest! good fellow,] *Steevens;*
Honest good fellow *Q;* Honest, good fellow *Q2;* Honest—good fellow! *Alexander.*
54. search] *Q;* scratch it *Steevens, conj. Mason.*　　look] *Q;* will look *Steevens.*
56. May] *Q;* Y'May *F3;* Nay *Steevens.*　　coast—] *Steevens;* coast: *Q.*　　57–
8. What . . . way] *As Malone;* Sea, / way *Q.*

51. *detect*] expose in wrongdoing.

53–5. *If . . . it*] obscure. Malone and
other edd. suggest that a phrase before
l. 52 is missing, in which Pericles
wishes the fishermen 'good day'. In
support of Steevens' 'scratch it', Mason
cites Beaumont and Fletcher, *The
Coxcomb*, Act IV (VIII, p. 362), 'I should
do something / That would quite
scratch me out o' th' Kelender', but,
as Maxwell comments, 'the resemblance in meaning is not close'. Ridley,
who adopts Steevens' 'will look' and
'scratch it', paraphrases: 'if the day is
one that fits the poor bedraggled creature you are, away with it from the
calendar and no one will miss it'. But
no one can claim really to have grasped
the meaning, and it seems useless to
cite others of the numerous doubtful
interpretations. I offer instead two
alternative interpretations for what
they are worth: (*a*) 'If there is a day in
the year that fits your character, go
and search for it in the calendar, but
let no one check it afterwards (for it is
sure not to be there)' or (*b*) 'If there is
a day in the year that irks you, away
with it . . .' (continue like Ridley);

cf. *Sonnet* 119, 'gives you a fit' (Staunton).

56. *May*] you may. Many edd. have
altered the text, but *may* without pronoun was common usage in Shakespeare's day and later. Cf. l. 128 below,
and Beaumont and Fletcher, *Wit
Without Money*, I. ii. 3 (Q1 text), 'much
good may do her' (Maxwell, privately).

57. *cast*] cast up, vomit.

60–1. *In . . . upon*] Metaphors from
tennis abound in Elizabethan literature. Edd. have quoted many parallels, among them *Arcadia*, V, 'in such a
shadow . . . mankind lives, that . . .
they . . . are like tenis bals tossed by the
racket of the higher powers' (Steevens),
but it would be wrong to assume that
this passage is necessarily the source.
At least two plays preceding *Pericles*,
but not extant, testify to the popular
interest in the game and its figurative
applications: Dekker's *Fortune's Tennis*
(1600) and Munday's *Set At Tennis*
(1602). The fact that the image occurs
frequently in the works of Day and
Wilkins is therefore of no significance
either.

1. Fish. No, friend, cannot you beg? here's them in our
country of Greece gets more with begging than we
can do with working.   65

2. Fish. Canst thou catch any fishes then?

Per. I never practis'd it.

2. Fish. Nay, then thou wilt starve, sure; for here's nothing to be got now-a-days, unless thou canst fish
for't.   70

Per. What I have been I have forgot to know;
But what I am, want teaches me to think on:
A man throng'd up with cold. My veins are chill,
And have no more of life than may suffice
To give my tongue that heat to ask your help;   75
Which if you shall refuse, when I am dead,
For that I am a man, pray you see me buried.

1. Fish. Die, quoth-a? Now gods forbid't, and I have a
gown here, come, put it on; keep thee warm. Now,
afore me, a handsome fellow! come, thou shalt   80
go home, and we'll have flesh for holidays, fish for
fasting-days, and moreo'er puddings and flap-jacks;
and thou shalt be welcome.

63-5. No ... working] *As Malone;* begge? | *Greece,* | working *Q.*   77. you] *Q;*
om. *Steevens.*   78. quoth-a?] *Malone;* ke-tha; *Q;* ko-tha *Rowe.*   forbid't, and
I] *Q;* forbid, I *Q4;* forbid! I *Malone.*   81. holidays] *Malone;* all day *Q;* ale-
days *conj. Mason.*   82. moreo'er] *Malone, conj. Farmer;* more; or *Q.*

69. *fish*] with a play upon the word.

73. *throng'd up*] overwhelmed (On.);
i.e. numbed.

76/7. *dead | buried*] This rhyme may
strike the modern reader as forced, but
cf. *Gent.*, IV. ii. 113, *Rom.*, IV. v. 63, and
Sonnet 31. 2.

78. *quoth-a?*] did he say? For Q's
spelling, cf. *O.E.D.* 'kether' (Deloney,
Works, ed. F. O. Mann, p. 57, l. 27)
and Udall, *Ralph Roister Doister*, I. ii.
111, ' "Enamoured", ka?', and III. iii.
21, 'Ko I'.

forbid't, and I] *and* = if, as often in
Elizabethan English. Miss Husbands,
cited by Sisson, was the first to notice
that this meaning of *and* applies here,
thus putting an end to centuries of
editorial muddle. Notwithstanding
widespread practice, there is no reason

why *and* should be contracted into
'an'.

79. *gown*] 'probably sea-gown, i.e. a
long coarse high-collared short-sleeved
garment' (Maxwell).

80. *afore me*] on my word.

81-2. *holidays . . . fasting-days*]
Malone's *holidays* for Q 'all day' is
almost certainly right considering
many passages in Jacobean drama,
where holidays or flesh-days and fasting-days are juxtaposed; e.g. Middleton, *The Family of Love* (1607), I. i. 43-
4, 'Love is like fasting days, but the
body is like flesh-days'. Maxwell regards Q 'all day' as an auditory error,
referring the reader to Kökeritz, p.
308, but only very few such errors can
be identified in the text.

82. *flap-jacks*] pancakes.

Per. I thank you, sir.

2. Fish. Hark you, my friend; you said you could not beg.   85

Per. I did but crave.

2. Fish. But crave? then I'll turn craver too, and so I shall
      'scape whipping.

Per. Why, are your beggars whipp'd then?

2. Fish. O, not all, my friend, not all; for if all your   90
      beggars were whipp'd, I would wish no better office
      than to be beadle. But, master, I'll go draw up the
      net.

                    [*Exeunt Second and Third Fishermen.*]

Per. [*Aside.*] How well this honest mirth becomes their labour!

1. Fish. Hark you, sir; do you know where ye are?   95

Per. Not well.

1. Fish. Why, I'll tell you: this is call'd Pentapolis, and
      our king, the good Simonides.

Per. The good Simonides, do you call him?

1. Fish. Ay, sir; and he deserves so to be call'd for his   100
      peacable reign and good government.

Per. He is a happy king, since he gains from his subjects
      the name of good by his government. How far is his
      court distant from this shore?

1. Fish. Marry, sir, half a day's journey. And I'll tell   105
      you, he hath a fair daughter, and to-morrow is her

89. your] *Yale;* you *Q;* all your *Q4.*   93. S.D.] *Dyce; not in Q.*   97. is] *Q2;*
I *Q.*   Pentapolis] *Rowe; Pantapoles / Q.*   100–8. Ay . . . parts of] *prose
Malone; irregular verse Q.*

87. *craver*] importunate asker, i.e.
beggar. Merely by employing an unusual term for his activity, the 2nd
Fisherman intimates in fun, he might
escape *whipping*, the regular punishment for beggars in Elizabethan days.
W. Lambard, *The Dueties of Constables*
. . . (1602, enlarged edn), pp. 38–41,
provides a legal definition of 'Rogue,
Vagabond, or sturdy Begger', and outlines his punishment, which is 'to be
striped naked from the middle up-
ward, and be openly whipped vntill
his or her body be bloudie, and shall
forthwith [be sent] . . . to the Parish
where such Rogue was borne, . . .'
Included among such rogues is 'euerie

person that calleth himselfe a *Schollar,*
and goeth about begging'.

89. *your*] Q 'you' is a common error
in Shakespeare quartos and the First
Folio for *your.* Most edd. have wrongly
followed Q4's 'all your', doubtless
because of *O, not all* in l. 90. But
Pericles' question is in general terms
(so Sisson).

92–93 S.D. *But . . .* Fishermen] Cf.
Wilkins, *P.A.,* 34. 1–4: 'When the
maister Fisherman commaunding his
seruants to goe dragge vp some other
nettes, which yet were abroade, he
seated himselfe by him . . .'

97. *is*] Q 'I' is a typical compositorial error.

birthday; and there are princes and knights come
from all parts of the world to joust and tourney for
her love.

Per. Were my fortunes equal to my desires, I could wish   110
to make one there.

1. Fish. O, sir, things must be as they may; and what a
man cannot get, he may lawfully deal for his wife's
soul.

Enter Second and Third Fishermen, drawing up a net.

2. Fish. Help, master, help! here's a fish hangs in the   115
net, like a poor man's right in the law; 'twill hardly
come out. Ha, bots on't, 'tis come at last, and 'tis
turn'd to a rusty armour.

Per. An armour, friends! I pray you, let me see it.

110–11. Were . . . there] *prose Malone;* desires, / there *Q.*   113–14. deal for his
wife's soul] *Q;* deal for—his wife's soul *Malone and Steevens;* steal for—his wife's
soul *D., conj. Williams;* deal for his wife's sole *conj. Staunton.*   114. S.D. *Second
and Third*] *Steevens subst., Dyce; the two / Q.*

---

112. *things . . . may*] proverbial; cf.
H5, II. i. 22.

112–14. *what . . . soul*] Knight comments: 'There are more riddles in this
play than that of Antiochus'. No ed. so
far has explained this one satisfactorily. Yet all the fisherman means is
that if a man cannot get rich any other
way, he may decide to deal for wealth
with his wife's soul, i.e. rent her out
to another man; cf. Marston, *Dutch
Courtezan,* I. i, 'A poore decayed
mechanicall mans wife, her husband is
layd up, may not she lawfully be layd
downe, when her husbands onely
rising is by his wifes falling. . . They
sell their bodies: doe not better persons
sell their soules?' (ed. Halliwell, vol. II,
pp. 114–15). The mocking 'lawfully' in
both passages may allude to a doctrine
of the religious sect satirized in Middleton's *The Family of Love* and in several
passages in Marston's play. Also cf.
(i) Day, *Ile of Gulls,* II. i (p. 26), 'and
with the Familie of Loue hold it lawfull to lie with her though she be another mans wife'; and (ii) the dia

logue in Middleton's *Phoenix,* I. iv.
250 ff.:
Phoenix. Why, does he mean to sell
his wife?
Tangle. His wife? Ay, by th' mass, he
would sell his soul if he knew.
. . . .
Tangle. . . . sold his wife t'other
day. . . .

115. *hangs*] can also mean 'is legally
delayed'; an appropriate verb for the
comparison that follows. Cf. Nashe,
The Terrors of the Night (1594), I. 373.
26–7, 'like a Chancerie sute, which
hangs two or three yeare ere it can
come to a judgement' (Maxwell, privately).

116. *right in the law*] so all edd., but
P.A., 35. 12 has 'case in the Lawe'
which may be correct.

117. *bots on't*] a plague upon it! A
common phrase in Elizabethan literature. *bots* is literally a maggot infection
in cattle or horses.

119. *An armour . . .*] Is it too farfetched to suggest that in this scene, so
full of Biblical echoes, the incident of

Thanks, Fortune, yet, that after all thy crosses   120
Thou giv'st me somewhat to repair myself;
And though it was mine own, part of mine heritage,
Which my dead father did bequeath to me,
With this strict charge, even as he left his life:
"Keep it, my Pericles; it hath been a shield   125
'Twixt me and death;"—and pointed to his brace—
"For that it sav'd me, keep it; in like necessity,
The which the gods protect thee from, may defend thee!"
It kept where I kept—I so dearly lov'd it—
Till the rough seas, that spares not any man,   130
Took it in rage, though calm'd hath given't again.
I thank thee for't; my shipwreck now's no ill,
Since I have here my father gave in his will.

1. Fish. What mean you, sir?

Per. To beg of you, kind friends, this coat of worth,   135
For it was sometime target to a king;
I know it by this mark. He lov'd me dearly,

---

120. thy] *Theobald MS, Delius, conj. Clarke;* not in *Q.*   122. And] *Q;* An *conj.*
S. Walker.   own, part] *Q5;* owne part *Q.*   127. it; in] *Theobald MS, Malone;*
it in *Q.*   128. from] *Malone;* Fame *Q.*   may] *Q;* may't *Staunton.*   130–1.
spares . . . hath] *Q2;* spares . . . haue *Q;* spare . . . 've *Malone.*   133. father gave]
Q; father's gift *Q4.*

Pericles' armour, which he inherited
from his father, echoes the 'armour of
the Lord' in the New Testament—e.g.
Ephesians, vi. 10 ff.? (John Levay,
privately.)

120. *all thy crosses*] *thy* is confirmed by
P.A., 35. 30, 'all her [= Fortune's]
crosses'.

122. *And though*] probably: 'even
though', Cf. II. Ch. 19, 'for though',
which is similarly obscure in meaning.
S. Walker and D. interpret *and* as 'if',
so that the phrase would mean 'even if
though'.

own, part] Q5's comma restores what
is the more probable sense of the
passage.

126. *brace*] mailed armpiece.

128. *from, may*] for *may*, see l. 56n.
above. Q's compositor seems to have
misread *from* as 'Fame'. Though less
likely, it is also possible that the com-

positor merely omitted the word *from*,
the original being 'from, Fame may'
('Fame' = honour).

129. *kept*] lodged.

130–1. *seas . . . spares . . . hath*] Maxwell and Sisson (but not Alexander)
follow the Q text, with support from
Abbott §§399–400. But the early regularization by a compositor in White's
shop, where both Q and Q2 were
printed, ought to be given some
weight, especially considering the
general corruption of the text. *hath*
was indeed retained by Ff 3–4 and
Rowe, who made many changes in
grammar. If Q2 and this ed. are right,
seas is to be regarded as a collective
singular. See also II. Ch. 31n. above.

133. *my father gave*] i.e. what my
father gave. Cf. I. i. 60, 61n.; yet Q4
may be right.

136. *target*] light shield.

And for his sake I wish the having of it;
And that you'd guide me to your sovereign's court,
Where with it I may appear a gentleman;   140
And if that ever my low fortunes better,
I'll pay your bounties; till then rest your debtor.

1. Fish. Why, wilt thou tourney for the lady?

Per. I'll show the virtue I have borne in arms.

1. Fish. Why, di'e take it; and the gods give thee good   145
on't!

2. Fish. Ay, but hark you, my friend; 'twas we that
made up this garment through the rough seams of
the waters: there are certain condolements, certain
vails. I hope, sir, if you thrive, you'll remember   150
from whence you had them.

Per. Believe't, I will.
By your furtherance I am cloth'd in steel;
And spite of all the rapture of the sea

---

141. fortunes] *Steevens, conj. Mason;* fortune's Q.   145. di'e] *uncorrected Q;* do'e
corrected Q.   151. them] Q; it *Malone.*   154. rapture] *Rowe (ii);* rupture Q.

141. *fortunes*] 'the emendation, with "better" as a verb, seems more pointed, and is supported by *P.A.*, 33. 25–6, "if ever his fortunes came to their ancient height" ' (Maxwell).

145. *di'e*] do ye. One of the few words which were changed by the press-corrector of Q—see Intro., p. xxxviii. The uncorrected form, though less usual, was in colloquial use and may render the MS copy justly. Cf. 'dee hear' in Day, *Parliament of Bees*, Q 1641, Char. III, sig. C4.

148. *made up*] fitted together; a tailor's term, and thus anticipating *seams*. The whole metaphor is daring and unusual.

149. *condolements*] meaning not clear. *O.E.D.*2b, which cites this passage as illustrating the definition 'tangible expression of sympathy', for once is clearly wrong. Rolfe, far more convincingly, regards it as a malapropism, 'blunderingly used by the fisherman—perhaps somehow confused with "dole" (= share, portion)'. Maxwell cites Dekker, who mocks this among

many high-flown terms in the subplot of *Patient Grissil*, II. i. 97–8, 'the magnitude of my condolement, hath bin eleuated the higher'. It is even possible that the fisherman's misusage is intended to be conscious, for malapropisms sweeten the act of begging, as some characters knew, at any rate, in Elizabethan drama; cf. Feste in *Tw. N.*, II. iii. 25, 'I did impetticos thy gratillity'. (See p. 188.)

150. *vails*] tips; leftovers of feasts or remnants of materials given to servants; here perhaps 'tailor's remnants', carrying on the metaphor of l. 148.

151. *them*] Q has been retained though the pronoun is grammatically incorrect, referring as it does to Pericles' armour. The intervening nouns, *condolements, certain vails*, may account for the plural.

154. *rapture*] in the literal sense: violent seizure. Rowe's emendation is confirmed by *P.A.*, 36. 8, 'raptures', where the term is also used in this sense. Q 'rupture' (= breaking) is therefore unlikely.

This jewel holds his building on my arm.   155
Unto thy value I will mount myself
Upon a courser, whose delightful steps
Shall make the gazer joy to see him tread.
Only, my friend, I yet am unprovided of a pair of
bases.   160
2. Fish. We'll sure provide; thou shalt have my best
gown to make thee a pair, and I'll bring thee to the
court myself.
Per. Then honour be but equal to my will,
This day I'll rise, or else add ill to ill.   [*Exeunt.*] 165

[SCENE II.—*The Same. A public Way leading to the Lists.
A Pavilion near it.*]

Enter SIMONIDES, *with* [*Lords and*] *Attendants, and* THAISA.

Sim. Are the knights ready to begin the triumph?

155. building] *Q;* biding *Malone.*   157. delightful] *F3;* delight *Q.*   159–
60. Only . . . bases] *As Q;* unprovided / bases *Malone.*   159. friend] *Q;* friends
Dyce.   161–3. We'll . . . myself] *prose Malone;* haue / paire; / selfe *Q.*   164.
equal] *Maxwell, conj. Staunton;* a Goale *Q;* egal *conj. Bullen.*   165. S.D.] *Rowe;
not in Q.*

Scene II

SCENE II] *Malone; not in Q.*   Location] *Malone (who adds: for the reception of the
King, Princess, Lords, etc.); not in Q.*   Entry. Lords and] *Malone; not in Q.*

155. *building*] place; an awkward
metaphor, but images of building are
frequent in the plays of Day, the probable author of this scene.

156. *Unto thy value*] 'to as high a
value (as the jewel will fetch)' (Round),
which will decide the quality of
Pericles' 'courser'.

159–60. *Only . . . bases*] Malone
probably versified these lines because
they form part of a speech otherwise in
verse. But the rhythm is quite different
from what goes before, and abrupt
transitions from verse to prose are
fairly common in Elizabethan drama.

160. *bases*] pleated skirt, worn by
knights on horseback, appended to the
doublet, and hanging down to the

knees. Cf. *P.A.*, 38. 10–11, 'his owne
Bases but the skirtes of a poor Fisher-
mans coate'.

164. *equal*] Q: 'a Goale' is strained in
sense and impossible verse. Staunton's
brilliant emendation finds support in
l. 110 above. Bullen's 'egal' is attractive only because it would be easier to
explain from it how the compositor of
Q made the slip.

Scene II

SCENE II] Except for additional
stage-directions and minor emendations, the text of this scene follows that
of Q. Comparison with Wilkins' prose
version in *P.A.* suggests strongly, however, that Q provides an imperfect

1. Lord. They are, my liege,
     And stay your coming to present themselves.
Sim. Return them we are ready; and our daughter,
     In honour of whose birth these triumphs are,   5
     Sits here like Beauty's child, whom Nature gat
     For men to see, and seeing wonder at.   [*Exit a Lord.*]

          [SIMONIDES *and* THAISA *take seats in the Pavilion,*
                    facing the public way.]

Thai. It pleaseth you, my royal father, to express
     My commendations great, whose merit's less.
Sim. It's fit it should be so; for princes are   10
     A model which heaven makes like to itself:
     As jewels lose their glory if neglected,
     So princes their renowns if not respected.
     'Tis now your honour, daughter, to entertain

2–3. They . . . themselves] *As Malone;* comming, / themselues *Q.*   4. daughter]
Malone; daughter heere *Q.*   7. S.D. *Exit a Lord*] *Malone; not in Q.*   S.D.
Simonides . . . way] *this ed.; not in Q.*   8. royal] *Q; not in Steevens.*   14. enter-
tain] *Q;* explain *Steevens;* entreat *conj. anon. apud Camb.*

report with some lines missing and
others replaced. See App. C. Neither
Gower nor Twine contains an equivalent for this scene, though a distant
analogue of the play does (see Intro.,
p. xviii). However, similar scenes are
not uncommon in Elizabethan drama:
Troil., I. ii; Kyd, *Spanish Tragedy,* I. v;
Soliman and Perseda, scene v; and
Middleton, *Your Five Gallants,* v. i.
What is more to the point, tournaments before royalty were frequently
held during the reigns of Elizabeth
and James I (who took great delight in
them), and usually began with a
'presentation' like that staged in this
scene.

Location. A Pavilion] Cf. *P.A.,* 36.
18–22: 'This is the day, this *Symonides*
Court, where the King himselfe, with
the Princesse his daughter, haue
placed themselues in a Gallery, to
beholde the triumphes of seuerall
Princes'. From this it would be wrong
to infer that the king and princess were

placed on the upper stage, for how in
that case would the squires present
their shields to them? See also ll. 57–
8n. below.
     1. *triumph*] here: tournament; a pub-
lic festivity of any kind.
     4. *Return*] answer (*O.E.D.*19b).
     daughter] on Q's 'daughter heere',
Maxwell comments, 'the reporter's anticipation of line 6'; or perhaps that of
the hasty compositor.
     6. *gat*] begat.
     11. *model*] image.
     12. *jewels*] piece of jewellery; used in
a wide sense.
     14. *honour*] honourable duty.
     entertain] probably 'receive', for
which meaning On. cites *Tim.,* I. ii.
194, 'Let the presents Be worthily entertain'd'. D. interprets, 'give reception to as they present themselves'.
Steevens' 'explain', adopted by many
edd., does not fit the context, for
it is not Thaisa but the King who
explains.

The labour of each knight in his device.   15
Thai. Which, to preserve mine honour, I'll perform.

*The First Knight passes by[, and his Squire presents his
Shield to the Princess].*

Sim. Who is the first that doth prefer himself?
Thai. A knight of Sparta, my renowned father;
    And the device he bears upon his shield
    Is a black Ethiop reaching at the sun;   20
    The word, *Lux tua vita mihi.*
                    [*She hands the Shield to* SIMONIDES *who
                    returns it through her to the Page.*]
Sim. He loves you well that holds his life of you.

The Second Knight [passes].

16. S.D. *and . . . Princess*] *Malone; not in Q.*   21. S.D.] *this ed.; not in Q.*   22.
S.D. *passes*] *Malone; not in Q.*

15. *The . . . device*] that is, the Knights' emblematic figures or designs (which here as usually were accompanied by a motto), wrought on their shields; or, possibly, the Knights' devices, upon which they have taken such pains. The interpretation depends somewhat on the meaning of *entertain* in the previous line. The following account conveys some idea of the intricacy and popularity of such emblematic devices:

'*Emblemes* and *Impresae's*, if ingeniously conceited, are of daintie device and much esteeme. The Invention of the Italian herein is very singular, neither doe our English wits come much behind them; but rather equall them every way. The best that I have seene, have beene the devises of Tiltings whereof many are reserved in the private Gallery at White Hall, of Sir *Philip Sidneys*, the Earle of *Cumberland*, Sir *Henry Leigh*, the Earle of *Essex*, with many others, most of which I once collected with intent to publish them, but the charge disswaded mee' (H. Peacham, *Compleat*

Gentleman, 1634 (1905 reprint), p. 234).

16. *honour*] reputation; perhaps echoes back to *renowns* in l. 13.

16. S.D.] Cf. Wilkins, *P.A.*, 37. 3–7, 'his shield . . . which being by the knights Page deliuered to the Lady, and from her presented to the King her father . . .'. See Intro., p. xlv.

17. *prefer*] present.

21. *word*] motto; frequent in Elizabethan English.

Lux . . . mihi] Thy light is life to me. Curiously enough, the motto of the Blount family of Soddington, Worcs., of which Edward Blount, the bookseller who registered a copy of *Pericles* in the Stationers' Register in 1608, was a member, ran similarly: 'Lux tua vita mea'. The crest, however, was different: an armed foot in the sun; see Green, *Emblem Writers*, p. 160.

21. S.D.] This direction is clearly indicated by Wilkins' account of the episode, quoted above, l. 16n. It is unnecessary to pack the text with similar directions for the other knights.

22. *holds . . . of*] regards as being dependent on.

> Who is the second that presents himself?
> *Thai.* A prince of Macedon, my royal father;
>   And the device he bears upon his shield   25
>   Is an arm'd knight that's conquer'd by a lady;
>   The motto thus, in Spanish, *Piùe per dolcezza che per*
>   *forza.*

27. *Piùe per dolcezza che per forza*] this ed., *conj.* Hertzberg *and* Schanzer; *Pue Per doleera kee per forsa* | Q; *Piu por dulzura que por fuerza* | Dyce; *Piu per dulçura que per fuerça* | Malone.

27. *in Spanish*, Piùe . . . forza] More by gentleness than by force. The text in Q is corrupt and edd. have not been able to agree on the correct wording. To turn the motto into Spanish would require very radical changes, into something like 'Mas por dulzura que por fuerza'. Other editors have settled on a mixture of Italian and Spanish, and others again have introduced a word or two of Portuguese. Hertzberg (*apud* Maxwell) was the first to suggest turning the motto into correct Italian: discussion with E.S. persuades me that this is the only sensible solution possible, though with some reservations.

Like the other mottos, this one was probably taken from some book of emblems, but the closest that has been discovered is in French: 'Plus par doulceur que par force' (= Emblem 28 in Corrozet, *Hecatomgraphie*, 1540, cited by Green, p. 165). This does not help matters. Wilkins' version is 'Pue per dolcera qui per sforsa', which is about as garbled as that of Q. But the fact that he does not name the language strengthens one's suspicion that we owe *in Spanish* to the play's reporter. And at least his version is useful in so far as it confirms two words in Q: 'Pue' and *per*, and also strongly suggests that in Q 'doleera', the first *e* should be emended to *c*; *e* for *c* being a common error in printing, attributable either to misreading of MS or foul case, an *e* in the *c* compartment. As the indications elsewhere in the text are strong that Q's compositor did *not*

make use of Wilkins' novel, it seems best to assume that he did not at this point; in that case one is justified in accepting those words which agree in the two versions as representing the original accurately—unless identical mistakes in the motto were made by the compositors of Q and of Wilkins' novel, a highly improbable assumption.

Yet two of the three words discussed are neither Italian nor Spanish. But they look like garbled Italian: 'dolcera' is probably an error for *dolcezza*, and 'Pue' for either Piú or poetical Piùe. Were it not for the correspondence of these corruptions in Wilkins' novel, one would be tempted to attribute them to Q's compositor, for omitted letters (*Piùe* > Pue) and misreadings of *z* for *r* (*dolcez(z)a* > dolcera) are common in Elizabethan printed texts. Under the circumstances the playwright himself must be held guilty. The two remaining words, though also garbled, offer less of a problem: 'kee' is an evident misinterpretation of Italian *che*, and 'forsa' a misspelling or auditory error of *forza*. For these two corruptions the reporter or anyone else may be responsible. I postulate, therefore, that the playwright wrote: 'Pue per dolcera che per forza', or something close to this. His intention was surely to quote the motto in its correct original Italian, which I have attempted to reconstruct and have defended at the risk of being comically prolix.

[The] Third Knight [passes].

Sim. And what's the third?
Thai.   The third of Antioch;
And his device, a wreath of chivalry;
The word, *Me pompae provexit apex.*   30

[The] Fourth Knight [passes].

Sim. What is the fourth?
Thai. A burning torch that's turned upside down;
The word, *Qui me alit, me extinguit.*
Sim. Which shows that beauty hath his power and will,
Which can as well inflame as it can kill.   35

---

27. S.D. *The . . . passes*] Malone; *3. Knight* | Q (*preceding S.H. of l. 28*).   28–30.
And . . . apex] *As Steevens;* third? | *deuice,* | *apex* | Q.   28. what's] *Q4;* with *Q;*
who *Maxwell.*   30. *pompae*] *Theobald MS, Steevens; Pompey* | Q.   30. S.D.]
Malone; 4. Knight | Q (*preceding S.H. of l. 31*).   33. *Qui*] *Q; Quod* | *Malone.*
34. his] *Q;* her *conj. S. Walker;* this *conj. Maxwell.*   and] Q (&); at *Maxwell.*

28. *what's*] Q4's emendation finds
support in ll. 31 and 39, and seems
more likely than Maxwell's 'who',
altered by analogy with ll. 17 and 23.
Probably a compositor's slip, resulting
from an abbreviation in the MS,
wrongly expanded: w^{ts} interpreted
wth (H.F.B.).

29. *wreath of chivalry*] a heraldic
term; 'the . . . twisted band by which
the crest is joined to the [knight's] hel-
met' (*O.E.D.*1c). Maxwell directs the
reader to the frontispiece of Scott-
Giles, *Shakespeare's Heraldry.*

30. *Me . . . apex*] The crown of the
triumph has led me on. Wilkins has
pompae and translates the motto, 'the
desire of renowne drew him to this
enterprise' (*P.A.*, 37. 13–15). Wilkins
almost certainly adapted this from
the English translation by P.S. of
Paradin's *Devises Héroïques* (1591),
sig. V3, p. 309, where the same
wreath is portrayed and the motto
translated: 'the desire of renowne hath
promoted me, or set me forward'. It is
a good guess that the King explained

the motto in similar words in the uncorrupted text.

33. *Qui . . . extinguit*] Who feeds me
extinguishes me. *Qui* is confirmed by
Wilkins, by Whitney, *Choice of Emblems,*
1583, p. 183 (Green, p. 173), and by
what is the evident source, Paradin
(see above), sig. z3, p. 357, who
describes the emblem as 'a burning
Torch turned vpside downe'. Several
Italian writers on emblems likewise
quote the motto with *Qui* (B. Pittoni
cites it as the motto of the Sig. de San
Valiere). Malone's emended *Quod*, on
the other hand, finds support only in
Daniel's translation of Paulus Jovius,
1585 (Green, p. 174). See also Lyly,
Euphues and his England, p. 18, 'The
Torch tourned downewards, is ex-
tinguished with the selfe same waxe
which was the cause of his lyght', and
cf. 1. Ch. 15–16 and n. above. Evidently, the motto merely reflects a
favourite conceit of the time.

34. *his*] its. Maxwell justly comments: 'But beauty is usually personi-
fied as feminine, hence Walker's conj.
"her". Perhaps "this" '.

[The] Fifth Knight [passes].

Thai. The fifth, an hand environed with clouds,
        Holding out gold that's by the touchstone tried;
        The motto thus, *Sic spectanda fides.*

*[The] Sixth Knight [*PERICLES, *passes in rusty Armour, without
Shield, and unaccompanied. He presents his Device directly to
THAISA.]

Sim. And what's the sixth and last, the which the knight
        himself
        With such a graceful courtesy deliver'd?   40
Thai. He seems to be a stranger; but his present is
        A wither'd branch, that's only green at top;
        The motto, *In hac spe vivo.*
Sim. A pretty moral;
        From the dejected state wherein he is,   45
        He hopes by you his fortunes yet may flourish.

---

35. S.D.] *Malone; 5. Knight* / Q (*preceding S.H. of l. 36*).   38. S.D.] *Malone;
6. Knight* / Q (*preceding S.H. of l. 39*).   39–40. And ... deliver'd] *As Steevens;
which,* / deliuered *Q.*   44–5. A ... is] *As Rowe; one line Q.*

---

37. *gold ... touchstone*] referring to the
old method of testing the genuineness
of metal by the colour of the streak
produced by it when rubbed on a piece
of quartz; proverbial, as a symbol of
fidelity (Tilley T 448).

38. *Sic ... fides*] Thus is faithfulness
to be tried. Both device and motto
occur in Whitney, *Choice of Emblems*,
p. 139 (Green, pp. 175–9), but the
probable source is again Claude Paradin, sig. O3, p. 213, where the picture
clearly shows 'an hand environed with
clouds ...' and the comment begins:
'The goodnes of gold is not onely tryed
by ringing, but also by the touchstone:
so the triall of godliness and faith is to
bee made not of wordes onely, but also
by the action & performance of the
deedes.'

38. S.D.] Pericles is the only knight
without shield and unaccompanied by
a page, and therefore delivers the
device to the Princess directly, as the

King's lines indicate. Cf. *P.A.*, 37. 27–
9: 'who hauing neither Page to deliuer his shield, nor shield to deliuer,
making his Deuice according to his
fortunes ...'.

40. *deliver'd*] presented.

41. *present*] object presented.

43. In ... vivo] In this hope I live.
No source for this motto has been
found; it may well have been invented
by the playwright.

45–6. *From ... flourish*] a reasonable
interpretation of Pericles' device and
motto. E.S. points out the absurd-
ity of the explanation of the same
device in Wilkins' account, 'which
prooued the abating of his body, decayed not the noblenesse of his mind'
(*P.A.*, 37. 30–38. 2). This serves to
show that even in this scene where
Wilkins' rendering seems sometimes
preferable to that of Q, it is not to be
trusted blindly.

45. *From*] emerging from (D.).

1. Lord. He had need mean better than his outward
          show
          Can any way speak in his just commend;
          For by his rusty outside he appears
          To have practis'd more the whipstock than the lance. 50
2. Lord. He well may be a stranger, for he comes
          To an honour'd triumph strangely furnished.
3. Lord. And on set purpose let his armour rust
          Until this day, to scour it in the dust.
Sim. Opinion's but a fool, that makes us scan   55
          The outward habit by the inward man.
          But stay, the knights are coming;
          We will withdraw into the gallery.   [*Exeunt.*]

Great shouts [heard from the lists], and all cry "The mean Knight!"

56. by] *Q; for conj. anon. apud Camb.*   57–8. coming / gallery] *Q;* withdraw /
gallery *Malone.*   58. S.D. *Exeunt*] *Rowe; not in Q.*   S.D. *heard . . . lists*] *Rowe
subst.; not in Q.*

48. *commend*] commendation.

50. *To have . . . whipstock*] literally: to
have worked more with the handle of a
whip, i.e. more like a carter.

55. *Opinion*] ignorant, and thus
slighting, opinion. Elizabethans frequently used the term in a derogatory
sense.

scan] judge, criticize (*O.E.D.*2).

56. *The outward . . . man*] Steevens
would transpose *outward* and *inward*,
but this would not restore the line's
meaning, which surely is that of *P.A.*,
38. 14–15, 'the outward habite was the
least table of the inward minde'. The
anonymous emendation 'for' for *by*,

though perhaps not restoring the
original correctly, does justice to what
the author meant.

57–8. *But . . . gallery*] that is, off-
stage, *not* to the upper stage; see above,
Loc. A Pavilion, n. We do not see the
King as a spectator of the lists, as we do
see Basilisco and Piston in the fifth
scene of *Soliman and Perseda* (1592, sig.
B2), where the stage-direction reads:
'They go up the ladders, and they
sound within to the first course'. Yet
the line in *Pericles* may have been
misplaced by the reporter, for cf.
Wilkins' account, summarized in
App. C.

[SCENE III.—*The Same. A Hall of State: a Banquet prepared.*]

Enter SIMONIDES, [THAISA, *Marshal, Ladies, Lords,*] *Knights from tilting*[*, and Attendants*].

Sim. Knights,
 To say you're welcome were superfluous.
 To place upon the volume of your deeds,
 As in a title-page, your worth in arms,
 Were more than you expect, or more than's fit,   5
 Since every worth in show commends itself.
 Prepare for mirth, for mirth becomes a feast.
 You are princes and my guests.
Thai.   But you, my knight and guest;
 To whom this wreath of victory I give,   10
 And crown you king of this day's happiness.
Per. 'Tis more by fortune, lady, than my merit.
Sim. Call it by what you will, the day is yours;
 And here, I hope, is none that envies it.
 In framing an artist, art hath thus decreed: 15
 To make some good, but others to exceed;

Scene III

SCENE III . . . *prepared*] *Malone; not in* Q.   Entry] *Malone* (*except for Marshal*),
this ed.; Enter the King and Knights from Tilting / Q.   1–2. Knights . . . super-
fluous] *As Malone; one line* Q.   3. To] *F4;* I Q.   8. princes and] *Q; not in
Steevens.*   13. yours] *Q3;* your Q.   15. an artist] *Q;* artists *Maxwell, conj.
Malone.*

SCENE III] The irregularity of the verse in much of this scene suggests considerable corruption by the reporter. But its undramatic character, with several asides, the whispering interlude between the King and Thaisa, and the wordiness and repetition in the dialogue between Thaisa and Pericles, betray also the hand of an inferior dramatist.

3. *To*] Q 'I', probably the result of misreading of MS copy.

4. *As . . . title-page*] Title-pages of early printed books were often embellished with the publisher's device, and sometimes with heraldic arms, pro-claiming the excellence of their contents.

6. *in show*] by being shown in action.

7. *becomes*] is fitting for.

8. *princes and*] omitted by Steevens on grounds of metre. But short lines occur frequently at the end of speeches in Shakespeare's later plays and, as Maxwell noted, the suitors are 'Princes Sones' in Gower, *C.A.*, 867.

15. *framing*] shaping.

an artist] Malone's conj. 'artists', adopted by Maxwell, improves the line metrically. But this is not sufficient ground for altering the text, particularly a 'bad' text like this one.

And you are her labour'd scholar. Come, queen o'th'
　　feast—
For, daughter, so you are—here take your place;
Marshal, the rest, as they deserve their grace.
Knights.　We are honour'd much by good Simonides.　　20
Sim.　Your presence glads our days; honour we love,
For who hates honour hates the gods above.
Marsh.　Sir, yonder is your place.
Per.　　　　　　　　　　　　Some other is more fit.
1. Knight.　Contend not, sir; for we are gentlemen
Have neither in our hearts nor outward eyes　　　　25
Envied the great nor shall the low despise.
Per.　You are right courteous knights.
Sim.　　　　　　　　　　　　Sit, sir, sit.
　　[*Aside.*] By Jove, I wonder, that is king of thoughts,

19. Marshal,] *this ed.; Martiall Q.*　　25–6. Have . . . / Envied . . . shall] *Sisson,*
conj. W. P. Trent; Haue . . . / Enuies . . . shall Q; That . . . / Envie . . . do Q4;
That . . . / Envy ' . . . shall Alexander.　28. S.D.] *Camb.; not in Q.*　28. By] *Q;*
Per. By Malone.

17. *her labour'd scholar*] i.e. the scholar
over whom art took special pains.

17–18. *queen . . . are*] Cf. *Wint.*, IV. iv.
67–8, 'present yourself / That which
you are, Mistress o'th' Feast'
(Steevens). The echo intimates that
the lines in *Pericles* may be Shakespeare's interpolation. One could say
the same, however, of very few other
lines in Acts I and II with any degree of
assurance, and the alternative is possible, that this effective phrase stuck in
Shakespeare's head, to be used in
Wint.

19. *Marshal,*] Not to include a
comma here is to leave room for mis-
understanding, and perhaps interpret
the word as a verb. It is a noun in the
vocative case. The King turns from his
daughter to the Marshal at this point,
as Wilkins' report makes clear:
'*Pericles* . . . with all the other Princes,
were by the Kings Marshall conducted
into the Presence . . .' (*P.A.*, 38. 24–7).
Up to now, edd. have curiously overlooked the Marshal, and not mentioned him in the Entry, though he is
given a speaking part.

23. *Sir . . . place*] Wilkins further
clarifies this episode: 'all being seated
by the Marshall at a table, placed
directly ouer-against where the king
and his daughter sate . . .' (*P.A.*, 39.
4–6).

25–6. *Have . . . Envied . . . shall*]
Trent's minor alteration, accepted by
Sisson and Maxwell, restores the
sense more plausibly than that of Q4,
which other edd. have followed. The
relative before *Have* is omitted—see
I. i. 15n.—and the mixture of tenses
presents no problem. Sisson comments: 'Here a plausible error on the
part of the Quarto compositor is
enuies for *envied*. The sense, moreover,
is superior with this simple emendation of Quarto. Logic is with the
sequence of thought, "we have not
envied the great, nor shall we despise
the low" ' (p. 293). The compositor
may have been predisposed to the
wrong 's' ending by *hearts* and *eyes*.

28–9. *Aside . . . upon*] Some edd.
have wrongly assigned these lines to
Pericles. That they belong to the King
is confirmed by *P.A.*, 39. 7–12: 'both

These cates resist me, he not thought upon.

Thai. [*Aside.*] By Juno, that is queen of marriage,   30
All viands that I eat do seem unsavoury,
Wishing him my meat. [*To Simonides.*] Sure he's
a gallant gentleman.

Sim. [*To Thaisa.*] He's but a country gentleman;
Has done no more than other knights have done;
Has broken a staff or so; so let it pass.   35

Thai. [*Aside.*] To me he seems like diamond to glass.

Per. [*Aside.*] Yon king's to me like to my father's picture,
Which tells me in that glory once he was;
Had princes sit like stars about his throne,
And he the sun, for them to reverence.   40
None that beheld him but, like lesser lights,
Did vail their crowns to his supremacy;
Where now his son's like a glow-worm in the night,
The which hath fire in darkness, none in light:

---

29. he not] *Q;* she not *Malone;* she but *Dyce* (i) *;* he but *D.*   30. S.D.] *Camb.;*
not in Q.   32. S.D. *To Simonides*] *this ed.; not in Q.*   33. S.D.] *To Thaisa*] *this
ed.; not in Q; Aside* / *Camb.*   33-5. He's . . . pass] *As Boswell;* more / *Staffe,* /
passe *Q.*   36, 37. S.D.] *Camb.; not in Q.*   37. Yon] *Q2;* You *Q.*   38. tells
me] *Q4;* tells *Q.*   43. son's like] *Malone;* sonne like *Q;* son's *Steevens.*

King and daughter, at one instant
were so strucke in loue with the noblenesse of his woorth, that they could not
spare so much time to satisfie themselues with the delicacie of their
viands, for talking of his prayses'.

29. *cates*] delicacies.

resist me] probably, repel me (On.
and *O.E.D.*4), 'go against my appetite' (D.). But I know of no other passage where resist is used in this sense.

31-2. *All . . . meat*] perhaps the corrupt rendering of what in the original
was a couplet ending in eat/meat
(Steevens). There is of course no inti-
mation of flirtation here, as in *Err.*, II.
ii. 116-17, 'That never meat sweet-
savour'd in thy taste, / Unless I spake,
or look'd, or touch'd, or carv'd to
thee'.

32, 33 S.Ds.] These directions have
merely been introduced to indicate
that not all of Simonides' and Thaisa's
lines in this passage are *Aside*, as the

Cambridge edd. suppose. To interpret ll. 32-5 as dialogue makes better
sense of them and seems more dramatic.

37-44. *Yon . . . light*] The images are
closely paralleled in a passage in Day's
Humour Out Of Breath. See App. B.

38. *tells me*] This emendation by Q4,
while restoring the metre and somewhat improving the sense, cannot be
regarded as certain.

42. *vail*] lower.

43. *Where*] whereas.

son's like] Malone's simple emendation restores the sense. The compositor's misreading of *s* for *e* (thus 'sonne')
is the probable explanation for Q's
error. Steevens and recently Maxwell
omit *like*, thus regularizing the metre.
like may well have been intruded by
the reporter, influenced by the string
of 'likes' preceding, and thus assimi-
lating a metaphor to the similes that
went before.

Whereby I see that Time's the king of men; 45
He's both their parent, and he is their grave,
And gives them what he will, not what they crave.
Sim. What, are you merry, knights?
1. Knight. Who can be other in this royal presence?
Sim. Here, with a cup that's stor'd unto the brim,— 50
As you do love, fill to your mistress' lips,—
We drink this health to you.
Knights.   We thank your grace.
Sim. Yet pause awhile;
Yon knight doth sit too melancholy,
As if the entertainment in our court 55
Had not a show might countervail his worth.
Note it not you, Thaisa?
Thai. What is't to me, my father?
Sim. O, attend, my daughter:
Princes, in this, should live like gods above, 60
Who freely give to every one that come to honour them;
And princes not doing so are like to gnats
Which make a sound, but kill'd are wonder'd at.
Therefore to make his entrance more sweet,

---

50. stor'd] *Malone;* stur'd *Q;* stirr'd *F3.*   51. you do] *Q4;* do you *Q.*   53–4.
Yet . . . melancholy] *As Dyce; one line Q.*   61. Who . . . them] *one line Q;* come /
them *Malone subst., Dyce.*   come] *Q;* comes *Q6.*   63. kill'd are] *Q;* kill'd no
more are *conj. Malone.*   64. entrance] *Q* (entraunce)*;* enterance *Q4;* entrance
now *F3;* entertain *Dyce, conj. S. Walker.*

---

50. *stor'd*] Malone's correction goes
unquestioned. Q 'stur'd' is obsolete for
'stirr'd', which does not make sense in
the context.

51. *to*] in honour of (D.).

mistress'] Round wrongly interprets
'mistresses''. Simonides means Thaisa
alone, who is *queen o'th' feast,* and for
whose hand all the knights are suitors.

56. *countervail*] counterbalance, be
equal to.

61. *Who . . . them*] a seven-foot line or
fourteener, that may possibly betray
an earlier version of the play, but the
text of the whole speech is probably
corrupt.

come] Most edd. since the eighteenth
century read *comes,* but 'every one that

come' is good seventeenth-century
English, and was therefore retained by
Ff3–4. For 'every one' used as a plural
noun, see Abbott §12.

63. *kill'd are*] Malone's conj. 'kill'd
no more are' would make a complete
but unnecessary alteration in the
sense, which Percy paraphrased:
'Only when they are dead do we realize how tiny the insects that have been
making such a noise are'.

64. *entrance*] trisyllabic, as indicated
in Q4's spelling. See On., who cites
other examples. Many edd. have
accepted Walker's conj. 'entertain',
but Sisson comments convincingly
that '*Entrance* surely gives good sense,
and refers back to "every one *that*

Here say we drink this standing-bowl of wine to him.   65
Thai. Alas, my father, it befits not me
    Unto a stranger knight to be so bold;
    He may my proffer take for an offence,
    Since men take women's gifts for impudence.
Sim. How?   70
    Do as I bid you, or you'll move me else!
Thai. [*Aside.*] Now, by the gods, he could not please me
    better.
Sim. Furthermore tell him, we desire to know
    Of whence he is, his name and parentage.
Thai. The king my father, sir, has drunk to you.   75
Per. I thank him.
Thai. Wishing it so much blood unto your life.
Per. I thank both him and you, and pledge him freely.
Thai. And further he desires to know of you
    Of whence you are, your name and parentage.   80
Per. A gentleman of Tyre; my name, Pericles;
    My education been in arts and arms;
    Who, looking for adventures in the world,

---

65. say we drink] Q; bear *conj. J. D. Wilson.*   70–1. How . . . else] *As Steevens;*
one line Q.   72. S.D.] *Rowe; not in* Q.   73. Furthermore . . . know] *This ed.,*
conj. H.F.B.; And furthermore . . . know of him Q; And further . . . know
Malone; And further, we desire to know of him *conj. J. D. Wilson.*

come to honour them" above (line 61)'
(p. 293, subst.).

65. *drink*] J. D. Wilson's conj. 'bear'
is hardly justified, for Wilkins' *P.A.*
(39. 22–5) gives as much support for
drink as for 'bear'. The King honours
Pericles by first drinking to him and
then asking his daughter to pass the
bowl to him.

standing-bowl] a bowl with a foot or
pedestal, sometimes referred to as
'standing-cup'.

73. *Furthermore . . . know*] The emendation was partly anticipated by
Malone. Not merely the impossible
metre, but also the awkward 'tell him
. . . know of him' in Q point to textual
corruption, and H.F.B. postulates
that the reporter's contamination
resulted from his anticipation of

l. 79, *And further . . . know of you.*

73–89. *Furthermore . . . shore*] The
manner of this dialogue, with its undramatic repetition, resembles that in
II. ii. Both are quite unShakespearean.

81–5. *A gentleman . . . shore*] reproduced almost word for word in *P.A.,*
40. 3–9. The source is Gower. In Twine
(Chapter v), the hero first answers
elusively, declaring his name and
origin only upon further importunity.

82. *been*] has been.

arts and arms] Cf. *LLL.,* II. i. 45, 'well
fitted in arts, glorious in arms'. Dugdale Sykes (*Sidelights on Shakespeare,*
pp. 171–2) makes much of Wilkins'
fondness for this collocation, but is
apparently unaware of its common-
ness in Elizabethan literature, especially in romance.

Was by the rough seas reft of ships and men,
And after shipwreck driven upon this shore.   85
Thai. He thanks your grace; names himself Pericles,
A gentleman of Tyre,
Who only by misfortune of the seas
Bereft of ships and men, cast on this shore.
Sim. Now, by the gods, I pity his misfortune,   90
And will awake him from his melancholy.
Come, gentlemen, we sit too long on trifles,
And waste the time, which looks for other revels.
Even in your armours, as you are address'd,
Will well become a soldier's dance.   95
I will not have excuse with saying this:
Loud music is too harsh for ladies' heads,
Since they love men in arms as well as beds.

[The Knights] dance.

87–8. A . . . seas] *As Collier; one line* Q.   88. only] Q; newly *conj. Elze.*   95.
Will well] Q; Will very well *F3;* Your steps will well *anon. conj. apud Camb.*
96–7. this: / Loud] *Maxwell;* this, / Lowd Q; that / Lowd *Q4;* this / Loud
Malone.   98. S.D.] *Malone; They daunce /* Q.

87–8. *A . . . Who*] As the broken line
suggests, some words, including the
verb of the sentence, seem to be missing, owing to the reporter's faulty
memory.

88–9. *Who only . . . cast*] perhaps:
'who only because of misfortune . . .
was cast'; but *only* may well be corrupt,
though Elze's conj. 'newly' (*Englische
Studien,* IX (1885), 282) is unconvincing.

91. *melancholy*] At this point, Wilkins in *P.A.* reports an additional incident. Pericles is presented with a steed
and spurs. This may well be a mere
expansion on Wilkins' part, but it
would make the development that
follows seem less abrupt.

94. *address'd*] dressed, furnished; i.e.
'just as you are'.

95. *will well*] The anon. conj. 'Your
steps will well' is attractive, since it
would improve syntax as well as restore metre.

96–7. *this: Loud . . . heads*] Edd.
usually follow Malone, interpreting

this as an adjective belonging to *Loud
music.* But such line-division is rare in
any poet, major or minor. The adver-
bial sense is therefore preferable. The
construction is paralleled elsewhere in
the play, e.g. I. i. 10 and I. ii. 12.
Accordingly, *this:* introduces Simonides' one-line quotation of what the
Knights may be going to say in objection, and then the next line, line 98, is
his reason for dismissing the objection.
By *Loud music,* probably 'the loud noise
made by the clashing of their armour'
(Malone) is meant.

98. *arms*] perhaps with a *double
entendre*: armed and in embrace. The
jocular sexual note in this line may be
echoed at more than one point later in
this speech.

S.D. The . . . dance] a sword dance
in armour. S. Singer (*Apollonius von
Tyrus,* p. 19) noted that Copland's
King Appolyn of Tyre (1510–15) has a
sword-play after dinner; Steevens,
that Twine has a 'daunsing in armour'
at the wedding.

So this was well ask'd, 'twas so well perform'd.
Come, sir, here's a lady that wants breathing too;   100
And I have heard, you knights of Tyre
Are excellent in making ladies trip,
And that their measures are as excellent.

Per. In those that practise them they are, my lord.

Sim. O, that's as much as you would be denied   105
Of your fair courtesy.

[*The Knights and Ladies*] *dance.*

101. have heard] *Q;* have often heard *Malone.*   106. S.D.] *Malone; They daunce | Q; Pericles and Thaisa dance | conj. J. H. Long.*

99. *So ... ask'd*] Usually paraphrased 'I did well when I asked for it', but perhaps Staunton's '*As* this was well asked' (interpreting *so ... so* = 'as ... so') is the correct interpretation, for which see *O.E.D. so* 18.

100. *breathing*] exercise. Cf. *Ham.*, v. ii. 171 and Jonson, *Every Man In*, I. v. 127, quoted by *O.E.D.* (*breathe* 11). See also l. 98n. above.

101. *have heard*] Malone's emendation is one of several attempts to provide a fifth foot for the line. While short lines are not uncommon in the blank verse drama of the period, the lameness of l. 100 serves to strengthen one's impression that the text is corrupt. H.F.B. ingeniously suggests that the *sir* of l. 100 should be placed after *heard.*

102. *trip*] dance a light, merry dance, with a *double entendre.* See l. 98n. above.

measures] grave or stately dances (*O.E.D.*20).

105–6. *that's ... courtesy*] Una Ellis-Fermor paraphrases: 'That's as much as to say you want to be refused (the honour, as if you were implying that you did *not* practise them and so backing out; but you are saying that only out of good manners).' Much less convincing is Maxwell, who interprets *Of ... courtesy* as a separate phrase, a request to Pericles to dance, and defines *denied* = 'contradicted', for which *O.E.D.* lends no support. D.'s para-phrase is quoted as a possible (though to me unconvincing) alternative: 'that answer is as much as if you would have it said that you yourself can claim no praise for such courtly accomplish-ments'. E.S. suggests that the bawdy undertone of some of the previous lines (see l. 98n. above) may echo still in this speech.

106. S.D. The ... dance] S. H. Long, in 'Laying the Ghosts in *Pericles*', *Sh.Q.*, VII (1956), 39–42, argues that this second dance is a duet involving Pericles and Thaisa only; that Pericles, having demonstrated his skills in tilting and in the artful sword-dance, is now examined for his fitness in the art of love, the last part of his 'threefold chivalric test'. But there is little in the play to suggest such a test in stages. Long makes much of the absence of 'Ladies' in the scene's open-ing S.D. in Q, but such omission means little in a play where so many S.D.s are either missing or incomplete. One would think it far more likely that all the Knights and Ladies participate in the dancing. The simple report in Wilkins, 'Much time beeing spent in daunting and other reuells' (*P.A.*, 40. 23–4), general as it is, indicates at any rate that the dances are not used to test but, on the contrary, to cheer Pericles and entertain the whole com-pany. Cf. the Masque of Cupid and the Amazons in *Tim.*, I. ii, where after the Ladies' dance, 'The Lords rise

Unclasp, unclasp!
Thanks, gentlemen, to all; all have done well,
[*To Pericles.*] But you the best. Pages and lights, to
    conduct
These knights unto their several lodgings!
Yours, sir, we have given order be next our own.   110
Per. I am at your grace's pleasure.
Sim. Princes, it is too late to talk of love,
And that's the mark I know you level at.
Therefore each one betake him to his rest;
To-morrow all for speeding do their best.   [*Exeunt.*] 115

108. S.D.] *Malone; not in* Q.   lights, to conduct] Q; lights, conduct *Steevens;*
lights conduct *Maxwell.*   109–10. lodgings! / own] Q; sir, / own *Malone.*
110. order be] Q; order to be *F3;* order should be *Maxwell.*   112. *Sim.*] Q4
(*King.*); not in Q.   115. S.D.] *Malone; not in* Q.

from table . . . and to show their loves,
each single out an Amazon, and all
dance . . .' The Knights, with their
soldiers' dance in *Pericles*, correspond
to the Masquers in *Timon*, and their
dance with Thaisa and (surely) her
Ladies corresponds to the 'revels' in
which the courtier-masquers, after the
'Main', danced with chosen members
of their audience.

108. *lights, to conduct*] The omission
of *to* would improve the metre, but the
purposive infinitive appears slightly
preferable to the imperative here. Yet
to may have been caught by the reporter from the previous line, or even
from l. 112. H.F.B. moreover suggests
that *lights* may mean 'light bearers',
paralleling the Elizabethan usage of
trumpet for trumpeter. If he is right,
this would be extra reason for omitting
to. However, *O.E.D.* (*light* 5e) lends
little support.

109–10. *These . . . own*] If the lineation is altered, as in most edd., some
such addition as 'to' or 'should' in l.
110 seems called for. The case for
'should' rests on the weak evidence of
P.A., 40. 27, '*Pericles* Chamber should
be next his owne'; weak, since Wilkins
paraphrases or transcribes far more
often than he quotes *verbatim.* 'To' is
more natural, but it seems best to let
the text stand, for the intention may
well have been to elide *we have.* The
source for the passage is Gower, *C.A.*,
801–3.

113. *level*] aim.

115. *speeding*] success.

S.D.] If one can trust Wilkins' report in *P.A.*, Pericles should make a
brief appearance on the stage with a
musical instrument, no words spoken,
somewhere between the end of this
scene and the opening of II. v. See
P.A., 45 and text, II. v. 25–6.

[SCENE IV.—*Tyre*.]

Enter HELICANUS *and* ESCANES.

Hel. No, Escanes, know this of me,
Antiochus from incest liv'd not free;
For which, the most high gods not minding longer
To withhold the vengeance that they had in store,
Due to this heinous capital offence,   5
Even in the height and pride of all his glory,
When he was seated in a chariot
Of an inestimable value, and his daughter with him,
A fire from heaven came and shrivell'd up
Their bodies, even to loathing; for they so stunk,   10
That all those eyes ador'd them ere their fall

Scene IV

SCENE IV] *Malone; not in Q.*   Location] *not in Q; Tyre. A room in the Governor's house. Malone.*   3–6. For . . . glory] *As Malone;* minding, / that / heynous / pride *Q.*   7–9. When . . . up] *As Dyce;* seated in / daughter / shriueld *Q.* 10. Their] *Steevens;* those *Q.*

3–9. *For . . . up*] Malone's and Dyce's traditional lineation has been adopted as the best possible rearrangement of Q's irregular and otherwise unsuitable verse. The resulting eighth line is hard to justify, though lines with six stresses are not infrequent in Elizabethan drama. The far more drastic changes made by the New Cambridge edd., with resulting broken lines, are not supportable. The true verse is irrecoverable from memorial losses.

3. *minding*] being inclined, intending.

6–12. *Even . . . burial*] probably a biblical echo; cf. *2 Kings*, i. 10 ff.: 'If I be a man of God, then let fire come down from heaven, and consume thee and thy fifty . . .'; also *Numbers*, xi. 1. But the passage may be indebted more directly to Greene's and Lodge's *Looking-Glass for London* (1594), where the incestuous Remilia is similarly struck by thunder and lightning. R. J. Kane, 'A Passage in *Pericles*', *MLN*, LXVIII (Nov. 1953), 483–4, further

points out that Gower and Twine relate Antiochus' retributive death by lightning, but not the noisome after-effects, and suggests that the playwright may have recollected the description of the fate of Antiochus IV (Epiphanes) in *2 Maccabees*, ix, who was stricken by the God of Israel with the plague and worms, so that he stunk intolerably. Another relevant biblical passage may be *Acts*, xii. 20–3, which describes the death of Herod (both Tyre and Antioch are mentioned in the context). (See p. 188.)

10. *Their*] Q 'those' may be owing to the reporter's or compositor's anticipation of the word in the next line. Cf. *P.A.*, 41. 24–42. 3: 'and strucke dead these prowd incestuous creatures where they sate, leauing their faces blasted and their bodies such a contemptfull obiect on the earth, that . . .', which does not provide clear support for Steevens' emendation.

11. *those eyes ador'd*] those eyes that adored; see I. i. 15n.

Scorn now their hand should give them burial.
Esca. 'Twas very strange.
Hel.   And yet but justice; for though
This king were great, his greatness was no guard
To bar heaven's shaft, but sin had his reward.   15
Esca. 'Tis very true.

Enter three Lords.

1. Lord. See, not a man in private conference
Or council has respect with him but he.
2. Lord. It shall no longer grieve without reproof.
3. Lord. And curs'd be he that will not second it.   20
1. Lord. Follow me then. Lord Helicane, a word.
Hel. With me? and welcome; happy day, my lords.
1. Lord. Know that our griefs are risen to the top,
And now at length they overflow their banks.
Hel. Your griefs! for what? wrong not your prince you love.
1. Lord. Wrong not yourself then, noble Helicane;   26
But if the prince do live, let us salute him,
Or know what ground's made happy by his breath.
If in the world he live, we'll seek him out;
If in his grave he rest, we'll find him there;   30
And be resolv'd he lives to govern us,

13. justice] *Q; just Steevens.*   13–15. And . . . reward] *As Malone;* great, / shaft, / reward *Q.*   16. S.D. *three] Malone; two or three / Q.*   22. welcome; happy] *Malone subst.;* welcome happy *Q.*   25. your] *Q;* the *Steevens.*   28. breath] *Q;* death *conj. J. D. Wilson.*

12. *Scorn*] perhaps vivid historical present through attraction of *now.* Yet considering that the rest of Helicanus' narrative is all in the past tense, the original may have been 'Scornd', misread by the compositor as 'Scorne'.

14–15. *guard / . . . reward*] The rhyme makes Malone's relineation certain.

15. *his*] its.

18. *he*] i.e. Escanes.

19. *grieve*] annoy (*O.E.D.*5) or offend (*O.E.D.*6); be grievous (to us).

23, 25. *griefs*] grievances.

25. *your*] Steevens' 'the' is possible. The MS may well have read 'ye', which the compositor misinterpreted as 'yr' (H.F.B.). But Q's repeti-

tion and emphasis may be deliberate.

27. *salute*] greet.

28. *what . . . breath*] what country is made happy by his presence. For *ground* = country, cf. *Oth.,* I. i. 29 and *Ham.,* I. i. 15. J. D. Wilson's conj. 'death' would, as Maxwell explains, make 'lines 27 and 28 antithetic in the same way as lines 31 to 32'. But Q's line follows so naturally upon *But . . . salute him* as to render such a hypothesis improbable.

31–3. *be resolv'd . . . gives . . . leaves us*] a much debated passage. Some edd. interpret *be resolv'd* as an imperative, but it is surely future tense, as the previous line suggests, and hence means:

Or dead, gives cause to mourn his funeral
And leaves us to our free election,
2. *Lord.* Whose death indeed the strongest in our censure,
And knowing this kingdom is without a head—   35
Like goodly buildings left without a roof
Soon fall to ruin—your noble self,
That best know how to rule and how to reign,
We thus submit unto—our sovereign.
All. Live, noble Helicane!   40
Hel. By honour's cause, forbear your suffrages;
If that you love Prince Pericles, forbear.
Take I your wish, I leap into the seas,
Where's hourly trouble for a minute's ease.
A twelvemonth longer, let me entreat you   45
 † To forbear the absence of your king;
 ⁞

32. gives] *Q5;* giue's *Q.*   33. leaves] *Malone;* leaue *Q.*   34. death indeed] *Q;*
death's indeed *Malone.*   censure,] *Q;* censure: *Malone.*   35. this kingdom
is] *Q;* this kingdom if *Malone;* this: kingdoms *Maxwell.*   39. unto—our]
Alexander; vnto our *Q.*   41. By] *Theobald MS, Alexander;* Try *Q;* For *Dyce.*
46. forbear] *Q;* forbear choice i' *Steevens.*

'will be satisfied'. The emendations
gives for 'give's' and *leaves* for 'leave'
are by analogy with *lives* in l. 31: 'Will
be satisfied that he lives to govern us,
or, if he is dead, that he gives cause ...
and that he leaves us ...'

34–5. *Whose death .   head*] *the
strongest* = the most compelling sup-
position; *censure* = judgment. But like
the previous lines this passage has been
subject to much emendation and
varied interpretation. Q has been retained in this edn, since, as Sisson
shows (II, p. 293), it makes sense. I
interpret: 'Believing in fact his death
as the more likely, and aware as we
consequently are that this kingdom
. . .' Should Malone's 'death's' be
thought correct, Maxwell's 'this:
kingdoms' is an attractive additional
emendation, in line with the style of
much of Act I and Act II. H.F.B.'s conjecture that an 's' dropped out after
indeed, deserves serious consideration,
if only because Q has a comma after
'in deed'. A reading 'in deeds' in the
MS might easily have prompted mis-

correction, the 's' not being recognized as ' 's' for 'is'. In that case, the
miscorrector either took the final 's'
for a comma, or he added the comma
believing the next clause to be paren-
thetic.

41. *By . . . forbear*] again, a difficult
line. Q's 'Try' does not make sense,
even if it is interpreted as meaning
'weigh', for Helicanus is objecting to
his acclamation as sovereign. Most
modern edd. accept Dyce's 'For',
which has the support of II. v. 60, but
By is more plausible on graphic
grounds. Alexander, when adopting
By, was apparently unaware that it
had been suggested two centuries
earlier by Theobald in a MS note in a
copy of Q4.

43. *Take I*] if I should accept.

44. *hourly*] an hour's, literally, but in
the sense not only of long-lasting, but
also of recurrent.

46. *forbear*] memorial corruption: a
recollection from ll. 41–2, betrayed by
disturbance of the verse. The original
is irrecoverable. Satisfactory guesses

If in which time expir'd he not return,
I shall with aged patience bear your yoke.
But if I cannot win you to this love,
Go search like nobles, like noble subjects,   50
And in your search spend your adventurous worth;
Whom if you find and win unto return,
You shall like diamonds sit about his crown.

1. Lord. To wisdom he's a fool that will not yield;
And since Lord Helicane enjoineth us,   55
We with our travels will endeavour it.

Hel. Then you love us, we you, and we'll clasp hands:
When peers thus knit, a kingdom ever stands.   [*Exeunt.*]

[SCENE V.—*Pentapolis.*]

Enter SIMONIDES, *reading of a letter at one door; the Knights meet him.*

1. Knight. Good morrow to the good Simonides.
Sim. Knights, from my daughter this I let you know,

---

56. endeavour it] *Steevens;* endeauour *Q;* endeavour us *Dyce.*   58. S.D.]
Rowe; not in Q.

Scene v

SCENE v] *Malone; not in Q.*   Location] *not in Q; Pentapolis. A room in the palace.*
Malone.   Entry. Simonides] *Malone; the King | Q.*

may be made, but we could never have real reason to feel confident that one of them restored the original reading. Thus Steevens' sweeping attempt to restore both sense and metre must be rejected. Considering the transitive form of *forbear*, the suggestion that its sense here is, as in *Lr.*, II. iv. 107, 'bear, be patient during' is highly improbable. My own guess, for what it is worth, is that the original 'further to bear' was contaminated by the reporter, influenced by the association with ll. 41–2.

57. *Then . . . hands*] perhaps the worst of numerous inferior lines in this scene, many of which should be blam-ed on the collaborating playwright, and only some on the reporter. See Intro., pp. xxxv and liv.

Scene v

SCENE V] In Q, this scene is un-usual for the absence of any palpable major errors. Yet in it, one has reason to suspect memorial contamination by the reporter as much as elsewhere; e.g. in ll. 1–6 and 18–22.

1. *to . . . Simonides*] The parallel greeting of Pericles in l. 24 makes one suspicious of memorial assimilation, and thus textual corruption in either line.

That for this twelvemonth she'll not undertake
A married life.
Her reason to herself is only known,   5
Which from her by no means can I get.
2. Knight. May we not get access to her, my lord?
Sim. Faith, by no means; she has so strictly tied
Her to her chamber that 'tis impossible.
One twelve moons more she'll wear Diana's livery;   10
This by the eye of Cynthia hath she vow'd,
And on her virgin honour will not break it.
3. Knight. Loath to bid farewell, we take our leaves.

                                        [*Exeunt Knights.*]

Sim. So,
They are well dispatch'd; now to my daughter's letter:
She tells me here, she'll wed the stranger knight,   16
Or never more to view nor day nor light.
'Tis well, mistress; your choice agrees with mine;
I like that well: nay, how absolute she's in't,
Not minding whether I dislike or no!   20
Well, I do commend her choice,

4–5. A . . . known] *As Steevens; one line Q.*   6. Which from] *Q;* Which yet from
F3.   7. get] *Q;* have *Maxwell, conj. S. Walker.*   8–9. strictly tied / Her to]
Globe; strictly / Tyed her to *Q;* strictly ty'd her / To *Malone.*   13. S.D.] *Dyce;*
Exit / Q2; not in Q.   14–16. So . . . knight] *As Malone;* dispatcht: / heere, /
Knight *Q.*   21–3. Well . . . it] *As Malone;* longer / comes, / it *Q.*

7. *get access*] 'have access' is, as Maxwell remarks, the more common
phrase, and 'get' may have been recollected from l. 6. Yet the case for emendation is not strong enough.

10. *One twelve moons*] a common
idiom—cf. *Cor.*, iv. i. 55, 'one seven
years' (D.). '*Moons* is appropriate in
connection with Diana' (Maxwell).

11–12. *This . . . it*] I do not think this
statement is to be taken at its face
value, as it is by Kenneth Muir (*N&Q*,
193 (1948), p. 362), who interprets it
as a clue to Thaisa's misfortunes in
Act III. These misfortunes, he argues,
are brought about by Diana, the play's
presiding goddess, who is incensed by
Thaisa's breaking of her vow. In that
case, Diana's role in the play would
parallel Apollo's in *Wint.* But favour-

ably inclined towards Pericles as the
King already is, he is merely inventing
a good excuse for ridding himself of
the other knights and thus of Pericles' possible rivals. See also Intro.,
p. lxxxi.

16–17. *She . . . light*] summarized
from Gower, *C.A.*, 898–903.

17. *to view*] i.e. will view. The con-
struction is odd, but paralleled in
AYL., v. iv. 21–2: 'Keep your word,
Phebe, that you'll marry me, / Or else,
refusing me, to wed this shepherd;'
(Maxwell).

19–21. *nay . . . Well*] The irregular
metre of these lines encourages the
suspicion that *nay* and *Well* are actors'
preluding.

19. *absolute*] positive, decided
(On. 3).

And will no longer have it be delay'd.
Soft, here he comes: I must dissemble it.

Enter PERICLES.

Per. All fortune to the good Simonides!
Sim. To you as much: sir, I am beholding to you   25
For your sweet music this last night. I do
Protest my ears were never better fed
With such delightful pleasing harmony.
Per. It is your grace's pleasure to commend;
Not my desert.
Sim.   Sir, you are music's master.   30
Per. The worst of all her scholars, my good lord.
Sim. Let me ask you one thing:
What do you think of my daughter, sir?
Per. A most virtuous princess.
Sim. And she is fair too, is she not?   35
Per. As a fair day in summer, wondrous fair.
Sim. Sir, my daughter thinks very well of you;
Ay, so well, that you must be her master,
And she will be your scholar: therefore look to it.
Per. I am unworthy for her schoolmaster.   40
Sim. She thinks not so; peruse this writing else.
Per. [*Aside.*] What's here?
A letter that she loves the knight of Tyre!
'Tis the king's subtlety to have my life.—
[*Kneels.*] O, seek not to entrap me, gracious lord,   45
A stranger and distressed gentleman,
That never aim'd so high to love your daughter,

25. much: sir,] *Q; much, sir! Steevens.* 26–7. For . . . fed] *As Malone; night:* /
fedde *Q.* 32–3. Let . . . sir?] *verse Q; prose Camb.* 42. S.D.] *Malone; not in Q.*
42–3. What's . . . Tyre!] *As Malone; one line Q.* 45. S.D. Kneels] *this ed., conj.*
E. Schanzer; not in Q.

25. *beholding*] 'beholden', indebted.
The active pple for the passive pple
(D.). Frequent in Elizabethan drama.
26. *music . . . last night*] See II. iii. 115.
S.D. n.

30. *Not my desert*] Cf. II. iii. 12.

37. *Sir . . . you*] bad verse and generally trite, but not untypical of Acts I
and II.

41. *else*] i.e. if you do not believe me.
Cf. *John*, IV. i. 108, 'see else yourself'
(D.).

45. S.D. Kneels] This S.D. is suggested by Wilkins' account: 'foorthwith prostrating himselfe at the kings
feete, hee desired . . .' (*P.A.*, 49. 25–6)
(E.S.).

47. *to*] as to; see Abbott §281. The

But bent all offices to honour her.

Sim. Thou hast bewitch'd my daughter, and thou art
A villain.

Per.   By the gods, I have not: 50
Never did thought of mine levy offence;
Nor never did my actions yet commence
A deed might gain her love or your displeasure.

Sim. Traitor, thou liest.

Per.   Traitor?

Sim.   Ay, traitor.

Per. Even in his throat—unless it be the king—   55
That calls me traitor, I return the lie.

Sim. [*Aside.*] Now, by the gods, I do applaud his courage.

Per. My actions are as noble as my thoughts,
That never relish'd of a base descent.
I came unto your court for honour's cause,   60
And not to be a rebel to her state;
And he that otherwise accounts of me,
This sword shall prove he's honour's enemy.

Sim. No?
Here comes my daughter, she can witness it.   65

49–50. Thou . . . villain] *As Malone;* daughter, / villaine *Q.*   50–3. By . . .
displeasure] *As Rowe;* thought / actions / loue, / displeasure *Q.*   54. Traitor?]
Q; traitor! *F3.*   57. S.D.[*Malone; not in Q.*   61. her] *Q;* your *Hudson, conj.*
S. Walker.   64–5. No . . . it] *As Malone; one line Q.*

idiomatic omission of *as* is not uncommon in modern English.

48. *bent all offices*] applied my whole
duty; *offices* in the Latin sense, as frequently in Shakespeare.

49. *Thou hast bewitch'd my daughter*]
Cf. *MND.,* I. i. 27 and *Oth.,* I. ii.
62–3 and I. iii. 59–64. See also n. to
l. 65 below.

51. *levy*] 'apparently misused for
level = aim' (On.); possibly by the
reporter. See *O.E.D. levy* 7, where two
other instances of *levy* for 'level' are
cited.

53. *deed might*] deed that might; cf.
I. i. 15n.

55–6. *Even . . . lie*] a common phrase
in Elizabethan drama; cf. *Ham.,* II. ii.
568–9, 'gives me the lie i' th' throat As

deep as to the lungs' (D.), *Shr.,* IV. iii.
129, and *Tw. N.,* III. iv. 149.

59. *relish'd*] had a trace of; cf. *Ham.,*
III. i. 119.

61. *her state*] *state* = majesty, power.
S. Walker's 'your' finds some support
in Wilkins' paraphrase in *P.A.,* 50.
17–9: 'affirming, that he came into his
court in search of honour, and not to be
a rebell to *his* State' (my italics). Yet
Q her can be defended as referring back
to *honour,* which was commonly per-
sonified as a goddess. Pericles' honour
has been slurred by the King's accusa-
tion, and his rebuttal throughout is a
defence of his honour.

65. *Here . . . it*] This line was almost
certainly derived by the playwright
from *Oth.,* I. iii. 170, 'Here comes the

Enter THAISA.

Per. Then, as you are as virtuous as fair,
        Resolve your angry father, if my tongue
        Did e'er solicit, or my hand subscribe
        To any syllable that made love to you.
Thai. Why, sir, say if you had, who takes offence   70
        At that would make me glad?
Sim. Yea, mistress, are you so peremptory?
        Aside. I am glad on't with all my heart.—
        I'll tame you, I'll bring you in subjection.
        Will you, not having my consent,   75
        Bestow your love and your affections
        Upon a stranger? *Aside.* who, for aught I know,
        May be (nor can I think the contrary)
        As great in blood as I myself.—
        Therefore hear you, mistress: either frame   80
        Your will to mine; and you, sir, hear you:
        Either be rul'd by me, or I'll make you—
        Man and wife.
        Nay, come, your hands and lips must seal it too;
        And being join'd, I'll thus your hopes destroy,   85
        And for further grief,—God give you joy!

70-1. offence? / glad] *Q*; had, / glad *Malone.* 73, 77. S.D. *Aside*] *Q* (*after ll.* 74, 78). 75. you, not] *Q4*; you not, *Q.* 79-83. As . . . wife] *As Q*; There-fore / mine, / by me, / wife *conj. Elze.* 82. I'll] *Q*; I will *Steevens.*   you—] *Q4*; you, *Q.* 84-7. Nay . . . pleas'd] *As Malone*; hands, / ioynd, / griefe: / pleased *Q.* 86. further] *Q*; a further *Malone.*

lady; let her witness it'. See also l. 49n. above.

    67. *Resolve*] assure, inform.

    70-1. *Why . . . glad*] In the original *had* and *glad* may have formed a rhyme, as Malone's rearrangement suggests. In that case, there was possibly some memorial loss. One cannot be sure.

    71. *that would*] that which would; cf. I. i. 15n. and l. 53 above.

    72. *peremptory*] resolved, determined.

    79-83. *As . . . wife*] But for the short l. 83, necessary for the lines following it, Q's lineation has been retained. Elze's rearrangement (in *Englische*

Studien IX (1886), 283) is attractive in more than one way, eliminating as it does the short makeshift line. But the great emphasis of and strong pauses in the King's speech point against the resulting heavy accentuation in ll. 80-1.

    86. *further*] so Q. Malone's 'a fur-ther', for the sake of regularizing the metre, is to be distrusted, though most edd. have followed him. The long pause after *grief* replaces, as often in Shakespeare, a syllable in the five-foot line. For this principle, see Preface to *The Cambridge Shakespeare*, section D.

What, are you both pleas'd?

Thai.   Yes, if you love me, sir.

Per. Even as my life my blood that fosters it.

Sim. What, are you both agreed?

Both. Yes, if't please your majesty.   90

Sim. It pleaseth me so well, that I will see you wed;

And then, with what haste you can, get you to bed.

Exeunt.

88. my blood] *Q;* or bloud *Q4.*

88. *my blood*] Many nineteenth-century edd. have followed Q4's 'or', but the sense is clearly: 'Even as my life loves the blood which fosters it' (D.).

[ACT III]

Enter GOWER.

Now sleep y-slacked hath the rout;
No din but snores the house about,
Made louder by the o'er-fed breast
Of this most pompous marriage-feast.
The cat, with eyne of burning coal, 5
Now couches 'fore the mouse's hole;
And crickets at the oven's mouth
Sing the blither for their drouth.
Hymen hath brought the bride to bed,
Where by the loss of maidenhead 10
A babe is moulded. Be attent,

ACT III

ACT III] *Malone; not in* Q. 1. y-slacked] Q; y-slaked Q2. 2. the house about] *Malone;* about the house Q. 6. 'fore] *Steevens, conj. Malone;* from Q. 7. crickets] *Rowe (iii);* Cricket Q. 7–8. at the oven's mouth / Sing] *Maxwell;* sing at the Ouens mouth, / Are Q; sing at . . . mouth, / As *Steevens;* sing at . . . mouth, / E'er *Dyce.* 10. Where by] Q2; Whereby Q.

ACT III] In F3, Act III starts at what is now Act III, Scene iii.

1–14. *Now . . . speech*] Cf. in mood and style *MND.*, v. i. 360 ff. (Hastings). *snores . . . house . . . mouse* are common to both passages, as is the occasion of the marriage-feast, the bridal bed, and the thought of 'issue there create' (v. i. 394) or *moulded.* The cluster of images and other associations the two passages have in common, and the freer, more varied and syncopated rhythm of this chorus, point to Shakespeare as the author. See Intro., pp. lv–lvi.

1. *y-slacked*] reduced to inactivity. Probably Q2 'yslaked' is merely an old variant spelling (see *O.E.D. slake*). But as in mod. English 'slack' and 'slake' have distinct meanings, it is not right to follow Q2, as many edd. have done.

rout] company, as in *Shr.*, III. ii. 177, 'the rout is coming'; and in Gower, *C.A.*, 571–2: 'Upon a time with his route / This lord to pleie goth him oute'; without the derogatory connotation, frequent in Shakespeare, as in 'the common rout'.

4. *pompous*] magnificent.

5. *eyne*] eyes; an archaic plural frequent in Shakespeare, e.g. *Lucr.*, 1229.

6. *'fore*] Q 'from' has been defended as meaning 'slightly away from', but *O.E.D.* lends no support to such an interpretation.

7. *crickets*] Cf. *Cymb.*, II. ii. 11.

7–8. *at . . . Sing*] Maxwell, whose emendation has been adopted, assumes that 'the reporter anticipated "sing" and so had to improvise the next line'.

75

> And time that is so briefly spent
> With your fine fancies quaintly eche;
> What's dumb in show I'll plain with speech.

[DUMB SHOW]

Enter PERICLES *and* SIMONIDES *at one door, with Attendants; a Messenger meets them, kneels, and gives* PERICLES *a letter;* PERICLES *shows it* SIMONIDES; *the Lords kneel to him. Then enter* THAISA *with child, with* LYCHORIDA, *a nurse; the King shows her the letter; she rejoices; she and* PERICLES *take leave of her father, and depart [with* LYCHORIDA *and their Attendants. Then exeunt* SIMONIDES *and the rest].*

> By many a dern and painful perch   15
> Of Pericles the careful search,
> By the four opposing coigns
> Which the world together joins,
> Is made with all due diligence
> That horse and sail and high expense   20
> Can stead the quest. At last from Tyre,
> Fame answering the most strange inquire,
> To th' court of King Simonides
> Are letters brought, the tenour these:
> Antiochus and his daughter dead,   25

---

13. eche] *Malone;* each *Q.*   14. dumb] *Q;* dark *Maxwell, conj. Daniel.*   14. *Dumb Show*] *Q5;* not in *Q.*   14. S.D. 5–7. with . . . rest] *Dyce;* not in *Q.*   17. coigns] *Rowe;* Crignes *Q.*   21. quest. At] *Malone;* quest; at *Rowe (iii);* quest at *Q.*   22. strange] *Q;* strong *Malone.*

---

13. *quaintly*] cleverly, skilfully, as in *Gent.,* III. i. 117, 'a ladder quaintly made of cords' (On.).

eche] supplement, augment; an old spelling of 'eke'; cf. *H5,* III. Ch. 35, 'And eche out our performance with your mind'.

14. *What's . . . speech*] This seems a natural way of introducing a dumb show. There is no need for Daniel's emendation.

plain] explain.

15. *dern*] dark, wild, drear; cf. *Lr.,* III. vii. 63, 'that dern time'.

painful] laborious, troublesome (*O.E.D.*3).

perch] measure of land; a square perch is 30¼ sq. yards.

17. *coigns*] corners, from French 'coin'. Cf. *Cor.,* v. iv. 1, 'coign a' th' Capitol'. For the image, cf. Donne, *Holy Sonnets,* VII. 1–2, 'At the round earths imagin'd corners, blow / Your trumpets, Angells...'

21. *stead*] assist, aid.

22. *Fame . . . inquire*] The problematical word in this line is *strange,* which probably means 'unfamiliar, outlandish'. A free paraphrase of the line would be: 'Rumour responding to this enquiry in distant (unfamiliar) regions'.

The men of Tyrus on the head
Of Helicanus would set on
The crown of Tyre, but he will none;
The mutiny he there hastes t'appease;
Says to 'em, if King Pericles   30
Come not home in twice six moons,
He, obedient to their dooms,
Will take the crown. The sum of this,
Brought hither to Pentapolis,
Y-ravished the regions round,   35
And every one with claps can sound,
"Our heir-apparent is a king!
Who dream'd, who thought of such a thing?"
Brief, he must hence depart to Tyre.
His queen with child makes her desire—   40
Which who shall cross?—along to go.
Omit we all their dole and woe.
Lychorida, her nurse, she takes,
And so to sea. Their vessel shakes
On Neptune's billow; half the flood   45
Hath their keel cut; but fortune's mood
Varies again; the grisled north
Disgorges such a tempest forth,
That, as a duck for life that dives,
So up and down the poor ship drives.   50
The lady shrieks and well-a-near

29. appease] *Steevens;* oppresse *Q.*   35. Y-ravished] *Theobald MS, Steevens;*
Iranyshed *Q;* Irony shed *Q2–6.*   36. can] *Q;* 'gan *Malone.*   41. cross?—]
Steevens; crosse *Q.*   46. fortune's mood] *Theobald MS, Malone;* fortune mou'd
Q.   47. grisled] *Q;* grislee *Q2–6;* grisly *F3.*

29. *he . . . t'appease*] Steevens' emendation, as Collier stated, is supported
by *P.A.*, 55. 8–9, 'appeased the stub-
borne mutiny of the *Tyrians*'. It provides a better rhyme for *Pericles* and,
more important, makes better sense.

32. *dooms*] judgments.

35. *Y-ravished*] enraptured; a rather
clumsy attempt at archaism, since the
prefix *y-*, reserved for past pples, is
here applied to the past ind. Yet
Steevens' emendation seems certain.
One can imagine the bewildered com-

positor trying to make sense of this
unusual term.

36. *can*] began; a M.E. variant of
'gan'.

sound] proclaim, declare.

39. *Brief*] in short (adverb).

42. *dole*] grief, dolour.

46. *fortune's mood*] The emendation
provides an acceptable rhyme for
flood.

47. *grisled*] horrible, grisly; an old
form.

51. *well-a-near*] alas; an obsolete

Does fall in travail with her fear;
And what ensues in this fell storm
Shall for itself itself perform.
I nill relate, action may   55
Conveniently the rest convey;
Which might not what by me is told.
In your imagination hold
This stage the ship, upon whose deck
The sea-tost Pericles appears to speak.   [*Exit.*]   60

[SCENE I.]

Enter PERICLES, *on shipboard.*

Per. The god of this great vast, rebuke these surges,

57. not what . . . told.] *Malone;* not? what . . . told, *Q.*   58–9. hold / This]
Malone; hold: / This *Q.*   60. sea-tost] *Rowe subst., Malone;* seas tost *Q.*
Pericles] *Q; prince Steevens.*   60. S.D.] *Q5 (Exit Gower) ; not in Q.*

Scene 1
SCENE I] *Malone; not in Q.*   Entry. *on*] *Q4; a* / *Q.*   1. The] *Q; Thou Rowe.*

north-country expression, probably
altered from 'well-a-way'. Skeat and
Mayhew in *A Glossary of Tudor and
Stuart Words* list an example from
Look About You (Hazlitt's *Dodsley,* VII,
p. 397). Another instance is found in
J.D.'s *The Knave of Graine* (1640), sig.
G2.

55. *nill*] will not (M.E.).

57. *Which . . . told*] an awkward-
sounding line, meaning 'which might
not conveniently convey what has
been told by me in a few lines'.

60. *Pericles*] Steevens' 'prince' would
reduce the line to a regular octo-
syllabic one. Possibly the copy for Q
merely read 'P.' or 'Pr.', leaving the
compositor to guess. Yet decasyllabic
lines occur elsewhere in the Gower
choruses. The longer line may here
mark the conclusion of the chorus; cf.
I. Ch. 41–2.

Scene 1
Entry] Cf. *P.A.,* 58. 20–1, 'her

princely husband being aboue the
hatches'.

1–14. *The . . . Lychorida*] It is generally agreed that this speech represents
a turning-point in the play from
mediocre language to dramatic poetry
with a sustained Shakespearean ring.
And yet the large number of emendations that have been made in its text
reflect the degree of apparent corruption, by reporter or perhaps other
agencies, during its transmission. Suspect also are the repeated exclamations
'oh', three times in this speech and
several times after in this scene, though
they may be said to fit the mood.

1. *The . . . surges*] Edd. have noted
two echoes to Scripture: (i) *Psalm* civ.
6–7, 'The waters stood above the
mountains;—at thy rebuke they fled;
at the voice of thy thunder they hasted
away' (Malone); (ii) *Matthew,* viii. 26,
'rebuked the winds and the sea' (Yale).
For *the* with the vocative, see Franz
§261; Maxwell cites *1H4,* I. ii. 152,

Which wash both heaven and hell; and thou that hast
Upon the winds command, bind them in brass,
Having call'd them from the deep! O, still
Thy deaf'ning, dreadful thunders; gently quench   5
Thy nimble sulphurous flashes! O, how, Lychorida,
How does my queen? Thou stormest venomously;
Wilt thou spit all thyself? The seaman's whistle
Is as a whisper in the ears of death,
Unheard. Lychorida!—Lucina, O   10
Divinest patroness, and midwife gentle
To those that cry by night, convey thy deity
Aboard our dancing boat; make swift the pangs
Of my queen's travails! Now, Lychorida!

Enter LYCHORIDA[, *with an infant*].

3–4. brass, . . . deep! O] *Malone;* Brasse; . . . deepe, ô *Q.*   7. Thou stormest]
Dyce; then storme *Q;* Thou storm, *Malone.*   8. spit] *Q* (speat).   10. Unheard. Lychorida!] *Malone;* Vnheard *Lychorida? Q.*   O] *Steevens;* oh! *Q.*
11. patroness] *Q4;* patrionesse *Q.*   midwife] *Steevens;* my wife *Q.*   14. S.D.
with an infant] *Steevens; not in* Q.

'Farewell, the latter spring!', where,
as in the present passage, edd. have
wrongly emended *the* to 'thou'. *vast =*
desolate expanse; cf. *Wint.*, I. i. 27,
'shook hands, as over a vast', where the
expression is also applied to the sea.

2–3. *thou . . . brass*] Cf. *2H6*, III. ii. 89,
'he that loos'd them forth their brazen
caves' (D.). *thou* refers to Aeolus, the
god of the winds. As a possible source,
P. Simpson (*Eliz. Drama*, 1955, p. 43)
suggests Virgil, *Aeneid*, I. 52–4:

hic vasto rex Aeolus antro
luctantis ventos tempestatesque
        sonoras
imperio premit ac vinclis et
        carcere frenat.

3–4. *brass, . . . deep!*] Malone's
changes in the punctuation are necessary, for *Having . . . deep* surely refers to
the *winds*, not the *thunders*.

6. *nimble sulphurous*] *sulphurous =*
lightning; cf. *Tp.*, I. ii. 203–4, 'the fire
and cracks / Of sulphurous roaring',
and *Lr.*, II. iv. 163, 'nimble lightnings',
and IV. vii. 34–5, 'the most terrible and

nimble stroke / Of quick, cross lightning' (D.).

7. *Thou stormest*] Q 'then storme' is
certainly corrupt. Dyce's emendation
is attractive on both literary and
metrical grounds and has been followed by most edd., but cannot be regarded as certain. The graphic error 'then'
for *thou* is frequent in Elizabethan
texts.

8. *spit*] Q 'speat' is an obsolete variant spelling of *spit*. But considering
l. 44, the true reading may possibly
be 'split'.

10–14. *Lucina . . . travails*] Malone
states that this passage may have been
suggested to Shakespeare by Terence,
in whose plays women in childbirth
are twice heard to pray: 'Iuno Lucina,
fer opem, serva me, obsecro' (*Andria*,
l. 473, and *Adelphoe*, l. 487). But classical lore of this kind was common pro-
perty in the Renaissance. More probably, the goddess was put into Shakespeare's mind by Twine's name for
Thaisa, which is also Lucina.

Lyc. Here is a thing too young for such a place,   15
      Who, if it had conceit, would die, as I
      Am like to do. Take in your arms this piece
      Of your dead queen.

Per.   How? how, Lychorida?

Lyc. Patience, good sir; do not assist the storm.
      Here's all that is left living of your queen,   20
      A little daughter: for the sake of it,
      Be manly, and take comfort.

Per.   O you gods!
      Why do you make us love your goodly gifts,
      And snatch them straight away? We here below
      Recall not what we give, and therein may   25
      Use honour with you.

Lyc.   Patience, good sir,
      Even for this charge.

Per.   Now, mild may be thy life!
      For a more blusterous birth had never babe;
      Quiet and gentle thy conditions! for
      Thou art the rudeliest welcome to this world   30
      That e'er was prince's child. Happy what follows!

16–18. Who ... Lychorida] *As Malone;* doe: / Queene. / Lychorida / *Q.*   26. Use]
Q; Vie *Steevens, conj. Mason.*   26–7. Use ... life] *As Malone;* you. / charge. /
life *Q.*   30. welcome] *Q;* welcom'd *Malone.*   31. e'er] *Q* (euer).   prince's]
F4; Princes *Q;* princess' *Maxwell, conj. Sykes.*

16–18. *Who ... queen*] Most modern
edd. have accepted Malone's lineation, though it splits the good line
'Take ... queen'.

16. *conceit*] understanding, mental
capacity.

19. *do ... storm*] Cf. *Tp.,* i. i. 14, 'you
do assist the storm' (Malone). Any
storm in the microcosm, the mind of
man, might arouse further the storm of
the macrocosm, the world at large, as
in *Lr.,* iii. The sympathetic analogy
between the two worlds was part of the
Elizabethan world picture.

26. *Use honour*] 'Make use of honour
with you, that is, use it in remonstrance
against the gods' (Porter and Clark).
Many edd., however, follow Mason,
who suggested that the compositor
misread *use* for 'vie'. For such an error,

Maxwell cites a parallel from H.
Lawes, *Ayres and Dialogues,* 1635, p. 15
(see *Library,* 5, Ser. viii (1953), 99).
Yet Q's reading is sufficiently good
Elizabethan English to justify reten-
tion.

27. *Even ... charge*] 'if only for the
sake of the babe left to your care' (D.).

29. *conditions*] 'mode of life' (*O.E.D.*
9).

30. *welcome*] The text is confirmed by
P.A., 59. 4–5, 'Thou arte as rudely
welcome to the worlde ...'

31. *prince's*] simply: 'royal'. Sykes
and Maxwell interpret 'princess' ', in
accord with *P.A.,* 59. 5 and with the
fairly common Elizabethan spelling of
'princess' as 'princes'. Yet the Elizabethan 'prince' was applied to sove-
reigns of both genders (see *O.E.D.* 1b).

Thou hast as chiding a nativity
As fire, air, water, earth, and heaven can make,
To herald thee from the womb. [Poor inch of nature!]
Even at the first thy loss is more than can   35
Thy portage quit, with all thou canst find here.
Now the good gods throw their best eyes upon't!

Enter two Sailors.

1. Sail. What courage, sir? God save you!
Per. Courage enough: I do not fear the flaw;
It hath done to me the worst. Yet for the love   40
Of this poor infant, this fresh-new seafarer,
I would it would be quiet.
1. Sail. Slack the bolins there! Thou wilt not, wilt thou?
Blow, and split thyself.

---

34. [Poor inch of nature!]] *this ed., conj. Collier; not in* Q.   41. fresh-new]
hyphenated Malone; unhyphenated Q.   43–53. Slack . . . straight] *prose Malone;
verse* Q.   43. Slack] *corrected* Q (Slacke); Slake *uncorrected* Q, Q2.

32. *chiding*] noisy, brawling.

34. *[Poor inch of nature]*] Many edd. have echoed Collier's belief that these words from Wilkins' report of the speech in *P.A.,* 59. 4 ff. are part of the original text of the play. They were incorporated in the play's production by the Birmingham Repertory Theatre in 1954, but they are here printed for the first time in the text. Whether the words are those of Shakespeare or some other author is a moot point.

36. *portage . . . here*] *portage* has puzzled most edd. Malone and On. interpret 'port-dues', without evidence. It certainly does not mean 'porthole', as in *H5*, III. i. 10, the only other instance of the word's use in Shakespeare. Possibly it is a figurative application of the sense listed in *O.E.D.*4, 'mariner's venture, in the form of freight or cargo, which he was entitled to put on board, if he took part in the common adventure and did not receive wages'; hence, fig. 'what a person starts with on life's voyage' (Maxwell). But it seems rather to be a

figurative use of the word's most common significance, 'carriage': i.e. during her entire voyage or carriage through life, Marina will hardly be able to make up for her initial loss (the death of her mother). *quit* = compensate for, requite.

38. S.H. 1. Sail.] probably the one in charge of the ship. In Q, the speechheadings of the mariners are left extremely vague, for which the reporter may be responsible. As Leo Kirschbaum (quoted by Maxwell) has pointed out, the 2nd Sailor's speeches, ll. 71 ff., also fit the ship's master.

39. *flaw*] Dyce (*Glossary*) cites Smith's *Sea-Grammar,* 1627, p. 46: 'A flaw of wind is a gust, which is very violent upon a sudden, but quickly endeth'.

43. *Slack*] changed by the presscorrector from 'Slake'. See Intro., p. xxxviii.

bolins] early form of 'bow-lines' = rope from weather-side of square sail to bow (*O.E.D.*).

43–4. *Thou . . . thyself*] For this apostrophe of the storm, Malone cites the

2. Sail. But sea-room, and the brine and cloudy billow   45
    kiss the moon, I care not.
1. Sail. Sir, your queen must overboard; the sea works
    high, the wind is loud, and will not lie till the ship be
    clear'd of the dead.
Per. That's your superstition.   50
1. Sail. Pardon us, sir; with us at sea it hath been still
    observ'd; and we are strong in custom. Therefore
    briefly yield 'er, for she must overboard straight.
Per. As you think meet. Most wretched queen!
Lyc. Here she lies, sir.   55
Per. A terrible childbed hast thou had, my dear;
    No light, no fire: th'unfriendly elements
    Forgot thee utterly; nor have I time
    To give thee hallow'd to thy grave, but straight
    Must cast thee, scarcely coffin'd, in the ooze;   60

---

52. custom] *Singer, conj. Boswell;* easterne *Q;* earnest *Steevens, conj. Mason;* , astern *Knight.*   53. for . . . straight] *As Malone; after* meet *in l. 55 Q.*   59. give] *Q;* bring *Q2.*   60. the ooze] *Steevens;* oare *Q.*

---

parallel in *Tp.*, I. i. 7. 'Blow till thou burst thy wind, if room enough', which is all the more remarkable considering the words *But sea-room* in the following line. It suggests a similar process of association in Shakespeare's mind while at work on the storm scenes in the two plays.

45. *and*] if.

cloudy billow] the image suggests either a cloud-like foam, or that the waves rise as high as the clouds.

47–8. *works high*] runs high, rages (*O.E.D.*34). Cf. *Oth.*, II. i. 2, 'a high-wrought flood', and Drayton, *Poliolbion*, XXII. 1082 (ed. 1622, p. 51), 'the high-working sea' (Craig quoted by D.).

48. *lie*] subside.

50. *superstition*] This belief is often referred to in classical and Elizabethan literature. See the discussion in *N&Q*, 9 Ser. VI (1900), 246–7, and VII (1901), 75–6. (D.).

51–2. *still observ'd*] perhaps not 'always complied with', as one would expect, but 'regularly noted by obser-

vation', for see *P.A.*, 60. 13–14, 'we that by long practise haue tried the proof of it' (Maxwell).

52. *strong*] zealous, unswerving.

custom] Q 'easterne' does not make sense (see also IV. i. 51, *the wind was north*), and looks like a graphic error by the compositor. Wilkins' free account of the master's speech in *P.A.*, 60. 5–7 gives some support to Boswell's emendation: 'But the Maister going on, tolde him, that by long experience they had tried, that a shippe may not abide to carry a dead carcasse, . . .'

53. *briefly*] immediately.

for . . . straight] The misplacement of this phrase in Q is evidence of a crowded MS.

55. *Here . . . lies*] In early productions of the play, Lychorida probably took Pericles to the inner stage or recess at these words.

60. *in the ooze*] For this remarkable emendation, Steevens cites *Tp.*, III. iii. 100, 'my son i'th'ooze is bedded'. Q's compositor misread *z* as *r*, and omitted *the*. Also cf. *Tp.*, v. i. 151.

Where, for a monument upon thy bones,
And e'er-remaining lamps, the belching whale
And humming water must o'erwhelm thy corpse,
Lying with simple shells. O Lychorida,
Bid Nestor bring me spices, ink and paper,   65
My casket and my jewels; and bid Nicander
Bring me the satin coffer; lay the babe
Upon the pillow; hie thee, whiles I say
A priestly farewell to her: suddenly, woman.

                                    [*Exit Lychorida.*]

2. Sail. Sir, we have a chest beneath the hatches, caulked   70
    and bitumed ready.
Per. I thank thee. Mariner, say what coast is this?
2. Sail. We are near Tharsus.
Per. Thither, gentle mariner,
    Alter thy course from Tyre. When canst thou reach it?
2. Sail. By break of day, if the wind cease.   76
Per. O, make for Tharsus!

---

62. And e'er—] *Globe;* The ayre *Q;* And aye— *Steevens, conj. Malone.*   64.
O] *Q; not in Steevens.*   65. paper] *Q2;* Taper *Q.*   67. coffer] *Malone;*
Coffin *Q.*   69. S.D.] *Malone; not in Q.*   70. chest] *Q* (Chist).   70–
1. Sir . . . ready] *prose Malone;* hatches, / ready *Q.*   75. from] *Maxwell,
conj. Collier;* for *Q.*

---

61. *for*] in place of.

62. *e'er-remaining lamps*] lamps ever
kept alight. An allusion to the Roman
custom of placing lighted lamps in
sepulchres.   Absent-mindedly, Q's
compositor spelt *e'er* as 'ayre'. Most
edd. have adopted Steevens' 'aye-
remaining', but Fleay notes that
Shakespeare has no compounds with
'aye-', but several with 'ever-' (*New
Sh. Soc. Transactions*, 1874, p. 238; cited
by Maxwell). (See p. 188.)

belching whale] Cf. *Troil.*, v. v. 23
(Malone).

64. *O*] perhaps to be omitted, as
Steevens suggested. Interjections of
this kind are a feature of reported
texts.

65. *paper*] Q 'Taper' may have been
suggested by *lamps* in l. 62. Cf. Heywood, *If you know not me*, Q 1605, sig.
E3, 'inke and paper'.

67. *coffer*] confirmed by III. iv. 2 and,
as Maxwell noted, by Gower, 1088 ff.
A satin *coffer* is anyhow more likely
than a 'satin coffin'. Q's compositor
may have been influenced by *coffin'd* in
l. 60. The coffin for Thaisa is surely the
chest referred to in l. 70. Nevertheless,
Q 'coffin' is possible for, as Knight
has shown, 'coffin' and 'coffer' were
synonyms as late as 1600.

69. *suddenly*] immediately.

71. *bitumed*] made watertight with
bitumen. For the Latinate form, see
Intro., p. xvii.

75. *from*] Q 'for' is defensible,
as Malone realized, paraphrasing:
'Change thy course which is now *for*
Tyre, and go to Tharsus'. Yet such a
reading would be excessively awkward, especially on the stage. Wilkins
moreover has 'alter the course *from*
Tyre' (*P.A.*, 61. 14).

There will I visit Cleon, for the babe
Cannot hold out to Tyrus; there I'll leave it
At careful nursing. Go thy ways, good mariner;   80
I'll bring the body presently   *Exeunt.*

SCENE II.—*Ephesus. A Room in Cerimon's House.*

Enter Lord CERIMON, *with a Servant [and another Poor Man,
both storm-beaten].*

Cer. Philemon, ho!

81. S.D.] *Rowe; Exit | Q.*

Scene II

SCENE II] *Malone; not in Q.*   Location] *not in Q; Ephesus. A room in Cerimon's
house. Malone.*   Entry. *and . . . storm-beaten*] *this ed.; not in Q; and some Persons
who have been shipwrecked | Malone.*

79. *Tyrus*] For Elizabethan literature, there is nothing unusual in this
use of the Latinized form only five
lines after the more regular 'Tyre'.

80. *Go thy ways*] go on your way.

Scene II

Entry—10. S.D. Exeunt . . . Poor
Man] Malone realized that the S.D.s
in Q are quite incomplete, but his own,
followed by most edd. since, misinter-
pret the episode. As Q's entry does not
account for the 'poor men' in l. 3, edd.
since Malone have expanded the S.D.,
judging the Servant to be one of Cerimon's men, and adding 'shipwrecked
persons'. But in that case, why should
Cerimon have to call especially for
Philemon? A better solution is to take
the *Servant* of Q's entry to be one of the
'poor men' given a speaking part in
ll. 5–6. Cerimon in l. 7 refers to his
'master', and far from enjoying the
protection of Cerimon's house, the
Servant has evidently experienced the
brunt of the storm.

This, however, he did probably
near by on land, and not in a ship, as
Malone's stage-direction would assume. Neither the play's text nor

Wilkins' account of the same episode
gives the slightest support to the view
that the men receiving help from
Cerimon are from anywhere else but
his own country.

That the Servant is not the only
'poor' man on the stage is made clear
by the words *these poor men* (*poor* obviously referring to their plight rather
than their economic status), as well as
by the fact that the last sentence of
Cerimon's third speech must be
directed at another person than the
Servant. According to the traditional
interpretation this sentence is addressed to Philemon, Cerimon's aid. Yet
after ll. 3–4, Philemon must be expected to be busy off-stage preparing fire
and meat. They can, therefore, only be
intended for another of the *poor* men,
who does not, like the Servant, require
help for his dying master, but medicine
for himself. This interpretation is supported by Wilkins: 'This Lord *Cerimon*
. . . being this morning in conference
with some that came to him both for
helpe for themselves, and reliefe for
others . . .' (*P.A.*, 62. 17–22). And it is
consistent with what must obviously
be the main dramatic purposes of the

Enter PHILEMON.

Phil. Doth my lord call?

Cer. Get fire and meat for these poor men;
            'T has been a turbulent and stormy night.

                                        [*Exit Philemon.*]

Serv. I have been in many; but such a night as this,   5
            Till now, I ne'er endur'd.

Cer. Your master will be dead ere you return;
            There's nothing can be minister'd to nature
            That can recover him. [*To Poor Man*] Give this to
                the 'pothecary
            And tell me how it works. [*Exeunt Servant and Poor Man.*]

Enter two Gentlemen.

1. Gent. Good morrow.   11

2. Gent. Good morrow to your lordship.

Cer. Gentlemen, why do you stir so early?

1. Gent. Sir,
                Our lodgings, standing bleak upon the sea,   15
                Shook as th'earth did quake. The very principals
                Did seem to rend and all to topple. Pure

---

4. S.D. *Exit Philemon*] *this ed.; not in Q.*   6. ne'er] *Q* (neare).   9. S.D. *To Poor Man*] *this ed., conj. H.F.B.; not in Q*; To Philemon | *Malone.*   10. S.D. *Exeunt . . . Man*] *this ed.; not in Q*; Exeunt all but Cerimon | *Malone.*   13. Gentlemen . . . early*] one line Q;* Gentlemen / . . . early *Steevens.*   14–15. Sir . . . sea] *As Steevens; one line Q.*   16–18. Shook . . . house] *this ed.;* quake: / topple: / house *Q;* quake; / rend, / fear / house *Malone.*   17. all to topple] *Q;* all-to topple *Singer* (ii); all to-topple *Dyce.*

---

opening of this scene; namely to establish this scene as sequel to the previous one—storm and morning after the storm—and to establish Cerimon's benevolence as well as prepare for his skill as a physician in resuscitating Thaisa. He shows his medical skill by his prognosis that one servant's master will die before his return—even by report the signs of death are intelligible to him—and also by his prescription to the second man, who can be helped (H.F.B. in part).

5–6. *but . . . endur'd*] Malone quotes *Mac.*, II. iv. 1–4, *Lr.*, III. ii. 45–8, and

Cæs., I. iii. 5–10, where experiences of severe storms are similarly described.

6. *ne'er*] See I. iv. 105n.

9. *'pothecary*] aphetic form of 'apothecary'.

16–18. *Shook . . . house*] Q's lineation is manifestly wrong. Most edd. follow Malone's arrangement, which includes two very short lines, 'Shook . . . quake' and 'Made . . . house'. The new arrangement is more regular.

16. *as*] as if.

principals] principal rafters of a house, corner-posts.

17. *all to topple*] To hyphenate *to* and

Surprise and fear made me to quit the house.
2. *Gent.* That is the cause we trouble you so early;
　　'Tis not our husbandry.
Cer.　　　　　　　　　O, you say well.　　　　　　20
1. Gent. But I much marvel that your lordship, having
　　Rich tire about you, should at these early hours
　　Shake off the golden slumber of repose.
　　'Tis most strange,
　　Nature should be so conversant with pain,　　　　25
　　Being thereto not compell'd.
Cer.　　　　　　　　　　I hold it ever,
　　Virtue and cunning were endowments greater
　　Than nobleness and riches; careless heirs
　　May the two latter darken and expend,
　　But immortality attends the former,　　　　　　30
　　Making a man a god. 'Tis known I ever
　　Have studied physic, through which secret art,

21–4. But . . . strange] *As Malone;* Lordship, / howers, / strange *Q.*　　26–41. I
. . . bags] *As Malone;* Cunning, / Riches; / expend; / former, / god: / Physicke: /
Authorities, / famyliar, / dwels / of the / cures; / delight / or / Bagges *Q.*　　26.
hold] *Q;* held *Theobald MS, Malone.*

---

topple, as Dyce does, would be to interpret *to* as an intensive prefix. Singer
hyphenates *all-to,* to mean 'altogether'.
But more probably the expression
simply means '(seem'd) quite to
topple', rendering such changes unnecessary (see Abbott §28); the alternative interpretation, 'everything
(seem'd) to topple' is also possible.

Pure] sheer.

20. *husbandry*] zeal for work (which
makes for early rising).

21–2. *having . . . you*] *tire* = equip-
ment, outfit (*O.E.D.*1); perhaps an
aphetic form of 'attire'. At any rate,
the term should be understood in a
broad sense, 'luxury', and not narrowly as 'bed-furniture', as On. defines it.

23. *Shake . . . repose*] Cf. *Tp.,* i. ii. 308–
9 (Henry H. Wolff, privately).

24. *'Tis most strange*] Such short lines
are sometimes encountered in good
Shakespearean texts, yet something
may well be missing here.

25. *pain*] trouble.

26–41. *I . . . bags*] Q's lineation is
chaotic. Malone's arrangement is the
best solution possible, but the original
is probably beyond restoration. See
also below, ll. 38–9n.

26. *hold it ever*] have always held.
Many edd. accept Malone's 'held',
which agrees with 'were'. But for the
use of the present tense with temporal
adverb for an action beginning in the
past and continuing in the present, see
Abbott §346, who cites *Ham.,* iii. i. 91,
'How does your honour for this many
a day?'

27–8. *Virtue . . . riches*] a commonplace idea, which the dramatist might
have met with in Boethius or in Mon-
taigne, *Essais,* iii. 73. *cunning* = skill.

28. *nobleness*] nobility, i.e. social
rank.

29. *darken*] sully the gloss of. Cf.
Ant., i. iv. 11, 'Evils enow to darken all
his goodness'(D.).

expend] Wilkins has 'dispend' (*P.A.,*
62. 7), which may echo the true text.

By turning o'er authorities, I have,
Together with my practice, made familiar
To me and to my aid the blest infusions   35
That dwells in vegetives, in metals, stones;
And can speak of the disturbances that
Nature works, and of her cures; which doth give me
A more content in course of true delight
Than to be thirsty after tottering honour,   40
Or tie my treasure up in silken bags,
To please the fool and death.

36. dwells] *Q;* dwell *F4.*   37. And can] *Q;* And I can *Malone.*   38.
doth give] *Q;* gives *Theobald MS, Malone.*   41. treasure] *Steevens;* pleasure *Q.*

35. *my aid*] may mean 'my beneficial use' but preferably as Yale interprets, 'my assistant (Philemon)', who in Twine's version plays a much larger part in the revival of Thaisa.

35–6. *infusions . . . vegetives*] natural characteristics that are inherent in plants. Cf. *Rom.,* II. iii. 15–16, 'O, mickle is the powerful grace that lies / In plants, herbs, stones, and their true qualities' (Steevens).

dwells] for the verbal form, see II. Ch. 31n.

37. *And can*] Malone added 'I' to fit his lineation, which has not been adopted.

38–9. *which . . . more*] The awkwardness of expression and irregular metre in Q indicate serious corruption of text. *More* = greater (*O.E.D.*2 and Abbott §17). Theobald's suggestion 'gives' for *doth give,* independently adopted by Malone, would make the text more readable, but as corruption probably lies much deeper, Q has been retained.

41. *treasure . . . bags*] Q 'pleasure' is an anticipation of *please* by reporter or compositor. The sequence 'treasure . . . bags' echoes *Luke,* xii. 33 (*Geneva*), 'make you bagges, which waxe not olde, a treasure that can neuer faile in heauen' (Maxwell).

42. *To . . . death*] Steevens states that he remembers having seen an old

Flemish print in which Death is shown in the act of plundering a miser of his bags, while the Fool stands behind grinning (Boswell and Malone's edn of Shakespeare, 1821, vol. 21, p. 116). While I have been unable to find any woodcut which fits this description closely, he was certainly right in finding in this passage a close echo to the *Danse macabre,* or the Dances of Death. The Fool and Death were regular companions in these Dances, as portrayed all over Europe in paintings on walls, cloisters, or windows, or in woodcuts of the fifteenth and sixteenth centuries. The most famous of these representations are the forty-one woodcuts by Holbein, usually known as the *Imagines Mortis,* which were reproduced numerous times during the sixteenth century. Several of these include both a Fool and Death.

Acquaintance with one or other of these pictorial representations can be assumed for the Jacobean audience who would thus understand the allusion in this play without difficulty, unlike the modern reader. It would also seem highly probable that such a popular conception was frequently echoed in late mediaeval literature, including the drama. Yet Douce's contention that the passage directly alludes to a stock feature of moralities and early Tudor interludes cannot be

2. Gent. Your honour has through Ephesus pour'd forth
          Your charity, and hundreds call themselves
          Your creatures, who by you have been restor'd;   45
          And not your knowledge, your personal pain, but even
          Your purse, still open, hath built Lord Cerimon
          Such strong renown as time shall never [raze].

          Enter two or three [Servants] with a chest.

1. Serv. So; lift there.
Cer.   What's that?
1. Serv.   Sir, even now
          Did the sea toss up upon our shore this chest;   50
          'Tis of some wreck.
Cer.   Set't down; let's look upon't.
2. Gent. 'Tis like a coffin, sir.

43–6. Your . . . even] *As Malone; Ephesus,* | themselues, | restored; | payne, *Q.*
48. never raze] *Dyce;* neuer. *Q;* never— *Malone;* ne'er decay *Staunton.*   48. S.D.
Servants] Malone; not in Q.   49–51. So . . . upon't] *arranged this ed.;* there. | that? |
shore | wracke. | upon't *Q;* there. | that? | Sir, | shore | wreck. | upon't *Malone.*
50. up upon] *Q;* upon *Malone;* up on *Maxwell, conj. Fleay.*   52–3. 'Tis . . .
straight] *As Malone;* sir. | heauie; | straight *Q.*

well substantiated for the simple reason that Death is a character in only a
very small number of the surviving
plays; in fact, not a single surviving
morality in English illustrates completely the situation postulated by the
phrase in *Pericles,* though the 'fool'
occurs in most in the form of a comic
Vice figure, a descendant sometimes
from the Seven Deadly Sins, sometimes directly from the Devil. Thus in
Dekker's *Old Fortunatus,* I. iii, the Vice
carried 'hornes on her head' and 'her
garments [are] painted behind with
fooles faces and divels heads' (*Dramatic
Works,* I, p. 132). For Elizabethans,
Fortunatus himself was the stock example of one who ties his *treasure up
in silken bags To please the fool and
death,* as the popularity of the story
and play testifies. Among Don
Quixote's adventures is that with a
waggon-load of stage players, who
include the Devil, Death, and a
Fool (Cervantes, *Don Quixote,* Pt 2,

Ch. 11; Seldon's tr., 1620, p. 66).
Cf. *Meas.,* III. i. 11–13, though that
passage does not really illuminate
ours.

46. *pain*] labour; probably 'alone' is
to be understood.

48. *never raze*] In Q, the last word of
the line was probably missed by the
hasty compositor. Dyce's *raze* will do
as well as any. Malone's 'never-', suggesting an interrupted speech, is unconvincing.

49–62. *So . . . sense*] It seems probable
that in the original the whole passage
was meant to be in verse. The text,
however, is evidently corrupt—see nn.
to ll. 55–6 and 57–8 below—and I
could not find a satisfactory way of
setting ll. 57–62 in verse. But see
App. D, pp. 184–5.

50. *toss up upon*] so Q, which makes
good sense, but Malone's simplification may be correct; cf. 'get up upon
him' in Vasari's *Life of Guilio Romano,*
tr. 1719, p. 320.

Cer.   Whate'er it be,
    'Tis wondrous heavy. Wrench it open straight.
    If the sea's stomach be o'ercharg'd with gold,
    'Tis a good constraint of fortune   55
    It belches upon us.
2. Gent.   'Tis so, my lord.
Cer. How close 'tis caulked and bitumed! Did the sea cast
    it up?
1. Serv. I never saw so huge a billow, sir, as tossed it upon
    shore.   60
Cer. Wrench it open: soft! it smells most sweetly in my
    sense.
2. Gent. A delicate odour.
Cer. As ever hit my nostril. So, up with it.
    O you most potent gods! what's here? a corse!   65
1. Gent. Most strange!
Cer. Shrouded in cloths of state; balmed and entreasured
    with full bags of spices! A passport too! Apollo, per-
    fect me in the characters!

57–62. How . . . sense] *prose Q; verse Malone.*   57. bitumed] *Theobald MS,
Malone;* bottomed *Q.*   61. open: soft!] *Malone;* open soft; *Q.*   68. too!
Apollo,] *Malone;* to *Apollo,* | *Q.*

55–6. '*Tis . . . us*] If the Q text, adopted here, is sound, 'that' may be understood after *fortune,* so that the meaning would be: 'It is a good compulsion that Fortune has exerted, to make the sea vomit upon us [this chest]'. But more probably, the passage is corrupt, and the intended meaning was: 'it is fortunate that it is compelled to vomit upon us'. In that case, perhaps the text should read: ' 'Tis *by* a good constraint . . .'.

57. *caulked and bitumed*] Malone's correction seems certain considering the parallel in III. i. 71, which in turn is confirmed by *P.A.,* 60. 20.

57–8. *Did . . . up?*] It seems very odd for Cerimon to ask this question after the precise statements that have gone before. The passage and the 1st Servant's answer have probably been disarranged by the reporter. For a more convincing if speculative arrangement, see Appendix D, pp. 184–5.

61. *Wrench . . . soft!*] If the text is sound, a strong punctuation mark after *open* is certainly called for, but the repetition of the remark *Wrench . . . open* is suspect; see App. D. *soft* = gently now (the box at last giving way).

63–4. *A . . . nostril*] Cf. *Ant.,* II. ii. 216, 'A strange invisible perfume hits the sense' (Maxwell).

64. *up with it!*] prise up the lid!

68. *passport*] In Shakespeare's day, this term was used in a wider sense than customary now.

Apollo] Malone comments: 'Cerimon, having made physick his peculiar study, would naturally, in any emergency, invoke Apollo. On the present occasion, however, he addresses him as the patron of learning.'

68–9. *perfect . . . characters*] instruct me fully in the letters.

[Reads from a scroll.]

> *Here I give to understand,*   70
> *If e'er this coffin drives a-land,*
> *I, King Pericles, have lost*
> *This queen, worth all our mundane cost.*
> *Who finds her, give her burying ;*
> *She was the daughter of a king.*   75
> *Besides this treasure for a fee,*
> *The gods requite his charity!*

If thou livest, Pericles, thou hast a heart
That even cracks for woe! This chanc'd to-night.
2. Gent. Most likely, sir.
Cer.   Nay, certainly to-night;   80
For look how fresh she looks! They were too rough
That threw her in the sea. Make a fire within;
Fetch hither all my boxes in my closet.   *[Exit a Servant.]*
Death may usurp on nature many hours,
And yet the fire of life kindle again   85
The o'erpress'd spirits. I heard of an Egyptian

---

69. S.D. *Reads . . . scroll*] *Malone subst., Camb.; not in* Q.   71. *drives*] Q; *driue* Q4.
76. *Besides*] Q4; *Besides,* Q.   79. *even*] Q4; *euer* Q.   80–3. *Most . . . closet*]
As Malone; sir. / looks / sea. / Closet Q.   81. look . . . looks] Q; see . . . looks
conj. Maxwell.   rough] Q; *rash conj. Malone.*   83. S.D.] *Dyce; not in* Q.
84–7. Death . . . dead] *As Malone;* yet / spirits : / dead Q.   86. I heard] Q; I have
heard *Malone.*

70–7. Here . . . charity] closely paraphrased from Gower, *C.A.,* 1120–30.

76. treasure] i.e. the jewels mentioned in III. i. 66 (D.).

79. *even cracks*] Q 'euer cracks' would
mean, 'is broken forever', but *P.A.,*
63. 15 confirms Q4's correction : 'thou
hast a bodie euen drowned with
woe'.

to-night] last night.

81. *look . . . looks*] as Maxwell suggests, this repetition smacks of memorial corruption. Yet to substitute 'see'
were only to produce a jingle with *sea*
in the next line. The possibility should
not be ruled out that the line was written by one of Shakespeare's collaborators who sometimes liked such repetitions.

too rough] apparently 'over-hasty';

cf. our 'rough and ready' (D.). Yet the
reading is doubtful, and *P.A.,* 65. 9–10,
'condemning them for rashnesse'
gives some support to Malone's conj.
'rash'.

83. S.D.] Maxwell postulates that
Cerimon gives orders to a servant off-
stage, 'as indeed "within" suggests'.
Yet Dyce's S.D. seems preferable.

86. *o'erpress'd*] overburdened, oppressed with pain.

spirits] In Galenic physiology, the
spirits were 'certain subtle highly re-
fined substances or fluids, supposed to
permeate the blood and chief organs
of the body' (*O.E.D.*1b).

I heard] In Elizabethan English, the
preterite was frequently used where
we would use the perfect.

86–8. *I . . . recovered*] Most modern

That had nine hours lien dead,
Who was by good appliance recovered.

Enter Servant, with [boxes,] napkins, and fire.

Well said, well said; the fire and cloths.

†   The still and woeful music that we have,   90
Cause it to sound, beseech you. [*Music*]
The viol once more; how thou stirr'st, thou block!
The music there! [*Music*] I pray you, give her air.

---

88. S.D. *Servant*] *Steevens; one | Q.*   *boxes*] *Steevens; not in Q.*   90. *still*] *Max-well, conj. Delius;* rough *Q.*   91, 93. S.D.] *this ed.; not in Q.*   92. *viol*] *Q* (Violl); viall *Q4.*

edd. agree that the passage is corrupt and that the original spoke of Egyptian physicians rather than of an Egyptian patient, as in *P.A.*, 63. 29–64. 4: 'I haue read of some Egyptians, who after foure houres death, . . . haue raised impouerished bodies, like to this, vnto their former health' (so Collier). E.S. points out that Wilkins' words, with the omission indicated, convey the true Shakespeare original, for they can be set up as regular and otherwise convincing verse, the lines ending: read / death / this, / health. The story may have been suggested by Lucian's *Philopseudes* or *The Lover of Lies*, where the physician Antigonus reports: 'I know a man who came to life more than twenty days after his burial, having attended the fellow both before his death and after he came to life' (*Lucian*, Loeb Classical Library, tr. A. M. Harmon, III, p. 361).

87. *lien*] lain; a common form in Elizabethan literature.

88. S.D. boxes] See l. 83 above.

89. *Well said*] well done; frequent in Elizabethan literature.

90. *still*] Q 'rough' is manifestly wrong. The reporter seems absent-mindedly to have repeated the word from l. 81. The emendation finds a little support in *P.A.*, 65. 5–6, 'they should commaund some still musicke to sound', but is of course quite uncertain.

91, 93. S.D. Music] For the restorative power of music, cf. *Lr.*, IV. vii (D.). Previous edd. do not comment on exactly when and how often the viol is played in this episode. The text encourages the view that music is played twice, whatever one's interpretation of *once more* (see note below). Such stage-business would allow Cerimon time to revive Thaisa.

92. *viol*] See I. i. 82n. Many edd., including Malone and Maxwell, follow Q4 'viall' = phial. In support of this reading, Malone cites Gower, I 199, 'And putte a liquor in hire mouth', which is rendered in *P.A.*, 64. 30, 'powring a precious liquor into her mouth' (Wilkins' words are far too close to echo the play here, as L. Kirschbaum *apud* Maxwell contends. On the contrary, the passage is evidence that Wilkins knew Gower; see Intro., p. xliii). But the entire context of ll. 90–3 is devoted to music, and Q4's 'viall' is merely an old variant spelling of *viol*; cf. Heywood, *1 Edward IV* (Q 1600), sig. B2v, 'a base Viall', and Middleton and Dekker, *The Roaring Girl* (Q 1611), sig. D4v, H2v, H3, etc., for the same spelling.

once more] probably 'once again', but Rolfe's interpretation, 'I say once more' (impatiently, like the following words), should be considered.

how thou stirr'st] ironically, 'how quick you are!'

Gentlemen, this queen will live.
Nature awakes a warm breath out of her.   95
She hath not been entranc'd above five hours;
See, how she 'gins to blow into life's flower again!
1. Gent. The heavens, through you, increase our wonder,
And set up your fame forever.
Cer.   She is alive!
Behold, her eyelids, cases to those   100
Heavenly jewels which Pericles hath lost,
Begin to part their fringes of bright gold.
The diamonds of a most praised water
Doth appear to make the world twice rich. Live,
And make us weep to hear your fate, fair creature,   105
Rare as you seem to be.   *She moves.*
Thai.   O dear Diana,
Where am I? Where's my lord? What world is this?
2. Gent. Is not this strange?
1. Gent. Most rare.

94–9. Gentlemen . . . forever] *As Q;* Gentlemen, / warmth / entranc'd / blow /
heavens / up *Steevens and Malone.*   95. awakes a warm breath] *Q2;* awakes a
warmth breath *Q;* awakes; a warmth breathes *Steevens.*   99. set] *Malone;* sets *Q.*
99–101. She . . . lost] *this ed.;* eyelids, / lost *Q;* behold, / jewels / part *Camb., conj.*
S. Walker.   103–7. The diamonds . . . this] *As Malone;* appeare, / weepe. /
bee. / Lord? / this *Q.*   104. Doth] *Q;* do *Sewell.*   rich. Live] *Malone (1780);*
rich, liue *Q;* rich. O live *Malone (1790).*

95. *awakes . . . breath*] Steevens'
'awakes; a warmth breathes' may be
right, and is followed by many edd.;
but Q2 makes sense, and carries some
weight.

96. *entranc'd*] in a swoon.

99. *set*] Q 'sets' is possible (cf.
Abbott §333), but *set* is in accordance
with *increase*.

100–4. *eyelids . . . twice rich*] Sykes'
interpretation, though pedantically
expressed, is worth citing: 'The world
is made "twice rich" because it is
blessed with the sight not only of the
cases with golden fringes (Marina's
[sic] eyelids) but of the jewels that they
contain (her eyes)' (*Sidelights on Shakespeare*, p. 196). But perhaps *twice* in this
conceit simply means 'doubly' in the
broad sense of 'greatly'. Steevens cites
Arcadia, II. 27, 'Her faire liddes then

hiding her fairer eyes, seemed unto
him sweete boxes of mother of pearle,
rich in themselves, but containing in
them farre richer Jewells'. *cases* =
'containers' (Maxwell), with perhaps
a suggestion of 'window-shutters'
(J. D. Wilson); not 'sockets', as
defined by *O.E.D.* and On. For *fringes
of bright gold*, cf. *Tp.*, I. ii. 408, 'The
fringed curtains of thine eye advance'
(Malone) and *Mer. V.*, v. i. 59,
'patines of bright gold'. *water* = lustre,
as in *Tim.*, I. i. 20.

104. *Doth*] for the singular form in
-*th* applied to the third person plural,
see Franz §156.

107. *Where . . . this*] directly adapted
from Gower, *C.A.*, 1206–7,
  Ha wher am I?
  Where is my Lord, what world is
    this?

Cer. Hush, my gentle neighbours!   110
    Lend me your hands; to the next chamber bear her;
    Get linen: now this matter must be look'd to,
    For her relapse is mortal. Come, come;
    And Aesculapius guide us!   *Exeunt, carrying Thaisa away.*

[SCENE III.—*Tharsus.*]

Enter PERICLES *with* CLEON *and* DIONYZA[, *and* LYCHORIDA
with MARINA *in her arms.*]

Per. Most honour'd Cleon, I must needs be gone;
    My twelve months are expir'd, and Tyrus stands
    In a litigious peace. You and your lady,
    Take from my heart all thankfulness! the gods
    Make up the rest upon you!
Cle.   Your strokes of fortune,   5

110–14. Hush . . . us] *As Malone;* hands, / linnen: / relapse / vs Q.   114. S.D.]
Q *subst.* (*They carry her away. Exeunt omnes*).

Scene III

SCENE III] *Malone; not in Q; Actus Tertius F3.*   Location] *Q* (*Atharsus*); *Tharsus.*
A room in Cleon's house. Malone.   Entry] *Dyce subst.; Enter Pericles, Atharsus, with
Cleon and Dionisa / Q.*   1–4. Most . . . gods] *As Malone; prose Q.*   5–6. Make
. . . glance] *As Maxwell, conj. S. Walker; prose Q.*   5. strokes] *Round;* shakes Q;
shafts *Steevens.*

110–14. *Hush . . . us*] Malone's rearrangement of the verse, though not
completely convincing, has been adopted.
    112. *now*] immediately.
    113. *is mortal*] would be fatal.
    114. *Aesculapius*] the classical god of
healing, son of Apollo and Coronis or
Arsinoë. His invocation is especially
apt, because before his apotheosis he
raised a dead man, Hippolytus, to life.
Zeus feared that by his aid men might
cheat death altogether, and so slew
him and the raised Hippolytus with
a thunderbolt.

Scene III

3. *litigious*] 'disturbed by constant
bickerings' (D.). H.F.B. remarks on

the Shakespearean boldness of this
epithet with *peace*.
    4. *Take*] i.e. receive.
    5. *Make . . . you*] Show you all the
gratitude, for which my heart is in-
adequately conditioned.
    5–7. *strokes . . . hurt . . . woundingly*]
Commentators are agreed that Q
'shakes . . . hant . . . wondringly' is corrupt, but not on how to emend the
text. I have, after consultation with
H.F.B., adopted three emendations
which are graphically plausible and
which make fair sense, if one interprets
full = 'very' or 'enough' (i.e. *woundingly* enough), a not unusual meaning
in Elizabethan English. The passage
then means: Fortune's stroke, namely
the loss of Thaisa, is mortal for

Though they hurt you mortally, yet glance
Full woundingly on us.

Dion.   O your sweet queen!
That the strict fates had pleas'd you had brought her
    hither,
To have bless'd mine eyes with her!

Per.   We cannot but obey
The powers above us. Could I rage and roar   10
As doth the sea she lies in, yet the end
Must be as 'tis. My gentle babe Marina,
Whom, for she was born at sea, I have nam'd so, here
I charge your charity withal; leaving her
The infant of your care; beseeching you   15
To give her princely training, that she may
Be manner'd as she is born.

Cle.   Fear not, my lord, but think
Your grace, that fed my country with your corn,
For which the people's prayers still fall upon you,
Must in your child be thought on. If neglection   20
Should therein make me vile, the common body,

---

6. hurt] *Steevens;* hant *Q;* hate *F3;* hunt *conj. Steevens.*   7. woundingly] *D.,*
conj. Schmidt and Kinnear; wondringly *Q;* wand'ringly *Steevens.*   7–9. O . . .
her] *As F4 subst., Rowe; prose Q.*   9–17. We . . . born] *As Steevens subst., Maxwell;*
vs; / in, / *Marina,* / so, / leauing her / giue her / borne *Q.*   17–25. Fear . . .
generation] *As Malone;* Grace, / which, / child / vile, / reliev'd, / that, / it /
generation *Q.*   19. still] *Q;* dayly *Q2.*

Pericles, but by glancing off him also
wounds Cleon and Dionyza, who are
deprived of her company. Cf. *Shr.,* v.
iv. 61 f., 'as the jest did glance away
from me, / 'Tis ten to one it maim'd
you two outright'; the same metaphor,
though there the ricochet does the
worse damage. Steevens' 'shafts' for
'shakes' cannot be defended on graphic
grounds, though it has literary at-
tractiveness. Should Q 'wondringly'
be correct, it might have the sense
of 'wondrously, mysteriously', but
O.E.D. gives no support, and *woundingly* fits the context better.

9–12. *We . . . 'tis*] These lines sound
like Shakespeare—not all do in this
scene. For the sentiment, cf. *Lr.,* v. ii.
9–11 and *Ham.,* v. ii. 212–16, 'there is a

special providence in the fall of a
sparrow . . . the readiness is all'. The
mood of these passages is similar; not
exactly alike.

13. *for*] because.

14. *withal*] with.

leaving] H.F.B. suspects memorial
assimilation to *beseeching* in the following line, for 'and leave' would make
better verse.

18. *grace*] favour, generosity.

19. *still*] always. The reason for Q2's
'dayly', paralleling the change at III. i.
5 ('dayly' for *gently*), is hard to fathom.

20. *neglection*] neglect. *O.E.D.* lists no
example earlier than Shakespeare. See
1H6, IV. iii. 49 and *Troil.,* I. iii. 127.

21. *common body*] common people,
cf. *Ant.,* I. iv. 44.

By you reliev'd, would force me to my duty.
But if to that my nature need a spur,
The gods revenge it upon me and mine,
To the end of generation!
Per.   I believe you;   25
Your honour and your goodness teach me to't,
Without your vows. Till she be married, madam,
By bright Diana, whom we honour, all
Unscissor'd shall this hair of mine remain,
Though I show ill in't. So I take my leave.   30
Good madam, make me blessed in your care
In bringing up my child.
Dion.   I have one myself,
Who shall not be more dear to my respect
Than yours, my lord.
Per.   Madam, my thanks and prayers.
Cle. We'll bring your grace e'en to the edge o'th' shore,   35
Then give you up to the mask'd Neptune and
The gentlest winds of heaven

25–9. I . . . remain] *As Malone;* goodnes, / maried, / honour, / remayne *Q.*
28. honour, all] *Q;* honour all, *Malone.*   29. Unscissor'd . . . hair] *Steevens;*
vnsisterd . . . heyre *Q.*   30. show ill] *Theobald MS, Singer (ii), conj. Malone;*
shew will *Q.*   32–41. I . . . lord] *As Malone; prose Q.*   36. mask'd] *Q;* moist
conj. S. Walker.

23. *need a spur*] Other edd. have cited
Mac., I. vii. 25–6 and *Cæs.,* II. i. 123, but
the image is of course common in
many writers.

25. *To . . . generation*] 'throughout
my posterity' (Round); see *O.E.D.*3
and 3b.

26. *teach . . . to't*] *to* has the force of
'of', i.e. 'convince me of it'. This usage
of *teach to* is both obsolete and uncommon, and not listed in *O.E.D.* However, 'instruct me to do it' would be
sound contemporary usage in the same
syntactical context.

27–9. *Without . . . remain*] These
lines are paraphrased from Gower,
C.A., 1301–6.

28. *honour, all*] Malone's change in
punctuation may be correct, but Q
makes good sense and has therefore
been left standing; also cf. *P.A.,* 68.

24, cited in n. 30 below.

29. *Unscissor'd . . . hair*] Steevens'
emendation is confirmed by *P.A.,* 68.
23, 'his head should grow vncisserd',
and 70. 28. The compositor misread
c > t in Q 'vnfifterd' (Maxwell).

30. *show ill*] Theobald's and
Malone's conjecture is much more
likely than Q 'shew will', and finds
support in *P.A.,* 68. 24, 'himselfe in all
vncomely'.

33. *to my respect*] in my esteem.

36. *mask'd*] i.e. 'deceivingly calm'.
The conjectural emendations by
Walker and others are weak. Delius
and Maxwell quote *Arcadia,* II. 7 (p.
191), 'with so smooth and smiling a
face, as if *Neptune* had then learned
falsely to fawne on Princes'. Steevens
cites Lucretius, 'subdola pellacis ridet
clementia ponti'.

Per.   I will embrace
Your offer. Come, dearest madam. O, no tears,
Lychorida, no tears;
Look to your little mistress, on whose grace   40
You may depend hereafter. Come, my lord.   [*Exeunt.*]

[SCENE IV.—*Ephesus.*]

Enter CERIMON *and* THAISA.

Cer. Madam, this letter and some certain jewels
Lay with you in your coffer; which are
At your command. Know you the character?
Thai. It is my lord's. That I was shipp'd at sea
I well remember, even on my eaning time;   5
But whether there deliver'd, by the holy gods,
I cannot rightly say. But since King Pericles,
My wedded lord, I ne'er shall see again,
A vestal livery will I take me to,

41. S.D.] *Rowe; not in Q.*

Scene IV

SCENE IV] *Malone; not in Q.*   Location] *not in Q; Ephesus. A room in Cerimon's house. | Malone.*   Entry. Thaisa] *Q4; Tharsa | Q.*   2–3. Lay ... character?] *As Malone;* command; / Character? *Q.*   Lay ... command] *Q;* which are at your command, lay in your coffer *conj. C. B. Young.*   coffer] *Q;* coffin *conj. Dyce.*   are] *Q;* are now *Malone.*   4–6. It ... gods] *As Rowe;* prose *Q;* lord's / remember / there / gods *Steevens.*   5. eaning] *F3;* learning *Q;* yielding *conj. Mason;* yeaning *conj. Mason;* bearing *conj. Ridley.*   6. deliver'd] *Q;* delivered or no *Malone;* I was deliver'd *conj. Dyce.*   7–10. I ... joy] *As Steevens; prose Q.*   9. vestal] *F3;* vastall *Q.*

40. *grace*] see l. 18n. above.

Scene IV

2. *Lay ... are*] metrically irregular. Malone was probably right in supposing that a word is missing after *are*, but what word is pure conjecture.

coffer] See III. i. 67n. 'coffre' is Gower's word in *C.A.*, 1157 and 1174.

3. *character*] handwriting.

4–6. *It ... gods*] Rowe's lineation to which this edition returns is clearly preferable to Steevens', where l. 6 is metrically incomplete. Malone's con-

jecture for l. 6 is not satisfactory.

5. *eaning time*] F3's emendation is more probable than any of the numerous alternative changes that have been suggested; this in spite of the fact that the expression *eaning time* was more commonly applied to the breeding of sheep, as in Jonson, *The Sad Shepherd*, I. iv. 10. Mason cites 'yielded there' at v. iii. 48 in support of his conj. 'yielding', but the parallel is not close enough.

9. *A ... to*] 'I will live the life of a vestal virgin' (D.). For *vestal livery*, cf.

      And never more have joy.   10
Cer. Madam, if this you purpose as ye speak,
      Diana's temple is not distant far,
      Where you may abide till your date expire.
      Moreover, if you please, a niece of mine
      Shall there attend you.   15
Thai. My recompense is thanks, that's all;
      Yet my good will is great, though the gift small. *Exeunt.*

---

11. you . . . ye] *Q;* you . . . you *Walker (1734).*   17. S.D.] *Rowe; Exit | Q.*

Rom., II. ii. 8 (Maxwell) and *MND.*, I. i. 70.

   13. *till . . . expire*] 'till you die' (Malone); *date* = term of life (*O.E.D.* 4).

   16. *My . . . all*] Maxwell compares *R2*, II. iii. 65 (Q text), 'evermore thank's the exchequer of the poor'. Cf. note to that passage in the revised Arden edn, which points to - second parallel in *Tw. N.*, III. iii. 14–15.

[ACT IV]

Enter GOWER.

Imagine Pericles arriv'd at Tyre,
Welcom'd and settled to his own desire.
His woeful queen we leave at Ephesus,
Unto Diana there's a votaress.
Now to Marina bend your mind,   5
Whom our fast-growing scene must find
At Tharsus, and by Cleon train'd
In music's letters; who hath gain'd
Of education all the grace,
Which makes her both the heart and place   10
Of general wonder. But, alack,
That monster envy, oft the wrack
Of earned praise, Marina's life
Seeks to take off by treason's knife;
And in this kind hath our Cleon   15

ACT IV

ACT IV] *Malone; not in* Q.   4. there's] Q (ther's)*; there Malone; there as Camb.*
8. music's letters] Q (Musicks letters)*; music, letters Tonson.*   10. her . . .
heart] *Steevens;* hie . . . art Q.   14. Seeks] *Rowe;* Seeke Q.   15–16. hath our
Cleon / . . . a wench full-grown] *Steevens;* our *Cleon* hath / . . . a full growne
wench Q.

4. *there's*] there as. For the elision of
as, cf. Jonson, *Catiline*, v. 298, 'Life,
and fauour's well' (Maxwell).

6. *fast-growing scene*] Cf. *Wint.*, IV. i.
16–17, 'I turn my glass, and give my
scene such growing / As you had slept
between' (Malone).

8. *music's letters*] the study of music
(see On., *letter* 5).

9. *grace*] graceful accomplishment.
To do everything with grace was the
ideal of courtly education in the
Renaissance.

10–11. *the heart . . . wonder*] 'the very
centre of heartfelt wonder' (D.). If

Steevens' *heart* is correct, Q 'art' may
be an auditory error on the reporter's
part; see, however, Intro., p. xxxvi.

12. *envy*] 'Here and at line 37,
though the modern sense is in place,
the commoner Shakespearean meaning "ill-will, malice" is also present'
(Maxwell).

wrack] ruin; see II. Ch. 32 n.

14. *Seeks*] Misreading of *e* for *s*, common in Elizabethan MSS, accounts
for Q 'Seeke'.

treason] treachery.

15–16. *And . . . wench*] Steevens' rearrangement, followed by most edd.,

One daughter and a wench full-grown,
Even ripe for marriage-rite. This maid
Hight Philoten; and it is said
For certain in our story, she
Would ever with Marina be: 20
Be't when she weav'd the sleided silk
With fingers long, small, white as milk;
Or when she would with sharp neele wound
The cambric, which she made more sound
By hurting it; or when to th'lute   25
She sung, and made the night-bird mute
That still records with moan; or when

---

17. ripe] *Q2;* right *Q.*   rite] *Collier;* sight *Q;* fight *Theobald MS, Malone.*
21. she] *Malone;* they *Q.*   23. neele] *Maxwell;* needle *Q;* neeld *Malone.*
25. it; or] *Q2 subst.;* it or *Q.*   26. night-bird] *Theobald MS, Malone;* night bed *Q.*

---

is a sensible solution, for the errors postulated are natural, the reporter's memory wrongly restoring the normal prose order of the words in both lines. Yet corruption may lie deeper, considering the error in l. 17. Worthy of consideration is also E.S.'s alternative solution, necessitating two alterations (one of them slight): 'And in this kind our Cleon has / One daughter, and a fullgrown lass' (cf. 'a lass unparallel'd', *Ant.,* v. ii. 314). As *this* has no antecedent, the meaning of *this kind* is not clear; possibly 'the same category (as Marina)' (H.F.B.).

17. *ripe . . . marriage-rite*] Although perhaps purely editorial, Q2's correction sounds plausible and has been generally followed. As so often in this text, the error may be ascribed to the reporter's faulty memory. He remembered the assonance *ripe . . rite* (sometimes spelt 'right', as in *MND.* (Q 1600), iv. i. 138), but got it wrong as 'right . . . sight'. But this substitution of words of like sound as well as of like appearance may also be the copyist's.

18. *Hight*] is called; present or past tense of the passive verb 'hoten'; cf. German 'sie heisst' = she is called.

21. *she*] Malone's emendation, by analogy with l. 23.

sleided] an irregular variant of 'sleaved' = divided into filaments, 'to be used in the weaver's sley or slay' (Percy). *O.E.D.* lists only one other example of this spelling: *Comp.,* 48, but note also *Troil.* (F version), v. i. 35, 'sleyd silk'. These parallels of an unusual spelling are evidence that Shakespeare had at least a hand in this chorus.

22. *small*] slender.

23. *neele*] needle; so spelt in v. Ch. 5. Both *neele* and 'neeld' were common variants of 'needle' in Elizabethan English. If Q's spelling 'needle' is correct, it was at any rate pronounced as a monosyllable; so also in *Lucr.,* 319 and *R2,* v. v. 17. See Abbott §465, who notes that in *Gammer Gurton's Needle,* I. iii. 23, 'needle' rhymes with 'feele'.

23–4. *Or . . . cambric*] Cf. *MND.,* III. ii. 203 ff. where Helena recalls how Hermia and she herself had 'with our needles created both one flower'.

23–5. *wound . . . it*] Maxwell cites Sidney, *Arcadia,* III. 10 (p. 402), 'the cloth loking with many eies upon her, & lovingly embracing the wounds she gave it'.

26. *night-bird*] nightingale.

27, 29. *still*] always.

27. *records with moan*] sings doleful-

She would with rich and constant pen
Vail to her mistress Dian; still
This Philoten contends in skill   30
With absolute Marina: so
With dove of Paphos might the crow
Vie feathers white. Marina gets
All praises, which are paid as debts,
And not as given. This so darks   35
In Philoten all graceful marks,
That Cleon's wife with envy rare
A present murderer does prepare
For good Marina, that her daughter
Might stand peerless by this slaughter.   40
The sooner her vile thoughts to stead,
Lychorida, our nurse, is dead;
And cursed Dionyza hath
The pregnant instrument of wrath
Prest for this blow. The unborn event   45
I do commend to your content;
Only I carried winged time

---

29. Dian; still] *Malone; Dian* still, Q.   32. With dove] *J. Munro;* The Doue *Q;*
With the dove *Steevens, conj. Mason.*   might the] *Steevens, conj. Mason;* might
with the Q.   38. murderer] *Q;* murder *conj. S. Walker.*   44. wrath] *F3;*
wrath. Q.   47. carried] *Q;* carry *Steevens.*

---

ly; cf. *Gent.*, v. iv. 5–6 (Maxwell).
  29. *Vail*] do homage (see *O.E.D.*
11b).
  31. *absolute*] perfect in accomplishments.
  32. *With . . . crow*] proverbial (Tilley
C 853); cf. *Rom.*, I. v. 46–7. Q's word
order 'The . . . crow' seems at first
sight more normal though the meaning is obviously wrong. But I am not
sure whether the error was occasioned
by the reporter (Maxwell) or by the
compositor who was puzzled by a
corrected MS copy. The omission of
'the' does not merely regularize the
metre but is also Gowerish in style.
  dove of Paphos] sacred to Venus, who
was believed to have risen from the
waves near Paphos, a town in Cyprus,
which thence became a shrine in her
worship. See *Tp.*, IV. i. 92–4.

  34. *All . . . debts*] a common notion.
Cf. *Wint.*, I. ii. 94, 'Our praises are
our wages' (Henry H. Wolff, privately).
  35. *darks*] darkens, puts in the
shade.
  37–8. *envy . . . murderer*] Cf. Dekker
and Wilkins, *Jests to Make you Merrie*,
II. 305 (Grosart ed.), 'O envy thou
fore-runner of murther'.
  41. *stead*] aid.
  44. *pregnant*] apt to be influenced.
  45. *Prest*] ready, from the Old
French *prest.*
  46. *content*] i.e. pleasure.
  47. *carried*] have carried. Steevens'
'carry', implying compositorial error
'carri'd' for 'carrie' by assimilation to
winged, may be right.
  winged time] Time was often conceived as *winged* in the Renaissance;

Post on the lame feet of my rime;
Which never could I so convey,
Unless your thoughts went on my way.   50
Dionyza does appear,
With Leonine, a murtherer.   *Exit.*

[SCENE I.—*Tharsus, near the Sea-shore.*]

Enter DIONYZA *with* LEONINE.

Dion. Thy oath remember; thou hast sworn to do't.
'Tis but a blow, which never shall be known.
Thou canst not do a thing in the world so soon,
To yield thee so much profit. Let not conscience,

48. on] *Q2;* one *Q.*   52. murtherer] *Q;* murderer *Q4.*

Scene 1

SCENE I . . . *shore*] *Malone subst.; not in Q.*   Entry. *with*] *Q; and* / *Q4.*   1–4. Thy
. . . *conscience*] *As Rowe; prose Q.*

cf. *Wint.*, iv. i. 3–4 and Dekker, *Whore
of Babylon* (Q 1607), Prologue (*Works*,
ii, p. 499).
  48. *Post*] in post haste (D.).

Scene 1

  1. *Thy . . . do't*] Cf. *Mac.*, i. vii. 58 ff.
where Lady Macbeth holds her reluc-
tant husband similarly to his oath.
  4–6. *Let . . . nicely*] *nicely* = over-
scrupulously. But the passage is one of
the play's textual cruces. Q does not
make sense, and of many alternative
emendations suggested, none is completely convincing. D.'s solution, the
best to my mind, has been adopted. It
is open to the criticism that it requires
no fewer than three alterations in the
text: *or* for 'in', *enslave* for 'enflame',
and the transposition of *love* and *thy.*
But, as D. justly maintains, this is not
the only point where transposition of
words is needed to restore the text, and
the two other emendations are defensible on graphic grounds. The long *s* in
enslave could, in Elizabethan secretary
hand, easily be mistaken for *f*, simi-

larly *v* for *m.* Some word to replace Q's
'inflame' is needed, for it is hard 'to
understand how "*cold* conscience" can
"inflame" ' (D.), and it seems likely
that the compositor was predisposed
by *flaming love.* The juxtaposition
resulting from the other two changes
is also attractive on literary grounds:
*conscience, which is but cold, or flaming
love.* And for the combination of fear,
love, and pity as motives, D. cites
3H6, v. vi. 68.
  Among the alternative solutions put
forward, Theobald's proposition seems
attractive only because it requires
such a slight change of Q's text; yet
'low bosom' makes little sense. Sisson,
who thinks that the copy was 'foul
papers', 'with corrections *currente
calamo* in line and margin' (*New Readings*, ii. 296), emends Q by dropping
'in flaming' and 'bosom'. As Malone
had already done, he postulates a mar-
ginal 'enflame too nicely'. But his
assumption of 'foul papers' for copy is
unwarranted (see Intro., p. xxxix),
and the literary objection against 'cold

Which is but cold, or flaming love thy bosom   5
Enslave too nicely; nor let pity, which
Even women have cast off, melt thee, but be
A soldier to thy purpose.
Leon. I will do't; but yet she is a goodly creature.
Dion. The fitter then the gods should have her.   10
Here she comes weeping for her only mistress' death.
Thou art resolv'd?
Leon.   I am resolv'd.

Enter MARINA, *with a basket of flowers.*

Mar. No, I will rob Tellus of her weed,
To strew thy green with flowers; the yellows, blues,
The purple violets, and marigolds,   15

5–8. Which . . . purpose] *As D.; prose Q.*   5–6. or flaming love thy bosom /
Enslave] *D.;* in flaming, thy loue bosome, enflame *Q;* inflaming thy low bosom,
inflame *Theobald MS;* thy love inflame *Sisson.*   11. only] *Q;* old *conj. Percy.*
mistress' death] *Q;* mistress. Death— *Malone;* nurse's death *Theobald MS, conj.*
Percy.   12. resolv'd?] *Q2* (resolude?); resolude. *Q.*   13–20. No . . . friends]
As Rowe; prose Q.   14. green] *Q;* Grave *F3.*

(conscience) thy love inflame' has
been stated.
    8. *A soldier . . . purpose*] Cf. *Cym.,* III.
iv. 181–2, 'This attempt / I am soldier
to' (Clarke).
    9–12. *I will . . . resolv'd*] H.F.B.
postulates the following lineation:
yet / then / for / resolv'd? / resolv'd.
    9. *goodly creature*] Cf. *Tp.,* v. i. 182.
    10. *The fitter . . . her*] proverbial
(Tilley G 251). Steevens compares
Q text of *R3,* I. ii. 104–5:
Anne. Oh he was gentle, milde, and
                    vertuous.
Glo. The fitter for the King of
                    Heauen that hath him.
    11. *only mistress'*] probably that of
Lychorida, the nurse, for though
Marina speaks of her mother in l. 18
below, Dionyza can hardly be referring to her. The adjective *only* is here
used in the sense of 'dear' as well as in
that of 'sole', as in 'only son' and perhaps in the 'onlie begetter' of Shakespeare's Sonnets. If the passage is corrupt, no convincing emendation has

yet been put forward, though it is just
conceivable that 'nurse's' could have
been misread as 'mistress'. But the
emphasis of 'only nurse' in *Rom.,* I. iii.
68 is quite different.
    12. *resolv'd . . . resolv'd*] Cf. Macbeth
to the murderers, *Mac.,* III. i. 137–8.
    12. S.D. Enter . . . flowers] Like
Perdita in *Wint.,* IV. iv, Marina is presented as a flower-maiden. See also
following n. for a parallel in *Cym.* These
resemblances make Shakespeare's
authorship of part of this scene highly
probable, though the idea of a flower-
maiden is not original with him.
    13–17. *No . . . last*] Cf. the very
similar passage in *Cym.,* IV. ii. 219–25,
especially the words 'Whilst summer
lasts' (Malone).
    13. *Tellus*] the earth.
    weed] dress (of flowers); from O.E.
wǽd, a garment (D.).
    14. *green*] 'the green turf with which
the grave of Lychorida was covered'
(Lord Charlemont, who cites a parallel
from Fairfax's *Tasso, apud* Malone).

Shall as a carpet hang upon thy grave,
While summer-days doth last. Ay me! poor maid,
Born in a tempest, when my mother died,
This world to me is as a lasting storm,
Whirring me from my friends.   20
Dion. How now, Marina! why do you keep alone?
How chance my daughter is not with you?
Do not consume your blood with sorrowing:
Have you a nurse of me! Lord, how your favour's
Chang'd with this unprofitable woe!   25
Come, give me your flowers. On the sea-margent
Walk with Leonine; the air is quick there,

---

17. doth] *Q; do Q5.*   19. is as a] *Maxwell, conj. Camb.;* is a *Q;* is like a *Q4.*
21. keep alone] *Q;* weepe alone *Q2.*   24. Have you] *Q;* You have *Q4;* Have
you not *Malone.*   26. flowers. On the sea-margent] *Hudson;* flowers, ere the
sea marre it, *Q;* flowers. O'er the sea-margin *Theobald MS.*

---

16. *carpet*] piece of tapestry or em-
broidery, used for window-seats or
table-cloths.

17. *doth*] Cf. III. ii. 104.

17–19. *last... lasting*] The repetition
smacks of the reporter (unless it be
merely the result of hasty composition). But *lasting* does not require
emendation. To Marina, life is a constant, a perpetual storm.

19. *is as a*] A word seems missing in
Q. Most edd. follow Q4 'is like a', but
Q4 has no authority, and Cambridge's
conj., followed by Maxwell, seems
much better.

20. *Whirring*] whirling, hurrying
along (*O.E.D.*1b).

21. *keep alone*] Malone restored the
Q text, quoting *Mac.,* III. ii. 8, 'How
now, my Lord! why do you keep
alone'. As *Macbeth* was in Shakespeare's mind all through this scene
and IV. iii, the textual echo is not to be
blamed on the reporter, as has been
suggested.

22. *How chance . . . ?*] How does it
happen . . .?

23. *Do . . . sorrowing*] 'Alluding to the
old notion that each sigh took a drop of
blood from the heart' (Rolfe *apud* D.).
Cf. *MND.,* III. ii. 97, 'With sighs of love

that costs the fresh blood dear' and
2H6, III. ii. 61, 'blood-consuming
sighs'.

24. *Have you*] Most edd. have followed Q4 'You have', but Q makes
sense if Dionyza's statement is interpreted as an imperative, 'Take *me* as
a nurse'.

favour] looks, appearance.

26–31. *Come . . . come*] Several features in these lines suggest memorial
contamination of the text by the reporter: (i) the treble repetition of
come, a frequent characteristic of corrupt texts; (ii) the incredible statement: *it pierces and sharpens the stomach;*
(iii) the halting and irregular verse;
(iv) the error in l. 26.

26. *On the sea-margent*] Hudson's
ingenious emendation, partly anticipated by Theobald, fits the context.
Herford, who keeps Q 'ere the sea
marre it', suggests that 'it' = the
flowers collectively, but in that case,
more would remain to be explained.
Hudson was influenced by *MND.,* II.
i. 85, 'in the beached margent of the
sea'. The reading finds even stronger
support in *Tp.,* IV. i. 69–70, where 'sea-
marge' and *air* are closely linked.

27. *quick*] fresh.

And it pierces and sharpens the stomach.
Come, Leonine, take her by the arm, walk with her.
Mar. No, I pray you; I'll not bereave you of your servant. 30
Dion. Come, come;
I love the king your father and yourself
With more than foreign heart. We every day
Expect him here; when he shall come and find
Our paragon to all reports thus blasted,   35
He will repent the breadth of his great voyage;
Blame both my lord and me, that we have taken
No care to your best courses. Go, I pray you,
Walk, and be cheerful once again; reserve
That excellent complexion, which did steal   40
The eyes of young and old. Care not for me;
I can go home alone.
Mar.   Well, I will go;
But yet I have no desire to it.
Dion. Come, come, I know 'tis good for you.
Walk half an hour, Leonine, at the least.   45
Remember what I have said.
Leon.   I warrant you, madam.
Dion. I'll leave you, my sweet lady, for a while.
Pray, walk softly, do not heat your blood.
What! I must have care of you.
Mar.   My thanks, sweet madam.
                                        [*Exit Dionyza.*]
Is this wind westerly that blows?
Leon.   South-west.   50
Mar. When I was born, the wind was north.

31–43. Come . . . it] *As Rowe; prose Q.*   39. reserve] *Q; resume Maxwell.*
44–6. Come . . . said] *As Q4; prose Q.*   47–9. I'll . . . madam] *As Rowe; prose Q.*
49. S.D.] *Malone; not in Q.*   50–6. Is . . . deck] *As Malone; prose Q.*   50. this]
Q; the Q2.

33. *With . . . heart*] as if I was closely
related to him. For *foreign*, cf. *Oth.*, IV.
iii. 86 (Maxwell).

35. *Our paragon . . . reports*] i.e. what
is according to all reports our very
model of excellence.

38. *to . . . courses*] 'to what was best
for you' (Steevens).

39. *reserve*] guard, preserve. Malone

compares *Sonnet* 32. 7, 'Reserve them
for my love'. J. D. Wilson conjectures
'resume', because *reserve* would contradict ll. 24–5. But there is no need for
Dionyza to be precisely consistent in
her remarks to Marina.

51. *When . . . north*] Cf. *Cym.*, I. iii. 36,
'like the tyrannous breathing of the
north'.

Leon.   Was't so?

Mar. My father, as nurse says, did never fear,
        But cried "Good seamen!" to the sailors, galling
        His kingly hands, haling ropes;
        And, clasping to the mast, endur'd a sea   55
        That almost burst the deck.

Leon. When was this?

Mar. When I was born.
        Never was waves nor wind more violent;
        And from the ladder-tackle washes off   60
        A canvas-climber. "Ha!" says one, "wolt out?"
        And with a dropping industry they skip
        From stem to stern; the boatswain whistles, and
        The master calls and trebles their confusion.

Leon. Come, say your prayers.   65

Mar. What mean you?

Leon. If you require a little space for prayer,

---

52. says] Q (ses); saith *Q4*; said *Malone*.   58–62. When . . . skip] *As Rowe;
prose in Q.*   61. wolt out] *Q;* wilt out *Q4*; woltou *conj. Hoeniger*.   63–4. From
. . . confusion] *As Malone; prose Q.*   63. stem] *Malone;* sterne *Q.*   67–81. If
. . . danger] *As Malone; prose Q.*

52. *says*] is accustomed to say. Like
Sisson, I have retained Q, but most
edd. follow Malone's 'said'. Cf. l. 61
below, where the present tense is also
used for an event that lies well back in
the past. Marina is not the only one
who, having lost a loved one, fails
sometimes to change *says* into 'used to
say'.

54. *haling ropes*] *haling* = dragging,
drawing with force (*O.E.D.*). Edd.
have wrongly emended this term, yet
a phrase is clearly missing. H.F.B. suggests that the original had what gave
rise to a homoeoteleuton from *haling* to
another participle; possibly 'haling
and drawing ropes' (though this
sounds a little flat). Cf. Drake's
famous declaration in *The World En-
compassed*, that he 'must have the
gentleman to hale and draw with
the mariner'.

55. *clasping*] clinging; 'Shakespeare
does not elsewhere use the intransitive
verb with to' (D.).

59. *was*] See Abbott §§333, 335 (D.).

61. *wolt out?*] probably: 'wilt thou
out?' *wolt*, 'wot', and 'woult' (see
The Puritan, I. iv. 135) were common
variant forms of 'wilt'—see *O.E.D.
will v.I.*A3. But what the phrase
means is not clear. Some commentators interpret it as being addressed to
the storm, but more probably it is, as
Ridley suggests, 'a rather brutally
humorous remark to the man who has
been washed off'; thus: 'you're off, on
your way, are you?' It is also possible
that the original reading was 'woltou?'
or 'woltowe?' (*O.E.D. will v.I.*A6),
meaning 'wilt thou?', in the sense of
'wilt thou really?' To my mind, this
would make better sense, but one cannot be sure whether even in colloquial
speech, these forms survived until
1600.

62. *dropping*] dripping wet. Cf. Heywood, *2 If you know not me* (ed. Pearson,
1874, I. 268): 'We shall be dropping
dry if we stay here' (D.).

I grant it. Pray, but be not tedious;
For the gods are quick of ear, and I am sworn
To do my work with haste.

Mar.   Why will you kill me?   70

Leon. To satisfy my lady.

Mar. Why would she have me kill'd?
Now, as I can remember, by my troth,
I never did her hurt in all my life.
I never spake bad word, nor did ill turn   75
To any living creature; believe me la,
I never kill'd a mouse, nor hurt a fly;
I trod upon a worm against my will,
But I wept for't. How have I offended,
Wherein my death might yield her any profit,   80
Or my life imply her any danger?

Leon. My commission
Is not to reason of the deed, but do't.

Mar. You will not do't for all the world, I hope.
You are well favour'd, and your looks foreshow   85
You have a gentle heart. I saw you lately,
When you caught hurt in parting two that fought.
Good sooth, it show'd well in you. Do so now.

72–3. kill'd? / Now] *Malone;* kild now? *Q.*   76. la] *Q* (law).   78. I]
Q; Nor *conj. Daniel.*   79. for't] *Q;* for it *Q4.*   82–90. My . . . weaker]
As Rowe; *prose Q.*

73. *as*] as far as.

76. *la*] indeed; an exclamation in-
tensifying a statement. Q 'law' was a
common Elizabethan variant of *la.*
See, for instance, *LLL.,* v. ii. 414 (Q
and F), 'so God helpe me law', and
Day, *Ile of Gulls* (Q 1606), sig. G4, 'that
may you do lawe'.

78. *I trod . . . will*] Cf. Middleton,
Phoenix, IV. i. 158–61 (ed. Bullen),
'using the world in his right nature but
to tread upon; one that would not
bruise the cowardliest enemy to man,
the worm, that dares not show his
malice till we are dead'.

It is probably mere coincidence that
the closest known parallel to the similar image of the mole, I. i. 101–3, is
also in Middleton. But cf. *Meas.,* III. i.

80–2, 'And the poor beetle that we
tread upon / In corporal sufferance
finds a pang as great / As when a giant
dies'.

79–82. *How . . . commission*] The
verse is suspicious. The reporter may
have omitted some words either before
or after *How . . . offended.* In that case,
the verse would run *death / life / commission* (H.F.B.).

80. *Wherein*] sc. 'have I offended
that'.

85. *well favour'd*] good-looking.
foreshow] show forth, betray (*O.E.D.*
3).

85–6. *your looks . . . heart*] Cf. *John,* IV.
i. 88 (Arthur to Hubert about the 1st
Executioner), 'He hath a stern look
but a gentle heart'.

Your lady seeks my life; come you between,
And save poor me, the weaker.

Leon.   I am sworn,   90
And will dispatch.   [*Seizes her.*]

Enter Pirates.

1. Pir. Hold, villain!   [*Leonine runs away.*]
2. Pir. A prize! a prize!
3. Pir. Half-part, mates, half-part! Come, let's have her
aboard suddenly.   95
                    Exeunt [*Pirates with Marina.*]

Enter LEONINE.

Leon. These roguing thieves serve the great pirate Valdes;
And they have seiz'd Marina. Let her go;
There's no hope she'll return. I'll swear she's dead
And thrown into the sea. But I'll see further;
Perhaps they will but please themselves upon her,   100
Not carry her aboard. If she remain,
Whom they have ravish'd must by me be slain.   *Exit.*

89. life; come you] *Q2 subst.;* lifeCome, you *Q.*   90–1. I . . . dispatch] *As
Malone; one line Q.*   91. S.D. *Seizes her*] *Globe; not in Q.*   92. S.D. *Leonine . . .
away*] *Malone; not in Q.*   95. S.D. *Exeunt . . . Marina*] *Malone; Exit / Q.*   96–
101. These . . . remain] *As Rowe; prose Q.*   96. roguing] *Q; roving conj. Mason.*
98. she'll] *Malone;* she will *Q.*

93–4. *A prize . . . half-part!*] Cf. Hutton, *Discovery of a London Monster called
the Black Dogg of Newgate*, n.d. (1600?):
'A prize, a prize in a buckram bag! a
prize! halfe part, quoth the gentleman'
(Halliwell-Philips, Scrapbook). *Half-
part* = go shares.

96. *roguing thieves*] As thieves are
usually 'rogues', Mason suggested
'roving'.

Valdes] Malone comments: 'The
Spanish Armada, I believe, furnished
our author with the name. Don Pedro
de *Valdes* was an admiral in that fleet,
and had commanded the great galleon
of Andalusia. His ship being disabled,
he was taken by Sir Francis Drake, on
the 22nd July 1588, and sent to Dart-
mouth. . . The making one of this
Spaniard's ancestors a pirate was prob-

ably relished by the audience of those
days'. Contrary to Maxwell, I regard
this conjecture as very plausible. In
Dekker, *The Whore of Babylon* (1607),
which in all probability was staged
only shortly before *Pericles*, a list of the
Spanish captains is given, part of
which runs:

Flores de Valdes guides the third,
          the fourth
Followes the silken streamers of
          the haughty
Pedro de Valdes that tryed warrior.
          (*Works*, II, p. 564).
The first audience of *Pericles* must have
been familiar with these names.

98. *hope*] i.e. fear.

she'll] Malone's simple emendation
regularizes the metre and is in tune
with *I'll.*

[SCENE II.—*Mytilene. In front of a Brothel.*]

Enter Pandar, Bawd, and BOULT.

Pand. Boult!

Boult. Sir?

Pand. Search the market narrowly; Mytilene is full of
gallants. We lost too much money this mart by being
too wenchless.   5

Bawd. We were never so much out of creatures. We have
but poor three, and they can do no more than they
can do; and they with continual action are even as
good as rotten.

Pand. Therefore let's have fresh ones, whate'er we pay for   10
them. If there be not a conscience to be us'd in every
trade, we shall never prosper.

Bawd. Thou say'st true; 'tis not our bringing up of poor
bastards, as I think I have brought up some eleven—

Boult. Ay, to eleven; and brought them down again. But   15
shall I search the market?

Scene II

SCENE II] *Malone; not in Q.*   Location] *this ed., conj. H.F.B.; not in Q; Mytilene.*
A room in a brothel | Malone.   Entry] *F3; Enter the three Bawdes | Q.*   3. Myti-
lene] *Q (Mettelyne).*   4. much] *Q2; much much Q.*   5. too] *Q; omit conj.*
Maxwell.   8. and they with] *Q; and with Malone.*   14. eleven—] *Malone;*
eleuen. *Q.*

S.D. *In front of a Brothel*] Ll. 50,
Wife, take her in, and 122, *take her home*,
indicate that this scene was not intended to take place within the brothel, as
Malone and edd. since have interpreted (H.F.B.).

3. *Mytilene*] a city in Lesbos. *Mytilene*
is the usual modern spelling in atlases.
Q has various spellings, including
'Mittelyne', 'Mittelin', 'Metaline',
'Metiline', etc.

4. *mart*] market-time.

11–12. *If . . . prosper*] The pandar's
meaning is clear, however illogical the
expression. His words are a good example of Shakespeare 'sympathizingly
cognizant with the talk of the illogical
classes' (Bagehot, *Shakespeare: The
Man*, ed. 1901, p. 30, who refers to

Mistress Quickly's answer to Falstaff
in *2H4*, II. iv. 79–91; quoted by Maxwell).

14. *as*] What Ingleby (*Shakespeare,
The Man and the Book*, I, p. 147) calls
'the conjunction of reminder, being
employed by Shakespeare to introduce
a subsidiary statement, qualifying, or
even contradicting what goes before,
which the person addressed is required
to take for granted'. Cf. *Meas.*, II. iv.
88–90 (D.). 'The modern equivalent
would usually be a parenthesis introduced by "and"' (Maxwell).

eleven—] 'that will bring us prosperity' is understood (D.).

15. *eleven*] i.e. years of age.

brought them down] Cf. J. Heywood,
Play of the Wether (in Gayley, *Represen-*

Bawd. What else, man? The stuff we have, a strong wind
    will blow it to pieces, they are so pitifully sodden.
Pand. Thou sayest true; there's two unwholesome, a'
    conscience. The poor Transylvanian is dead, that   20
    lay with the little baggage.
Boult. Ay, she quickly poop'd him; she made him roast-
    meat for worms. But I'll go search the market.   *Exit.*
Pand. Three or four thousand chequins were as pretty a
    proportion to live quietly, and so give over.   25
Bawd. Why to give over, I pray you? is it a shame to get
    when we are old?
Pand. O, our credit comes not in like the commodity, nor
    the commodity wages not with the danger; there-
    fore, if in our youths we could pick up some pretty   30
    estate, 'twere not amiss to keep our door hatch'd.

19. there's two] *Q; they're too Malone.*   19. a'] *Q* (a); *in Q4;* o' *Malone.*

---

tative English Comedies, 1, 1. 860), 'Longe
be women in bryngyng up & sone
brought downe' (Steevens).

18. *sodden*] stewed; literally: 'subjected to treatment by the sweating
tub' (Maxwell). Cf. *Troil.,* III. i. 40,
'Sodden business! There's a stewed
phrase indeed!' (Delius).

19. *unwholesome*] diseased.

there's two] Malone emended,
'they're too', for 'the complaint had
not been made of *two* but of *all the stuff*
they had' (Malone). This is true, yet a
major emendation of a passage which
makes good sense in the original cannot be justified. Sisson defends Q: 'The
Pandar is precise in reply to the Bawd.
"You are quite right; there are two of
them that are badly diseased (unwholesome a conscience), and the
little one actually killed the Transyl-
vanian" '. That only *two* should be
unwholesome is a highly comic under-
statement.

19–20. *a' conscience*] on my conscience. The phrase, with *a*, occurs
frequently in Middleton's comedies.
Modernization, 'o' conscience', seems
undesirable, as it might obscure some
of the low-class idiom of this scene.

22. *poop'd*] usually defined as 'de-
ceived, cozened' (*O.E.D.*2) but this
does not fit the context; rather 'overcome' (J. S. Farmer, *Slang and its
Analogues,* v. 251, who cites *Gammer
Gurton's Needle,* II. i, 'But there ich was
powpte indeed'); perhaps a figurative
application of the sense listed in
*O.E.D.*3, of a towering wave hitting
the stern of a ship (and thus sometimes
sinking it). In Eliz. English, the term
often had a sexual connotation (see
Partridge, *A Dict. of Slang*). (See p. 188.)

24. *chequins*] Italian 'zecchini' = gold
coins worth about 8s. in Shakespeare's
day; three thousand chequins would
thus have been a considerable fortune.

25. *proportion*] portion, share, fortune (*O.E.D.*1, which cites *H5,* I. ii.
304). See also n. in (old) Arden edn of
Meas., v. i. 217; frequently so used.

give over] retire.

26. *get*] gain, earn money.

28. *credit*] reputation.

29. *commodity*] profit.

wages not] is not commensurate with,
contends not in rivalry with. Cf. *Ant.,*
v. i. 30–1, 'His taints and honours /
Wag'd equal with him' (Steevens).

31. *hatch'd*] with the hatch shut. The

Besides, the sore terms we stand upon with the gods
will be strong with us for giving o'er.

Bawd. Come, other sorts offend as well as we.

Pand. As well as we? ay, and better too; we offend worse.   35
Neither is our profession any trade; it's no calling.
But here comes Boult.

Enter BOULT, *with the Pirates and* MARINA.

Boult. Come your ways, my masters; you say she's a
virgin?

1. Pir. O, sir, we doubt it not.   40

Boult. Master, I have gone through for this piece you see.
If you like her, so; if not, I have lost my earnest.

Bawd. Boult, has she any qualities?

Boult. She has a good face, speaks well, and has excellent
good clothes; there's no farther necessity of qualities   45
can make her be refus'd.

38. ways, my masters;] *Q subst.* (wayes my maisters,); ways. My masters, *Malone.*

hatch, a common feature of brothels, was the lower half of a divided door, admitting people into the vestibule where they could be interviewed. Steevens adorns his edn with a woodcut of a brothel with hatch from *Holland's Leaguer*, 1632.

34. *sorts*] classes of people.

36. *trade*] recognized business (Maxwell).

calling] i.e. high calling; with a reference to the doctrine of a man's vocation in a divinely-ordered universe, as expressed in *1 Corinthians*, vii. 20, 'Let every man abide in the same vocation wherein he was called' (*Geneva Bible*, quoted by J. D. Wilson, ed. *2H6*, pp. xl–xli; also cf. Tilley C 23, cited there).

38. *Come . . . masters;*] so Q. Many edd. have followed Malone, who believed that *come your ways* is addressed to Marina, because Boult uses these very words towards her several times.

41. *gone through*] Cf. *P.A.*, 81. 18–19, 'in the end, went thorow, and bar-

gained to haue her'. Scholars have not been able to agree on the meaning of either passage. On. cites *Meas.*, II. i. 258, 'I do it for some piece of money, and go through with all', and interprets: 'do one's utmost', which I find quite unconvincing. Maxwell's paraphrase, 'completed the process of bargaining', seems much better, in spite of the apparent difficulty of reconciling it with the passage from Wilkins. Boult has concluded that process of bargaining which results in a price being stated—she cannot be had at less than a thousand pieces—and has paid a deposit or *earnest*, which is sufficient security for the pirates to end their auction. If Maxwell's paraphrase seems too strong, perhaps: 'got an option on by paying a deposit'.

42. *earnest*] a deposit put down to secure ultimate possession, and irrecoverable if the bargain was not carried through.

43. *qualities*] accomplishments (*O.E.D.*2b).

45-6. *no . . . refus'd*] a blending of

Bawd. What's her price, Boult?

Boult. I cannot be bated one doit of a thousand pieces.

Pand. Well, follow me, my masters; you shall have your
  money presently. Wife, take her in; instruct her what   50
  she has to do, that she may not be raw in her entertainment.   [*Exeunt Pandar and Pirates.*]

Bawd. Boult, take you the marks of her, the colour of her
  hair, complexion, height, her age, with warrant of
  her virginity, and cry "He that will give most shall   55
  have her first." Such a maidenhead were no cheap
  thing, if men were as they have been. Get this done as
  I command you.

Boult. Performance shall follow.   *Exit.*

Mar. Alack that Leonine was so slack, so slow!   60
  He should have struck, not spoke; or that these pirates
  Not enough barbarous, had not o'erboard
  Thrown me for to seek my mother!

Bawd. Why lament you, pretty one?

Mar. That I am pretty.   65

Bawd. Come, the gods have done their part in you.

Mar. I accuse them not.

Bawd. You are light into my hands, where you are like
  to live.

---

48. *Boult.* I] *Q ; 1. Pirate.* I *Lillo, conj. Malone; Boult.* It *Dyce.*   52. S.D.] *Malone;*
not in Q.   54. her age] *Q ;* age *Q4.*   60–3. Alack . . . mother!] *As Malone;*
prose Q.   61. struck] *Q* (strooke).   63. me for to] *Q ;* me, to *Malone.*

'there's no need of any other qualities
to make her acceptable' and 'there's
no such want of qualities as to cause
you to refuse her' (D.).

48. Boult. *I*] As the collation indicates, ever since the eighteenth century, edd. have questioned the Q text.
Yet it is, I believe, vindicated by the
following parallel in a little-known
play, J.D.'s *The Knave in Graine* (1640),
sig. I–Iv:

 Julio. . . . but you will bate nothing
  of your price?

 Mercer. I protest sir, I cannot . . .
By analogy, if the speech in *Pericles*
were to be given to the 1st Pirate, his
words would be 'I cannot bate one

doit . . .'. The passive form is appropriate for Boult. The sense is therefore:
'I cannot get them to bate me . . .' or 'I
cannot get the price lowered to me
by . . .'.

 bated] reduced.

 doit] smallest coin, worth a fraction
of a farthing.

 51. *raw*] inexperienced.

 51–2. *entertainment*] manner of reception (Maxwell).

 61. *struck*] Q 'strooke' was a variant spelling and pronunciation common in Elizabethan literature. Today it still persists in northern England.

 68. *are light*] have chanced to fall.

Mar. The more my fault   70
   To 'scape his hands where I was like to die.
Bawd. Ay, and you shall live in pleasure.
Mar. No.
Bawd. Yes, indeed shall you, and taste gentlemen of all
   fashions. You shall fare well; you shall have the dif-   75
   ference of all complexions. What do you stop your
   ears?
Mar. Are you a woman?
Bawd. What would you have me be, and I be not a wo-
   man?   80
Mar. An honest woman, or not a woman.
Bawd. Marry, whip thee, gosling; I think I shall have
   something to do with you. Come, you're a young
   foolish sapling, and must be bow'd as I would have
   you.   85
Mar. The gods defend me!
Bawd. If it please the gods to defend you by men, then
   men must comfort you, men must feed you, men stir
   you up. Boult's return'd.

70-1. The . . . die] *As Malone; prose Q.*
What] *Q;* What, *Rowe;* What! *Malone.*
Q; men must stir *Q4.*

71. was like to] *Q4;* was to *Q.*   76.
82. thee] *Q4;* the *Q.*   88. men stir]

70. *fault*] mischance. Cf. *Wiv.,* I. i.
83-4 and III. iii. 193.
   71. *was like to*] Q4's emendation
effects a better balance between
Marina's and the Bawd's speeches and
restores a decasyllabic line.
   75-6. *the difference . . . complexions*]
'men of every variety of race' (D.).
   What] why (a meaning that obviously escaped Malone).
   81. *honest*] honourable, and therefore 'chaste'. Cf. *Wint.,* I. ii. 288 and
II. iii. 70.
   82. *whip thee*] *whip* is a mild excra-
tion = confound, hang (*O.E.D.*11b).
Cf. *Oth.,* I. i. 49, 'whip me such honest
knaves' and *Lingua* (1607), III. iii,
'Untruss thy points, and whip thee
. . .' (D.). *thee* for Q 'the' is not abso-
lutely inevitable since expressions of
indignation sometimes do take the
third person construction. Yet the

accusative personal pronoun after
whip is far more common; and as *thee*
was often printed 'the' and thus the Q
text itself is open to interpretation, it
hardly seems proper to speak of an
emendation here. Maxwell objects because Marina is addressed as *you* in the
following sentence, but a shift from
thee to *you* is common in Elizabethan
literature.
   gosling] greenhorn.
   82-3. *have . . . you*] have trouble with
you.
   83-5. *you're . . . you*] Cf. Tilley T 632,
'Best to bend while it is a twig'.
   88. *men stir*] If this (Q's) reading is
correct, 'must' is understood.
   89. *Boult's return'd*] so Q; but it seems
an unnecessary statement, and sounds
like the reporter's hasty note for the
S.D., Enter Boult, supplied by later
edd.

[*Enter* BOULT.]

Now, sir, hast thou cried her through the market?   90
Boult. I have cried her almost to the number of her hairs;
    I have drawn her picture with my voice.
Bawd. And I prithee tell me, how dost thou find the in-
    clination of the people, especially of the younger
    sort?   95
Boult. Faith, they listen'd to me as they would have
    hearken'd to their father's testament. There was a
    Spaniard's mouth water'd and he went to bed to
    her very description.
Bawd. We shall have him here to-morrow with his best   100
    ruff on.
Boult. To-night, to-night. But, mistress, do you know
    the French knight that cowers i' the hams?
Bawd. Who? Monsieur Verolles?

89. S.D.] *Q4; not in Q.*   98. water'd and] *this ed.;* watred, and *Q;* so watered, that *Q4.*   103. i' the] *Q* (ethe).   104. Verolles] *Malone* (Veroles); *Verollus* / *Q.*

90–2. *Now . . . voice*] Mason suggested that Evanthe's lines in Fletcher, *Wife for a Month,* I. i, may have been influenced by this passage:

    I had rather thou hadst delivered
        me to Pirats
    Betray'd me to Uncurable diseases,
    Hung up my Picture in a Market-
        place,
    And sold me to wild Bawds.
                    (*Works,* v, p. 12)

91. *almost . . . hairs*] any number of times (D.). Cf. *Oth.,* v. ii. 78, 'Had all his hairs been lives, my great revenge Had stomach for them all' (H.F.B.).

98. *Spaniard's . . .*] The list of potential customers of different nationalities may owe something to Mary Faugh's similar catalogue in Marston, *The Dutch Courtezan,* I. ii. Her idiom, too, resembles that of the Bawd; e.g. her phrase 'Go thy ways'. Or is this merely testimony to the accurate realism of both authors?

mouth . . . and] The Spaniard's going *to bed to her very description* is not necessarily a result of his *mouth* watering, as many edd., who have followed Q4, seem to assume. Boult may merely be describing two separate symptoms of the Spaniard's condition. Still more plausibly, to my mind, *and* is to be understood not as a conjunction, but as having the sense of 'as if'—for which cf. *MND.,* I. ii. 73. If this interpretation is sound, the only change that needs to be made in the text is the removal of Q's comma before *and.*

103. *cowers . . . hams*] 'here, apparently, in consequence of his diseased condition' (D.). Q's 'ethe' for *i' the* is an unusual spelling.

104. *Verolles*] Malone's change from Q 'Verollus' is clearly warranted, considering the preceding *Monsieur* and the term's derivation from French *vérole* = pox. Cf. 'Doctor *Verolles* bottles' in Chapman, *The Widow's Tears,* IV. ii. 144, and 'Monsieur Parolles' in *All's W.*

Boult. Ay, he; he offer'd to cut a caper at the proclama-   105
    tion; but he made a groan at it, and swore he would
    see her to-morrow.
Bawd. Well, well; as for him, he brought his disease
    hither: here he does but repair it. I know he will
    come in our shadow, to scatter his crowns in the   110
    sun.
Boult. Well, if we had of every nation a traveller, we
    should lodge them with this sign.
Bawd. [*To Marina.*] Pray you, come hither awhile. You
    have fortunes coming upon you. Mark me: you   115
    must seem to do that fearfully which you com-
    mit willingly; despise profit where you have most
    gain. To weep that you live as ye do makes pity
    in your lovers: seldom but that pity begets you

---

105. Ay, he; he] *Globe;* I, he, he *Q;* I, he *Q4;* Ay, he *Rowe.*   114. S.D.] *Dyce;* not in *Q.*   117. despise] *Q;* to despise *Malone.*   119. lovers: seldom] *Malone;* Louers seldome, *Q.*

---

105. *offer'd*] attempted (frequent in Shakespeare).

caper] a dancing movement, taking the form of a leap in the air during which the feet are beaten together. (See *Shakespeare's England*, II. 447).

109. *repair*] renew (*O.E.D.v2*.3). Cf. *Err.*, II. i. 99; with a possible sarcastic undertone.

110–11. *come . . . sun*] Perhaps simply: 'seek the shelter of this house to spend his money there' (Mason subst.). 'Crowns of the sun' were French gold coins current in Shakespeare's England; cf. Massinger, *Unnatural Combat*, I. i, 'Present your bag, crammed with crowns of the sun'. Quite possibly the original read 'of the sun' for *in the sun*. The phrase 'Has crowns to scatter' occurs in Middleton, *Phoenix*, II. ii. 62.

But, as Malone already suggested, a secondary bawdy meaning is probably intended, for 'french crown' was also a term for baldness caused by syphilis; for this meaning, cf. *Meas.*, I. ii. 50, *MND.*, I. ii. 86–7, and *All's W.*, II. ii. 21. And Mason, quoting a piece

of bawdy dialogue from Fletcher, *The Custom of the Country*, III. iii (*Works*, I, p. 341),

   Sulpicia. What's become of the
      Dane?
   Jaques. Who? goldly-locks?
      He's foul i th' touch-hole . . .

   . . . .

      He lies at the sign of the *Sun*,
      to be new breech'd,
suggests, though on inadequate evidence, that Jacobean brothels frequently carried the sign of a sun.

113. *this sign*] i.e. Marina's signal charms; for a possible other meaning, see previous note.

115. *fortunes . . . you*] so *Mac.*, I. iii. 144, 'New honours come upon him' (Maxwell).

117. *despise*] Malone's 'to' is unnecessary, though it would indicate more clearly the dependance of *despise* on *seem*.

119. *lovers: seldom*] Q's 'Lovers seldome,' provides one of the many instances in early printed texts of Elizabethan drama where the comma indicates a pause before and emphasis

a good opinion, and that opinion a mere profit.   120
Mar. I understand you not.
Boult. O, take her home, mistress, take her home; these
    blushes of hers must be quench'd with some present
    practice.
Bawd. Thou sayest true, i'faith, so they must; for your   125
    bride goes to that with shame which is her way to
    go with warrant.
Boult. Faith, some do, and some do not. But, mistress, if
    I have bargain'd for the joint,—
Bawd. Thou mayst cut a morsel off the spit.   130
Boult. I may so?
Bawd. Who should deny it? Come, young one, I like the
    manner of your garments well.
Boult. Ay, by my faith, they shall not be chang'd yet.
Bawd. Boult, spend thou that in the town; report what a   135
    sojourner we have; you'll lose nothing by custom.
    When nature fram'd this piece, she meant thee a

---

125. *Bawd.*] *F3; Mari.* / *Q.*   129. joint,—] *Malone;* ioynt. *Q.*   131. so?] *D.;*
so. *Q.*

upon the previous word; thus the emendation.

   120. *mere*] sheer, downright (*O.E.D.* 4).

   122. *take her home*] simply: take her inside; but probably with the strong secondary meaning of 'tell her your mind' (E.S. and Maxwell subst.), as in 'tax him home' (*Ham.*, III. iii. 29), but I have not been able to find a parallel phrase with *take.*

   125. S.H. *Bawd*] F3's correction is beyond debate. But though the Bawd's words follow naturally upon Boult's, corruption in Q may be larger, for Q's faulty S.H. *Mari.* at the top of sig. G1ᵛ is anticipated by the catchword 'Mari' on sig. G1, and faulty catchwords are comparatively rare even in the work of inexperienced compositors. The possibility suggests itself that the compositor rather omitted a few words of Marina's—perhaps merely an exclamation, for her remarks obviously did not disrupt the flow of conversation.

Such a hypothesis might also serve to account for the unusually wide blank space, surrounding the final *Exit* of this scene on the same page, sig. G1ᵛ, in Q, though again there may be a simpler explanation.

   126–7. *which . . . go*] 'to which she is entitled to go' (Malone).

   128–30. *if . . . spit*] As Maxwell has noted, this phrase occurs at the point corresponding to IV. vi. 127 ff. in *P.A.*, 93. 13–15. Three possible explanations occur to me: (*a*) that the reporter misplaced this part of the dialogue in the play; (*b*) that Wilkins misplaced it in his prose report; (*c*) that the dialogue was shifted in a revision of the play. With the meagre facts of the play's transmission at one's disposal, it is impossible to go beyond this listing of possibilities.

   134. *they . . . yet*] possibly equivocal.

   136. *by custom*] i.e. by our getting customers (for Boult can expect a share of the takings).

good turn; therefore say what a paragon she is, and
thou hast the harvest out of thine own report.

Boult. I warrant you, mistress, thunder shall not so   140
awake the bed of eels as my giving out her beauty
stirs up the lewdly inclin'd. I'll bring home some
to-night.

Bawd. Come your ways; follow me.

Mar. If fires be hot, knives sharp, or waters deep,   145
Untied I still my virgin knot will keep.
Diana, aid my purpose!

Bawd. What have we to do with Diana? Pray you, will
you go with us?   *Exeunt.*

[SCENE III.—*Tharsus.*]

Enter CLEON *and* DIONYZA.

Dion. Why are you foolish? Can it be undone?

142. stirs] *Q;* stir *Malone.*   149. S.D. *Exeunt*] *F3; Exit | Q.*

Scene III

SCENE III] *Malone; not in Q.*   Location] *not in Q; Tharsus. A room in Cleon's
house. Malone.*   1. are] *Q4;* ere *Q.*

140–1. *thunder . . . eels*] Whalley
(*apud* Steevens) remarks: 'Thunder is
not supposed to have an effect on fish
in general, but on eels only, which are
roused by it from the mud, and are
therefore more easily taken', and cites
Marston, *Scourge of Villainy*, II. vii. 78–
80:

They are naught but Eeles, that
    neuer will appeare,
Till that tempestuous winds or
    thunder teare
Their slimy beds.

Cf. also Beaumont and Fletcher, *The
False One*, IV. ii. 200–1:

And you'll see me how I'll break
    like thunder
Amongst these beds of slimy Eeles'
                    (Craig *apud* D.).

I have not consulted any modern
scientists about this.

142. *stirs*] so Q. Malone's 'stir'
would regularize the grammar of the
statement, in accordance with *shall not
so awake*, but this use of the vivid present suits Boult.

144. *Come your ways*] come along.

145. *If . . . deep*] Malone compares
Oth., III. iii. 392–4, where the same
three modes of death are listed among
five.

Scene III

SCENE III] This interview between
Cleon and Dionyza, as Steevens and
other commentators have noted, resembles that of Macbeth and Lady
Macbeth immediately after the murder of Duncan. The similarity with
that of Albany and Goneril in *Lr.*, IV.
ii is even closer (E.S.). In all three
cases, the women are the instigators of

Cle. O Dionyza, such a piece of slaughter
        The sun and moon ne'er look'd upon!
Dion. I think you'll turn child again.
Cle. Were I chief lord of all this spacious world,   5
        I'd give it to undo the deed. A lady,
        Much less in blood than virtue, yet a princess
        To equal any single crown o'th' earth
        I'th' justice of compare! O villain Leonine!
        Whom thou hast poison'd too.   10
        If thou hadst drunk to him, 't had been a kindness
        Becoming well thy fact. What canst thou say
        When noble Pericles shall demand his child?
Dion. That she is dead. Nurses are not the fates,
†   To foster it, not ever to preserve.   15

5–43. Were ... epitaphs] *As Malone; prose Q.*   6. A] *Maxwell, conj. Delius;* O *Q.*
8. o'th'] *Q* (ath).   12. fact] *Dyce and Singer* (ii); face *Q;* feat *conj. Mason.*
15. not] *Q;* nor *Q4.*

the crime. Cleon and Albany, unlike
Macbeth, have no share in it, though
in the end, Cleon as head of a criminal
family is held responsible. At some
points, the resemblance of the scenes
extends to the wording.

4. *you'll ... again*] Cf. *Mac.*, II. ii.
53–4, ' 'tis the eye of childhood / That
fears a painted devil'.

5–6. *Were ... deed*] Cf. *King Leir* (ed.
Lee), IV. vii. 267–9, 'Oh, had I now to
give thee / The monarchy of all the
spacious world / To save his life, I
would bestow it on thee' (Maxwell,
private communication). This may
well be the source of the image, as
'spacious world' occurs nowhere else
in Shakespeare. It is, however, also
found in G.W.'s (Wilkins'?) *Historie of
Iustine* (1606), p. 102v.

6. *A*] Delius' conj. has been adopted,
for 'an apostrophe to Marina sounds
most unnatural' (Maxwell). As E.S.
pertinently comments, the emendation finds some support in *Lr.*, IV. ii.
41 ff., 'A father, and a gracious man...'
where, after lamenting the enormity of
Goneril's misdeed, Albany, like Cleon,
proceeds to describe the excellence of
the victim.

7. *Much ... virtue*] i.e. even 'more
so in point of virtue than of descent'
(D.).

9. *I' ... compare*] in a just comparison; *of compare* is an unusual expression.

10. *Whom ... too*] This suspiciously
short line suggests that the reporter
dropped some words either in this line
or before *O villain* in l. 9.

11. *drunk to him*] See Steevens' paraphrase in the following n.

12. *fact*] deed. Singer's correction
makes better sense than Q 'face', and
fact is Shakespeare's usual term for a
gross misdeed; see for instance *Wint.*,
III. ii. 86. The error arose from $e > t$
misreading, common in Elizabethan
times. Retaining 'face', Steevens paraphrases: 'hadst thou poisoned thyself
pledging him, it would have been an
action well becoming thee'.

14–15. *Nurses ... not ... preserve*] Like
most edd., D. accepts Q4's 'nor' for
not, and paraphrases: 'nurses ..., however great their care, are not the
fates to foster a child or keep it alive'.
But Maxwell justly comments that
this 'leaves the reference to *it* obscure,
and carries the odd implication that
the fates, unlike nurses, *do* foster life

> She died at night; I'll say so. Who can cross it?
> Unless you play the pious innocent,
> And for an honest attribute cry out
> "She died by foul play."

Cle.   O, go to. Well, well.
> Of all the faults beneath the heavens, the gods   20
> Do like this worst.

Dion.   Be one of those that thinks
> The petty wrens of Tharsus will fly hence,
> And open this to Pericles. I do shame
> To think of what a noble strain you are,
> And of how coward a spirit.

Cle.   To such proceeding   25
> Who ever but his approbation added,
> Though not his prime consent, he did not flow
> From honourable sources.

Dion.   Be it so, then.
> Yet none does know but you how she came dead,
> Nor none can know, Leonine being gone.   30

---

17. pious] *Collier, conj. Mason;* impious *Q; not in Q4.*   21. thinks] *Q;* think *Tonson.*   22. petty] *Q;* pretty *Q4.*   27. prime] *Dyce;* prince *Q.*   28. sources] *Dyce;* courses *Q.*

---

forever'. He plausibly suggests that some words are missing in the text. Making a similar assumption, H.F.B. thinks that a whole line has dropped out after *fates*, which read somewhat like this: 'To save a life or slay; their part is but'. This of course is mere conjecture but seems the only way of making sense of the passage.

16. *cross*] contradict.

17. *pious*] Mason's conj. is confirmed by *P.A.*, 80. 11, 'pious innocent'. The printer of Q4 was so puzzled by Q's 'impious' that he dropped it altogether.

18. *attribute*] reputation.

19. *go to*] used to express disapprobation or contempt; not unlike modern 'come, come'.

21. *thinks*] This grammatical error is still common in ordinary speech.

22-3. *The . . . Pericles*] Dionyza is

referring to the folk-belief in the revelation of hidden murders by a tell-tale bird. Cf. *Mac.*, III. iv. 123-5 (E. Schanzer, 'Four Notes on Macbeth', *MLR*, LII, No. 2 (April 1957), 225-7). Many ballads illustrate this belief; e.g. 'Young Hunting' (Child, *English and Scottish Popular Ballads*, No. 68).

23. *shame*] So Lady Macbeth feels ashamed of her husband, *Mac.*, II. ii. 63-4.

27. *prime*] The minim error *nc* for *m* is frequently found in Elizabethan printing and explains Q 'prince'.

27-8. *he . . . sources*] i.e. he does not stem from an honourable family. Retaining Q, Sisson defends 'courses' as meaning 'water-courses'. But this would make very odd sense, and is unlikely considering *All's W.*, II. i. 138-9, 'Great floods have flown / From simple sources'.

She did distain my child, and stood between
Her and her fortunes. None would look on her,
But cast their gazes on Marina's face,
Whilst ours was blurted at and held a malkin
Not worth the time of day. It pierc'd me through;   35
And though you call my course unnatural,—
You not your child well loving—yet I find
It greets me as an enterprise of kindness
Perform'd to your sole daughter.

Cle.   Heavens forgive it!

Dion. And as for Pericles,   40
What should he say? we wept after her hearse,
And yet we mourn. Her monument
Is almost finish'd, and her epitaphs
In glitt'ring golden characters express
A general praise to her, and care in us   45
At whose expense 'tis done.

Cle.   Thou art like the harpy,

---

31. distain] *Dyce, conj. Steevens;* disdaine *Q.*   33. Marina's] *Q2; Marianas | Q.*
34. malkin] *Q* (Mawkin).   35. through] *Q* (thorow).   44–6. In . . . done]
As Dyce; prose Q.   46–8. Thou . . . talons] *As Q4; prose Q.*

31. *She . . . child*] She made my child
look colourless.

33. *Marina's*] For a discussion of Q
'*Mariana's*', see *Dramatis Personae* n.

34. *blurted at*] treated with scorn.

malkin] slut; often spelt 'mawkin',
in Shakespeare's day.

35. *the . . . day*] greeting.

38. *greets*] gratifies (On.).

40–2. *And . . . monument*] The traditional lineation, here reproduced,
seems best in the context of the surrounding lines; something may well
have dropped out of the text, or, as
H.F.B. conjectures, *And as* may be
actor's preluding. In that case, the
original lines may have been: 'For
Pericles, what should he say? We
wept / After her hearse, and yet we
mourn. Her monument / '.

42. *yet*] still.

43. *epitaphs*] The plural is appropriate, as it was customary to affix to
the hearse or grave more than one

laudatory poem or 'epitaph' (D.).

44. *characters*] letters.

46–8. *Thou . . . talons*] *with thine
angel's face* = with that angel face of
yours. The expression seems confused
because on first reading one inclines to
link *seize* with *face*, and because *thine*
refers directly to Dionyza. Yet the
sense is plain: 'You are like the harpy
who seizes with its eagle talons that
which its angel-like appearance has
deluded' (D.). Emendations have not
been listed, as they are all quite absurd.
Perhaps, H.F.B. suggests, what Shakespeare had begun as simile, so far as
like to the Harpie | Which to betray, then
turned to metaphor, so that instead of
continuing 'does with an Angells
Face / Ceaze with an Eagles talents',
it continued with *doest . . . thine . . .
thine*, making *Which* (= Who) now
refer to Dionyza instead of to the
Harpy. Q's 'talents' was a common
variant spelling for *talons*; see the

  Which, to betray, dost with thine angel's face,
  Seize with thine eagle's talons.
Dion. Ye're like one that superstitiously
  Do swear to th' gods that winter kills the flies;   50
  But yet I know you'll do as I advise.   [*Exeunt.*]

[SCENE IV.—*Before the monument of Marina at Tharsus.*]

[*Enter*] GOWER.

Thus time we waste, and long leagues make short;

48. talons] *Rowe;* talents *Q.*   50–1. Do . . . advise] As *Q4;* kills / youle / aduise
Q.   50. Do] *Q;* Doth *Q4;* Does *conj. Maxwell.*   51. S.D.] *Rowe;* not in *Q*
Exit / Q4.

Scene IV
Scene IV] *Malone; not in Q; Actus Quartus / F3.*   Location] *Malone; not in Q.*
Enter Gower] *Q4; Gower / Q (as S.H. only).*   1. long] *Q;* longest *Malone.*

quibble in *LLL.*, IV. ii. 61–2, 'If a
talent be a claw, look how he claws
him with a talent' (Dyce). As no pun
is intended here, Rowe's modernization has been adopted.

The image of the harpy was a common one in literature, and was popu-
larized by pictorial representation; cf.
Gosson, *Schoole of Abuse* (ed. Arber,
p. 20), 'The Harpies haue Virgins
faces and Vultures Talentes' (Maxwell, privately), and J. Day, *Peregrinatio*, p. 54, 'her fingers naild with
Harpeis tallents'.

49–50. *like one . . . flies*] This passage
has been interpreted in a variety of
ways, e.g. 'You are one of those who
superstitiously appeal to the gods on
every trifling and natural event'
(Mason); and 'like one who with
religious naivety complains to the gods
of the rigour of the seasons' (D.). But
none of these interpretations really
squares with Cleon's attitude as
scorned by Dionyza. She is evidently
satirizing Cleon's view of the gods as
well as his, to her, 'needless' fears of
their being suspected of Marina's
murder. And she fails to make a distinction between deceiving Pericles
and deceiving the gods. The equation
of the crime of killing Marina with
such an insignificant act as the killing
of flies is sheer sophistry, of course.
Thus the probable meaning of the
comparison is: 'like one so afraid of the
power and so sure of the suspicious
vengeful character of heaven, that he
needlessly swears, "please, it wasn't
me", when winter kills the flies' (paraphrased with the help of E.S. and
H.F.B.).

50. *Do*] Q4's 'Doth' is tempting but,
as Maxwell notes, 'agreement with the
subject of the main clause is not unnatural' in seventeenth-century literature.

Scene IV
1. *waste*] annihilate (*O.E.D.*5, Maxwell).

long] Most edd. adopt Q4's 'longest',
which regularizes the metre. But
deliberate metrical irregularity in
imitation of Gower, whose metre
Elizabethans held to be uncertain, is a
distinct possibility (Sisson). So is a
disyllabic pronunciation of *leagues*.

Sail seas in cockles, have and wish but for't;
Making, to take our imagination,
From bourn to bourn, region to region.
By you being pardon'd, we commit no crime   5
To use one language in each several clime
Where our scene seems to live. I do beseech you
To learn of me, who stand i' th' gaps to teach you
The stages of our story. Pericles
Is now again thwarting the wayward seas,   10
Attended on by many a lord and knight,
To see his daughter, all his life's delight.
Old Helicanus goes along. Behind

2. and] *Q; an Dyce.*   3. Making,] *Malone (1780); Making Q.*   our] *Q; your
Malone; not in Hudson.*   7. scene seems] *Maxwell; sceanes seemes Q; sceanes
seeme Q4.*   8. i' th'] *Maxwell, conj. Bullen; with Q; i the Malone; in Q4.*
you] *F4; you. Q.*   9. story.] *Tonson; storie Q; story, F4.*   10. the] *Q2; thy Q.*
13–16. Old . . . estate] *As Q; ll. 15–16 followed by ll. 14, 13 Steevens.*   13. along.
Behind] *Daniel; along behind, Q; along behind. Steevens.*

2. *Sail . . . cockles*] Malone sees here
an allusion to the folk-belief that
witches could sail in egg-shells,
cockles, or mussel-shells through tempestuous seas. E.S. points out that the
opening two lines of this chorus fit in
well with the general fairy-tale atmosphere of the play.

and . . . for't] by merely wishing
for it.

3. *Making . . . imagination*] to take our
imagination has been a much debated
phrase, but it seems unnecessary to
adopt Malone's 'your' or to omit *our*
altogether, as some edd. have done.
J. D. Wilson's interpretation, 'moving
in order to capture the imagination'
seems less convincing than 'moving, *in*
(and with the help of) our imagination, from . . .' It would also be possible 'to omit the comma after *Making*
(so Q) and treat *take* as intransitive,
"causing our imagination to make its
way"' (Maxwell subst.). E.S. suggests
that *take* here means, as fairly frequently in seventeenth-century literature, 'delight, captivate, enchant'
(*O.E.D.*10), and accordingly interprets the sense of the passage as,

'Making our way, to delight our
imagination, from . . .'.

4. *bourn*] frontier.

7. *scene*] dramatic performance. Cf.
l. 48 below, *Ham.*, II. ii. 586, 'the very
cunning of the scene', and *H5*, I.
Ch. 4–5, 'princes to act / And monarchs to behold the swelling scene',
which gives strong support to Maxwell's emendation.

8. *i' th' gaps*] The idea of a *gap* of time
appears frequently in Shakespeare's
plays from *Ant.* on; e.g. *Ant.*, I. v. 5,
Cym., III. ii. 61–2, *Wint.*, IV. i. 7 and
v. iii. 154. Bullen's emendation (from
Malone) gets support from *Wint.*, v.
iii. 154, 'in this wide gap'. Should Q
'with gappes' be sound after all, the
sense can only refer to the interrup-
tions in the action proper which
Gower himself fills out.

10. *thwarting*] crossing.

wayward] untoward; from 'awei-
ward' = turned away, perverse (D.,
citing Skeat, *Etym. Dict.*).

13. *along. Behind*] Daniel's simple
emendation restores the sense much
better than Steevens' transposition of
lines. The resulting contorted word-

Is left to govern it, you bear in mind,
Old Escanes, whom Helicanus late   15
Advanc'd in time to great and high estate.
Well-sailing ships and bounteous winds have brought
This king to Tharsus—think his pilot thought;
So with his steerage shall your thoughts grow on—
To fetch his daughter home, who first is gone.   20
Like motes and shadows see them move awhile;
Your ears unto your eyes I'll reconcile.

[DUMB SHOW]

Enter PERICLES *at one door, with all his train;* CLEON *and* DIONYZA
at the other. CLEON *shows* PERICLES *the tomb; whereat* PERICLES
makes lamentation, puts on sackcloth, and in a mighty passion departs.

[*Then exeunt* CLEON, DIONYZA, *and the rest.*]

14. govern it, you] Q; govern, if you *conj. Maxwell.*   mind,] *Malone;* mind. Q;
minde Q2.   16. time] Q; Tyre *conj. S. Walker.*   18. his pilot thought]
Steevens; this Pilat thought Q; this pilot—thought *conj. Mason.*   19. grow
on] *Malone;* grone Q; go on *Maxwell, conj. Malone.*   20. first] Q; since *conj.
Kellner.*   22. *Dumb Show*] *Malone; not in* Q.   S.D. 4. *Then* . . . *rest*] *Camb.;
not in* Q.

order is not unlike other passages in the
play.

14. *govern it, you*] Maxwell's conj.
'govern, if you' is attractive, though in
Elizabethan drama 'and' usually
takes the place of 'if' in unemphatic
conditional clauses.

mind,] Once the emendation of
l. 13 is accepted, the comma is essential.

16. *time*] Walker's 'Tyre' is plausible, for it would supply a belated
antecedent for *it* (l. 14), and makes
better sense.

18–19. *think . . . grow on*] Q is manifestly corrupt, and edd., unable to
agree on the text's meaning, have
changed it in various ways. The two
emendations adopted in this text,
Steevens' *his thought* for 'this thought'
and Malone's *grow on* for 'grone', not
merely restore tolerable sense to the
passage—'think that Pericles' pilot is
thought (i.e. as swift as thought). Thus

shall your own thoughts proceed,
steered by him (i.e. by thought acting
as your pilot also)'—but they are
likewise defensible on bibliographical
grounds. As Maxwell suggests, Q's
compositor caught up 'this' from the
beginning of l. 18, and he might easily
have misinterpreted *grow on* as 'grone'
in a difficult MS; or, as H.F.B. thinks,
having set up scribal *grow on* as far as
"gro", then unconsciously so completed the line as to make an eye-rhyme
with the next. Mason's interpretation
of 'think this pilot thought' as 'keep
this leading circumstance in your mind,
which will serve as a pilot to you' is not
convincing. The parallel in *H5*, III.
Ch. 1–3 and 18 supports one's impression that Shakespeare had a hand in
this chorus.

20. *who . . . gone*] who left before; for
this use of *first*, see *O.E.D.*B2.

21. *motes*] particles of dust in a sun-
beam.

See how belief may suffer by foul show!
This borrow'd passion stands for true-ow'd woe;
And Pericles, in sorrow all devour'd,　　　　　　　25
With sighs shot through and biggest tears o'ershower'd,
Leaves Tharsus and again embarks. He swears
Never to wash his face, nor cut his hairs.
He puts on sackcloth, and to sea. He bears
A tempest, which his mortal vessel tears,　　　　　　30
And yet he rides it out. Now please you wit
The epitaph is for Marina writ
By wicked Dionyza.
　　　　　[*Reads the inscription on Marina's monument.*]
The fairest, sweet'st and best, lies here,
Who wither'd in her spring of year.　　　　　　35
She was of Tyrus the king's daughter,

---

24. true-ow'd] *Maxwell, anon. conj. apud Camb.;* true olde *Q.*　　　29. puts]
Malone; put *Q.*　　　sea. He bears] *Malone;* Sea he beares, *Q;* sea, he bears
Sewell.　　　33. S.D.] *Malone; not in Q.*　　　34. sweet'st and] *Malone; sweetest, and | Q;*
sweetest | *Steevens.*

---

23. *suffer . . . show*] be abused by
hypocrisy.

24. *borrow'd*] pretended, counterfeit.

true-ow'd] sincerely owned. In support of the emendation, Round cites
Comp., 327 'that borrowed motion,
seeming owed'; *true-ow'd* seems inten-
tionally antithetical to *borrow'd*. If it is
correct, the error in Q may either be
a graphic one, the compositor misreading *ow'd* as 'ould' (Maxwell) or an
auditory one resulting from a silent *l*.
Yet Q 'true olde' is just possible.

29. *puts*] present tense, to accord
with the context.

30. *vessel*] biblical for 'body'; cf.
Tim., v. i. 199, 'nature's fragile vessel';
yet consciously used as an image.

31. *rides it out*] sustains it without
irreparable damage. (The nautical
metaphor is continued.)

wit] know.

34–43. The . . . flint] After a fairly
tolerable beginning, this epitaph
deteriorates into sheer poetic drivel.
The facts that ll. 34–7 only are para-

phrased from Gower (see *C.A.*, 1535–
8), and that in Wilkins' report, *P.A.*,
79. 9–12, the first two lines are almost
identical, while the remaining eight
are replaced by the couplet, 'In
Natures garden, though by growth a
Bud, / Shee was the chiefest flower, she
was good', support Maxwell's notion
that ll. 38–43 were not part of the
original play but improvised by the
reporter. And yet they may have at
least a Shakespearean substratum, for
the idea of the sea encroaching upon
the land is frequent in Shakespeare,
and sometimes the imagery is similar;
cf. *Sonnet* 65: 'boundless sea' . . . 'rage'
. . . 'batt'ring days' . . . 'rocks impreg-
nable', the phrase, 'the battery that
you make' (*Complaint*, 277), the linking
of 'rages' and 'batters' in Ulysses'
description of Achilles' pride (*Troil.*,
II. iii. 170–1; cf. Thetis' pride), and the
association of water and flint in *Tit.*,
II. iii. 141 (H.F.B.).

34. sweet'st and] Steevens' 'sweetest' (omitting 'and') is a possible alternative to Malone's simple alteration.

> On whom foul death hath made this slaughter.
> Marina was she call'd; and at her birth,
> Thetis, being proud, swallow'd some part o' th' earth.
> Therefore the earth, fearing to be o'erflow'd,   40
> Hath Thetis' birth-child on the heavens bestow'd;
> Wherefore she does, and swears she'll never stint,
> Make raging battery upon shores of flint.

No visor does become black villainy
So well as soft and tender flattery.   45
Let Pericles believe his daughter's dead,
And bear his courses to be ordered
By Lady Fortune; while our scene must play
His daughter's woe and heavy well-a-day
In her unholy service. Patience, then,   50
And think you now are all in Mytilen.   *Exit.*

[SCENE V.—*Mytilene.*]

Enter[, from the brothel,] two Gentlemen.

1. Gent. Did you ever hear the like?

2. Gent. No, nor never shall do in such a place as this, she
    being once gone.

39. *Thetis*] Q; *That is* Q2–6, F3–4, *Rowe.*   48. scene] *Malone* (*1790*)*;* Steare Q*;*
tears *Malone* (*1780*)*.*   49. well-a-day] Q (welladay).   51. Mytilen] Q
(*Mittelin*).

Scene v

Scene v] *Malone; not in* Q.   Location] *not in* Q*; Mytilene. A street before the
brothel. Malone.*   Entry. *from the brothel*] *Malone; not in* Q.

39. Thetis . . . earth] The swelling of
the sea is ascribed 'to the pride Thetis
felt at the birth of Marina in her element' (Mason). Naturally the earth
revenges herself upon Marina. But
Mason does not comment that here,
Thetis, the sea-nymph and mother of
Achilles, is confused, as in *Troil.,* i. iii.
39 and elsewhere in Elizabethan literature, with Tethys, the wife of Oceanus
(E.S.). Q2's 'That is' provides a
dramatic illustration of how much a
compositor could play havoc with a
text, even with a printed version as
a copy. Theobald (marginalia in

copy of Q4) was the first to restore Q.

42. *she*] i.e. Thetis.
does] i.e. *does make . . . battery.*
stint] cease.

43. *visor*] mask.

47. *bear . . . ordered*] suffer his actions
to be regulated (D.).

48. *scene*] By far the most plausible
emendation of Q 'Steare'. The corruption can be accounted for in two
possible ways: either as a reporter's 'recollection' of 'Steerage' in l. 19 above,
or, which is more likely, as a graphic
error, misreading *t* for *c* and *r* for *n.*

49. *well-a-day*] grief.

1. Gent. But to have divinity preach'd there! did you ever
      dream of such a thing?   5
2. Gent. No, no. Come, I am for no more bawdy-houses.
      Shall's go hear the vestals sing?
1. Gent. I'll do anything now that is virtuous; but I am
      out of the road of rutting for ever.   *Exeunt.*

[SCENE VI.—*Mytilene. In the Brothel.*]

Enter Pandar, Bawd, and BOULT.

Pand. Well, I had rather than twice the worth of her she
      had ne'er come here.
Bawd. Fie, fie upon her! she's able to freeze the god
      Priapus, and undo a whole generation. We must
      either get her ravish'd or be rid of her. When she   5
      should do for clients her fitment and do me the kind-
      ness of our profession, she has me her quirks, her
      reasons, her master-reasons, her prayers, her knees;
      that she would make a puritan of the devil, if he
      would cheapen a kiss of her.   10
Boult. Faith, I must ravish her, or she'll disfurnish us of

9. S.D.] *F3; Exit Q.*

Scene VI

SCENE VI ... *Brothel*] *Malone subst.; not in Q.*   Entry] *Malone; Enter Bawdes 3. | Q.*
8. master-reasons] *hyphenated Q4; unhyphenated Q.*

7. *Shall's*] a mixture of 'let us' and
'shall we' (Jespersen *apud* Franz §285).
Cf. *Cym.*, IV. ii. 234, 'Say, where shall's
lay him?' The illiterate use of *us* for
'we' is still common in some parts of
England.

9. *rutting*] fornication.

Scene VI

4. *Priapus*] God of fertility; to Elizabethans the embodiment of lechery.
Possibly suggested by Twine, p. 296,
'hee brought her into a certain chappel
where stoode the idoll of Priapus made
of gold' (Steevens), but references to

this figure were common in Elizabethan literature.

6. *fitment*] an unusual expression:
duty (On.); what befits her as a prostitute. The brothel-keepers are aston-
ished and dismayed at Marina's con-
travening the inverted morality of the
bawdy house.

6–7. *do me ... has me*] For the use of
the 'ethical dative', see Abbott §220
and Franz §294 who, among many
examples in Shakespeare, cites *Troil.*,
I. ii. 113, 'she came and puts me her
white hand to his clown chin'.

10. *cheapen*] bargain for.

all our cavalleria, and make our swearers priests.
Pand. Now, the pox upon her green-sickness for me!
Bawd. Faith, there's no way to be rid on't but by the way
    to the pox. Here comes the Lord Lysimachus, dis-   15
    guis'd.
Boult. We should have both lord and lown, if the peevish
    baggage would but give way to customers.

Enter LYSIMACHUS.

Lys. How now! How a dozen of virginities?
Bawd. Now, the gods to bless your honour!   20
Boult. I am glad to see your honour in good health.
Lys. You may so; 'tis the better for you that your resorters
    stand upon sound legs. How now, wholesome ini-
    quity, have you that a man may deal withal, and
    defy the surgeon?   25

---

12. cavalleria] *Alexander, anon. conj. apud Camb.;* Caualereea *Q;* Caualeres *Q2.*
make our] *Q;* make all our *F3.*   20. to bless] *unhyphenated Q; hyphenated Malone,*
conj. Tyrwhitt.   22. may so;] *Malone;* may, so *Q;* may so *Q4.*   23–4.
iniquity, have] *Malone subst.;* iniquitie haue *Q.*

---

12. *cavalleria*] Italian, 'body of
gentlemen', 'knighthood'. The colourful Italianate word seems appropriate
in the atmosphere of a brothel. Q
'Caualereea' spelt the word as it
sounds, with a stress on the penulti-
mate syllable, as in *Cavalleria
Rusticana.* Q2 'Caualeres' = cavaliers
is plausible, but probably the press-corrector's
or compositor's guess.

our swearers] those who swear by
us; or 'our freeswearing customers'.

13. *green-sickness*] literally an anae-
mic disorder to which young women
are subject; but here obviously a metaphor for excessive squeamishness in
sexual matters, attributed to in-
experience.

for me] say I. Cf. *All's W.,* IV. iii. 245
(F text), 'A pox upon him for me'
(E.S.).

15. *pox*] syphilis.

15–16. *disguis'd*] In Twine also, but
not in Gower, Lysimachus arrives in
disguise. Yet in Twine he is Marina's
first customer (Maxwell).

17. *lown*] loon, low-bred fellow; cf.
Oth., II. iii. 85; still in use in parts of
northern England.

19. *How*] at what price; cf. *2H4,*
III. ii. 37–8, 'How a good yoke of
bullocks at Stamford fair?' (D.).

20. *to bless*] 'I pray' is understood.
Many edd. hyphenate 'to-bless' =
bless entirely (*to* being an intensive
prefix).

23–4. *wholesome iniquity,*] Lysimachus
so addresses the Bawd ironically (D.).
Some edd. follow Q's punctuation,
taking the words as the object of *have
you.* In support of Q, P. Edwards
writes: 'Lysimachus has just reminded
the Bawd that it is lucky for her that
he, "a resorter", is in good health, and
then goes straight on to demand a
piece of healthy sin, a sound prostitute,
so that he may continue in good
health' (*Sh.Q.,* VIII, No. 4 (1957), 537).
D.'s interpretation is more convincing
and equally comic.

24. *deal withal*] have sexual inter-
course with.

Bawd. We have here one, sir, if she would—but there
    never came her like in Mytilene.
Lys. If she'd do the deeds of darkness, thou wouldst
    say.
Bawd. Your honour knows what 'tis to say well enough.   30
Lys. Well, call forth, call forth.
Boult. For flesh and blood, sir, white and red, you shall
    see a rose; and she were a rose indeed, if she had
    but—
Lys. What, prithee?   35
Boult. O, sir, I can be modest.
Lys. That dignifies the renown of a bawd no less than it
    gives a good report to a number to be chaste. [*Exit Boult.*]
Bawd. Here comes that which grows to the stalk; never
    pluck'd yet, I can assure you.   40

[*Enter* BOULT *with* MARINA.]

Is she not a fair creature?
Lys. Faith, she would serve after a long voyage at sea.
    Well, there's for you; leave us.

28. deeds] *Q;* deede *Q5.*   32, 36. *Boult.*] *Q; Bawd. | Grant White.*   34. but—]
Malone; but. *Q.*   37. dignifies] *Q4;* dignities *Q;* dignity is *conj. Malone.*
38. number] *Q;* whore *conj. E. Thiessen;* wanton *anon. conj. apud Camb.*   38.
S.D.] *Dyce; not in Q.*   40. S.D.] *Dyce; not in Q.*

28. *deeds of darkness*] Though the
singular, 'deed of darkness', is more
common, the plural form is not unusual; see, for instance, Wilkins, *Miseries of Inforst Marriage,* p. 525 (Hazlitt's *Dodsley,* 1874, IX), and J.D., *The
Knave in Graine* (1640), sig. H4.

30. *what . . . say*] 'What one should
say to express my meaning' (D.).

32, 36. S.H. Boult] Grant White
attributes these speeches to the Bawd,
because of Lysimachus' answer, l. 37.
But it should be kept in mind that the
term 'bawd' could be applied to both
male and female, and to both owners
and employees of brothels, as exempli-
fied in Q's opening S.D. to this scene:
'Enter Bawdes 3'. See also Greene,
A Notable Discovery of Cosnage (1591),
sig. C4v (among a list of the terms of

coney-catching): 'The Bawde, if it be
a woman [is called], a Pandar'.

34. *but—*] 'a thorn' is understood,
according to the saying, 'no rose without a thorn' (Tilley R 182); 'thorn' has
frequently a bawdy implication; cf.
ATL., III. ii. 101–2 (Maxwell).

38. *number*] Sisson (II, pp. 297–8)
comments on the passage: 'The sense
is plain and pregnant: "Modesty (in
speech) gives a reputation for chastity
to many (who are unchaste in act)" '.
No emendation is necessary, once *to be*
is interpreted in its Elizabethan sense
of 'for being'. *Viz.* 'the dignity that
modesty gives to bawds is just as spe-
cious as the reputation it gives to many
for being chaste' (H.F.B.).

42. *Faith . . . sea*] a sardonic remark,
belittling the Bawd's praise; all the

Bawd. I beseech your honour, give me leave a word, and
    I'll have done presently.   45

Lys. I beseech you, do.

Bawd. [*To Marina.*] First, I would have you note, this is
    an honourable man.

Mar. I desire to find him so, that I may worthily note
    him.   50

Bawd. Next, he's the governor of this country, and a man
    whom I am bound to.

Mar. If he govern the country, you are bound to him
    indeed; but how honourable he is in that I know
    not.   55

Bawd. Pray you, without any more virginal fencing, will
    you use him kindly? he will line your apron with
    gold.

Mar. What he will do graciously, I will thankfully re-
    ceive.   60

Lys. Ha' you done?

Bawd. My lord, she's not pac'd yet; you must take some
    pains to work her to your manage. Come, we will
    leave his honour and her together. Go thy ways.

            [*Exeunt Bawd, Pandar, and Boult.*]

Lys. Now, pretty one, how long have you been at this   65
    trade?

---

44. leave a] *Q*; leave: a *Malone*.   47. S.D.] *Malone; not in Q.*   64. Go thy
ways] *Q; Lys.* Go thy ways *Malone; not in Q4.*   S.D.] *Malone; not in Q; Exit
Bawd | Q4.*

more ironic in a play about voyages.

    44. *give . . . word*] a possible expres-
sion for 'give me leave awhile', *a
word* being treated as a measure of
time.

    45. *presently*] immediately, instant-
ly.

    49. *worthily note*] respect.

    56. *virginal fencing*] quibbling about
your chastity.

    59. *graciously*] like a gentleman.
Quite possibly the word's religious
sense is also present: 'while he remains
in a state of grace'.

    62–3. *pac'd . . . manage*] *pac'd* =
broken in, taught her paces; images

taken from the schooling of horses.

    64. *Go thy ways*] Go along. Whores
seem to have been fond of this phrase
see IV. ii. 98n.

    65–90. *Now . . . come*] here printed as
prose, as in Q and most edd. But
H.F.B. strongly argues for verse which
would (i) fit this dialogue of noble personages; (ii) fit an episode of emotional
and dramatic climax; (iii) provide a
contrast with the prose of the brothel-
keeper episodes. If the passage is verse,
however, it can only be reconstructed
in part, for memorial damage is considerable; see App. D. I am not entirely persuaded by H.F.B.'s argu-

Mar. What trade, sir?

Lys. Why, I cannot name't but I shall offend.

Mar. I cannot be offended with my trade. Please you to
name it.   70

Lys. How long have you been of this profession?

Mar. E'er since I can remember.

Lys. Did you go to't so young? Were you a gamester at
five or at seven?

Mar. Earlier too, sir, if now I be one.   75

Lys. Why, the house you dwell in proclaims you to be a
creature of sale.

Mar. Do you know this house to be a place of such resort,
and will come into't? I hear say you're of honourable
parts and are the governor of this place.   80

Lys. Why, hath your principal made known unto you
who I am?

Mar. Who is my principal?

Lys. Why, your herb woman; she that sets seeds and
roots of shame and iniquity. O, you have heard   85
something of my power, and so stand aloof for more
serious wooing. But I protest to thee, pretty one, my
authority shall not see thee, or else look friendly upon
thee. Come, bring me to some private place; come,
come.   90

Mar. If you were born to honour, show it now;

68. Why, . . . name't] *F3;* Why, . . . name *Q;* What . . . name *Steevens.*   86.
aloof] *Rowe;* aloft *Q.*   91–3. If . . . it] *As Rowe; prose Q.*

ment, for cf. the fifth scene of *Tw. N.*
where Olivia and Viola continue to
speak in prose for some time after being
left alone.

68. *Why . . . name't*] Steevens supports his emendation, 'what . . . name'
feebly, citing *Meas.,* I. ii. 129. Yet Q
'name' is just possible.

73. *go to't*] copulate; cf. *Lr.,* IV. vi.
112, 122 (Maxwell).

gamester] wanton; 'one addicted to
amorous sport' (*O.E.D.*5).

86. *aloof*] Q 'aloft' can only mean
'up high' which makes no sense here.

87–8. *my authority . . . thee*] 'you have
nothing to fear from me in my capacity

as governor; I shall wink at your
manner of life' (D.).

91–3. *If . . . it*] If *put upon you* = If
honour was bestowed upon you. Cf.
Tw. N., II. v. 129–30, 'Some are born
great . . . some have greatness thrust
upon 'em' (Maxwell). From the two
following speeches of Lysimachus it
would appear probable that in the
original text Marina made a much
longer and more eloquent plea than Q
reports. As the text stands, Marina
spends more time in shaming Boult
than in shaming Lysimachus. Wilkins,
however, has Lysimachus visit the
brothel with wicked intent, which was

If put upon you, make the judgement good
That thought you worthy of it.
Lys. How's this? how's this? Some more; be sage.
Mar.   For me,
That am a maid, though most ungentle fortune   95
Have plac'd me in this sty, where, since I came,
Diseases have been sold dearer than physic—
That the gods
Would set me free from this unhallow'd place,
Though they did change me to the meanest bird   100
That flies i'th' purer air!
Lys.   I did not think
Thou couldst have spoke so well; ne'er dreamt thou
couldst.
Had I brought hither a corrupted mind,

94–8. For . . . gods] *As Collier; prose Q. prose Q.*

99–106. Would . . . thee!] *As Rowe; prose Q.*

surely not Shakespeare's intention in the play, though Lysimachus throws off his mask only at l. 101. See the following notes and Intro., pp. xlvi–xlviii.

94. *be sage*] See previous n. Many edd. quote Malone, 'with a sneer—"proceed with your fine moral discourse"', but even if Lysimachus maintains his mask until l. 101, such a negative reaction would be out of character. Rather one would expect the intended effect of the words to be non-committal, even ambiguous: 'be wise and virtuous', or 'be a good whore'.

94–114. *For . . . thief*] The arrangement of the verse by Rowe, Malone, and Collier cannot be improved upon, though several of the resulting lines are metrically irregular or incomplete. These irregularities may well have resulted from omissions, transpositions, or faulty paraphrases in the text by the reporter. For instance, the incomplete l. 98, preceding as it does a line that seems genuinely Shakespearean, makes one suspect that a phrase before *That* has been lost (see also n. to ll.

178–9 below). Ll. 108–9 are suspect for several reasons: they are bad verse; the repetition *For me . . . for to me*, with the echo back to l. 94, seems memorially corrupt; and the statement would seem more appropriate after *hap alter'd it* in l. 104. L. 113 may also be corrupt, for it is a short line and merely repeats, but for one word, l. 104 (H.F.B.). At any rate, the original seems irrecoverable, and for reasons stated in Intro., pp. xlviii–xlix, Wilkins' different and more extensive account of this episode cannot be relied upon either.

97. *physic*] medicine.

100–1. *meanest bird . . . air*] undoubtedly a Shakespearean image. In *Cym.*, possibly written immediately after *Pericles*, Imogen is several times described as a bird—e.g. IV. ii. 198–9, 'the bird is dead That we have made so much on'—and meanness (in the earlier, non-pejorative sense of the term) is an important theme in that play; e.g. I. i. 149–50, and the incident discussed in V. iii, where the meanly-dressed Posthumus and the two roya sons rescue Cymbeline's army.

Thy speech had alter'd it. Hold, here's gold for thee.
Persever in that clear way thou goest,   105
And the gods strengthen thee!

Mar. The good gods preserve you!

Lys. For me, be you thoughten
That I came with no ill intent; for to me
The very doors and windows savour vilely.   110
Fare thee well. Thou art a piece of virtue, and
I doubt not but thy training hath been noble.
Hold, here's more gold for thee.
A curse upon him, die he like a thief,
That robs thee of thy goodness! If thou dost   115
Hear from me, it shall be for thy good.

[*Enter* BOULT.]

Boult. I beseech your honour, one piece for me.

Lys. Avaunt thou damned door-keeper! Your house,
But for this virgin that doth prop it,
Would sink and overwhelm you. Away!   [*Exit.*]   120

Boult. How's this? We must take another course with
you. If your peevish chastity, which is not worth a
breakfast in the cheapest country under the cope,
shall undo a whole household, let me be gelded
like a spaniel. Come your ways.   125

108–14. For ... thief] *As Malone; prose Q.*
prose Q.   116. S.D.] *Malone; not in Q.*
prose Q.   120. S.D.] *Rowe; not in Q.*

115–16. That ... good] *As Dyce;*
118–20. Avaunt ... Away!] *As Camb.;*

---

105. *clear*] blameless; possibly disyllabic. Cf. *Tp.*, III. iii. 81–2, 'Nothing but heart's sorrow / And a clear life ensuing'.

108. *be you thoughten*] think, i.e. assure yourself. An odd phrase, though, as D. remarks, participles in *-en* are frequent in Shakespeare.

111. *piece of virtue*] 'of the very stock of virtue' (Steevens). So *Tp.*, I. ii. 56 (Steevens) and *Ant.*, III. ii. 28 (Malone).

118–20. *Your . . . you*] K. Muir (*N&Q* CXCVII (1952), 555) quotes S. Harsnett, *Declaration of Egregious Popishe Impostures* (1603), p. 10, 'I mar-

uaile that the house sinketh not for such wickedness committed in it'. For Shakespeare's indebtedness to this tract in *Lr.*, see Arden edn of *Lr.*, App. 7.

118. *door-keeper*] pandar; cf. *Oth.*, IV. ii. 91–2.

122. *peevish*] perverse.

123. *cope*] sky, heaven; frequent in Elizabethan literature.

125–30. *Come your ways . . . I say*] for *Come your ways* see IV. ii. 144n. These speeches are suspicious in their present position. Ll. 125–7 are repeated in substance at ll. 152–3, where they follow the Bawd's instructions, and 'it

Mar. Whither would you have me?

Boult. I must have your maidenhead taken off, or the
common hangman shall execute it. Come your
ways. We'll have no more gentlemen driven away.
Come your ways, I say.   130

Enter Bawd and Pandar.

Bawd. How now! what's the matter?

Boult. Worse and worse, mistress; she has here spoken
holy words to the Lord Lysimachus.

Bawd. O abominable!

Boult. She makes our profession as it were to stink afore   135
the face of the gods.

Bawd. Marry, hang her up for ever!

Boult. The nobleman would have dealt with her like a
nobleman, and she sent him away as cold as a
snowball; saying his prayers too.   140

Bawd. Boult, take her away; use her at thy pleasure.
Crack the glass of her virginity, and make the rest
malleable.

Boult. And if she were a thornier piece of ground than
she is, she shall be plough'd.   145

Mar. Hark, hark, you gods!

Bawd. She conjures: away with her! Would she had
never come within my doors! Marry, hang you!

130. ways] *Dyce;* way *Q.*   S.D.] *Maxwell; Enter Bawdes | Q; Enter Bawd | Rowe.*
135. She] *Rowe;* He *Q.*   137. Marry] *Q4; Marie Q.*

is not likely that Boult would take the
responsibility upon himself' (Maxwell). On the other hand, *We'll . . .
away* seems to belong here. Part of the
present passage, then, may represent
the reporter's anticipation of ll. 152–
3, with a certain amount of impro-
visation for the present context.

128. *execute*] 'with a play on the
"head" of "maidenhead"; cf. *Rom.*,
i. i. 23–6' (Maxwell).

130. *ways*] Dyce's emendation, by
analogy with ll. 64 and 129, though Q
'way' is repeated at l. 152. 'Go thy
ways' (plural) occurs three times in
Shr., 'come thy ways' in *Tw. N.*, ii. v. 1.

133–4. *holy words . . . abominable!*]
Shakespearean in humour.

135. *She*] The emendation is made
certain by ll. 138–40.

137. *Marry*] a corruption of 'Mary',
as used in invocations to the Virgin.
Here an expression of indignation.

142. *Crack . . . virginity*] Malone
points to the parallel in the version of
Apollonius of Tyre in the *Gesta Romanorum*, 'dixit, duc eam ad te, et frange
nodum virginitatis ejus' (ed. H.
Oesterley, 1872, p. 524).

147. *conjures*] invokes supernatural
aid.

148, 150. *Marry*] See l. 137n.

She's born to undo us. Will you not go the way of
women-kind? Marry, come up, my dish of chastity   150
with rosemary and bays!   [*Exeunt Bawd and Pandar*.]

Boult. Come, mistress; come your ways with me.

Mar. Whither wilt thou have me?

Boult. To take from you the jewel you hold so dear.

Mar. Prithee, tell me one thing first.   155

Boult. Come now, your one thing.

Mar. What canst thou wish thine enemy to be?

Boult. Why, I could wish him to be my master, or rather,
    my mistress.

Mar. Neither of these are so bad as thou art,   160
    Since they do better thee in their command.
    Thou hold'st a place, for which the pained'st fiend
    Of hell would not in reputation change;
    Thou art the damned door-keeper to every
    Coistrel that comes inquiring for his Tib;   165
    To the choleric fisting of every rogue
    Thy ear is liable; thy food is such
    As hath been belch'd on by infected lungs.

Boult. What would you have me do? go to the wars,

151. S.D.] *Maxwell; not in Q; Exit | Q4.*   152. ways] *F3; way Q.*   160-3.
Neither . . . change] *As Rowe; prose Q.*   161. in their] *Q; in conj. H.F.B.*
164-8. Thou . . . lungs] *As Malone; prose Q.*   165. Coistrel] *Q (custerell).*
166. fisting] *Q; fist conj. H.F.B.*

150-1. *dish . . . bays*] 'Anciently many
dishes were served up with this garni-
ture, during the season of Christmas.
The Bawd means to call her a piece of
ostentatious virtue' (Steevens). I cannot agree with J. D. Wilson who sees in
rosemary an ironic reference to Marina's
'marriage' with Boult.

152. *ways*] See above, l. 130n.

157. *What . . . be?*] a riddle, with a
view to gaining the initiative whatever Boult's answer. *enemy* is used
in the biblical sense (cf. *Mac.*, III. i.
68), and anticipates *pained'st fiend
Of hell*.

160-8. *Neither . . . lungs*] Minor corruptions probable. For a bold reno-
vation of this text, see App. D.

161. *Since . . . command*] 'since they

are at all events in authority, while you
are but a slave' (D.).

164. *door-keeper*] See l. 118n.

165. *Coistrel*] originally = groom,
which degenerated in meaning to
'base fellow, scoundrel'; cf. *Tw. N.*,
I. iii. 37.

Tib] low woman, strumpet; a common term in Elizabethan literature.

166-7. *To . . . liable*] D. paraphrases:
'the meanest fellow in the world would
not hesitate, if angry, to box your
ears'. *fisting* = punching. But this
word occurs nowhere else in Shakespeare as a verbal noun, and the *-ing*
may well have been stuck on by the
reporter or compositor, by assimilation with *inquiring* in the previous line;
'fist' would improve the line metrically.

would you ? where a man may serve seven years for   170
the loss of a leg, and have not money enough in the
end to buy him a wooden one ?

Mar. Do any thing but this thou doest. Empty
Old receptacles, or common shores, of filth;
Serve by indenture to the common hangman: 175
Any of these ways are yet better than this;
For what thou professest, a baboon, could he speak,
Would own a name too dear. That the gods
Would safely deliver me from this place!
Here, here's gold for thee.   180
If that thy master would gain by me,
Proclaim that I can sing, weave, sew, and dance,
With other virtues, which I'll keep from boast;
And will undertake all these to teach.
I doubt not but this populous city will   185
Yield many scholars.

Boult. But can you teach all this you speak of?

Mar. Prove that I cannot, take me home again,
And prostitute me to the basest groom
That doth frequent your house.   190

Boult. Well, I will see what I can do for thee; if I can
place thee, I will.

173–86. Do . . . scholars] *As Malone; prose* Q.   178. That] *Q; O that* Q4.
184. And will] *Q; And I will* Rowe.   188–90. Prove . . . house] *As Rowe; prose* Q.

174. *common shores*] 'no man's land
by the water-side, where filth was
allowed to be deposited for the tide to
wash away' (*O.E.D.*4); common
sewers.

175. *by indenture*] 'i.e. as an apprentice: he is not only to choose the most
objectionable profession, but to start
at the bottom even in that. For the
notion of the pimp turned hangman,
cf. *Meas.*, IV. ii. 14–16' (Maxwell).

177. *baboon*] stressed, as Maxwell
points out, on the first syllable, as in
Mac., IV. i. 37.

178. *Would . . . dear*] would claim to
possess too high a reputation, i.e.
'would think his tribe dishonoured by
such a profession' (Steevens); *dear* may
be disyllabic.

178–9. *That . . . place!*] a paraphrase
of ll. 98–9 above. While some appeal
to the gods is in place here, the wording
of the passage is probably assimilated
by the reporter and thus corrupt.
The unsatisfactory verse confirms
this.

181. *If . . . me*] This and the following
lines are an adaptation of Gower,
C.A., 1449 ff.

184. *And will*] Rowe's 'And I will',
which edd. have almost uniformly
adopted, makes the metre more regular, but Q's line makes sense as it
stands, and it is useless trying to tinker
with metre in what is manifestly a
corrupt speech.

189. *groom*] stable lad; i.e. low fellow.

Mar. But amongst honest women.

Boult. Faith, my acquaintance lies little amongst them.
    But since my master and mistress hath bought you, 195
    there's no going but by their consent; therefore I
    will make them acquainted with your purpose, and
    I doubt not but I shall find them tractable enough.
    Come, I'll do for thee what I can; come your ways.

                          Exeunt.

195. hath] *Q;* have *F4.*

193. *honest women*] so in Gower,   195. *hath*] Cf. III. ii. 104n.
C.A., 1457 (Staunton).

[ACT V]

Enter GOWER.

Marina thus the brothel 'scapes, and chances
Into an honest house, our story says.
She sings like one immortal, and she dances
As goddess-like to her admired lays.
Deep clerks she dumbs, and with her neele composes   5
Nature's own shape, of bud, bird, branch, or berry,
That even her art sisters the natural roses;
Her inkle, silk, twin with the rubied cherry:
That pupils lacks she none of noble race,
Who pour their bounty on her; and her gain   10
She gives the cursed bawd. Here we her place,
And to her father turn our thoughts again,
Where we left him on the sea. We there him lost,

ACT V

Act V] *Malone; not in Q.*   5. neele] *Q;* needle *Q4;* neeld *Malone.*   7. roses;] *Malone;* Roses *Q.*   8. silk, twin] *Malone;* Silke Twine *Q;* Silke, Twine *Q2.* 13. lost] *Malone;* left *Q.*

1 ff. *Marina . . .*] Only in this Chorus are the lines rhymed alternately.

2. *honest house*] hyphenated in Q; apparently as antithesis to 'bawdy-house' (Maxwell).

4. *goddess-like*] so in *Cym.*, III. ii. 8 and *Wint.*, IV. iv. 10 (Hastings).

5–8. *neele . . . cherry*] Cf. *MND.*, III. ii. 203–9; a Shakespearean reminiscence.

5. *neele*] needle. See n. to IV. Ch. 23.
clerks . . . dumbs] Cf. *MND.*, V. i. 93–8 (Malone).

7. *sisters*] Malone comments justly on the rarity of the verbal use of this word in Elizabethan writing, but cites *Comp.* 2, 'a sist'ring vale'.

8. *inkle*] linen thread or yarn (*O.E.D.*2).

silk, twin . . . cherry] = 'silk, in colouring are twin . . . cherry'. Malone's emendation is undoubtedly correct, for cf. *TNK.*, I. i. 178–9, 'Her twinning cherries shall their sweetness fall / Upon thy tasteful lips' (Steevens), and *Cor.*, IV. iv. 15, 'who twin, as 'twere, in love / Unseparable', where Ff2–4 also print 'twine' (E.S.). Further, cf. *MND.*, III. ii. 208–9, where Helena berates Hermia for ingratitude, after their years of doing needle-work together, and uses the image 'So we grew together / Like to a double cherry'.

13. *lost*] The emendation restores the rhyme with *coast*, yet corruption may lie deeper. The original phrase may have ended 'tost'.

136

Whence, driven before the winds, he is arriv'd
Here where his daughter dwells; and on this coast   15
Suppose him now at anchor. The city striv'd
God Neptune's annual feast to keep; from whence
Lysimachus our Tyrian ship espies,
His banners sable, trimm'd with rich expense;
And to him in his barge with fervour hies.   20
In your supposing once more put your sight;
Of heavy Pericles, think this his bark,
Where what is done in action, more, if might,
Shall be discover'd; please you sit and hark.   *Exit.*

14. Whence,] *Steevens;* Where *Q;* And *Q4.*   20. fervour] *corrected Q, Q2;*
former *uncorrected Q.*   21-2. sight; . . . Pericles,] *Q* (sight, . . . *Pericles,*); sight
. . . Pericles, *Q4.*   22. his] *Q;* the *Malone.*   24. discover'd; please] *Malone;*
discouerd, please *Q.*

14. *Whence*] Q 'Where' is possible,
but probably an erroneous repetition
from l. 13.

driven . . . winds] a close paraphrase
of Gower, *C.A.*, 1607, 'tofor the wynd
thei dryve'.

16. *Suppose . . . anchor*] The similarity
in phrasing to other choruses in early
seventeenth-century drama is not surprising. Cf. 'suppose him now at sea' in
Day, Wilkins, and Rowley, *The Travels
of the Three English Brothers*, p. 40 (Day,
Works), and Dekker, *Old Fortunatus*, II.
Ch. 10 and 35.

17. *Neptune's annual feast*] a hilarious
festival held on 23 July. This special
occasion was perhaps regarded as suitable for the reunion between father
and daughter, but if there was any
such significance in the original
romance of Apollonius of Tyre, it has
been lost. The corresponding passage
in the *Gesta Romanorum* runs: '. . . ad
Machilenam civitatem . . . venerunt.
Gubernator autem cum omnibus
magnum plausum dedit. Ait Apollonius: "quis sonus hilaritatis aures meas
percussit?" Ait gubernator: "gaude,
domine, quia hodie Neptunalia cele-
brantur". Appollonius ingemuit et ait:
"et omnes diem festum celebrent preter
me!" Tunc vocavit dispensatorem
suum et ait ei: "sufficiat famulis meis

pena mea ac dolor—dona eis X
aureos, et emant, si que voluerint, et
diem festum celebrent. Et quicunque
vocaverit me vel gaudium mihi fecerit,
crura illorum frangi jubeo" ' (cited by
Smyth, p. 106; Oesterley, ed., *Gesta
Romanorum*, p. 525.)

19-20. *His . . . him*] Its . . . it.

19. *sable*] because of his mourning
for Marina, and emblematic of his
melancholy stupor.

20. *fervour*] a press-correction in Q;
see Intro., p. xxxviii.

21. *In . . . sight;*] 'put your sight
under the guidance of your imagination' (Malone). This interpretation is
preferable to D.'s 'once more imagine
you behold Pericles' with Q4's punctuation (except for semi-colon after
'Pericles').

22. *Of . . . his*] If Malone's interpretation of l. 21 is sound, the construction
of l. 22 is awkward, but it may be
defended as a pseudo-archaism (so
Maxwell). Malone's 'the' for *his* is
plausible.

heavy] sorrowful.

23. *more, if might*] and more if it were
possible (Clarke subst.).

24. *discover'd . . . hark*] Retaining Q's
comma, Maxwell interprets: 'discovered, if you please to sit and hark'
but this seems rather forced.

[SCENE I.—*On board Pericles' ship, off Mytilene. A Pavilion on deck, with a curtain before it;* PERICLES *within it, reclined on a couch, unkempt and clad in sackcloth. A barge lies beside the Tyrian vessel.*]

Enter HELICANUS, *to him two Sailors*[, *one belonging to the Tyrian vessel, the other to the barge*].

Tyr. Sail. Where is Lord Helicanus? he can resolve you.
    O, here he is.
    [*To Helicanus.*] Sir, there is a barge put off from
        Mytilene,
    And in it is Lysimachus the governor,
    Who craves to come aboard. What is your will?   5
Hel. That he have his. Call up some gentlemen.
Tyr. Sail. Ho, gentlemen! my lord calls.

Enter two or three Gentlemen.

1. Gent. Doth your lordship call?
Hel. Gentlemen, there is some of worth would come aboard;

Scene 1

SCENE I] *Malone; not in* Q.   Location. *On . . . couch*] *Malone; not in* Q.   *unkempt . . . sack-cloth*] *Maxwell; not in* Q.   *A . . . vessel*] *Malone; not in* Q.   Entry. *one . . . barge*] *Malone; not in* Q.   1. *Tyr. Sail.*] *Malone; 1. Say. / Q.*   1–5. Where . . . will?] *As Steevens; prose* Q.   2–3. is. / Sir] *Rowe; is Sir* Q.   3. S.D.] *this ed.; not in* Q.   7. *Tyr. Sail.*] *Malone; 2. Say. / Q.*   8–9. Gentlemen . . . fairly] *As Steevens; prose* Q.

SCENE I . . . vessel] Malone's description of the scene is in harmony with the text. J. W. Saunders (in V aulting the Rails', *Shakespeare Survey* 7, 1954, p. 76) reconstructs simply the staging of the opening episode at the Globe. The deck, where the main action takes place, was, he thinks, represented by the main platform, the pavilion by the study (or 'inner' stage), and the barge by the yard alley. However, there is insufficient evidence to show that the yard alley of the Globe was used in that way. Yet earlier reconstructions, which place most of this scene on the upper stage, seem absurd.

1, 7, 11. S.H. Tyr. Sail.] Though divided between the two Sailors in Q, these speeches probably all belong to the Tyrian Sailor, as Malone first indicated. If any speech is to be attributed to the 2nd (Mytilenian?) Sailor, it should be ll. 11–13. These lines were first given to Helicanus in Q (see Intro., p. xxxviii), but changed over by the press-corrector to the 1st Sailor (so some copies of Q). Similar confusion or ambiguity of speech-headings in a text is often regarded as a mark of 'foul papers', but here it is evidence of a bungling reporter. For this, see n. to ll. 11–13.

1. *resolve you*] satisfy you.

6–9. *Call . . . gentlemen*] I doubt whether there were four speeches in the original; the text seems corrupt.

9. *some*] some one.

I pray, greet him fairly.   [*Gentlemen and Sailors descend,
                                  and go on board the barge.*]

Enter [*from thence*] LYSIMACHUS [*and Lords; with them the
                Gentlemen and Sailors.*]

Tyr. Sail. Sir,   11
        This is the man that can, in aught you would,
        Resolve you.
Lys. Hail, reverend sir! the gods preserve you!
Hel. And you, to outlive the age I am,   15
        And die as I would do.
Lys.   You wish me well.
        Being on shore, honouring of Neptune's triumphs,
        Seeing this goodly vessel ride before us,
        I made to it to know of whence you are.
Hel. First, what is your place?   20
Lys. I am the governor of this place you lie before.
Hel. Sir,
        Our vessel is of Tyre, in it the king;
        A man who for this three months hath not spoken
        To any one, nor taken sustenance   25
        But to prorogue his grief.

10. S.D. *Gentlemen . . . barge*] *Malone; not in Q.*   S.D. *Enter . . Sailors*] *Malone
subst.; Enter Lysimachus* | *Q.*   11. *Tyr. Sail.*] *Malone; 1. Say.* | *corrected Q; Hell.
uncorrected Q.*   11–13. Sir . . . you] *As Malone; prose Q.*   14. reverend] *Rowe;
reuerent Q.*   15–16. And . . . do] *As Malone; prose Q.*   15. you, to] *Q; you,
sir, to Malone (1790).*   16–19. You . . . are] *As Rowe; prose Q.*   22–6. Sir
. . . grief] *As Steevens; prose Q.*

11–13. *Sir . . . you*] See n. to ll. 1, 7, 11 above. The similarity of these lines to v. iii. 59–61 makes them all the more look like the reporter's interpolation (Edwards). The verse of the opening lines of this scene is likewise unsatisfactory. However, *Sir* is perhaps extra-metrical, in which case it belongs to the following line.

14. *Hail . . . preserve you*] See similar phrases in l. 38 below and in IV. vi. 107. Here the phrase fits the context better than in IV. vi, where it may be corrupt. *reverend* = worthy of reverence; Q 'reverent'. The two spellings were

mutual variants in Shakespeare's day, as they no longer are.

15. *you, to*] Malone's 'you, sir, to', adopted by many edd. would regularize the metre, but this is not sufficient grounds for dabbling with the text.

17. *Neptune's triumphs*] public festivities in honour of Neptune. See n. to v. Ch. 17.

20. *place*] official position. But considering that *place* is used in a different sense in l. 21, textual corruption is probable (H.F.B.).

26. *prorogue*] prolong.

Lys. Upon what ground is his distemperature?
Hel. 'Twould be too tedious to repeat;
But the main grief springs from the loss
Of a beloved daughter and a wife.   30
Lys. May we not see him?
Hel. You may;
But bootless is your sight; he will not speak
To any.
Lys.   Yet let me obtain my wish.
Hel. Behold him.   [*Pericles discovered.*]
                    This was a goodly person,   35
Till the disaster that, one mortal night,
Drove him to this.
Lys. Sir king, all hail! the gods preserve you!
Hail, royal sir!
Hel. It is in vain; he will not speak to you.   40
1. Lord. Sir,
We have a maid in Mytilene, I durst wager,
Would win some words of him.
Lys.   'Tis well bethought.

28–30. 'Twould . . . wife] *As Malone; prose Q.*   32–4. You . . . any] *As Collier;
prose Q.*   33. bootless is] *Q4;* bootlesse. Is *Q.*   sight; he will] *corrected Q*
(sight, hee will); sight see, will *uncorrected Q.*   34–6. *Lys.* Yet . . . wish. | *Hel.*
Behold . . . Till] *Q4;* [*Hel.*] yet . . . wish. | *Lys.* Behold . . . person. | *Hell.* Till *Q.*
35–7. Behold . . . this] *As Malone; prose Q.*   35. S.D.] *Malone; not in Q.*
36. night] *Malone;* wight *Q.*   38–9. Sir . . . sir!] *As Dyce; prose Q.*   41–3. Sir
. . . him] *As Dyce; prose Q.*   43–62. 'Tis . . . sorrow] *As Malone; prose Q.*

27. *distemperature*] mental disturbance.

33. *bootless*] unavailing.
sight; he will] emended by the press-
corrector of Q; see Intro., p. xxxviii.

34–6. S.H.s] The confusion in Q's
attribution of speeches may be the
fault of the compositor, who perhaps
failed to interpret sensibly his corrected MS copy.

35. S.D. Pericles discovered] In
Shakespeare's theatre, the inner stage
with its curtain would have been the
natural place for such a discovery (so
Malone). But the later developments
of this scene were almost certainly
enacted on the main or outer stage, in
full view of the audience.

36. *that . . . night*] i.e. the night of
his wife's death. The emendation
night seems certain. Possibly the original read, 'Of one mortal night'.
Maxwell notes that Pericles' state 'is
due not to that but to the news of his
daughter's death', but it is surely due
to the effect on him of both. Moreover,
the two deaths are closely connected.
Pericles would not have entrusted
Marina to Dionyza's care but for her
mother's death.

38–9. *hail . . . sir*] See n. to l. 14
above. The verse is of course unsatisfactory, and the repetition is perhaps
the reporter's, not Shakespeare's.

41. *Sir*] Perhaps extra-metrical; see
ll. 11–13n. above.

She, questionless, with her sweet harmony
And other chosen attractions, would allure,   45
And make a batt'ry through his deafen'd ports,
Which now are midway stopp'd.
She is all happy as the fairest of all,
And with her fellow maids is now upon
The leavy shelter that abuts against   50
The island's side.
        [*Whispers a Lord, who goes off in the barge of Lysimachus.*]
Hel. Sure, all effectless; yet nothing we'll omit
That bears recovery's name. But, since your kindness
We have stretch'd thus far, let us beseech you
That for our gold we may provision have,   55
Wherein we are not destitute for want,
But weary for the staleness.
Lys.   O, sir, a courtesy
Which, if we should deny, the most just God

---

46. deafen'd] *Q* (defend) ; defended *Q2.*   ports] *Maxwell, conj. Steevens;* parts *Q.*
49. with her fellow maids is now] *Malone;* her fellow maides, now *Q.*   50. leavy]
Q (leauie).   51. S.D.] *Malone subst., Camb.; not in Q.*   52. all] *Q;* all's *Lillo,*
Malone.   58. God] *Q;* gods *Dyce, conj. S. Walker.*

---

45. *chosen*] choice.

46. *make a batt'ry*] literally: 'assault with artillery'.

deafen'd ports] Maxwell cites *TNK.,* v. i. 135–7 (ed. Skeat), 'thine ear . . . into whose port / Ne'er enter'd wanton sound' and Crashaw, *Hymn of St. Thomas,* 9–10, 'Your ports are all superfluous here, / Save that which lets in faith, the ear', providing strong support for Steevens' emendation in what has been a much debated passage.

49. *with . . . now*] Malone's emendation restores the sense of a passage corrupted by compositor or reporter. E.S. plausibly suggests that the true reading is 'maid' not *maids,* which would facilitate the explanation of Q's graphic error, and would be consistent with l. 77, 'my companion maid'.

50. *leavy*] covered with foliage; the earlier and more common form of

'leafy' (*O.E.D.*); yet not merely a variant spelling but also a variant pronunciation, *v* being voiced. Cf. *Ado,* ii. iii. 65–8 (Balthasar's Song), where *leavy* rhymes with 'heavy'.

52. *all*] entirely.

56–7. *Wherein . . . for*] Of which . . . because of.

57. *weary . . . staleness*] Cf. *Ham.,* i. ii. 133, 'How weary, stale, flat . . .' for a similar collocation (Maxwell).

58. *God*] Most modern edd. follow S. Walker's 'gods', pointing to the Act of Abuses of 1606 which forbade the use of the names of Christ and God in the theatre, to invocations to the gods (plural) elsewhere in the play—see, for instance, iv. vi. 98 and v. i. 79— and to the fact that the deities in the play are pagan. Nevertheless, Q *God* seems to me right. The *God* referred to reminds one in his behaviour rather of the 'just' God of Israel than of Neptune or Diana. Pagan and Old Testament

> For every graff would send a caterpillar,
> And so inflict our province. Yet once more   60
> Let me entreat to know at large the cause
> Of your king's sorrow.

Hel.   Sit, sir, I will recount it to you.
> But see, I am prevented.

> [*Enter Lord from the barge, with* MARINA *and one
> of her Companions.*]

Lys. O, here's the lady that I sent for.
> Welcome, fair one! Is't not a goodly presence?   65
Hel. She's a gallant lady.
Lys. She's such a one that, were I well assur'd
> Came of gentle kind and noble stock,
> I'd wish no better choice, and think me rarely wed.
> Fair one, all goodness that consists in beauty,   70

62–3. Sit . . . prevented] *As Collier; prose Q.*   63. S.D.] *Malone subst.; not in Q;*
Enter Marina / *Q4.*   65. presence] *Malone;* present *Q.*   67–9. She's . . . wed]
As Q4; assurde / wish / wed *Q.*   69. I'd] *Q4;* I do *Q.*   rarely wed] *Q4;* rarely
to wed *Q.*   70. one, all] *Malone;* on all *Q.*   beauty] *Q;* bounty *Steevens.*

notions of the deity were often com-
bined in the Renaissance—Every-
man's God is 'the highest Jupiter of
all'—and the many biblical echoes as
well as the dominant moral tone suggest that this is the case in *Pericles*. As
for the Act of Abuses, it seems reasonable to suppose that the censors often
winked at minor trespasses: Q *God* was
left unchanged in later quartos! And
God (singular) occurs also at II. v. 86.

59. *graff*] the old form of 'graft',
grafted plant.

60. *inflict*] from Latin 'infligere' =
cause damage to, afflict.

61. *at large*] in full.

63. *prevented*] forestalled.

65. *goodly presence*] comely personage
(On. 4).

66–70. *She's . . . beauty*] Apart from
obvious errors in Q, which have been
corrected, there are other signs of textual corruption, and the original is
probably irrecoverable: (i) l. 69 is
hypermetrical and sounds flat; (ii)

gentle kind and *noble stock* are suspiciously synonymous. See ll. 71–4n. below.

67–8. *were . . . stock*] for the construction, cf. *Ado,* IV. i. 153–4, 'Who lov'd
by her so, that, speaking of her foul-
ness, / Wash'd it with tears' (Abbott
§399).

68. *Came . . . kind*] descended from a
gentle family.

70. *all . . . beauty*] *consists* = resides.
The phrase is not to be taken as an
object of *expect*, but as an appositive to
Fair one, the comma after *beauty* having
almost the force of a colon. As this
interpretation of Q is at least possible,
it seems wise to retain the text, though
Steevens' 'bounty' for *beauty*, with a
stronger punctuation mark after
patient, is attractive, not least on
account of the simpler sentence structure his emendation assumes. But that
goodness should express itself through
beauty was a neo-platonic commonplace of the Renaissance. See, for
instance, Spenser's *Foure Hymnes.*

Expect even here, where is a kingly patient,
If that thy prosperous and artificial feat
Can draw him but to answer thee in aught,
Thy sacred physic shall receive such pay
As thy desires can wish.

Mar.   Sir, I will use   75
My utmost skill in his recovery, provided
That none but I and my companion maid
Be suffer'd to come near him.

Lys.   Come, let us leave her;
And the gods make her prosperous!   [*They withdraw.*]

MARINA *sings.*

Mark'd he your music?
Mar.   No, nor look'd on us.   80
Lys. See, she will speak to him.
Mar. Hail, sir! my lord, lend ear.
Per. Hum, ha!   [*pushing her back.*]

---

71. patient,] *Q; patient: Steevens.*   72. prosperous . . . feat] *Collier, conj. Percy;* prosperous . . . fate *Q;* prosperous artifice and fate *conj. Mason.*   75–8. Sir . . . him] *As Malone; prose Q.*   78–9. Come . . . prosperous!] *As Steevens; prose Q.*   79. S.D. *They withdraw*] *Maxwell; not in Q.*   S.D. *Marina sings*] *Malone; The Song | Q.*   80. Mark'd] *Q4;* Marke *Q.*   83. S.D. *pushing her back*] *this ed., conj. Camb.; not in Q; roughly repulses her | Maxwell.*

71–4. *Expect . . . pay*] For the situation, cf. *All's W.*, II. i. 189 ff., where Helena promises to cure the King. *artificial* = skilful, skilled in the art of medicine; *physic* = medicine; Q 'fate' is listed by *O.E.D.* as an early variant spelling of *feat.* If the text is sound as it stands, *Expect* governs the clause *Thy . . . pay* (so J. D. Wilson). As, however, the sentence-structure is both complex and awkward, and l. 72 is hypermetrical, the text is probably corrupt. The original cannot be recovered, but H.F.B. convincingly suggests that in Shakespeare's text, *kingly patient* was the object of *Expect* (*where is* being interpolated by the reporter) and *thy . . . feat* a full line. See ll. 66–70n. above.

78. *come . . . Come*] The second *Come* may be memorial or actor's preluding.

79. *prosperous*] See l. 72. Such repetitions are frequent in this reported text, yet in this case surely intended by the author, for *prosperous* is a key-word in v. i.

79. S.D. Marina sings] The song, like many others that once adorned the Elizabethan drama, has been lost. Only verses infinitely superior to those given by Wilkins (*P.A.*, 103–4), who copied Twine almost word for word, would have been appropriate.

83. S.D. pushing her back] Ll. 100 and 126 indicate the need for such a direction. Dover Wilson's more violent S.D. is not suitable, since it is in harmony rather with the prince's behaviour and character in Gower, Twine, and Wilkins, than with that of Pericles in the play. See Intro., pp. lxxxvi–lxxxvii, where it is argued that Shakespeare changed the hero's character significantly.

Mar. I am a maid,
    My lord, that ne'er before invited eyes,   85
    But have been gaz'd on like a comet; she speaks,
    My lord, that, may be, hath endur'd a grief
    Might equal yours, if both were justly weigh'd.
    Though wayward fortune did malign my state,
    My derivation was from ancestors   90
    Who stood equivalent with mighty kings;
    But time hath rooted out my parentage,
    And to the world and awkward casualties
    Bound me in servitude. [*Aside.*] I will desist;
    But there is something glows upon my cheek,   95
    And whispers in mine ear "Go not till he speak".
Per. My fortunes— parentage— good parentage—
    To equal mine—was it not thus? what say you?
Mar. I said, my lord, if you did know my parentage,
    You would not do me violence.   100
Per. I do think so. Pray you, turn your eyes upon me.
    You're like something that—What countrywoman?
    Here of these shores?

84–100. I . . . violence] *As Malone; prose Q.*   94. S.D.] *Malone; not in Q.*
101–3. I . . . these shores] *As Dyce; prose Q.*   102. You're] *Q* (your); y'are *Q4;*
You are *Malone.*   102–3. countrywoman? / Here] *Malone, conj. Charlemont;*
Countrey women heare *Q.*   103. shores? . . . shores;] *Malone, conj. Charlemont;*
shewes? . . . shewes, *Q.*

---

84. *I . . . maid*] Thaise uses the same
words in Gower's version, *C.A.*, 1696,
but the development leading up to the
recognition is handled quite differently.

86. *like a comet*] Cf. *1H4*, III. ii. 47
(Malone).

89. *wayward*] capricious, change-
able.

   did malign] dealt malignantly with.

93. *awkward casualties*] adverse
chances.

95. *something . . . cheek*] 'some inward
prompting causes my cheek to glow
with expectation' (D. subst.). Maxwell's suggestion (p. xvi in his edn)
that this line may be a misplaced reference to a blow on the cheek
Marina has received from Pericles

seems quite improbable. See following
note.

100. *You . . . violence*] See S.D. to l.
83. These words do not indicate any
crude behaviour on Pericles' part towards her, but merely refer to his pushing her back. In previous versions of
the story, the hero treats his daughter
much more roughly. See Intro., p.
lxxxvii. Cf. however, Posthumus'
treatment of Imogen in *Cym.*, v. v.
228–9.

102. *What countrywoman?*] Of what
country? Cf. *Shr.*, I. ii. 186 and IV. ii.
77 and *Tw. N.*, v. i. 223.

103. *shores? . . . shores*] The Earl of
Charlemont's emendation restores a
passage that makes nonsense in Q.
The compositor's misreading of his

Mar.   No, nor of any shores;
   Yet I was mortally brought forth, and am
   No other than I appear.
Per.   I am great with woe   105
   And shall deliver weeping. My dearest wife
   Was like this maid, and such a one
   My daughter might have been: my queen's square
      brows;
   Her stature to an inch; as wand-like straight;
   As silver-voic'd; her eyes as jewel-like   110
   And cas'd as richly; in pace another Juno;
   Who starves the ears she feeds, and makes them hungry
   The more she gives them speech. Where do you live?
Mar. Where I am but a stranger; from the deck
   You may discern the place.
Per.   Where were you bred?   115
   And how achiev'd you these endowments which
   You make more rich to owe?
Mar. If I should tell my history, 'twould seem

103–4. No . . . am] *As Malone; prose Q.*   105–7. No . . . one] *arranged this ed.;*
prose Q.   108–32. My . . . open'd] *As Malone; prose Q.*   111. cas'd] *Q* (caste);
cast *Q2.*

---

difficult MS copy is probably to be
blamed for the corruption of ll. 102–3;
shores in an Elizabethan hand might be
misread as 'shewes'.

104. *mortally*] humanly (with emphasis); i.e. not by spirits.

105–7. *I . . . one*] In most modern
edd. this speech begins a new line, but
the present arrangement is preferable,
I am great with woe completing Marina's
hemistich.

106. *deliver weeping*] Among the
many interpretations of these two
words perhaps the most convincing is
that of Malone, who, pointing to the remarkable parallel of the image in *R2*,
II. ii. 61–6, suggests that Pericles' *woe* is
so overpowering that he will deliver
his tears as a mother frees herself from
her burden in the process of birth. But
perhaps simply: 'be delivered of my

burden [of woe] with tears'. Yet see
l. 160n. below.

111. *cas'd as richly*] Cf. III. ii. 100–4,
'cases . . . rich' (Mason) and *Tp.*, I. ii.
40–8. Q's spelling is ambiguous, witness Q2.

in pace . . . Juno] See *Tp.*, IV. i. 102,
'Great Juno, comes; I know her by her
gait' (Malone). Both passages echo
Virgil, *Aeneid*, I. 405, 'vera incessu
patuit dea'.

112–13. *Who . . . speech*] Cf. *Ant.*, II.
ii. 241–2, 'she makes hungry / Where
most she satisfies' (Malone), *Ham.*, I.
ii. 144–5, 'As if increase of appetite
had grown / By what it fed on', and
Sonnet 75, 'Sometimes all full with
feasting on your sight, / And by and by
clear starved for a look'.

117. *to owe*] to own, i.e. by owning
them.

Like lies, disdain'd in the reporting.

Per.   Prithee, speak;
Falseness cannot come from thee, for thou look'st   120
Modest as Justice, and thou seem'st a palace
For the crown'd Truth to dwell in. I will believe thee,
And make my senses credit thy relation
To points that seem impossible; for thou look'st
Like one I lov'd indeed. What were thy friends?   125
Didst thou not say when I did push thee back,
Which was when I perceiv'd thee, that thou cam'st
From good descending?

Mar.   So indeed I did.

Per. Report thy parentage. I think thou said'st
Thou hadst been toss'd from wrong to injury,   130
And that thou thought'st thy griefs might equal mine,
If both were open'd.

Mar.   Some such thing I said,
And said no more but what my thoughts
Did warrant me was likely.

---

120. look'st] *Malone;* lookest *Q.*   121. seem'st] *Q4; seemest Q.*   palace]
Lillo, Malone; Pallas / Q.   122. I will] *Q;* I'll *Malone.*   123. make my
senses] *Q4;* make senses *Q.*   124. look'st] *Q4;* lookest *Q.*   126. say] *Malone;*
stay *Q.*   131. thought'st] *Q* (thoughts).   132–4. Some . . . likely] *As Collier;*
prose Q.

119. *in the reporting*] in the very act of utterance.

122. *crown'd Truth*] Cf. *Rom.,* III. ii. 93–4, 'For 'tis a throne where honour may be crown'd / Sole monarch . . .', and *Sonnet* 37, 5–7, 'For whether beauty . . . do crowned sit', cited by Malone who comments: 'It is observable that our poet, when he means to represent any quality of the mind as eminently perfect, furnishes the imaginary being whom he personifies, with a crown'. But this usage was common among other Elizabethan writers also.

125. *friends*] relations.

126. *push thee back*] See S.D. to l. 83 above and n.; also Intro., p. lxxxvii.

128. *descending*] descent, lineage.

129–30. *I . . . injury*] Maxwell com-

ments: 'She has not said this in Q, but Wilkins (*P.A.,* 105. 22–3) inserts "I haue bin tossed from wrong to iniurie" into a speech otherwise derived from Twine'. But the implication that a speech or part of a speech of Marina's has been lost in the text is not warranted. One must not take *thou said'st* too literally.

131. *thought'st*] For the euphonic avoidance of *tst* before *th* in Q 'thoughts', cf. *R2,* IV. i. 270, 'thou torments' and see Abbott §340 and Kökeritz, p. 303.

132–4. *Some . . . likely*] Cf. Iago in *Oth.,* V. ii. 177–8:

I told him what I thought, and told no more
Than what he found himself was apt and true.

Per.   Tell thy story;
    If thine consider'd prove the thousandth part   135
    Of my endurance, thou art a man, and I
    Have suffer'd like a girl; yet thou dost look
    Like Patience gazing on kings' graves, and smiling
    Extremity out of act. What were thy friends?
    How lost thou them? Thy name, my most kind virgin?
    Recount, I do beseech you. Come, sit by me.   141
Mar. My name is Marina.
Per.   O, I am mock'd,
    And thou by some incensed god sent hither
    To make the world to laugh at me.
Mar.   Patience, good sir,
    Or here I'll cease.

134–44. Tell . . . at me] *As Malone; prose* Q.   135. thousandth] *Sewell;* thousand
Q.   140. thou them? Thy] *Malone;* thou thy Q.   144–50. Patience . . .
Marina?] *As Steevens subst.; prose* Q.

135–7. *If thine . . . girl*] 'if yours when considered prove a thousandth part as great as what I have endured, then you deserve the title of a man, and I to be called a girl for the weakness which I have shown' (D.). Q 'thousand' is an obsolete spelling of the adjective, which also occurs in *AYL.*, IV. i. 46 (F text).

138–9. *Like . . . act*] For this, perhaps the most famous image of the play, cf. *Tw. N.*, II. iv. 113–14, 'like Patience on a monument, / Smiling at grief' (Malone), and see the comments, too long to quote here, by G. Wilson Knight in *The Crown of Life*, p. 65, and by K. Muir in *Shakespeare as Collaborator*, p. 94. But no one seems to have noticed the obvious: that the inspiration for the two images in *Per.* and *Tw. N.* was derived from statues of Patience and probably even from figures on tombs. See the illustration of a 'monumental' and smiling Patienza in Cesare Ripa, *Iconologia . . .*, Rome, 1603, p. 381 (W. S. Heckscher, privately). For *extremity* = the utmost of calamity, cf. *Err.*, v. i. 306, 'O, time's extremity' and *TNK.*,

I. i. 118–19, 'Extremity, that sharpens sundry wits, / Makes me a fool.' For *out of act*, c.. *All's W.*, I. ii. 30 (D.). Literally, *smiling . . . act* would seem to mean, 'smiling despair out of committing the extreme act' (i.e. suicide), the usual interpretation given to these words. But I would interpret more broadly, 'smiling extreme calamity out of existence' (i.e. making it melt away), whatever the dictionaries say. The appeal of the image is primarily to the imagination, and a prosaic and literal paraphrase cannot do it justice. Though the meaning is very different, the words 'monument', 'smile', and 'patience' are also closely linked in *Meas.*, v. i. 231–3.

139. *friends*] See l. 125n. above.

140. *thou them? Thy*] Malone's excellent emendation restores both sense and metre. He was probably right in attributing Q's 'thou thy' to the negligent compositor, who is responsible for a good share of the havoc in the text of this great scene—cf. l. 103n. above.

142–4. *Marina . . . laugh at me*] Cf. recognition scene in *Lr.*, IV. vii. 59 and 68–70.

Per.   Nay, I'll be patient.   145
    Thou little know'st how thou dost startle me,
    To call thyself Marina.
Mar.   The name
    Was given me by one that had some power,
    My father, and a king.
Per.   How, a king's daughter?
    And call'd Marina?
Mar.   You said you would believe me;
    But, not to be a troubler of your peace,   151
    I will end here.
Per.   But are you flesh and blood?
    Have you a working pulse, and are no fairy
    Motion? Well, speak on. Where were you born,
    And wherefore call'd Marina?
Mar.   Call'd Marina   155
    For I was born at sea.
Per.   At sea! what mother?
Mar. My mother was the daughter of a king;
    Who died the minute I was born,

150–2. You . . . here] *As Malone; prose Q.*   153–4. fairy / Motion? Well]
Malone (1790), conj. Mason; Fairie? / Motion well *Q;* fairy? / No motion?—well
Steevens; fairy? / Motion! well; *Dyce;* fairy? / Motion as well? *Maxwell.*   155–
60. Call'd . . . weeping] *As Malone; prose Q.*

152–6. *But . . . sea*] The arrangement of these lines, which is partly Malone's, seems unsatisfactory, but has been adopted here in want of a better solution. *But* should perhaps form the beginning of a metrical line.

153–4. *Have . . . Well*] Edd. have not been able to agree on the text. Mason, whose conjecture I have adopted, paraphrases: 'Have you really life in you, or are you merely a puppet formed by enchantment? the work of fairies?' For this reading, only a slight alteration of Q is required, the shifting of a question-mark; slight at any rate in this text, considering Q's chaotic punctuation. And Mason's interpretation fits Marina's insistent *mortally* in l. 104. Pericles is still afraid that he may be mocked by supernatural powers, which renders the interpretation of *motion* as 'puppet' (as in *Gent.,* II. i. 100) reasonable. Cf. also Jonson, *Epicoene,* III. iii: 'Why, did you think you had married a statue, or a motion only?'

Steevens' 'No motion' has been widely adopted, partly it seems for metrical reasons. But the lineation is quite uncertain, and one should keep in mind the possibility of pauses here as elsewhere in Shakespearean verse replacing syllables in a metrical line. Maxwell's 'motion as well?' (*motion* = movement) is more attractive as it fits in well with the preceding lines.

156. *For*] because.

158. *Who . . . born*] 'A lame line, repeated in substance at lines 210–11 in what sounds a more Shakespearian form' (Maxwell).

As my good nurse Lychorida hath oft
Deliver'd weeping.
Per.   O, stop there a little!   160
This is the rarest dream that e'er dull'd sleep
Did mock sad fools withal; this cannot be
My daughter, buried; well; where were you bred?
I'll hear you more, to th' bottom of your story,
And never interrupt you.   165
Mar. You scorn; believe me, 'twere best I did give o'er.
Per. I will believe you by the syllable
Of what you shall deliver. Yet, give me leave:
How came you in these parts? where were you bred?
Mar. The king my father did in Tharsus leave me,   170
Till cruel Cleon, with his wicked wife,
Did seek to murder me; and having woo'd
A villain to attempt it, who having drawn to do't,

160–2. O . . . withal] *As Malone;* dreame / withall *Q.*   161. dull'd] *Q; dull Q4.*
162–9. this . . . bred] *As Malone; prose Q.*   162–3. be / My daughter, buried;]
Q subst. (be my daughter, buried,)*;* be my daughter; buried! *F3;* be. / My
daughter's buried, *Steevens;* be / My daughter—buried!— *Sisson, Maxwell.*
166. You scorn; believe] *Q subst.* (scorn,)*;* You'll scarce believe *Malone;* You
scorn to believe *Staunton.*   172–3. Did . . . do't] *As Malone;* villaine / doo't *Q.*
172. murder] *Q* (murther).

160. *Deliver'd weeping*] stated in
tears. Edwards and Maxwell regard
these words as repeated by the blun-
dering reporter from l. 106. In fact, the
whole speech may be textually corrupt; see previous note. Yet one should
not rule out the possibility that Shakespeare himself repeated the words.
There are plenty of 'memorial echoes'
on Shakespeare's part. See Intro.,
p. xxxiv.
161. *dull'd sleep*] so Q, but most edd.
print 'dull sleep'. Q may mean: 'the
sleep of one who has been dulled', and
has therefore been retained; see
Abbott §374 on 'passive participles
used as epithets to describe the state
which would be the result of the active
verb'. The reading is less debatable in
Day, *Law Tricks* (Q 1608), sig. G1v,
'when a hath bene duld at his study'.
161–2. *that . . . withal;*] with which
. . .;

162–3. *be . . . buried;*] As Q's text,
with the slight change of *buried;* for
'buried,', makes good sense in its context, it has been adopted in preference
to Steevens' emendation, which is
otherwise attractive and has been
widely followed. The much more ex-
pressive punctuation of F3, Sisson, and
Maxwell is, to my mind, wrong in each
case. An exclamation, even a mild
one, is hardly compatible with
Pericles' puzzled musings. Rather, his
thoughts are: 'this cannot be my
daughter, who after all was buried
long ago'.
166. *You scorn*] After ll. 162–3,
Marina's lines come naturally.
Malone's ingenious emendation is
scarcely necessary.
173–4. *A . . . me*] The awkward
wordiness of the passage as well as its
metrical irregularity are indicative of
serious corruption. The reporter may

A crew of pirates came and rescu'd me;
Brought me to Mytilene. But, good sir,   175
Whither will you have me? Why do you weep? It
    may be
You think me an impostor: no, good faith;
I am the daughter to King Pericles,
If good King Pericles be.

Per. Ho, Helicanus!   180
Hel. Calls my lord?
Per. Thou art a grave and noble counsellor,
Most wise in general. Tell me, if thou canst,
What this maid is, or what is like to be,
That thus hath made me weep?

Hel.   I know not;   185
But here's the regent, sir, of Mytilene,
Speaks nobly of her.

Lys.   She never would tell
Her parentage; being demanded that,
She would sit still and weep.

Per. O Helicanus, strike me, honour'd sir!   190
Give me a gash, put me to present pain,
Lest this great sea of joys rushing upon me

---

175. Brought] *Q; And brought MS in Bodl. copy of Q.*   175–9. But . . . be] *As
Steevens; prose Q.*   177. impostor] *Q (imposture).*   180. S.H. *Per.*] *Q4;
Hell. / Q.*   183–7. Most . . . her] *As Malone; prose Q.*   187–9. She . . .
weep] *As Malone;* parentage, / weepe *Q.*   190–4. O . . . hither] *As Malone;
prose Q.*

have assimilated *having* from the previous line and expanded 'rescu'd' into
came and rescu'd; in that case, the original text was closer to: 'A villain to
attempt it, who being drawn / To
do't, a crew of pirates rescu'd me'
(H.F.B.).

   176. *Whither . . . me?*] 'to what point
are you drawing me on by your
inquiries?' (D.).

   177. *impostor*] Q's spelling 'imposture' survived until the eighteenth
century. Cf. *All's W.,* ii. i. 155.

   179. *be*] i.e. be alive.

   180. Per. *Ho*] Q's mistaken S.H.
'Hell.' is in part accounted for by the
inadequate catchword 'Hoe' on sig.

H4v, and thus an error which arose
during printing.

   184. *like*] likely.

   187. *never would*] H.F.B. conjectures
'would never', and compares *Tw. N.,*
ii. iv. 109, 'She never told her love',
from the same passage already echoed
in ll. 138–9.

   192–4. *Lest . . . sweetness*] For a similar thought, Malone cites *Mer. V.,* iii.
ii. 111–14; and for a similar image,
Maxwell refers to *Troil.,* iii. ii. 18–25
and *Tp.,* v. i. 79–82. In each case, the
similarity is not very close, yet, in the
two latter passages at least, close
enough to corroborate that the lines in
Pericles are Shakespeare's.

O'erbear the shores of my mortality,
And drown me with their sweetness. O, come hither,
Thou that beget'st him that did thee beget;   195
Thou that wast born at sea, buried at Tharsus,
And found at sea again. O Helicanus,
Down on thy knees! thank the holy gods as loud
As thunder threatens us: this is Marina.
What was thy mother's name? tell me but that,   200
For truth can never be confirm'd enough,
Though doubts did ever sleep.

Mar. First, sir, I pray, what is your title?

Per. I am Pericles of Tyre: but tell me now
My drown'd queen's name, as in the rest you said   205
Thou hast been godlike perfect, the heir of kingdoms,
And another life to Pericles thy father.

Mar. Is it no more to be your daughter than
To say my mother's name was Thaisa?
Thaisa was my mother, who did end   210
The minute I began.

204–5. I . . . said] *As Steevens;* my / sayd *Q.*   207. another life] *Steevens, conj.*
Mason; a mother like *Malone (1790);* an other like *Q.*   208–11. Is . . . began]
As Malone; prose Q.

195. *beget'st*] i.e. gives new life to; this unquestionably Shakespearean line is echoed by Wilkins (*P.A.,* 106. 30–107. 1) in a passage otherwise taken from Twine. See Intro., p. xlii. The relation between father and daughter is dramatically contrasted with that in I. i of Antiochus and 'Hesperides'.

202. *Though . . . sleep*] 'though all doubts were laid to rest' (D.).

203–11. *First . . . began*] See App. D for a conjectural reconstruction.

205–7. *as . . . father*] probably corrupt. Many edd. have reshuffled the lines without effecting real improvement, and several suggestions of missing words have been put forward, none of which is convincing. Like the Cambridge edd., I have therefore reproduced Q's lineation; see however Appendix D, pp. 187–8.

206. *godlike perfect*] perfect = 'per-

fectly informed'; for so far Marina has repeated the facts without errors or omission; but, as Maxwell comments, *godlike* suggests the other meaning of perfect (= faultless, ideally great) as well; cf. E. J. Dobson on 'perfit', *RES,* n.s. VI (1955), 407.

207. *another life*] In support of Mason's emendation, consider l. 195 and Wilkins' rendering of it in *P.A.,* 106. 30–107. 1, 'to begette life in the father who begot her' (Maxwell). For Q's error, cf. also l. 244 below.

208–9. *Is . . . say*] Is all that is needed to make me accepted as your daughter, the saying that . . .

209–10. *Thaisa? Thaisa*] Possibly an intentional repetition by the author, yet I suspect reporter's duplication, since the repetition weakens the total effect. See App. D.

210–11. *end . . . began*] Cf. *Wint.,* v.

Per. Now, blessing on thee! rise; thou art my child.
     Give me fresh garments. Mine own, Helicanus,
     She is not dead at Tharsus, as she should have been,
     By savage Cleon; she shall tell thee all,   215
     When thou shalt kneel, and justify in knowledge
     She is thy very princess. Who is this?
Hel. Sir, 'tis the governor of Mytilene,
     Who, hearing of your melancholy state,
     Did come to see you.
Per.   I embrace you.   220
     Give me my robes; I am wild in my beholding.
     O heavens bless my girl! But hark, what music?
     Tell Helicanus, my Marina, tell him
     O'er point by point, for yet he seems to doubt,

212. thou art] *Q4;* th'art *Q.*   213–20. Give . . . see you] *As Malone; prose Q.*
213. garments. Mine own, Helicanus,] *Steevens;* garments, mine owne *Helicanus,*
Q; garments, mine own Helicanus; *Sewell.*   220–5. I . . . music?] *As Malone;*
robes. / girle, / *Marina,* / doat. / musicke? *Q.*   220. you] *Q;* you, sir *Steevens.*
222. music? / Tell Helicanus, my] *Steevens;* Musicke tell, *Hellicanus* my *Q.*
224. doubt] *Malone;* doat *Q.*

iii. 45, 'Dear queen that ended when
I but began' (Malone).

212. *thou art*] Q 'th'art' is a fairly
common elision in Elizabethan plays,
e.g. *Tw. N.,* II. iii. 12 and 113.
Modern edd., including Dover Wilson
and Alexander, follow F in the passages from *Tw. N.,* but, like this ed.,
adopt Q4's emendation here. The
much more formal occasion and poetic
speech of this passage justify this procedure.

213. *Give . . . garments*] Cf. *Lr.,* IV. vii.
22, where Lear's resumption of his
royal garments symbolizes his return
to spiritual health (so Traversi,
Shakespeare: The Last Phase, p. 41).
Consider also the dramatic use of
'robes' in *Ant.,* v. ii and in *Tp.,* and see
l. 221 below.

garments . . . Helicanus] Steevens'
punctuation has been adopted in substance as the only one which makes
good sense; for the words *mine own*
surely refer to Marina and not, as
Maxwell suggests and Sewell's punc-

tuation implies, to Helicanus; nor, as
J. D. Wilson thinks, to Pericles' garments. The words are addressed, not
to Marina as is sometimes thought,
but to Helicanus who has access to
Pericles' store.

214. *should have been*] was said to be.

215. *By*] at the hands of. Cf. *Ham.,*
IV. v. 125, 'Laer. Where is my father?
King. Dead. *Queen.* But not by him'
(Maxwell).

216. *justify in knowledge*] D.'s free
paraphrase, 'assure yourself beyond all
doubt' seems preferable to 'acknowledge as true' (*O.E.D.*5c) and Maxwell's 'confirm'.

221. *wild . . . beholding*] highly
elated (almost to distraction) at what
I see; for *wild,* see *O.E.D.*10–12.

224. *point by point*] so Gower, *C.A.,*
1725, 'Fro point to point al sche him
tolde' (Malone).

doubt] A possible explanation for
Q's error 'doat' is that the compositor misread *a* for *u* in 'dout', a common Elizabethan spelling.

How sure you are my daughter. [*Music.*] But what
    music?   225
Hel. My lord, I hear none.
Per. None?
    The music of the spheres! List, my Marina.
Lys. It is not good to cross him; give him way.
Per. Rarest sounds! Do ye not hear?   230
Lys. Music, my Lord? I hear.
Per.   Most heavenly music!
    It nips me unto list'ning, and thick slumber
    Hangs upon mine eyes; let me rest.   [*Sleeps.*]
Lys. A pillow for his head. So, leave him all.
    Well, my companion friends,   235
    If this but answer to my just belief,
    I'll well remember you.   [*Exeunt all but Pericles.*]

---

225. S.D.] *this ed.; not in* Q.   227–8. None . . . Marina] *As Malone; one line* Q.
227. None?] *Q4;* None, Q.   231. *Lys.* Music . . . music!] *Q;* [*Music*] *Lys.*
My Lord . . . music. *Dyce; Lys.* Music, my Lord? / *Per.* I hear . . . music. *Maxwell,
conj. Camb.*   232. nips] *Q;* raps *Collier.*   233. S.D.] *Malone; not in* Q.
235–7. Well . . . you] *As Steevens; prose* Q.   237. S.D. *Exeunt . . . Pericles*] *Malone;
not in* Q.

225. S.D.] Dyce introduced this
S.D. after l. 231—see n. below—but
many edd. have objected, pointing out
that Pericles is the only one who hears
the music. He is indeed the only one
(apart perhaps from Marina) because
his state of mind alone is attuned to the
music of the spheres. As this music is
real to him, it must be shared by the
audience from the beginning, to avoid
the absurd impression of Pericles being
deluded. Similar views are expressed
in a recent article by J. P. Cutts,
'Pericles' "Most Heauenly Musicke"',
N&Q, n.s., VII (1960), 172–4. See
Intro., p. lxxviii–lxxix for a discussion
of the place of music in this play.

228. *music . . . spheres*] heavenly
music; more precisely, the music
made by the heavenly bodies in their
circular revolution around the earth,
according to the Ptolemaic sys-
tem of astronomy. See *Tw. N.*, III.
i. 107, *Mer. V.*, v. i. 61–3 and, for
a longer contemporary account, Spen-

ser's *An Hymn of Heavenly Beauty.*

231. Lys. *Music . . . music!*] This
passage at a vital and beautiful
moment in the play also presents a
challenge to the modern ed., as many
different interpretations have been
given. Both Dyce, who interprets the
first *Music* as a S.D., and Maxwell,
who accepts the small but important
transposition suggested by the Camb.
edd., may be right, for similar
changes have to be made at other
places in this text. Yet, as Sisson points
out (II, p. 299), Lysimachus' words are
fully in accord with l. 229. But see
225 S.D. n. above.

232. *nips me unto*] a very unusual
expression, not cited in *O.E.D.*, and
perhaps metaphorical; 'compels me
to'.

236–7. *If . . . you*] obscure, and perhaps the reporter's padding. Possibly:
'If Marina is really a princess (and
therefore a fit marriage-partner), I
shall well reward you' (E.S.).

DIANA [*appears to* PERICLES *in a Vision.*]

Dia. My temple stands in Ephesus; hie thee thither,
    And do upon mine altar sacrifice.
    There, when my maiden priests are met together,   240
    [   ] before the people all,
    Reveal how thou at sea didst lose thy wife.
    To mourn thy crosses, with thy daughter's, call
    And give them repetition to the life.
    Or perform my bidding, or thou liv'st in woe;   245
    Do't, and happy; by my silver bow!
    Awake, and tell thy dream.   [*Disappears.*]
Per. Celestial Dian, goddess argentine,
    I will obey thee. Helicanus!

[*Enter* LYSIMACHUS, HELICANUS, *and* MARINA.]

Hel.   Sir?
Per. My purpose was for Tharsus, there to strike   250
    The inhospitable Cleon; but I am
    For other service first; toward Ephesus
    Turn our blown sails: eftsoons I'll tell thee why.

237. S.D. *Diana ... Vision*] *Globe; Diana.* | *Q; Actus Quintus* | *Diana* | *F3.*   238–
47. *My ... dream*] *As Rowe; Ephesus,* | *then prose Q.*   244. *life*] *Malone, conj.
Charlemont;* like *Q.*   245. *Or perform*] *Q;* Perform *Malone.*   liv'st] *Malone;*
liuest *Q.*   246. *and happy*] *Q;* and be happy *Malone.*   247. S.D.] *Malone
subst., Camb.; not in Q.*   249. S.D.] *Malone; not in Q.*   250–61. *My ... her*]
As Malone; strike, | first, | sayles, | *then prose Q.*

237. S.D. *Diana*] A clue to the cos-
tume of the goddess in the original
production may be afforded by
Daniel's description of her appearance
in his masque *The Vision of the Twelve
Goddesses,* 1604. There she was 'in a
greene Mantle imbrodered with siluer
halfe Moones, and a croissant of pearle
on her head'. As goddess of hunting,
she 'presents a Bow and a Quiuer'.

239–41. *sacrifice ... all*] The short
l. 241 and the absence of a rhyme for
sacrifice are indicative of textual corruption. 1½ lines seem to be missing
between *together* and *before* (H.F.B.).

243. *crosses*] trials, misfortunes.
call] loudly give voice (D.).

244. *give ... life*] recount them in

life-like detail (Maxwell); see n. to l.
207. The rhyme with *wife* makes the
emendation certain; again, a compositor's error.

245. *Or perform ... woe*] The elision
of *liv'st* for the sake of a smoother metre
is more easily justifiable than Malone's
omission of *Or.*

248. *argentine*] silvery. For this, in
Shakespeare, unique word, P. Simpson, *Studies in Elizabethan Drama,* 1955,
p. 39, quotes Ovid, *Heroides,* XVIII. 71,
'... cum fulges radiis argentea puris'
(also referring to Diana), with the pertinent note that no similar line is found
in Turberville's Elizabethan translation of Ovid.

253. *blown*] inflated by the winds.

    Shall we refresh us, sir, upon your shore,
    And give you gold for such provision   255
    As our intents will need?
Lys. Sir,
    With all my heart; and when you come ashore,
    I have another suit.
Per.   You shall prevail,
    Were it to woo my daughter; for it seems   260
    You have been noble towards her.
Lys. Sir, lend me your arm.
Per.   Come, my Marina.   *Exeunt.*

[SCENE II.—*The Temple of Diana at Ephesus; Thaisa standing
near the Altar, as High Priestess; a Number of Virgins on each Side;
Cerimon and other Inhabitants of Ephesus attending.*]

[*Enter*] GOWER.

    Now our sands are almost run;
    More a little, and then dumb.
    This, my last boon, give me,
    For such kindness must relieve me,
    That you aptly will suppose   5

259. suit] *Malone;* sleight *Q.*

Scene II

SCENE II] *Malone; not in Q.*   Location and Heading] *Malone (at the head of* v. iii.*),
Maxwell; not in Q.*   Enter Gower] *Q4;* Gower | *Q (as S.H. only).*   2. dumb] *Q*
(dum); dun *F4;* done *Rowe.*

eftsoons] afterwards (*O.E.D.*3);
found nowhere else in Shakespeare,
but frequent in Spenser and other
Elizabethan writers; included in
Withal's *Dictionary,* 1608, p. 170.
    256. *intents*] purpose.

Scene II

    2. *dumb*] F4's emendation, 'done',
for the sake of the rhyme, is unconvincing. Sisson, who adopts it, comments that 'the spelling *dum* for *dumb*
is very unusual', but *O.E.D.* cites

instances from Skelton and others and
the similar spelling 'dom' from Q.
Elizabeth, *Boethius* (*E.E.T.S.*), 31. If
the Queen or her amanuensis could
drop a *b,* so could Shakespeare and
his printer. Imperfect *n–m* rhymes are
common in this play (e.g. ll. 19–20
below), and *dumb* is used similarly by
the chorus in Dekker, *Old Fortunatus,*
IV. Ch. 33.
    3–4. *This . . . me*] Cf. *Tp.,* Epil. 15–16
and 20 (Maxwell).
    5. *aptly*] readily.

What pageantry, what feats, what shows,
What minstrelsy and pretty din,
The regent made in Mytilin
To greet the king. So he thriv'd,
That he is promis'd to be wiv'd   10
To fair Marina; but in no wise
Till he had done his sacrifice,
As Dian bade: whereto being bound,
The interim, pray you, all confound.
In feather'd briefness sails are fill'd,   15
And wishes fall out as they're will'd.
At Ephesus the temple see
Our king and all his company.
That he can hither come so soon,
Is by your fancies' thankful doom.   [*Exit.*]   20

---

7. and pretty] *Q;* what pretty *Q2*.   8. Mytilin] *Q4 subst.* (*Metalin.*) *Q.*   9. So he] *Q;* So well he *conj. H.F.B.*   12. sacrifice,] *Q4;* sacrifice. *Q.*   14. interim, pray you,] *Malone; Interim* pray, you *Q.*   17. Ephesus . . . see] *this ed., conj. Maxwell; Ephesus* . . . see, *Q;* Ephesus, . . . see, *Malone.*   20. fancies'] *Camb., conj. S. Walker;* fancies *Q;* fancy's *Rowe.*   S.D.] *Q4; not in Q.*

9. *So . . . thriv'd*] An adverb is missing in the text (H.F.B.); the heavy emphasis on *So* seems awkward and improbable.

9–10. *thriv'd . . . wiv'd*] a common proverbial phrase in Elizabethan drama. See Tilley T 264 and cf. *Shr.,* I. ii. 53–4, 'And I have thrust myself into this maze, / Happily to wive and thrive as best I may'.

12. *he*] i.e. Pericles, whereas *he* in ll. 9–10 is Lysimachus.

14. *confound*] 'consume' (Malone, *O.E.D.*1e) or 'bring to nought' (*O.E.D.*1b); 'do away with in thought' (Young, quoted by Maxwell).

15. *In . . . briefness*] with winged speed (D.).

17. *At Ephesus . . . see*] At the temple of Ephesus see (Maxwell conj.). Necessitating only a slight adjustment in punctuation, this interpretation seems better than Malone's, which edd. usually follow. *Ephesus the temple* is both a classicism and a Chaucerism; cf. 'Thebes the citee' ('Knight's Tale', *Canterbury Tales*, A 939).

20. *Is . . . doom*] *doom* = judgment; is due to the judgment of your imagination, for which I am thankful. Gower thus compliments the audience.

fancies'] or 'fancy's' (Rowe); Q allows of either interpretation.

[SCENE III.—*The Same.*]

[*Enter* PERICLES, *with his Train;* LYSIMACHUS, HELICANUS,
and MARINA.]

Per. Hail, Dian! to perform thy just command,
    I here confess myself the king of Tyre;
    Who, frighted from my country, did wed
    At Pentapolis the fair Thaisa.
    At sea in childbed died she, but brought forth   5
    A maid-child call'd Marina; who, O goddess,
    Wears yet thy silver livery. She at Tharsus
    Was nurs'd with Cleon, who at fourteen years
    He sought to murder; but her better stars
    Brought her to Mytilene; 'gainst whose shore   10

Scene III

SCENE III] *Malone; not in* Q.   *The Same*] *Maxwell subst., this ed.; not in* Q.
Entry] *Malone subst.; not in* Q.   3–13. Who . . . daughter] *As Rowe and* (*ll. 10–11*)
Malone; prose Q.   6–8. who . . . who] *F4*; whom . . . who *Q*; who . . . whom
Tonson.   9. He] *Q*; Her *conj. Elze.*

SCENE III] In accordance with
tradition and in order to keep the
choruses separate from scenes of
dialogue, this scene is divided from v.
ii. Yet they are of course continuous,
with Thaisa, Cerimon, and their
Attendants present on the stage from
the start of v. ii.

3. *country*] perhaps pronounced tri-
syllabically.

4. *At . . . Thaisa*] a rough line which
may be corrupt. Malone suggests
moving *At Pentapolis* to the end of the
line.

6. *maid-child*] An early example of
this expression is found in Wycliffe's
Bible, *Genesis*, xxiv. 55 and 57 (Halli-
well-Philipps, Scrapbook). Used only
once in Shakespeare.

who] so F4 and most edd. since, and
accepted in this edn so as not to con-
fuse the modern reader unnecessarily,
as a modernization. But Q's ungrammatical 'whom' for nominative *who* is
found fairly often in Elizabethan

literature—see *O.E.D. whom* 11. An-
other instance is Wapull, *The Tyde
taryeth no Man* (1576), ll. 665–6 (ed.
E. Ruehl, *Sh. Jahrbuch* (1907): 'Helpe.
Who is it . . .? *Courtyer*. Euen I a
Gentleman *whome* money doe lack'.

7. *silver livery*] white robe; *silver* is the
colour of chastity; cf. *Mer. V.*, II. vii.
22, 'the silver with her virgin hue'
(J. D. Wilson). The link with Diana,
the moon-goddess or 'goddess argentine' of v. i. 248, is appropriate.

8. *with Cleon*] in Cleon's family.

fourteen years] so Twine, p. 320;
not in Gower (L. Kirschbaum *apud*
Maxwell).

8–9. *who . . . He*] ungrammatical
who for 'whom' is as common in
Elizabethan drama as in modern
colloquial English. What has troubled
edd. is that *who*, though evidently referring to Marina, is placed after
Cleon, thus confusing the meaning of
the passage. But Elze's conj. 'Her' is
unconvincing.

Riding, her fortunes brought the maid aboard us,
Where, by her own most clear remembrance, she
Made known herself my daughter.

Thai.   Voice and favour!
You are, you are—O royal Pericles!   [*Faints.*]
Per. What means the nun? she dies, help, gentlemen!   15
Cer. Noble sir,
If you have told Diana's altar true,
This is your wife.
Per.   Reverend appearer, no:
I threw her overboard with these very arms.
Cer. Upon this coast, I warrant you.
Per.   'Tis most certain.   20
Cer. Look to the lady. O, she's but o'erjoy'd.
Early one blustering morn this lady was
Thrown upon this shore. I op'd the coffin,
Found there rich jewels; recover'd her, and plac'd her
Here in Diana's temple.
Per.   May we see them?   25
Cer. Great sir, they shall be brought you to my house,
Whither I invite you. Look, Thaisa is
Recovered.
Thai.   O, let me look!
If he be none of mine, my sanctity

13–14. Voice . . . Pericles!] *As Malone; prose Q.*   14. S.D.] *Rowe; not in Q.*
15. nun] *MS in Capell copy of Q, Collier;* mum *Q.*   16–36. Noble . . . drown'd]
As Malone; prose Q.   18. Reverend] *Q2;* Reuerent *Q.*   21. o'erjoy'd]
Q (ouer-joyde).   22. one] *Malone;* in *Q.*   28–9. look! / If] *Malone;* looke
if *Q;* look; if *Rowe.*

---

11. *Riding*] as we rode at anchor
(D.).

13. *favour*] looks, face.

15. *nun*] In the Capell copy of Q,
'mum' has been corrected in ink by an
early hand. The correction is confirmed by *P.A.*, 107. 27, where we are
told that Thaisa was 'placed to be a
Nunne' in the temple.

18. *Reverend*] See v. i. 14n.

appearer] one who appears; the only
instance of this word in Shakespeare.
But Shakespeare seems to have been
fond of inventing unusual nouns in *-er*
during his last years; cf. 'abandoner'

(*TNK.*, v. i. 138) and 'rejoicer' (*TNK.*'
i. i. 121).

21. *Look . . . lady*] Cf. *Mac.*, ii. iii. 125
and *Ham.*, v. ii. 295, 'Look to the
queen'.

22. *one*] Q's 'in' was probably a miscorrection of 'on' (Maxwell), a frequent spelling of *one* in Elizabethan
literature, as for instance in Q at
v. i. 70.

25. *Here . . . temple*] 'The same situation occurs again in *Errors*, where
Aegeon loses his wife at sea, and finds
her at last in a nunnery' (Steevens);
see also Intro., p. lxiv.

Will to my sense bend no licentious ear,   30
But curb it, spite of seeing. O, my lord,
Are you not Pericles? Like him you spake,
Like him you are. Did you not name a tempest,
A birth and death?
Per.   The voice of dead Thaisa!
Thai. That Thaisa am I, supposed dead   35
And drown'd.
Per. Immortal Dian!
Thai.   Now I know you better.
When we with tears parted Pentapolis,
The king my father gave you such a ring.
                    [*Points to his ring.*]
Per. This, this: no more. You gods, your present kindness   40
Makes my past miseries sports. You shall do well,
That on the touching of her lips I may
Melt and no more be seen. O come, be buried

32. spake] *Q;* speak *Q2.*   37. Immortal] *Q4;* I mortall *Q.*   37-45. Now . . .
bosom] *As Malone; prose Q.*   39. S.D.] *Cowden Clarke; not in Q; Shows a ring* /
Malone.   40. no more. You gods,] *this ed.;* no more, you gods, *Q;* no more,
you gods! *Malone.*

29-31. *If . . . seeing*] 'If he is not my
husband, my holiness will not listen
licentiously to what my eyes tell me'.
Maxwell is right in taking *sense* to mean
primarily 'sense of sight', though no
doubt there is an overtone of 'sensual
passion' (Steevens), called forth by the
epithet *licentious* and by our consciousness of the delicacy of Thaisa's
situation.

32. *spake*] not a certain reading, considering Q2's early change to 'speak',
yet not without precedent; see, for
instance, *Err.,* II. i. 50, 'Spake he so
doubtfully'.

37. *Immortal Dian!*] sc. be praised
for bringing this about.

38. *parted*] departed from.

39. S.D. Points . . . ring] Most edd.
have accepted Malone's S.D., 'shows
a ring', evidently supposing that
Thaisa and Pericles wear identical
rings. My preference is indicated by
my choice.

40. *no more. You gods,*] The punctua-

tion, suggested to me by E.S., is different from that usually adopted in
modern edd. ('no more, you gods!')
but equally close to Q's. It seems best
to interpret *no more* as simply meaning:
'no more is needed to confirm that you
are Thaisa', though the possibility
should be kept in mind that he may be
anticipating the sentiment of the following lines: 'Let my emotion not
grow greater or it will destroy me'
(H.F.B.).

41-3. *You . . . seen*] *You shall . . . That*
= you will do well if; i.e. the embrace
with Thaisa will be such an ecstasy
that if the gods were at that moment
to dissolve Pericles' human existence,
they would do so fittingly. Cf.
Pericles' recognition of Marina, v. i.
191-4, where extreme joy and death
are similarly associated, and also
Oth., II. i. 187-91.

43-4. *be buried . . . arms*] Cf. *Wint.,* IV.
iv. 131-2, 'not to be buried, / But
quick, and in mine arms' (Malone).

                A second time within these arms.
Mar.   My heart
        Leaps to be gone into my mother's bosom.   45
                                [*Kneels to Thaisa.*]
Per. Look, who kneels here, flesh of thy flesh, Thaisa;
        Thy burden at the sea, and call'd Marina
        For she was yielded there.
Thai.   Bless'd, and mine own!
Hel. Hail, madam, and my queen!
Thai.   I know you not.
Per. You have heard me say, when I did fly from Tyre,   50
        I left behind an ancient substitute;
        Can you remember what I call'd the man?
        I have nam'd him oft.
Thai.   'Twas Helicanus then.
Per. Still confirmation!
        Embrace him, dear Thaisa; this is he.   55
        Now do I long to hear how you were found,
        How possibly preserv'd, and who to thank,
        Besides the gods, for this great miracle.
Thai. Lord Cerimon, my lord; this man,
        Through whom the gods have shown their power; that
            can   60
        From first to last resolve you.
Per.   Reverend sir,
        The gods can have no mortal officer
        More like a god than you. Will you deliver
        How this dead queen re-lives?
Cer.   I will, my lord.
        Beseech you, first go with me to my house,   65
        Where shall be shown you all was found with her;
        How she came plac'd here in the temple;
        No needful thing omitted.

45. S.D.] *Malone; not in* Q.   46–58. Look . . . miracle] *As Rowe; prose* Q.
50. *Per.*] *Q4; Hell.* Q.   59–64. Lord . . . re-lives] *As Steevens; prose* Q.   59. this
man] *Q; this is the man Dyce* (ii), *conj. S. Walker.*   64–8. I will . . . omitted]
As Malone; prose Q.

48. *yielded*] brought forth.   67. *How . . . temple*] The similarity in
57. *possibly*] by any existing means.   wording to ll. 24–5 above suggests
61. *resolve*] satisfy.   cross-contamination of the two pass-
63. *deliver*] relate.   ages by the reporter (H.F.B.).

Per.   Pure Dian,
    I bless thee for thy vision, and will offer
    Night-oblations to thee. Thaisa,   70
    This prince, the fair betrothed of your daughter,
    Shall marry her at Pentapolis. And now
†   [   ] this ornament
    Makes me look dismal will I clip to form;
    And what this fourteen years no razor touch'd   75
    To grace thy marriage-day I'll beautify.
Thai. Lord Cerimon hath letters of good credit, sir,
    My father's dead.
Per. Heavens make a star of him! Yet there, my queen,
    We'll celebrate their nuptials, and ourselves   80
    Will in that kingdom spend our following days.
    Our son and daughter shall in Tyrus reign.
    Lord Cerimon, we do our longing stay
    To hear the rest untold: sir, lead's the way.   [*Exeunt.*]

68–71. Pure Dian . . . daughter] *As Steevens; prose Q.*   68–9. Dian, / I . . . and]
Malone (Diana)*; Dian blesse thee . . . and Q; Dian, bless thee . . . vision; I F3.*
70. Night-oblations] *Malone;* night oblations *Q;* My night oblations *Steevens;*
nightly oblations *Maxwell.*   thee. Thaisa] *Q4 subst., Malone;* thee Thaisa / *Q.*
72–3. Shall . . . ornament] *arranged this ed.; prose Q.*   74–8. Makes . . . dead] *As
Dyce; prose in Q.*   77. credit, sir] *Q4;* credit. Sir *Q.*   79–82. Heavens . . .
reign] *As Rowe; prose Q.*   84. S.D.] *Q4;* Finis *Q.*

68–73. *Pure . . . ornament*] It is
impossible to recapture the Shakespearean original of these lines. Maxwell's 'nightly oblations' for *night-
oblations* is a distinct possibility.
Several words seem to have been
omitted by either reporter or compositor, and the lines therefore do not
lend themselves to convincing metrical
arrangement. The best has been made
here of a bad job, and the result may at
least be closer to the original than Q's
prose. Some such word as 'Dear'
or 'Come' seems to have dropped
out before *Thaisa* (H.F.B.), and a
phrase may be missing before *this
ornament.*

69–70. *Dian, I . . . and*] Q's omission
may have resulted from two causes:
either the reporter misinterpreted *Dian*
as the subject of *bless* (Maxwell subst.);
or the hurried compositor simply

missed a word plus the punctuation
mark after *Dian.* See n. above.

74. *Makes*] which makes.

75. *fourteen years*] Cf. l. 8 above.

78. *My father's dead*] The conj. 'that'
is omitted. For the incident, cf. *LLL.*,
where, also close to the end of the play,
the heroine is informed of her father's
death.

79. *Heavens . . . him*] Cf. *Rom.*, III. ii.
21 ff. The primary reference is un-
doubtedly to the translation of Julius
Caesar's soul to a star at the end of
Ovid's *Metamorphoses*, echoed in *1H6*,
I. i. 55–6.

83. *we . . . stay*] not: 'we will delay
for a while our longing' (D.), but
rather '(with all this talk) we are
delaying our longing' (after Maxwell).

84. *untold*] i.e. that is yet untold.

lead's the way] so, or similarly, the

[EPILOGUE]

[Enter] GOWER.

In Antiochus and his daughter you have heard
Of monstrous lust the due and just reward.
In Pericles, his queen and daughter, seen,
Although assail'd with fortune fierce and keen,
Virtue preserv'd from fell destruction's blast,   5
Led on by heaven, and crown'd with joy at last.
In Helicanus may you well descry
A figure of truth, of faith, of loyalty.
In reverend Cerimon there well appears
The worth that learned charity aye wears.   10
For wicked Cleon and his wife, when fame
Had spread his cursed deed to th' honour'd name

Epilogue

Heading. EPILOGUE] *this ed.; not in Q.*   Entry.] *Q4; Gower. / Q.*   3. Pericles,]
Rowe; Pericles / Q.   5. preserv'd] *Tonson;* preferd *Q.*   12. his] *Q; their Q4.*
deed to th'] *Maxwell, conj. Collier;* deede, the *Q;* deed and *F3.*

last words of other plays; e.g. *Wint.*,
'hastily lead away', and Heywood,
1 If You Know Not Me (1605).

Epilogue

3. *Pericles,*] The comma is essential,
since 'Pericles his' would mean
'Pericles' ', which is not intended.

11–14. *when fame . . . to th' . . . turn . . .
burn*] so Q, except for *to th'* instead of
'the' and changes in punctuation.
fame = report. F3's 'and', though
found in many modern edd., makes no
sense whatsoever. Ridley and Kitt-
redge (whom E.S. would follow) are
the only two modern edd. who retain
Q completely. They presumably interpret: 'when report . . . deed,
Pericles' honoured name turns the
city to rage, so that . . . burn'. But in
that case, *turn* would require to be
explained. E.S. suggests that such an
irregular plural for singular is not uncommon in Elizabethan English; *turn*
could also be justified by interpreting
name (like 'race') as a plural. But I am

not persuaded. Possibly, as H.F.B.
remarks, the original read 'turnd . . .
burn'd', and the compositor, misinterpreting the passage, dropped the
d in 'turnd', and then adjusted the
rhyme. But to me, Collier's solution
seems preferable by far, making *city*
the subject of the main clause. See
nn. to ll. 12 and 14 for other emendations.

12. *his*] Q4's 'their' is given by most
edd., since Dionyza was the main
offender, and since Cleon himself did
not plan the *deed.* In that case one
might postulate that Q's compositor
caught *his* from the previous line. Yet
the emendation seems unnecessary.
Cleon did eventually adopt the deed,
and is, at any rate by Gower, regarded
as fully implicated in the murder.
Q *his* makes sufficient sense, referring
as it does to Cleon as the head of a
punishable family, which includes of
course Dionyza. The judgment upon
them is in strict accord with Cleon's
own words at III. iii. 23–5.

Of Pericles, to rage the city turn,
That him and his they in his palace burn:
The gods for murder seemed so content   15
To punish; although not done, but meant.
So on your patience evermore attending,
New joy wait on you! Here our play has ending.   *Exit.*

13. Pericles,] *Q;* Pericles *Ridley.*   14. him and his] *Q;* him and her *Halliwell.*
16. punish; although] *Q subst.* (punish,); punish them; although *Malone.*
18. S.D.] *Malone;* FINIS *Q.*

14. *his*] i.e. Cleon's whole family; not only Dionyza, as Halliwell supposes. See previous n.

16. *To . . . meant*] metrically rough and possibly corrupt: hence Malone's emendation. Yet the passage makes good sense as it stands. *although . . . meant* = although the murder was not carried out, only intended.

APPENDIX A

EXTRACT FROM LAURENCE TWINE

The Patterne of Painefull Aduentures, Q 1607, sig. F4ᵛ–Hv, Chapters
11–14. These chapters correspond to Act IV, scenes i, iii, and vi in
the play.

THE ELEVENTH CHAPTER.

*How after the death of Ligozides the nurce Dionisiades enuying at the
beautie of Tharsia, conspired her death, which should haue bin
accomplished by a villaine of the countrey.*

Tharsia much lamented the death of Ligozides her nurce, and
caused her bodie to be solemnly buried not farre of, in a field without the walles of the citie, and mourned for her an whole yeere
following. But when the yeare was expired, she put off her mourning atire, and put on her other apparel, and frequented the
schooles, and the studie of liberall Sciences as before. And when-
soeuer she returned from schoole, she would receiue no meate
before she had visited her nurces sepulchre, which she did daily,
entring thereinto, and carrying a flagon of wine with her, where
she used to abide a space, and to call vppon her father and mother.
Now on a day it fortuned, that as she passed through the street with
Dionisiades, and her companion Philomacia, the people beholding
the beautie and comlinesse of Tharsia, said: Happy is that father
that hath Tharsia to his daughter, but her companion that goeth
with her, is foule and euill fauoured. When Dionisiades heard
Tharsia commended, and her owne daughter Philomacia so dis-
praised, shee returned home wonderfull wroth, and withdrawing
her self into a solitary place, began thus secretly to discourse of yᵉ
matter. It is now fourteen yeares since Apollonius this foolish
girles father departed frō hence, and he neuer sendeth letters for
her, nor any remembrance vnto her, whereby I coniecture that he
is dead. Ligozides her nurce is departed, and there is no bodie now
of whom I should stande in feare, and therefore I will now slay her,
and dress vp mine owne daughter in her apparell and iewels. When
shee had thus resolued her selfe vppon this wicked purpose, in the

meane while there came home one of their countrey villaines called
Theophilus, whom shee called, and said thus vnto him: Theophilus, my trustie friend, if euer thou looke for libertie, or that I
shoulde doe thee pleasure, doe so much for me as to slay Tharsia.
Then said Theophilus: Alas mistresse, wherein hath that innocent
maiden offended, that she should be slaine? Dionisiades answered,
Shee innocent! nay she is a wicked wretch, and therefore thou shalt
not denie to fulfill my request, but doe as I commaund thee, or els
I sweare by God, thou shalt dearely repent it. But how shall I best
doe it, Mistres said the villaine? Shee aunswered: shee hath a custome as soone as shee returneth home from Schoole, not to eate
meat before that she haue gone into her Nurces sepulchre, where
I would haue thee stand readie, with a dagger drawn in thine hand;
and when she is come in, gripe her by the haire of the head, and
so slay her: then take her bodie and cast it into the Sea, and when
thou hast so done, I will make thee free, and besides reward thee
liberally. Then tooke the villaine a dagger, and girded himselfe
therewith, and with an heauy heart and weeping eies went forth
toward the graue, saying within himselfe, Alas poore wretch that
I am, alas poore Theophilus that canst not deserue thy libertie but
by shedding of innocent bloud: and with that hee went into the
graue, and drue his dagger, and made him readie for the deede.
Tharsia was now come from schoole, and made haste vnto the
grave with a flagon of wine as shee was wont to doe, and entred
within the vaut. Then the villaine rushed violently vpon her, and
caught her by the haire of the head, and threw her to the ground.
And while he was now readie to stab her with the dagger, poore
silly Tharsia, all amazed casting her eies vpon him, knew the
villain, and holding vp her handes, said thus vnto him: O Theophilus, against whom haue I so greeuously offended, that I must
die therefore? The villaine answered, Thou hast not offended, but
thy father hath, which left thee behind him in Stranguilios house
with so great a treasure in mony, and princely ornaments. O, said
the mayden, would to God he had not done so: but I pray thee
Theophilus, since there is no hope for me to escape with life, giue
mee licence to say my praiers before I die. I giue thee licence saide
the villaine, and I take God to record, that I am constrained to
murther thee against my will.

THE TWELFTH CHAPTER.

How certaine Pyrats rescued Tharsia when she should haue been slaine, and carried her vnto the citie Machilenta to be sold among other bondslaues.

As fortune, or rather the prouidence of God serued, while Tharsia was deuoutly making her praiers, certaine pyrats which were come aland, and stood vnder the side of an hill watching for some prey, beholding an armed man offering violence vnto a mayden, cried vnto him and said: Thou cruel tyrant! that maiden is our prey and not thy victorie, and therfore hold thine hands from her, as thou louest thy life. When the villain heard that, he ran away as fast as he could, and hid himselfe behind the sepulchre. Then came the pyrats and rescued Tharsia, and carried her away to their ships, and hoysed saile, and departed. And the villaine returned home to his mistres, and saide vnto her: that which you commaunded me to doe is dispatched, and therefore now I thinke it good, that you put on a mourning garment, and I also, and let vs counterfeit great sorrowe and heauinesse in the sight of all the people, and say that shee died of some greeuous disease. But Stranguilio himselfe consented not to this treason, but so soone as hee heard of the foule mischaunce, beeing as it were amort and mazed with heauinesse and griefe, he clad himselfe in mourning aray, and lamented that wofull case, saying: Alas in what a mischiefe am I wrapped? what might I doe, or say herein? The father of this mayden deliuered this citie from the peril of death, for this cities sake he suffered shipwracke, lost his goodes and endured penury, and now he is requited with euil for good. His daughter which he committed vnto me to be brought vp, is now deuoured by a most cruell Lionesse: thus I am depriued as it were of mine owne eies, & forced to bewaile the death of an innocent, and am vtterly spoiled through the fierce biting of a moste venemous serpent. Then casting his eies vp towards heauen, O God said hee, thou knowest that I am innocent from the bloud of silly Tharsia, which thou hast to require at Dionisiades handes, and therewithall he looked towards his wife, saying: Thou wicked woman, tell me, how hast thou made away prince Apollonius daughter? thou that liuest both to the slaunder of God, and man? Dionisiades answered in manie wordes euermore excusing herselfe, and moderating the wrath of Stranguilio, shee counterfeited a fained sorrowe by attiring her selfe and her daughter in mourning apparell, and in dissembling teares before the people of the citie, to whom shee saide: Dearely beloued friendes and Citizens of Tharsus, for this cause we doe weepe and mourne in your sight, because the ioy of our eyes and staffe of our olde age, the Mayden Tharsia is dead, leauing vnto vs bitter teares, and sorrowfull heartes. Yet haue we alreadie taken order for her funerals, and buried her according to her degree. These wordes were right greeuous vnto the people, and there was almost none that let not fall some teares for sorrowe. And they went with one accord vnto the market place, whereas her fathers image stood, made of brasse, and erected also another vnto her there with this inscription: *Vnto the virgin Tharsia in liew of her fathers benefites, the Citizens of Tharsus haue erected this monument.*

THE THIRTEENTH CHAPTER.

How the Pirats which stole away Tharsia brought her to the citie Machilenta, and solde her to a common bawd, and how she preserued her virginity.

The meane time while these troubles were at Tharsus, the Pirats being in their course vpon the Sea, by benefite of happie winde arriued at Machilenta, and came into the citie. Nowe had they taken manie mo men and women besides Tharsia, whom all they brought a shoare, and set them to sell as slaues for money. Then came there sundrie to buy such as they lacked for their purposes, amongst whom a moste vile man-bawd, beholding the beautie and tender yeeres of Tharsia, offered money largely for her. Howbeit Athanagoras, who was Prince of the same Citie, beholding likewise the noble countenance, and regarding the great discretion of the mayden in communication, out-bid the bawd, and offered for her ten sestercies of gold. But ye bawd, being loth to loose so commodious a prey, offered twenty. And I wil giue thirty said Athanagoras. Nay I wil giue forty said the bawd: and I fiftie quoth Athanagoras, and so they continued in outbidding one an other vntill the bawd offered an hundred sestercies of gold to be payed ready downe, and whosoeuer wil giue more, saide he, I will yet giue ten sestercies more than he. Then prince Athanagoras thus bethought him secretly in his minde: if I should contend with the bawd to buy her at so hie a price, I must needes sell other slaues to pay for her, which were both losse and shame vnto me. Wherefore I will suffer him to buy her, and when he setteth her to hire, I will be the first man that shall come vnto her, and I will gather the floure of her virginitie, which shall stand mee in as great steade as if I had bought her. Then the bawd payed the money, and tooke the maiden and departed home; and when he came into his house, hee brought her into a certaine chappel where stoode the idoll of Priapus made of gold, and garnished with pearls and pretious stones. This idoll was made after the shape of a man, with a mighty member vnproportionable to the body, alwayes erected, whome bawds and leachers doe adore, making him their god, and worshipping him. Before this filthy idoll he commaunded Tharsia with reuerence to fall downe. But she answered, God forbid master, that I should worship such an idoll. But (sir) said she, are you a Lapsatenian? Why askest thou, said the bawd? I aske, quoth she, because the Lapsatenians doe worship Priapus: this spake she of simplicitie, not knowing what he was. Ah wretch, answered he, knowest thou not that thou arte come into the house of a couetous bawd? When Tharsia heard that, she fell downe at his feet and wept, saying: O master, take compassion vpon my virginity, and do not hire out my body for so vile a gaine. The bawd answered, knowest thou not, that neither bawd nor hangman do regard teares or prayers? Then called he vnto him a certaine villaine which was gouernour ouer his maids, and said vnto him: Let this maiden be decked in virgins apparell, pretious and costly, and write vpon her: whoseeuer defloureth Tharsia shal pay ten peeces of golde, and afterward she shall be common vnto the people for one peece at a time. The villaine fulfilled his masters commaundement, and the third day after that she was bought, shee was with great solemnitie conducted through the streete with musicke, the bawd himselfe with a great multitude going before, and so conueyed vnto the brothell house. When shee was come thither, Athanagoras the Prince disguising his head and face, because hee woulde not be knowen, came first in vnto her, whome when Tharsia sawe, she threw her selfe downe at his feete, and saide vnto him: for the loue of God, Gentleman, take pitty on me, and by the name of God I adiure and charge you, that you do no violence vnto me, but bridle your lust, and hearken vnto my unhappy estate, and consider diligently from whence I am sprung. My father was poore Apollonius prince of Tyrus, whome force constrained to forsake his owne countrey. My mother was daughter to Altistrates king of Pentapolis, who died in the birth of me, poore wretch, vpon the sea. My father also is dead as was supposed, which caused Dionisiades wife to Stranguilio of Tharsus, to whom my father committed me of special trust to be brought vp being but an infant, enuying mine estate, and thirsting after my wealth, to seeke my death by the handes of a villaine, which had been accomplished, and I would to God it had before I had seen this day, but that I was suddenly taken away by the pyrates which solde me vnto this filthie bawd. With these or such like wordes declared shee her heauie fortune, eftsoones sobbing and bursting out into streames of tears, that for extreme griefe she could scarsly speake. When she had in this manner vttered her sorow, the good prince being astonied and mooued with compassion, said vnto her: Be of good cheere Tharsia, for surely I rue thy case, and I my selfe haue also a daughter at home, to whome I doubt that the like chances may befall.

And when he had so said, he gaue her twenty peeces of gold, saying: Holde heere a greater price or reward for thy virginitie, than thy master appointed: and say as much vnto others that come vnto thee as thou hast done to me, and thou shalt withstand them. Then Tharsia fell on her knees, and weeping saide vnto him: Sir, I giue you most hartie thankes for your great compassion and curtesie, and most hartily I beseech you vpon my knees, not to descry vnto any that which I haue saide vnto you. No surely, answered Athanagoras, vnless I tell it vnto my daughter, that she may take heede when she commeth vnto the like yeares, that she fall not into the like mishappe: and when he had so saide, he let fall a few teares, and departed. Now as he was going, he met with an other pilgrime that with like deuotion came for to seeke the same saint, who demaunded of him howe hee liked of the maidens company. Truly, answered Athanagoras neuer of any better. Then the yong man whose name was Aportatus entred into the chamber; and the maiden, after the manner, shut the doore to, and Athanagoras listned at the windowe. Then said Aportatus vnto Tharsia, How much did the prince giue vnto thee? She answered fortie peeces of golde. Then said he, receiue here of me an whole pound weight of golde. The Prince which heard this talke thought then in his minde, the more that you do giue her, the more she will weepe, as thinking that you would looke for recompence, the which shee meaneth not to perfourme.

The maiden receiued the money, and fell down on her knees at his feete, and declared vnto him all her estate with teares, as is before shewed. When Aportatus heard that, he was mooued with compassion, and he tooke her vp from the ground, saying: Arise Ladie Tharsia: we are al men, and subiect to the like chances, & therewithall he departed. And when he came foorth he found prince Athanagoras before the doore laughing at him, to whom he said: Is it wel done, my liege, thus to delude a poore gentleman? Was there none to whom you might beginne in teares but vnto me only? Then communed they further of the matter, and sware an othe betweene themselues, that they would not bewray those words vnto any, & they withdrew themselues aside into a secret place, to see the going in and comming foorth of other, and they sawe many

which went in and gaue their mony, and came foorth againe
weeping. Thus Tharsia through the grace of God, and faire per-
swasion, preserued her body vndefiled.

THE FOURTEENTH CHAPTER.

*How Tharsia withstoode a second assault of her virginitie, and by
what meanes she was preserued.*

When night was come, the master bawd vsed always to receiue
the money, which his women had gotten by the vse of their bodies
the day before. And when it was demaunded of Tharsia, she
brought him the money, as the price and hire of her virginitie.
Then said the bawd vnto hir: It is wel doone Tharsia, vse diligence
hencefoorth, and see that you bring mee thus much mony euery
day. When the next day was past also, and the bawd vnderstoode
that she remained a virgin stil, he was offended, and called vnto
him the villaine that had charge ouer the maides, and said vnto
him: Sirra, how chanceth it that Tharsia remaineth a virgin still?
Take her vnto thee, and spoile her of her maidenhead, or be sure
thou shalt be whipped. Then said the villaine vnto Tharsia, tel me,
art thou yet a virgin? She answered, I am, and shalbe as long as
God will suffer me. How then, said he, hast thou gotten all this
mony? She answered, with teares falling downe vpon her knees,
I haue declared mine estate, humbly requesting all men to take
compassion on my virginitie. And nowe likewise, falling then
downe at his feete also, take pitty on me, good friend, which am a
poore captiue, and the daughter of a king, and doe not defile me.
The villaine answered: Our master the bawd is very couetous and
greedie of money, and therefore I see no meanes for thee to continue
a virgin. Whereunto Tharsia replied: I am skilful in the liberal
sciences, and well exercised in all studies, and no man singeth or
playeth on instruments better than I, wherefore bring mee into the
market place of the citie, that men may heare my cunning. Or let
the people propound any maner of questions, and I will resolue
them: and I doubt not but by this practise I shall get store of money
daily. When the villaine heard this deuise, and bewailed the
maidens mishappe, he willingly gaue consent thereto, and brake
with the bawd his master touching that matter, who hearing of
her skill, and hoping for the gaine, was easily perswaded.

Now when she was brought into the market place, all the people
came thronging to see and heare so learned a virgin, before whom
shee vttered her cunning in musicke, and her eloquence in speaking, and aunswered manifestly vnto all such questions as were pro-

pounded vnto her with such perspicuitie, that all confessed themselues fully satisfied, and she wonne great fame thereby, and
gained great summes of money. But as for Prince Athanagoras, he
had euermore a speciall regard in the preseruation of her virginitie,
none otherwise than if she had been his owne daughter, and
rewarded the villaine very liberally for his diligent care ouer
her.

APPENDIX B

JOHN DAY—EVIDENCE FOR COLLABORATION

I

This Appendix provides the evidence for the tentative proposal
made in the Introduction, Section 3, p. lxii, that John Day was
one of the original authors of, or one of Shakespeare's collaborators
in, *Pericles*. This hypothesis was first made in my article, 'How
Significant are Textual Parallels? A New Author for *Pericles*?',
Sh.Q. xi, No. 1 (Winter 1960), 27–37. Some pages of this article are
closely followed here, but certain adjustments and additions have
been made.

As will be seen, much of the evidence is in the form of textual
parallels and close similarities in idiom and in syntax. The reliability of textual parallels as evidence for authorship has been
widely questioned, and doubt has also been expressed whether
style can be a safe criterion in the case of any authors but those of
the first rank. It has been stated, accurately though with slight
exaggeration, that many Elizabethan dramatists wrote blank
verse with the smoothness and anonymity of modern journalistic
prose. The following material is therefore presented with due
caution. I have kept in mind that Day's style sometimes resembles
that of Dekker and other of his contemporaries closely, and I have
tried to observe the 'five golden rules for the parallel-hunter' laid
down in an important article by M. St Clare Byrne.[1] Particularly,
a distinction has been observed between textual parallels or similarities in phrasing and idea which are proverbial or commonplace,
and those others which reflect more truly and sharply an author's
style and habits of mind. And in some cases, other kinds of evidence
have been cited in corroboration. Lastly, I have kept watch for possible indications that the reporter of *Pericles* prodded his faltering

---

1. 'Bibliographical Clues in Collaborate Plays', *The Library*, Ser. 4, 13 (1932–
3), 21–48.

memory with the help of passages recollected from other plays. But readers must judge the evidence on its particular merits.

II

The majority of Day's plays have perished. Many were probably never printed. The extant canon of Day's works consists of *The Blind Beggar* (with Chettle), *The Ile of Gulls*, *The Travels of the Three English Brothers* (with Wilkins and W. Rowley), *Law-Tricks*, *Humour out of Breath*, *The Parliament of Bees*, and a single piece of prose, *Peregrinatio Scholastica*.[1] A close reading of these works revealed to me a strikingly large number of textual parallels to *Pericles*. Further encouraged by the fact that no fewer than four of Day's surviving plays were first printed in 1606–8, that is the three years preceding the publication of Q of *Pericles*, I made a detailed list of all parallels, whether they in themselves seemed significant or not; everything, that is to say, from proverbial phrasing to striking correspondences of several successive lines or clusters of images. The resulting catalogue showed for most scenes of *Pericles* only one or two, and usually insignificant parallels, but for two scenes, namely II. i and II. iii, a much larger number of parallels, including some remarkable ones.

One of these parallels was pointed out long ago by Bullen and is well known. It involves the liveliest episode of the first two acts, the dialogue of the fishermen at II. i. 26–43. Bullen discovered that some of the fishermen's very phrases also occur in two scenes of *Law-Tricks*:

> *Joculo.* But, madam, do you remember what a multitude of fishes we saw at sea? and I do wonder how they can all live by one another.
> *Emilia.* Why, fool, as men do on the land; the great ones eat up the little ones.   (I. ii, p.15)[2]

> *Adam.* I knew one of that faculty in one term eat up a whole town, church, steeple and all.
> *Julio.* I wonder the bells rung not all in his belly.   (II. i, p. 26)

These remarkable parallels called for some explanation, and considering that *Law-Tricks* was first printed in 1608, the same year in which *Pericles* was entered in the Stationers' Register, Bullen decided that 'Day must either have seen the MS of *Pericles*, or must have carried away the words in his memory from the play-

---

1. An allegorical tract, first printed from Lansdowne MS 725 in Bullen's edn of Day, 1881. Another MS of the same tract is in the Huntington Library.

2. References are to Bullen's edn of Day, unless otherwise stated, but spelling has been modernized.

house'. Since then, however, E. K. Chambers[1] has found grounds for dating *Law-Tricks* as early as 1604, that is several years before *Pericles*. It has been stressed that the yarn echoed in the two passages is an old one,[2] but this is not true of the notion of the 'jangling of the bells' (*Per.*, II. i. 41), which is anticipated only by 'the bells rung not all in his belly' in *Law-Tricks*. The general proximity in wording surely suggests interdependence. What kind of interdependence, however, we are not as yet ready to decide. Even if *Law-Tricks* preceded *Pericles*, Shakespeare or some other possible author of II. i might have liked the two pieces in *Law-Tricks* enough to develop them in *Pericles*. The case would be altered, however, if it could be shown that other lines in the same scene are paralleled in thought as well as in wording in Day.

Such echoes can in fact be found, as the following list indicates:

(1) wat'ry grave . . . finny subject of the sea . . . wat'ry empire
(*Per.*, II. i. 10, 48–50)
    deceive the watry subjects   (*Humour*, I. ii, p. 11)
    scorning land, water shall be my grave
(*Parl. of Bees*, Char. VII, p. 49)

Fishes are nowhere else in Shakespeare referred to as 'subjects'.

(2) Fortune . . . shipwreck . . . till then, rest your debtor . . . jewel
(*Per.*, II. i. 120–55)

    Lisander. . . . shipwreck . . . notwithstanding, Fortune hath reserv'd me one jewel which . . . means to work my admittance to the Duke, I should become a true debtor to your love.   (*Ile of Gulls*, I. iv, p. 23)[3]

(*The Ile of Gulls* was printed in 1606 and thus definitely precedes *Pericles*. Not only are the same objects and thoughts closely associated in the two scenes, but Lisander's situation as well as intentions are akin to those of Pericles when he rediscovers his armour and plans to visit the court of Simonides. Lisander, like Pericles, was 'cast . . . on this shore' by 'wrathful Neptune'. Occurring as close as it does to Bullen's parallel of the fish in the sea, it constitutes strong evidence for the belief that the author of II. i of *Pericles* was much under the influence of the language of Day's contemporary plays, if not more.)

The following parallels are less striking but help to corroborate the evidence of the others in the same scene:

1. *The Eliz. Stage*, III. 285–6. Chambers has been supported by John Crow in the M.S.R. of Q of *Law-Tricks*.

2. See Commentary, II. i. 28–9 n.

3. The wording in Day's source, Sidney's *Arcadia*, is quite different.

(3) Which my dead father did bequeath to me,
    With this strict charge . . .   (*Per.*, II. i. 123–4)

who on his death-bed made me his heir, with this charge . . . ,
                                          (*Ile of Gulls*, II. i, p. 30)

(4) I can compare our rich misers to nothing so fitly as to a whale
                                          (*Per.*, II. i. 29–30)

I can compare my lord and his friend to nothing in the world
so fitly as to a couple of water buckets . . .
                                          (*Ile of Gulls*, II. iii, p. 40)

(Note that the two passages from Day are again from the early *Ile of Gulls*. However, the correspondence in the last parallel is not unique to the two plays, for compare Jonson, *Every Man In*, III. i. 222: 'I can compare him to nothing more happily than a drum'. Incidentally, for his comic dialogue Day learned much from Jonson.)

To other echoes in II. i still less weight is to be attached, but two may be worth while listing, considering the presence of more significant parallels. The metaphor of the 'vast tennis-court' on which Pericles was made 'the ball' for 'the waters to play upon' (II. i. 59–61) was evidently one dear to Day, for it occurs at least three times in his plays:

(1) You have courts for tennis (*Humour*, p. 7)

(2) *Dametas.* Manasses, how dost like my play at Tennis?
    Manasses. You play well, Sir, but you lose still.
    Dametas. . . . Court. . . .
    Manasses. By the Tennis-court I think you have.
                                          (*Ile of Gulls*, p. 14)

(3) *Parsim.* Suppose all kingdoms in this world were balls,
                And thou stood for a racket twixt four walls
                To toss *ad placitum*: how wouldst thou play?
    Acolastes. Why, as with balls, bandy 'em all away;
                They gone, play twice as many of the score.
    Parsim. A tennis-Court of Kings could do no more.
                                          (*Parliament*, Char. VII, p. 47)

Yet it was a popular metaphor in the early seventeenth century, witness the titles of two lost plays, Dekker's *Fortune's Tennis* (1600) and Munday's *Set at Tennis* (1602), and its use in *H5*, I. ii. 263. For the same reason, the similar style and thought in 'we'll have flesh for holidays, fish for fasting-days, and moreo'er puddings and flap-jacks' (*Per.*, II. i. 81–2) and 'I go wide ope Wensdays, I never lace myself but on Sundays, and that for fear I should burst with eating plum porridge' (*Ile of Gulls*, II. iv, p. 51) may merely reflect common talk of the time, as evidenced by other similar passages in Jacobean drama; e.g. *Every Man In*, III. ii. 175–218.

These facts make one wary of reading too much into verbal echoes or similarities in image or phrasing. Yet I believe that at least the first two parallels listed are remarkable, and that together with Bullen's, they make highly probable some close connection between the works of Day and the first scene of Act II of *Pericles*— a connection which indeed suggests identical authorship.

No other scene in *Pericles* echoes Day in so many places as this one, but II. iii contains some sufficiently startling parallels to attract notice. When, after having so surprisingly won the tournament held in Thaisa's honor at Simonides' court, Pericles is asked by Thaisa to reveal his identity, he answers:

> A Gentleman of Tyre; my name, Pericles;
> My education been in arts and arms;
> Who, looking for adventures in the world,
> Was by the rough seas reft of ships and men,
> And after shipwreck driven upon this shore,

whereupon Thaisa passes this information on to her father:

> He thanks your grace; names himself Pericles,
> A gentleman of Tyre,
> Who only by misfortune of the seas
> Bereft of ships and men, cast on this shore.

In *The Ile of Gulls*, Lisander dissembles his identity towards Dametas in a strikingly similar manner:

> My mother is the queen of Amazons,
> Myself a virgin married unto arms,
> And bold achievements, who have pac'd the world
> In quest of fair Antiope, my sister;
> And turning homeward, the inconstant winds
> And wrathful Neptune cast me on this shore.[1]

Not only in content but also in syntax and in the movement of the verse, a closer similarity (other than direct copy) between two passages in different plays is hard to imagine.

A second fairly close echo to a passage in II. iii of *Pericles* strengthens my impression that Day took at least a part in its composition. Simonides' royal generosity and the banquet over which he presides bring to Pericles' mind times when his own family enjoyed better fortunes:

---

1. *Ile of Gulls*, I. iv, pp. 21–2. The passage in the source, Sidney's *Arcadia*, is quite different.

> Yon king's to me like to my father's picture,
> Which tells me in that glory once he was;
> Had princes sit *like stars* about his throne,
> And he the *sun*, for them to reverence.
> None that beheld him but, *like lesser lights*,
> Did vail their crowns to his supremacy;
> Where now his son's *like a glow-worm* in the night,
> The which hath *fire* in darkness, none in light.   (ll. 37–44)

Compare the following passage from Day:

> we, *like inferior lights*,
> Take life from your reflection, for *like stars*
> Unto the *sun* are counsellors to kings:
> He feeds their orbs with *fire*, and their shine
> Contend to make his glory more divine;
> (*Humour out of Breath*, v. ii)[1]

and note, moreover, the same contrast between a glow-worm and a star (found nowhere else in Shakespeare) in this image from the *Ile of Gulls*:

> her face differs as far
> From others, as a glow-worm from a star.   (II. i, p. 27)

These passages show an impressive correspondence not only in conception but also in wording, a correspondence whose significance is not nullified by the consideration that the compound image itself may have been conventional.

The relevance of a third parallel in II. iii is much more doubtful, but considering its proximity to the two others just discussed, perhaps some importance should also be attached to it. During the banquet, both Simonides and Thaisa are singularly moved by Pericles' presence, but while Thaisa conveys her emotion frankly to her father, the latter playfully dissimulates, accepting Pericles as no more than 'a country gentleman'. Thaisa, however, has a will of her own: 'to me he seems like diamond to glass'. This simple contrast occurs nowhere else in Shakespeare, but Day, who is generally fond of the imagery of jewels and precious stones (there are several such images in the first two acts of *Pericles*), juxtaposes diamond and glass twice in *Law-Tricks*: 'Pure as diamond, clear as crystal glass' and 'This gilded copper, diamond of glass'. The comparison seems commonplace, but Day's liking for it and its

---

1. *Humour*, p. 70. The italics in the two quoted passages are mine. Note also the less obvious parallel in *Travels*, in a passage usually attributed to Wilkins:

> Thus like the *sun* in his meridian pride
> Attended by a regiment of *stars*,
> Stand we triumphant 'mongst our petty kings.

(Cited by D. Sykes in *Sidelights on Shakespeare*, 1.)p. 17

absence elsewhere in Shakespeare justify my mentioning it here.

The passages so far cited have relevance to two scenes of *Pericles* only: II. i and II. iii. Of parallels in Day for the rest of the play, few can be cited with any degree of conviction, but the following are worth pointing out:

(1) Drew sleep out of mine eyes, blood from my cheeks.
>> *(Per.,* I. ii. 96)

> The law shall fetch red water from his veins
> That hath drawn blood from your eyes
>> *(Humour,* III. i. p. 38)

> 'Tshall be to draw blood from detraction's vein
>> *(Parliament of Bees,* Commission, p. 8)

> You'd draw fair ladies' hearts into their eyes
>> *(Humour,* I. iii, p. 17)

> My fear dropt out of mine eyes in tears and fetch'd blood
> from my heart ... drew tears from thine eyes and blood from
> thy heart. *(Peregrinatio Scholastica,* pp. 75–6)

The eye–blood association common to these passages is probably not remarkable considering the widespread belief in the Renaissance that sighs and tears did actually impoverish the heart of blood. Yet the correspondence in the words 'draw ... eyes ... blood' is striking. Another feature of the second scene in *Pericles* is the frequent repetition and interplay of 'doubt' and 'fear'; together, the words occur nine times within the space of twenty-five lines (ll. 79–103). Playful use of the same terms in dialogue occurs twice in *Humour out of Breath*:

(2)   ... this doubt I fear ...
> ... I leave my fear with thee
> And follow doubt abroad.   (p. 20)

> 'Tis good to doubt, but 'tis not good to fear,
> Yet still to doubt will at the last prove fear;
> Doubt love, 'tis good, but 'tis not good to fear it.   (p. 28)

But there are probably other instances of the same word-play in Elizabethan literature.

Lastly, the opening lines of Character 8 in *The Parliament of Bees* seem to echo, in idea though less obviously in wording, the passage which introduces the daughter of Antiochus in the first scene of *Pericles*. The relevant lines in *The Parliament* are:

(3) Nature, save thee, hath no work worth the loving;
> For, when she fashion'd thee, she summon'd all
> The Graces and the Virtues Cardinal;

> Nay, the whole swarm of bees came loaden home,
> Each bringing thee a rich perfection;   (ll. 2–6)

Yet as the Commentary to the corresponding lines in *Pericles* (i. i. 10–12) indicates, the basic concept expressed in the two passages was a Renaissance commonplace. It is clear that the three parallels just discussed do not amount to strong evidence. If one concludes that Day had a share in *Pericles*, such a position can be held with conviction only for II. i and II. iii.

III

So far I have left out of consideration one of Day's plays, *The Travailes of the Three English Brothers*, 1607, for the simple reason that we know it to be a collaborate play. But in the light of the previous evidence given here, the close similarity in the general technique as well as the wording of the choruses of *Travailes* and of *Pericles*[1] may assume extra significance. The same holds true for other 'parallels' in the two plays, though again the author of the relevant passages in *Travailes* may well have been Wilkins or Rowley. I mention merely the following:

(i) The comparison of life to 'taper-light' in *Pericles*, i. Ch. 15–16 resembles in idea two lines in *Travailes*[2]: 'our liues are lighted tapers that must out' (sig. B2^v) and 'As candles lighted to burne out themselves' (sig. D.) Yet the notion was commonplace.

(ii) The word *countless* occurs only three times in the Shakespeare canon, two of which are in the 'non-Shakespearean' scenes of *Pericles*, and both of which refer to the stars in an image (i. i. 32 and 74). The word is used in the same way in *Travailes*, sig. B4v:

> The siluer moone, and those her cowntlesse eyes,
> That like so many seruants wait on her.

If the image is commonplace, it is at any rate not Shakespearean.

(iii) A much more remarkable correspondence, both in image and in syntax, is the following:

> Here many sink, yet those which see them fall
> Have scarce strength left to give them burial.
> (i. iv. 48–9)

> . . . Whose knees do buckle, and have scarce strength
> To beare mee further than a graues in length.
> (sig. Hv)

The idea is of course somewhat different, but in both cases 'scarce

---

1. See Introduction, pp. xxii–xxiii.
2. Passages from *Travailes* are cited from the quarto of 1607.

strength' is linked with the grave. Compare further 'scarce had strength to crawl' in *Travailes*, sig. C2v.

(iv) Finally, the unusual rhyme in *Pericles*, I. iii. 27–8, 'please/seas' is paralleled in *Travailes*, sig. D4.

We recall once more that all the cited passages from *Travailes* may be used equally well as evidence for Wilkins as for Day. One can hardly use one collaborate play to prove the authorship of another. And even if these passages could be proved to be Day's, the parallels are not substantial enough to warrant any addition to our previous conclusion: the case for the collaboration of Day in *Pericles* is strong only for two scenes. If he did write these scenes, he may well have contributed to others. To claim anything more specific would be idle speculation.

IV

No external evidence can be found which might give direct support for our conclusion. Yet what we do know about Day's career and about the general character of his work does not go contrary to it in any way. The dates of Day's works fit well, for four of his six extant plays were first printed between 1606 and 1608. Day seems to have been writing mainly for the Children of the Revels, who performed at Blackfriars, and for the Children of Paul's during the first years of King James's reign. Neither company survived beyond 1608, when the Blackfriars Theatre passed into the possession of Shakespeare's company. We do not know what happened to Day then, for his name is not linked to a single play between 1608 and 1623. He must have had a precarious reputation among his fellow-dramatists, considering his fatal stabbing, though in self-defence, of Henry Porter in 1599, and Jonson's dislike of him.

As for the character of his plays, it would be absurd to suggest any close kinship between them and *Pericles*. Some of them remind one rather of Shakespeare's early comedies, whose language is often imitated in them, or of Lyly or Dekker. They owe much to the themes and style of Elizabethan prose romance. Sparklingly witty at their best, Day's plays reflect a lightheartedness of spirit and a delicacy of imagination that distinguish them from most other writings of the period—including *Pericles* and Shakespeare's last plays. Yet we can find in them two or three features that have special relevance for this discussion. Day liked plots, suggested to him by one or other romance, of a more or less tragi-comic form. This is true of *Law-Tricks* and more pronouncedly of *Humour out of Breath*, both of which can be said to anticipate Shakespeare's last plays in one important feature. They present an action involving parents and children who are separated for some time, and who only after much suffering become reconciled and reunited. Though the action of *Humour out of Breath* is lighter than that of *Cymbeline* or *The Winter's Tale* and encompasses a much shorter period of time, it is like them a tragi-comedy of two generations. Its final scene presents the reconciliation of two arch-enemies, Octavio and Antonio, brought about by the love of their children.

Not unrelated to these scenes of reunion between parents and children, though not necessarily part of them, is the repeated echoing of the notion of birth and re-creation in Day's plays: 'Many a good thing has been buried quick and survived again' (*Humour*, III. ii, p. 52), 'You new create me, and breathe a second life Into my dying bosom' (*Humour*, v. ii, p. 71), 'Life begot in death' (*Parl. of Bees*, Char. x, p. 63). The relevance of these passages to the beautiful lines,

> Thou that beget'st him that did thee beget,
> Thou that wast born at sea, buried at Tharsus,
> And found at sea again,   (*Per.*, v. i. 195–7)

and to the scenes of reunion in Shakespeare's other Romances does not require further comment.

APPENDIX C

CONJECTURAL RECONSTRUCTIONS OF EPISODES

A

As stated in the Introduction, Section 2.4, Q's text of I. ii. 1–52, followed in this edition except for minor emendations, reveals confusion of a major kind. The following conjectural reconstruction of the order of this episode is based on the analysis by P. Edwards, pp. 26–7, and on a comparison with Wilkins' prose version in *The Painfull Aduentures*. Edwards comments:

Pericles fleeing from the fury of Antiochus whose dreadful secret he has unriddled, has just arrived at Tyre. The scene opens with the direction *Enter Pericles with his Lords*, but at the very first words—Pericles's 'Let none disturb vs'—the Lords are required to file out in silence as they came. After a soliloquy in which Pericles expatiates on his misery and his fear of an invasion by Antiochus, we find the Lords filing in once more—*Enter all the*

Lords to Pericles. Their behaviour now is not a little strange: they wish their prince *bon voyage*:

1. Lord. Ioy and all comfort in your sacred brest.
2. Lord. And keepe your mind till you returne to vs peacefull and comfortable.

Now Pericles has only just returned home and is purposing no fresh journey. When, indeed, shortly after this, he does hurriedly decide to leave his country, all is done with extreme secrecy and the Lords are told nothing until he has gone. Their clairvoyance here, therefore, is remarkable, but stranger things follow when Helicanus interrupts the remarks just quoted . . . with a tirade against flattery . . . and . . . most unexpected and unwarranted observations on the duty of kings to suffer reproach. The answer of Pericles to all this is first to send the Lords out *again*—this time with an injunction to see what ships are in the harbour—and then to remonstrate with Helicanus for his daring to do what there is nothing in the text to show that he actually did, namely, chide his Prince for his faults. Pericles then pardons him. . . .

If one reconstructs the scene according to the lines suggested by this attack, the result is somewhat like this:

Lines in Play	*Enter Pericles with Lords*
	1. Lord. Joy and all comfort in your sacred breast.
35	
1	*Per.* Let none disturb us; but let your cares o'erlook
49–51	What shipping and what lading is in our haven,
	And then return to us. *Exeunt Lords*
2–34	Why should this change of thoughts,
	The sad companion, . . .
	. . . before that he would punish.

Enter Helicanus

Hel. (chides Pericles for his retiredness; the lines are lost)
Per. (briefly answers Helicanus)
38–48   *Hel.* Peace, peace, and give experience tongue.
      They do abuse the king . . .
             . . . lower than my knees.
52 ff.   *Per.* Helicanus, thou hast mov'd us . . .

                            (to end of scene)

Unfortunately, Wilkins' description of the episode is very general and echoes only a few lines of the whole scene. Yet the following passage may provide a clue for the missing piece of dialogue in the scene, as reconstructed above:

[Pericles] In this sorrowe consisting, one *Helycanus* a graue and wise Counsellor of his (as a good Prince is euer knowne by his prudent Counsell) as much greeued in mind for his Princes distemperature, as his Prince was troubled with the feare of his subiects mishap, came hastily into the chamber to him, and finding him so distasting mirth, that he abandoned all familiar society, he boldely beganne to reprooue him, and not sparingly tolde him, he did not wel so to abuse himselfe, to waste his body there with pyning sorrow, vpon whose safety depended the liues and prosperity of a whole kingdome, that it was ill in him to doe it, and no lesse in his counsell to suffer him, without contradicting it.   (*P.A.*, 21.4–18)

B

Wilkins' report of II. ii differs in two important respects from the play as conveyed by Q, and may possibly present a juster account of the original.

(i) Instead of withdrawing 'into the gallery', as the King, Thaisa, and the Lords do at the end of the scene in the play, according to Wilkins, right at the beginning, 'the King himselfe, with the Princesse his daughter, haue placed themselues in a Gallery', and 'thus seated' they receive the knights with their shields and devices (*P.A.*, 36.19–21, 25). If Wilkins' account is correct, his 'Gallery' would of course be a piece of stage furniture; certainly not the balcony or 'tarras'.

(ii) The order of appearance of the knights is different in Wilkins, and moreover all are described fully, while in the play we are never told of the origin of the fourth and fifth knights. This omission may of course have been deliberate, in the interest of speed or brevity; yet the various descriptions and mottos in Wilkins seem to be fitted sensibly:

1st. Prince of Macedon
      Device: a black Ethiop reaching at the sun.
      Motto: Lux tua vita mihi.
      (Corresponds to 2nd Knight in the play, with device of the first).
2nd. Prince of Corinth
      Device: a Wreath of Chivalry
      Motto: Me pompae prouexet apex
      (No equivalent Knight in the play; but device of the third).
3rd. of Antioch
      Device: an armed knight, being conquered by a lady.
      Motto: Pue per dolcera qui per sforsa
      (Same Knight in the play, but carrying device of the 2nd).

4th. of Sparta
  Device: man's arm environed by the clouds, holding out gold that's by the touchstone tried
  Motto: Sic spectanda fides
  (1st Knight in the play, with device of the 5th).
5th. of Athens
  Device: flaming torch turned downward
  Motto: Qui me alit me extinguit
  (In the play, the Knight is unidentified; the device corresponds to that of the 4th).
6th. Pericles
  (as in the play).

It is not possible to say whether Q or Wilkins conveys the original more correctly.

APPENDIX D

CONJECTURAL RE-ARRANGEMENTS OF VERSE

(contributed by Harold F. Brooks)

I have here attempted, for five passages given as prose or halting verse in Q, to reconstruct texts in such verse as Shakespeare, in this later period of his style, might not inconceivably have composed. It seemed more proper to place them in an Appendix than to represent them by conjectures in the Collations and Commentary. Although I believe they stand a good chance of being closer than Q to the original, they depend too much on guesswork to be urged upon the editor for his adoption. Emending a text like Q is bound to be hazardous.[1] Too often one hypothetical correction may have no more to recommend it than another, so that neither can be made with confidence. Even where we think we recognize a familiar type of memorial error, which can be set right, the corruption may be worse than we suppose: the reporter's memory may have deviated so wildly from the original that the process of deviation, and consequently the true reading, are impossible to divine. My versions, therefore, must be regarded as speculative. They are not fanciful, however. As my notes are meant to show, I have emended only where I can postulate an error characteristic of reporters or of copyists; though in four or five instances[2] I have made a guess at what the error has obliterated.

1. See Introduction, pp. l–li.
2. Cf. in (4) below, the first line; in (3), *And* and *fair town*; in (2) *lady*; and in (1) *queasy*, which, however, I support from other places in Shakespeare.

(1) III. ii. 49–69[1]

> *Enter two or three [Servants] with a chest.*

1. Serv. So, lift there.

Cer.   What's that?

1. Serv.   Sir, even now
>   Did the sea toss upon[2] our shore this chest;
>   'Tis of some wreck.

Cer.   Did the sea cast it up?

1. Serv. I never saw so huge a billow, sir
>   As toss'd it upon shore.[3]

Cer.   Set't down, let's look upon't.[4]

2. Gent. 'Tis like a coffin, sir.

Cer.   Whate'er it be
>   'Tis wondrous heavy. Wrench it open straight!
>   [*They begin work on it.*]
>   If the sea's stomach be o'ercharg'd with gold,
>   'Tis [by] a good constraint of [queasy] Fortune[5]
>   It belches upon us.

2. Gent.   'Tis so, my lord.

Cer. How close 'tis caulk'd and [bitum'd!][6] Soft! It[7] smells
>   Most sweetly to my sense.

2. Gent.   A delicate odour.

1. This reconstruction proceeds from two assumptions: (i) that the whole passage was intended as verse; (ii) that the odd placing of Cerimon's question, *did the sea cast it up?* shows memorial confusion in Q.

2. Q *up upon.* I omit *up* as an inadvertent duplication, which, if I am right about the true position of *Did . . . up?*, was perhaps encouraged by the proximity of *cast it up?*

3. In Q, these two speeches follow [bitum'd], a position in which, after Cerimon's acceptance of the Servant's specific statement, his question is altogether unnatural. If both question and answer are fitted earlier into the dialogue, the whole, besides running better as verse, develops intelligibly. Cerimon is then directly answering the Servant's statement; his words mean: 'So the sea cast it up, did it?'

4. An Alexandrine divided between two speakers is not uncharacteristic of Shakespeare.

5. I assume memorial omissions. Appropriately for a physician, Cerimon takes his image from bodily sickness and relief. For the association or juxtaposition of physic, (potions), surfeits, (*o'ercharg'd*, superflux), *stomach, queasy*, (sick), *constraint, Fortune*, cf. *Lr.*, I. ii. 125 f., sick *in* fortune, *often the surfeits of our own behaviour*; III. iv. 33, 35, Take physic, *pomp*; . . . *shake the* superflux *to them*; II. i. 18 f. *a* queasy question . . . *Briefness and* Fortune, work!; *Ado*, II. i. 399 queasy stomach; *2H4*, I. i. 196 f., *with* queasiness, constrain'd / *As men* drink potions. (Italicization mine.)

6. Q *bottomed,*—see Commentary.

7. Q *Wrench it open soft; it.* I omit *Wrench it open* as memorial repetition from three lines above: *soft* does belong, I believe, to the present line, but *Wrench it open straight* was inopportunely recollected here as *Wrench it open soft*. It is improbable that Cerimon should have to repeat this command.

Cer. As ever hit my nostril; so, up with it.
Oh you most potent gods! What's here, a corse?
2. Gent. Most strange.
Cer.   Shrouded in cloth of state,
Balm'd and entreasur'd with full bags of spices;
A passport too![1] [*Business*] Apollo
Perfect me in the characters!

(2) III. ii. 94–106[2]

Gentlemen,
This Queen will live. Nature awakes a warm
Breath[3] out of her. She hath not been entranc'd
Above five hours. See how she 'gins to blow
Into life's flower again.
I. Gent.   The Heavens through you[4]
Increase our wonder, and set[5] up your fame
For ever[more].[6]
Cer.   She is alive, behold
Her eyelids, cases to those heavenly jewels
Which Pericles hath lost, begin to part
Their fringes of bright gold. The diamonds
Of a most praised water doth appear
To make the world twice rich; live [, lady, live],[7]

1 Q *to*—see Collations. There may be memorial omissions in the short lines *Most . . . state, A . . . Apollo*, but as elsewhere in Shakespeare, the 'missing' beats may be supplied by wonderment or stage-business.

2. Working back from the end of the passage in Q, and assuming a hiatus (the result of a skip) in the third line up, we can restore the verse with confidence as far as *She is alive, behold*. For the remaining lines, more than one rearrangement is feasible. If we work back just as before, the Gentleman's speech makes unexceptionable verse (cf. n. 3 below, Alexander's arrangement) but there is a 'missing' beat to be accommodated at some point, and if we carry it up beyond the last half-line of the preceding speech, we get an arrangement *Gentlemen, | This . . . awakes | A warm . . . been | Entranc'd . . . 'gins | To blow . . . again*, which even apart from the short line is somewhat unsatisfactory. On the present alternative, on Alexander's, and on Maxwell's, see nn. 3, 4 and 6 below.

3. Q *awakes a warmth breath*. This edition, following Q2 (see Commentary) assumes that an original *warm* was assimilated to *breath*. The line division is more acceptable if, following Steevens, we assume a stop was omitted and an original *breathes* assimilated to *warmth*, and so read, with Maxwell and Alexander: *Nature awakes; a warmth | Breathes out of her.*

4. Alexander locates the 'missing' beat here: *The Heavens | Through . . . up | Your . . . ever.*

5. Q *sets* (see Commentary).

6. Conjecturing that *ever* is a reporter's synonym. But the short line *For ever.* *Cer. She . . . behold*, accepted by Maxwell, is not unShakespearian, especially as it may allow for Cerimon's stage-business.

7. This supposes a skip by homoeoteleuton, from the first *live* to the second.

And make us weep to hear your fate, fair creature,
Rare as you seem to be.
Thai.   O dear Diana . . .

(3) IV. vi. 65–90[1]

Lys.   Now, pretty one, how long
Have you been at this trade?
Mar.   What trade, sir?
Lys.   Why,
I cannot name [it][2] but I shall offend.
Mar. I cannot be offended with my trade;
Please you to name it.
Lys.   How long have you been
Of this profession?
Mar.   Ere since I can remember.
Lys. Did you go to't so young? Were you a gamester
At five, or at seven?
Mar.   Earlier, too, sir
If now I be one.
Lys.   Why, the house you dwell in[3]
Proclaims you[4] a creature of sale.
Mar.   [And][5] do you know
This house to be a place of such resort
And will come into't? I hear say you are[6]
Of honourable parts, and are the Governor
Of this [fair town].[7]
Lys.   Why, hath your principal
Made known unto you who I am?
Mar.   Who is
My principal?

1. The reasons for regarding this passage as verse are discussed in the Commentary. But after *Who is | My principal?* (ll. 87–8), we have at best verse fragments; hence the conjectured omissions, indicated by asterisks.

2. Q's *name* (without *it*) must be emended for sense, even apart from metre; and not improbably Marina's *name it* repeats Lysimachus' exact words.

3. Of Lysimachus' seven speeches, four begin with *Why*, which in one or more of them may be intruded through recollection of the others. Since Wilkins has *This house wherein thou livest*, the true text may have read: *sir, if | Now I be one.* Lys. *This house wherein you live.*

4. Q *you to be*; I assume *to be* is caught from the line below.

5. A light syllable seems wanting. The *And* of surprised expostulation would sufficiently combine respect with reproach, and might easily slip the reporter's memory.

6. Q *you're*; the reporter's contraction, I suggest.

7. Q *the Gouernour of this place*. The identical phrase occurs at V. i. 21, and there is probably memorial contamination, perhaps even in *both* instances. Here *place* is most likely memorial from three lines above. Instead of *this* [*fair town*], possibly *Mytilene*.

Lys.   Why, your herb woman; she that sets seeds[1]
And roots of shame and iniquity. O you have
Heard something of my power, and stand aloof[2]
For   *   [3] more serious wooing,   *   *   *

*   *   *   *   *   *   *   *   *   *

But I protest [un]to[4] thee, pretty one,
My authority shall not see thee, or else look
Friendly upon thee.   *   *   *   *
Come, bring me to some private place, come, come.

(4) IV. vi. 160–8[5]

Mar.   Neither['s] so bad as thou [thyself], since they[6]
Do better thee in command;[7] thou holdst a place
For which the painedst fiend in hell would not
In reputation change. Thou art the damn'd
Doorkeeper to every coistrel comes[8]
Inquiring for his Tib; to the choleric fist[9]
Of every rogue thy ear is liable;
Thy food is such as hath been belch'd on by
Infected lungs.

(5) V. i. 202–11

          Though doubts did ever sleep.
Mar.   First, sir, I pray
What is your title?
Per.   I am Pericles
Of Tyre. But tell me now my drown'd queen's name.

1. *Why,* and *she* should perhaps be omitted as memorial expansions.

2. For *aloof* (Q *aloft*) see Commentary. Q *and so stand* makes more explicit the causal connection quite adequately conveyed in *and stand*; I take it for the reporter's expansion.

3. The original may have been something like *To prompt* or *For some.*

4. Reporter's synonym? Q *to.* Cf. *Rom.*, II. iv. 183, *I protest unto thee.*

5. Set as prose (wrongly, it is clear) in Q.

6. If one assumes that *since they* ends the first line, it requires only three minor emendations to rearrange the rest as verse after the late Shakespearian style. The result, with its frequent enjambements and banging stresses on b, p, d, c, and f, can be declaimed with conviction. The three emendations postulate small and not improbable errors of the reporter; in the first line we have to suppose a larger one: that Q *Neither of these are so bad as thou art* is his loose paraphrase of an original which may have been more succinct. I hold no brief for my version of this line.

7. Q *their command*: taking its cue from *they*, the reporter's memory perhaps intruded *their* in a misguided effort to clarify the sense, which is clearer without it: they are better (less *ignominiously* bad) than Boult in virtue of being in authority (over him).

8. Q *that comes*: memorial expansion, I assume, of the ellipsis.

9. Q *fisting*: perhaps by assimilation to *Inquiring.*

As in the rest[1] thou hast been godlike perfect,[2]

*   *   *   *   *   *   *   *   *   *

The heir of kingdoms, and another life[3]
To Pericles thy father.
Mar.[4]   Is it no more to be[5]
Your daughter than to say my mother's name?[6]
Thaisa was my mother, who did end
The minute I began.

1. Q *rest you sayd,*: redundant memorial expansion, presumably.

2. Like previous edd., we believe a phrase to be missing here; no doubt at least a line, importing:.'So be but right in that, thou art my daughter'.

3. Q *like.* The emendation is obvious.

4. Q sets this speech as prose.

5. Another Alexandrine split between two speakers (cf. above, III. ii. 49–69 n. 4). This one has an extra unstressed syllable at the caesura.

6. Q *name was Thaisa?* I omit *was Thaisa,* as a memorial expansion and duplication.

ADDITIONAL NOTES AND REVISIONS

I. iii. 11. *to question of.*] This reading must be credited to Steevens, not to Maxwell as in collation and note.

II. Ch. 5–6n.] One may interpret differently: *he* = Pericles.

II. i. 149. *condolements.*] See also discussion of this term in Hilda M. Hulme, *Explorations in Shakespeare's Language,* 1962, pp. 279–80.

II. iv. 6–12n.] The suggestion that some of the scene's detail may be indebted to the story of Antiochus Epiphanes in 2 Maccabees, ix was already made by S. Singer, *Apollonius von Tyrus,* 1895, p. 49.

III. i. 62n.] For references by sixteenth-century authors to inextinguishable monuments still burning in subterranean monuments in Italy, see Lynn Thorndike, *A History of Magic and Experimental Science,* VI. 279.

IV. ii. 22. *poop'd.*] Hulme, *opus cit.,* pp. 114–15, in a discussion of this word cites a relevant epigram by John Davies of Hereford (*Works,* ed. by A. B. Grosart, 1878, Vol. II, p. 41).